THE

SACRED BOOKS OF THE EAST

Translated by

VARIOUS ORIENTAL SCHOLARS

And Edited by

F. MAX MÜLLER

Vol. 3

SACRED BOOKS OF THE EAST

(50 VOLUMES)

Series Editor : *F. Max-Müller*

ISBN: 978-81-208-0101-1 (Set) Rs. 11000 (Each Vol. Rs. 250)

These volumes of the Sacred Books of the East series include translations of all the most important works of the seven non-Christian religions that have exercised a profound influence on the civilisations of the continent of Asia. The Vedic Brahmanic system claims 21 volumes, Buddhism 10, and Jainism 2; 8 volumes comprise Sacred Books of the Parsis; 2 volumes represent Islam; and 6 the two main indigenous systems of China. Translated by twenty leading authorities in their respective fields, the volumes have been edited by the late F. Max Müller. The inception, publication and the compilation of these books cover almost 34 years.

I. BUDDHISM

Vol. 49: Buddhist Mahayana Texts (2 Parts)
Vol. 11: Buddhist Suttas
Vol. 10: The Dhammapada and Sutta Nipata
Vols. 35 & 36: The Questions of King Milinda (2 Parts)
Vol. 21: The Saddharma Pundarika or the Lotus of the True Law
Vols. 13, 17 & 20: Vinaya Texts (3 Parts)

II. CHINESE

Vol. 19: The Fo-Sho-Hing-Tsan-King
Vols. 3, 16, 27, 28, 39 & 40: The Sacred Books of China (6 Parts)

III. A GENERAL INDEX

Vol. 50: A General Index to the Names and Subject-matter of the Sacred Books of the East

IV. ISLAM

Vols. 6 & 9: The Qur'an (2 Parts)

V. JAINISM

Vols. 22 & 45: The Jaina Sutras (2 Parts)

VI. PARSIS

Vols. 5, 18, 24, 37 & 47: Pahlavi Texts (5 Parts)
Vols. 4, 23 & 31: The Zend-Avesta (3 Parts)

VII. VEDIC-BRAHMANIC SYSTEM

Vol. 8: The Bhagavadgita with the Sanatsujatiya and the Anugita
Vols. 29 & 30: The Grihya-Sutras: Rules of Vedic Domestic Ceremonies (2 Parts)
Vol. 42: Hymns of the Atharva Veda together with Extracts from the Ritual Books and the Commentaries
Vol. 7: The Institutes of Vishnu
Vol. 25: The Laws of Manu
Vol. 33: The Minor Law Books
Vols. 2 & 14: The Sacred Laws of the Aryas as Taught in the Schools of Apastamba, Gautama, Vasishtha and Baudhayana (2 Parts)
Vols. 12, 26, 41, 43 & 44: The Satapatha Brahmana According to the Text of the Madhyandina School (5 Parts)
Vols. 1 & 15: The Upanishads (2 Parts)
Vols. 34 & 38: The Vedanta Sutras (2 Parts)
Vol. 48: The Vedanta-Sutras (with the commentary by Ramanuja)
Vols. 32 & 46: Vedic Hymns (2 Parts)

THE SACRED BOOKS OF CHINA

The Texts of Confucianism

Translated by

JAMES LEGGE

Part I

THE SHU KING
THE RELIGIOUS PORTION OF THE SHIH KING
THE HSIĀO KING

MOTILAL BANARSIDASS PUBLISHERS
PRIVATE LIMITED • DELHI

Reprint: Delhi, 1966, 1970, 1978, 1988, 1996, 2008
First published by the Clarendon Press, 1879

ISBN: 978-81-208-0104-2

MOTILAL BANARSIDASS
41 U.A. Bungalow Road, Jawahar Nagar, Delhi 110 007
8 Mahalaxmi Chamber, 22 Bhulabhai Desai Road, Mumbai 400 026
203 Royapettah High Road, Mylapore, Chennai 600 004
236, 9th Main III Block, Jayanagar, Bangalore 560 011
Sanas Plaza, 1302 Baji Rao Road, Pune 411 002
8 Camac Street, Kolkata 700 017
Ashok Rajpath, Patna 800 004
Chowk, Varanasi 221 001

UNESCO COLLECTION OF REPRESENTATIVE WORKS— Indian Series
This book has been accepted in the Indian Translation Series of the UNESCO Collection of Representative Works, jointly sponsored by the United Nations Educational Scientific and Cultural Organization (UNESCO) and the Government of India

PRINTED IN INDIA

BY JAINENDRA PRAKASH JAIN AT SHRI JAINENDRA PRESS,
A-45 NARAINA, PHASE-I, NEW DELHI 110 028
AND PUBLISHED BY NARENDRA PRAKASH JAIN FOR
MOTILAL BANARSIDASS PUBLISHERS PRIVATE LIMITED,
BUNGALOW ROAD, DELHI 110 007

Rashtrapati Bhavan,
New Delhi-4
June 10, 1962

I am very glad to know that the Sacred Books of the East, published years ago by the Clarendon Press, Oxford, which have been out-of-print for a number of years, will now be available to all students of religion and philosophy The enterprise of the publishers is commendable and I hope the books will be widely read.

S. Radhakrishnan

PREFATORY NOTE TO THE NEW EDITION

Since 1948 the United Nations Educational, Scientific and Cultural Organisation (UNESCO), upon the recommendation of the General Assembly of the United Nations, has been concerned with facilitating the translation of the works most representative of the culture of certain of its Member States, and, in particular, those of Asia.

One of the major difficulties confronting this programme is the lack of translators having both the qualifications and the time to undertake translations of the many outstanding books meriting publication. To help overcome this difficulty in part, UNESCO's advisers in this field (a panel of experts convened every other year by the International Council for Philosophy and Humanistic Studies), have recommended that many worthwhile translations published during the 19th century, and now impossible to find except in a limited number of libraries, should be brought back into print in low-priced editions, for the use of students and of the general public. The experts also pointed out that in certain cases, even though there might be in existence more recent and more accurate translations endowed with a more modern apparatus of scholarship, a number of pioneer works of the greatest value and interest to students of Eastern religions also merited republication.

This point of view was warmly endorsed by the Indian National Academy of Letters (Sahitya Akademi), and the Indian National Commission for UNESCO.

It is in the spirit of these recommendations that this work from the famous series "Sacred Books of the East" is now once again being made available to the general public as part of the UNESCO Collection of Representative Works.

PUBLISHER'S NOTE

First, the man distinguished between eternal and perishable. Later he discovered within himself the germ of the Eternal. This discovery was an epoch in the history of the human mind and the *East was the first to discover it.*

To watch in the Sacred Books of the East the dawn of this religious consciousness of man, must always remain one of the most inspiring and hallowing sights in the whole history of the world. In order to have a solid foundation for a comparative study of the Religions of the East, we must have before all things, complete and thoroughly faithful translation of their Sacred Books in which some of the ancient sayings were preserved because they were so true and so striking that they could not be forgotten. They contained eternal truths, expressed for the first time in human language.

With profoundest reverence for Dr. S. Radhakrishnan, President of India, who inspired us for the task; our deep sense of gratitude for Dr. C. D. Deshmukh & Dr. D. S. Kothari, for encouraging assistance; esteemed appreciation of UNESCO for the warm endorsement of the cause ; and finally with indebtedness to Dr. H. Rau, Director, Max Müller Bhawan, New Delhi, in procuring us the texts of the Series for reprint, we humbly conclude.

CONTENTS.

PAGE

PREFACE xiii

THE SHÛ.

INTRODUCTION.

CHAP.

I. THE NATURE AND HISTORY OF THE SHÛ 1

Meaning of the name Shû King. The Shû existed as a collection of documents before Confucius. Number of documents in it in his time. The Preface ascribed to him. The sources of the Shû. Destruction of the classical literature by the emperor of *Kh*in. Recovery of the Shû.

II. THE CREDIBILITY OF THE RECORDS IN THE SHÛ . . 12

Are the records reliable or not? The Books of *K*âu; of Shang; of Hsiâ. The Books of Thang and Yü are professedly later compilations; legendary; based on ancient documents. The Tribute of Yü. Yâo, Shun, and Yü are all historical personages.

III. ON THE CHRONOLOGY OF CHINA, AND THE PRINCIPAL ERAS IN THE SHÛ 20

No detailed chronological system can be made out from the Shû. Attempts at systematic chronology began in the Han period. Ancient method of determining the length of Chinese history. The period of the *K*âu dynasty; of the Shang; of the Hsiâ; of Yâo and Shun.

A CHART BY THE REV. PROFESSOR PRITCHARD, representing the principal zodiacal stars above the horizon of any place in central China, about the year B.C. 2300; with note, and table of the apparent positions of the principal stars in B.C. 2300, B.C. 1500, A.D. 1, A.D. 1000, and A.D. 1878 27-30

PART I. THE BOOK OF THANG.

The Canon of Yâo 31

PART II. THE BOOKS OF YÜ.

BOOK		PAGE
1.	The Canon of Shun	37
2.	The Counsels of the Great Yü	46
3.	The Counsels of Kâo-yâo	53
4.	The Yî and *K*î	56

PART III. THE BOOKS OF HSIÂ.

1.	The Tribute of Yü. Section i	64
	" " " ii	72
2.	The Speech at Kan	76
3.	The Songs of the Five Sons	78
4.	The Punitive Expedition of Yin	81

PART IV. THE BOOKS OF SHANG.

1.	The Speech of Thang	84
2.	The Announcement of *K*ung-hui	86
3.	The Announcement of Thang	89
4.	The Instructions of Î	92
5.	The Thâi *K*iâ. Section i	95
	" " ii	97
	" " iii	99
6.	The Common Possession of Pure Virtue	100
7.	The Pan-kăng. Section i	104
	" " ii	108
	" " iii	111
8.	The Charge to Yüeh. Section i	113
	" " " ii	115
	" " " iii	116
9.	The Day of the Supplementary Sacrifice to Kâo Ȝung	118
10.	The Chief of the West's Conquest of Lî	120
11.	The Count of Wei	121

PART V. THE BOOKS OF *K*ÂU.

1.	The Great Declaration. Section i	125
	" " " ii	127
	" " " iii	129
2.	The Speech at Mû	131
3.	The Successful Completion of the War	133
4.	The Great Plan	137
5.	The Hounds of Lü	149
6.	The Metal-bound Coffer	151

BOOK		PAGE
7.	The Great Announcement	156
8.	The Charge to the Count of Wei	161
9.	The Announcement to the Prince of Khang	164
10.	The Announcement about Drunkenness	171
11.	The Timber of the Rottlera	179
12.	The Announcement of the Duke of Shâo	181
13.	The Announcement concerning Lo	188
14.	The Numerous Officers	196
15.	Against Luxurious Ease	200
16.	The Prince Shih	205
17.	The Charge to *K*ung of 3hâi	211
18.	The Numerous Regions	213
19.	The Establishment of Government	219
20.	The Officers of *K*âu	226
21.	The *K*ün-*kh*ăn	231
22.	The Testamentary Charge	234
23.	The Announcement of King Khang	243
24.	The Charge to the Duke of Pî	245
25.	The *K*ün-yâ	250
26.	The Charge to *Kh*iung	252
27.	The Marquis of Lü on Punishments	254
28.	The Charge to the Marquis Wăn	265
29.	The Speech at Pî	267
30.	The Speech of the Marquis of *Kh*in	270

THE SHIH.

INTRODUCTION.

CHAP.

I. THE NAME AND CONTENTS OF THE SHIH 275

The meaning of the character Shih. The contents. Only the pieces of the fourth Part have professedly a religious character. Classification of the pieces from their form and style.

II. THE SHIH BEFORE CONFUCIUS, AND WHAT, IF ANY, WERE HIS LABOURS UPON IT 280

Statement of Sze-mâ *Kh*ien; in the Records of the Sui Dynasty; of *K*û Hsî. View of the author. Groundlessness of *Kh*ien's statement. What Confucius did for the Shih.

CHAP. PAGE

III. THE SHIH FROM THE TIME OF CONFUCIUS TILL THE GENERAL ACKNOWLEDGMENT OF THE PRESENT TEXT 285

From Confucius to the rise of the *Kh*in dynasty. The Shih was all recovered after the fires of *Kh*in. Three different texts:—of Lû; of *Kh*î; of Han Ying. The text of Mâo.

IV. THE FORMATION OF THE COLLECTION OF THE SHIH; HOW IT CAME TO BE SO SMALL AND INCOMPLETE; THE INTERPRETATION AND AUTHORS OF THE PIECES; ONE POINT OF TIME CERTAINLY INDICATED IN IT; AND THE CONFUCIAN PREFACE 290

The theory of the Chinese scholars about a collection of poems for governmental purposes. The music-master of the king got the odes of each state from its music-master; and the collected poems were disseminated throughout the states. How the Shih is so small and incomplete. The authors of the pieces. The year B.C. 776 clearly indicated. The Preface to the Shih.

ODES OF THE TEMPLE AND THE ALTAR.

1. The Sacrificial Odes of Shang 303
2. The Sacrificial Odes of *K*âu. Decade i 313
   „ „ „ „ ii 320
   „ „ „ „ iii 328
3. The Praise Odes of Lû 336

THE MINOR ODES OF THE KINGDOM.

Decade i. Odes 5, 6, 9 347
„ iv. Odes 5, 6, 7, 8, 9, 10 349
„ v. Odes 1, 2, 3, 4, 6, 9 358
„ vi. Odes 3, 5, 6, 7, 8 364
„ vii. Odes 1, 6 373
„ viii. Ode 5 376

THE MAJOR ODES OF THE KINGDOM.

Decade i. Odes 1, 2, 3, 4, 5, 6, 7, 9, 10 377
„ ii. Odes 1, 2, 3, 4, 5, 8, 9, 10 396
„ iii. Odes 1, 2, 3, 4, 5, 6, 7, 8, 10, 11 410

LESSONS FROM THE STATES.

Book 2. Odes 2, 4 430
„ 3. Odes 4, 15 433
„ 4. Odes 1, 3, 6 434

PAGE

Book 5. Ode 4 437
„ 6. Odes 1, 9 438
„ 10. Odes 8, 11 440
„ 11. Ode 6 442
„ 15. Ode 1 444

THE HSIÂO.

INTRODUCTION.

CHAP.

I. THE NAME OF THE CLASSIC; ITS EXISTENCE BEFORE THE HAN DYNASTY; ITS CONTENTS, AND BY WHOM IT WAS WRITTEN 449

Meaning of the character Hsiâo. Was the treatise called the Hsiâo King by Confucius? It existed before the Han dynasty during the time of the *K*âu. It came, probably, from the school of Ȝăng-ȝze.

II. THE RECOVERY OF THE HSIÂO UNDER THE HAN DYNASTY, AND ITS PRESERVATION DOWN TO THE PUBLICATION OF THE COMMENTARY OF THE THANG EMPEROR HSÜAN ȜUNG 452

Recovery of the Hsiâo. The shorter or modern text. The old or longer text. Was another copy in the old text discovered? Can we fully rely on the copies catalogued by Liû Hin? From Khung An-kwo to the emperor Hsüan Ȝung. The emperor's work. Hsing Ping's work.

III. CRITICISM OF THE HSIÂO SINCE THE THANG DYNASTY 458

Works on the old text by Sze-mâ Kwang and Fan Ȝû-yü. Sceptical criticism;—views of *K*û Hsî and Wû *Kh*ăng. Conclusion regarding the genuineness and integrity of the Hsiâo. Note on the translation.

1. The Scope and Meaning of the Treatise 465
2. Filial Piety in the Son of Heaven 467
3. Filial Piety in the Princes of States 468
4. Filial Piety in High Ministers and Great Officers . . 469
5. Filial Piety in Inferior Officers 470
6. Filial Piety in the Common People 471
7. Filial Piety in Relation to the Three Powers . . . 472

CHAP.		PAGE
8.	Filial Piety in Government	474
9.	The Government of the Sages	476
10.	An Orderly Description of the Acts of Filial Piety	480
11.	Filial Piety in Relation to the Five Punishments	481
12.	Amplification of 'the All-embracing Rule of Conduct' in Chapter I	481
13.	Amplification of 'the Perfect Virtue' in Chapter I	482
14.	Amplification of 'Making our Name Famous' in Chapter I	483
15.	Filial Piety in Relation to Reproof and Remonstrance	483
16.	The Influence of Filial Piety and the Response to it	484
17.	The Service of the Ruler	486
18.	Filial Piety in Mourning for Parents	487

Transliteration of Oriental Alphabets adopted for the Translations of the Sacred Books of the East 489

PREFACE.

WHILE submitting here some prefatory observations on the version of the Shû King presented in this volume, I think it well to prefix also a brief account of what are regarded as the Sacred Books of the Religions of China. Those religions are three:—Confucianism, Tâoism, and Buddhism.

I. I begin with a few words about the last. To translate any of its books does not belong to my province, and more than a few words from me are unnecessary. It has been said that Buddhism was introduced into China in the third century B.C.; but it certainly did not obtain an authoritative recognition in the empire till the third quarter of our first century[1]. Its Texts were translated into Chinese, one portion after another, as they were gradually obtained from India; but it was not till very long afterwards that the Chinese possessed, in their own language, a complete copy of the Buddhist canon[2]. Translations from the Sanskrit constitute the principal part of the Buddhistic literature of China, though there are also many original works in Chinese belonging to it.

---

[1] I put the introduction of Buddhism into China before our Christian era thus uncertainly, because of what is said in the article on the history of Buddhism in China, in the Records of the Sui Dynasty (A.D. 589-618), the compilers of which say that before the Han dynasty (began B.C. 202) Buddhism was not heard of in China. They refer to contrary statements as what 'some say,' and proceed to relate circumstances inconsistent with them. It is acknowledged on all sides that Buddhist books were first brought to China between A.D. 60 and 70.

[2] Mr. Beal (Catena of Buddhist Scriptures from the Chinese, pp. 1, 2) says that 'the first complete edition of the Buddhist Canon in China dates from the seventh century; that a second and much enlarged edition of it, called the Southern Collection, was prepared in A.D. 1410; that a third edition, called the Northern Collection, appeared about A.D. 1590; which again was renewed and enlarged in the year 1723.'

II. Confucianism is the religion of China par excellence, and is named from the great sage who lived in the fifth and sixth centuries B.C. Confucius indeed did not originate the system, nor was he the first to inculcate its principles or enjoin its forms of worship. He said of himself (Analects, VII, i) that he was a transmitter and not a maker, one who believed in and loved the ancients; and hence it is said in the thirtieth chapter of the Doctrine of the Mean, ascribed to his grandson, that 'he handed down the doctrines of Yâo and Shun, as if they had been his ancestors, and elegantly displayed the regulations of Wăn and Wû, taking them as his models.'

In fulfilling what he considered to be his mission, Confucius did little towards committing to writing the views of antiquity according to his own conception of them. He discoursed about them freely with the disciples of his school, from whom we have received a good deal of what he said; and it is possible that his accounts of the ancient views and practices took, unconsciously to himself, some colour from the peculiar character of his mind. But his favourite method was to direct the attention of his disciples to the ancient literature of the nation. He would neither affirm nor relate anything for which he could not adduce some document of acknowledged authority. He said on one occasion (Analects, III, ix) that he could describe the ceremonies of the dynasties of Hsiâ (B.C. 2205–1767) and Yin (B.C. 1766–1123), but did not do so, because the records and scholars in the two states of *K*âu, that had been assigned to the descendants of their sovereigns, could not sufficiently attest his words. It is an error even to suppose that he compiled the historical documents, poems, and other ancient books from various works existing in his time. Portions of the oldest works had already perished. His study of those that remained, and his exhortations to his disciples also to study them, contributed to their preservation. What he wrote or said about their meaning should be received by us with reverence; but if all the works which he handled had come down to us entire, we should have been, so far as it is possible for foreigners to be, in the same position as he was for learning the ancient religion of his country. Our text-books would be the same as his. Unfortunately most of the ancient books suffered loss and injury after Confucius had passed from the stage of life. We have reason, however, to be thankful that we possess so many and so much of them. No other literature, comparable to them for antiquity, has come down to us in such a state of preservation.

But the reader must bear in mind that the ancient books of China do not profess to have been inspired, or to contain what we should call a Revelation. Historians, poets, and others wrote them as they were moved in their own minds. An old poem may occasionally contain what it says was spoken by God, but we can only understand that language as calling attention emphatically to the statements to which it is prefixed. We also read of Heaven's raising up the great ancient sovereigns and teachers, and variously assisting them to accomplish their undertakings; but all this need not be more than what a religious man of any country might affirm at the present day of direction, help, and guidance given to himself and others from above. But while the old Chinese books do not profess to contain any divine revelation, the references in them to religious views and practices are numerous; and it is from these that the student has to fashion for himself an outline of the early religion of the people. I will now state what the books are.

First, and of greatest importance, there is the Book of Historical Documents, called the Shû and, since the period of the Han dynasty (began B.C. 202), the Shû King. Its documents commence with the reign of Yâo in the twenty-fourth century B.C., and come down to that of king Hsiang of the *K*âu dynasty, B.C. 651–619. The earliest chapters were not contemporaneous with the events which they describe, but the others begin to be so in the twenty-second century B.C. The reader will find a translation of the whole of this work without abridgment.

Second, and nearly as important as the Shû, there is the Shih, or the Book of Poetry. It contains in all 305 pieces, five of which are of the time of the Shang dynasty (called also the Yin), B.C. 1766–1123. The others belong to the dynasty of *K*âu, from the time of its founder, king Wăn, born B.C. 1231, to the reign of king Ting, B.C. 606–586. The whole is divided into four Parts, the last of which is occupied with 'Odes of the Temple and the Altar.' Many pieces in the other Parts also partake of a religious character, but the greater number are simply descriptive of the manners, customs, and events of the times to which they belong, and have no claim to be included in the roll of Sacred Texts. In this volume will be found all the pieces that illustrate the religious views of their authors, and the religious practices of their times.

The third work is the Yî, commonly called the Book of Changes. Confucius himself set a high value on it, as being fitted to correct and perfect the character of the learner (Analects, VII, xvi); and it is often spoken of by foreigners as the most ancient of all the Chinese classics. But it is not so. As it existed in the time of the sage, and as it exists now, no portion of the text is older than the time of king Wăn, mentioned above. There were and are, indeed, in it eight trigrams ascribed to Fû-hsî, who is generally considered as the founder of the Chinese nation, and whose place in chronology should, probably, be assigned in the thirty-fourth century B.C. The eight trigrams are again increased to sixty-four hexagrams. To form these figures, two lines, one of them whole (——) and the other divided (— —), are assumed as bases. Those lines are then placed, each over itself, and each over the other; and four binograms are formed. From these, by the same process with the base lines, are obtained eight figures,—the famous trigrams. Three other repetitions of the same process give us successively sixteen, thirty-two, and sixty-four figures. The lines in the figures thus increase in an arithmetical progression, whose common difference is one, and the number of the figures increases in a geometrical progression, whose common ratio is two. But what ideas Fû-hsî attached to his primary lines,—the whole and the divided; what significance he gave to his trigrams; what to the sixty-four hexagrams,—if indeed he himself formed so many figures; and why the multiplication of the figures was stayed at sixty-four:—of none of these points have we any knowledge from him. There is some reason to believe that there were texts to the hexagrams under the dynasties of Hsiâ and Shang, but none of them have been preserved. It may be that king Wăn and his equally famous son, the duke of *K*âu, adopted much of what they found already existing, and incorporated it with their own interpretations of the figures; but they, and they alone, are accepted as the authors of the text of the Yî. King Wăn, we are told, at a time when he was imprisoned by the tyrannical sovereign with whom the dynasty of Shang or Yin ended, took in hand the ever-changing hexagrams, and appended to each a brief explanation of the meaning which the trigrams composing it suggested by their union to his mind; and in some cases the practical course in affairs to which that meaning should direct. His son did for the separate lines of each hexagram what Wăn had done for the whole figure. Confucius is said to have entered into their labours about 600 years afterwards. Several appendixes are ascribed to him, in which there is an attempt to explain the origin of the Fû-hsî figures, and many of the interpretations of Wăn and his son. The early linear figures; the notes of Wăn and the duke of *K*âu; and the Confucian appendixes:—these constitute the Yî.

The work was from the first intimately connected with the practice of divination, which, we know from the Shû, entered largely into the religion of the ancient Chinese. This goes far to account for its obscure and enigmatical character; but at the same time there occur in it, though in a fragmentary manner, so many metaphysical, physical, moral, and religious utterances, that the student of it is gradually brought under a powerful fascination. In consequence, moreover, of its use in divination, it was exempted by the superstitious tyrant of *Kh*in from the flames to which he condemned all the other Confucian literature in B.C. 213. It has thus come down to us entire, and a translation of the whole of it will be given.

An additional interest belongs to the Yî as the fountain-head from which the comparatively modern philosophers of the Sung dynasty (began A.D. 960) professed to draw what has been called their 'atheo-political' system. As an appendix to the translation of the Yî, there will be given an outline of that system, and an attempt will be made to test the correctness of the interpretation of this classic by its authors.

The fourth of the great classics is the Lî *K*î, or the Record of Rites; but it is only one of a class that we may denominate the Constitutional and Ritual Books of ancient China, especially under the *K*âu dynasty. They are often mentioned together as 'the Three Rituals.' The first of them is called *K*âu Lî, the Rites of *K*âu, and also *K*âu Kwan, the Officers of *K*âu, which latter is the better name for it. It is the official book of the *K*âu dynasty. The prevailing opinion is that it was the production of the duke of *K*âu; and if it were not composed in its present form by him, it contains, no doubt, the substance of the regulations which he made for the administration of the government, after the dynasty of Shang had passed, through the achievements of his father and brother, into that of *K*âu. Under the various departments in which that administration was arranged, it enumerates the principal and subordinate officers belonging to each, and describes their duties. After the fires of *Kh*in, the work was recovered nearly complete in the first century B.C. A good translation of the whole work was published in 1851, at Paris, by M. Edouard Biot.

The second Ritual Collection bears the name of Î Lî, which has been translated 'the Decorum Ritual,' and 'the Rules of Demeanour.' It was recovered earlier than the former, and is as voluminous. It consists of the rules by which a scholar or officer should regulate his behaviour on social and state occasions. It has not yet, so far as I know, been translated into any European language.

The third Collection, more voluminous than either of the others, was made also under the Han dynasty. In the first century B.C., it was an immense compilation of 214 books arranged in five divisions. The 214 were reduced to eighty-five by Tâi Teh, a scholar of the time, and his eighty-five again to forty-six by a cousin, called Tâi *Kh*ăng. Three other books were added to these towards the end of the Han period, forming forty-nine in all, which have come down to us under the title of Lî *K*î, or 'the Record of Rites,' and have long constituted by imperial authority one of the five King. An abridgment of this work was translated by M. J. M. Callery, at Turin, in 1853, with the title,—'Lî *K*î, ou Memorial des Rites, traduit pour la première fois du Chinois, et accompagné de notes, de commentaires, et du texte original.' Callery's work, however, contains only thirty-six of the forty-nine books of the Lî *K*î, and most of those thirty-six in a condensed form. Whether it will be possible to give in these Sacred Books of the East translations of the whole of these Rituals; and if that be not possible, by what principles to be guided in the selection of portions of them:—these are questions to be determined after further deliberation. Many passages contain more of the mind of Confucius himself on the sacrificial worship of his country, and the ideas underlying it, than we find elsewhere.

But it must not be forgotten that these ritual books do not throw so valuable a light on the ancient religion of China as the older Shû and Shih. They belong to the period of the *K*âu dynasty, and do not go back as contemporaneous records to the dynasties beyond it and the still remoter age of Yâo and Shun. The views of Confucius, moreover, as given in them, do not come to us at first hand. They were gathered up by the Han scholars five and six centuries after his death, nor can we be sure that these did not sometimes put ideas of their own into the mouth of the sage, and make additions to the writings which were supposed, correctly or incorrectly, to have come from his immediate disciples.

We owe the fifth and last of the Kings of China to Confucius himself. It is what he called *Kh*un *Kh*iû, or 'the Spring and Autumn,' a very brief chronicle compiled by him of the annals of his native state of Lû for 242 years, from B.C. 722 to 481. But there is not much to be gleaned from it for the Sacred Texts; and if we were to launch out into the three supplements to it of Ʒo *Kh*iû-ming, Kung-yang, and Kû-liang, the result would not repay the labour. A translation of the whole of Ʒo's supplement, much the most important, is given in my work on the *Kh*un *Kh*iû, published at Hong Kong in 1872.

There is another short treatise attributed to Confucius,—the Hsiâo King, or 'Classic of Filial Piety.' Though not like one of the five great works that have been described, it was the first to receive the denomination of a King,—and that from the lips of the sage himself,—if the account which we have received of the matter is to be relied on. This little work does not come to us, like the *Kh*un *Kh*iû, as directly from the pencil of Confucius, but in the shape of conversations between him and his disciple Ʒăng-ʒze, put on record in the first place, probably, by some members of Ʒăng's school. No portion of the ancient literature has more exercised the minds and engaged the attention of many of the emperors of successive dynasties. The Hsiâo seems to me an attempt to construct a religion on the basis of the cardinal virtue of Filial Piety, and is open to criticism in many respects. A translation of it is given in the present volume.

The classical books are often spoken of as being 'the five King' and 'the four Shû.' The King have all been separately referred to above; the four Shû is an abbreviation for the Shû or Books of the four Philosophers. The first is the Lun Yü, or 'Discourses and Conversations,' occupied chiefly with sayings of Confucius and conversations between him and many of his disciples. The second is the Works of Mencius, perhaps the greatest thinker and writer of the Confucian school after the Master. I hope to be able to give both these works. The third of the Shû is the Tâ Hsio, or 'Great Learning,' ascribed, like the Hsiâo, to Ʒăng-ʒze. The fourth is the *K*ung Yung, or 'Doctrine of the Mean,' the production of Ʒze-sze, the sage's grandson. Both of these treatises, however, are taken from the Lî *K*î. The whole of the Four Books were translated and published by me in 1861.

III. The third Religion in China is what is called Tâoism. It was, like Confucianism, of native origin, and its acknowledged founder was Lî *R*, called also Lî Po-yang, and, after his death, Lî Tan. More commonly he is designated Lâo-ʒze, translated by some 'the Old Philosopher,' and by others 'the Old Boy' from a fabulous story that his mother carried him in her womb for seventy-two years, so that when he was at length cut out of it, his hair was already white. His birth is referred to the year 604 B.C., so that he was between fifty and sixty years older than Confucius. There are accounts, hardly reliable, of interviews and discussions between the two men.

Lâo-ʒze's system often goes with English writers by the name of Rationalism; but if that name be retained, the term must be taken in quite a peculiar sense. His doctrine was that of the Tâo, but it is not easy to determine what English term will best express the meaning of the Chinese character. The only record which we have of Lâo-ʒze's views is the Tâo-teh King, or 'Classic of Tâo and Virtue,' a treatise of no great length. It was published at Paris in 1842, with a translation in French, by the late Stanislas Julien, under the title of 'Le Livre de la Voie et de la Vertu.' Appealing to the views of *K*wang-ʒze and other writers of the Tâoist school, M. Julien says that 'Le Tâo est dépourvu d'action, de pensée, de jugement, d'intelligence,' and adds that 'it appears impossible therefore to take it for the primordial reason, the Sublime Intelligence, which created and rules the world.'

A translation in English was published, in 1868, by the Rev. Dr. Chalmers of Canton, under the title of 'the Speculations in Metaphysics, Polity, and Morality, of "the Old Philosopher."' Dr. Chalmers retains the term Tâo in his English Text, and says, 'I have thought it better to leave the word Tâo untranslated, both because it has given the name to the sect,—the Tâoists,—and because no English word is its exact equivalent. Three terms suggest themselves,—the Way, Reason, and the Word; but they are all liable to objection. Were we guided by etymology, "the Way" would come nearest to the original, and in one or two passages the idea of a Way seems to be in the term; but this is too materialistic to serve the purpose of a translation. Reason again seems to be more like a quality or attribute of some conscious Being than Tâo is. I would translate it by the Word in the sense of the Logos, but this would be like settling the question which I wish to leave open, viz. what amount of resemblance there is between the Logos of the New Testament and this Tâo, which is its nearest representative in Chinese.'

Two other translations of the Tâo-teh King have appeared, both in German:—'Lao-tsze's Tao Te King, aus dem Chinesischen ins Deutsche übersetzt, eingeleitet, und commentirt, von Victor von Strauss (Leipzig, 1870),' and 'Lao-tse, Tao-te-king, "Der Weg zur Tugend," aus dem Chinesischen übersetzt und erklärt von Reinhold von Plänckner,' also published at Leipzig. Strauss closely follows Julien, while Plänckner allows himself great freedom in dealing with his original. Notwithstanding these four attempts to give the meaning of 'the Old Philosopher' in three European languages, there is room for a new version, which will be submitted to the reader in due course. It is only by an intense and long-continued study of the original that we can come to an agreement as to the meaning of the Tâo. I propose not only to give a translation of the Tâo-teh King, but also of the works of *K*wang-ʒze, the most remarkable of the early writers of the Tâoist school.

Whatever Lâo-ʒze intended by the Tâo, Tâoism has, in the course of time, borrowed largely, both from Confucianism and Buddhism. It inculcates a morality of a high order in some respects, and has developed a system of grotesque beliefs and practices, ministering to superstition, and intended to refine and preserve the breath of life. Its practical teachings will be exhibited in the most popular of all the Tâoist writings,—the treatise on 'Actions and their Recompenses,' and perhaps in one or more, besides, of the characteristic productions of the system.

The version of the Shû that appears in this volume is substantially the same as that in the third volume of my large edition of the Chinese Classics, and which was published in 1865. I wrote out the whole afresh, however, having before me not only my own version, but the earlier translations of P. Gaubil in French and Dr. Medhurst in English. Frequent reference was made likewise to a larger apparatus of native commentaries than I had formerly used. Going to the text anew, after more than twelve years devoted mainly to the continuous study of the Chinese classics, I yet hardly discovered any errors which it was necessary to correct. A few verbal alterations were made to make the meaning clearer. Only in one case will a reader, familiar with the former version, be struck with any alteration in this. The Chinese character 帝 (Tî), applied repeatedly to the ancient Yâo and Shun in the commencing books of the classic, and once in the 27th Book of the fifth Part, was there translated by 'emperor,' while it is left untranslated in the present volume, and its name transferred to the English text.

Before adopting this change, I had considered whether I ought to translate Tî in all other instances of its occurrence in the Shû (and invariably in the Shih), and its intensified form Shang Tî (上 帝), by our term 'God.' Gaubil rendered Tî for the most part by 'le Seigneur,' and Shang Tî by 'le Souverain Maître,' adding sometimes to these names Tî and Shang Tî in brackets. Medhurst translated Tî by 'the Supreme,' and 'the Supreme Ruler,' and Shang Tî by 'the Supreme Ruler.' More than twenty-five years ago I came to the conclusion that Tî was the term corresponding in Chinese to our 'God,' and that Shang Tî was the same, with the addition of Shang, equal to 'Supreme.' In this view I have never wavered, and I have rendered both the names by 'God' in all the volumes of the Chinese Classics thus far translated and published.

What made me pause before doing so in the present volume, was the consideration that the object of 'the Sacred Texts of the Religions of the East, as I understand it, is to give translations of those texts without any colouring in the first place from the views of the translators. Could it be that my own view of Tî, as meaning God, had grown up in the heat of our controversies in China as to the proper characters to be used for the words God and Spirit, in translating the Sacred Scriptures? A reader, confronted everywhere by the word God, might be led to think more highly of the primitive religion of China than he ought to think. Should I leave the names Tî and Shang Tî untranslated? Or should I give for them, instead of God, the terms Ruler and Supreme Ruler? I could not see my way to adopt either of these courses.

The term Heaven (天, pronounced Thien) is used everywhere in the Chinese Classics for the Supreme Power, ruling and governing all the affairs of men with an omnipotent and omniscient righteousness and goodness; and this vague term is constantly interchanged in the same paragraph, not to say the same sentence, with the personal names Tî and Shang Tî. Thien and Tî in their written forms are perfectly distinct. Both of them were among the earliest characters, and enter, though not largely, as the phonetical element into other characters of later formation. According to the oldest Chinese dictionary, the Shwo Wăn (A. D. 100), Thien is formed, 'by association of ideas,' from yî (一), 'one,' and tâ (大), 'great,' meaning—what is one and undivided, and great. Tâi Thung, of our thirteenth century, in his remarkable dictionary, the Liû Shû Kû, explains the top line of it as indicating 'what is above,' so that the significance of the character is 'what is above and great.' In both these dictionaries Tî (帝) is derived from 丄 or 二 (shang), 'above,' or 'what is above:' and they say that the whole character is of phonetical formation, in which I am not able to follow them[1];

[1] It is said in the Shwo Wăn that the phonetical element in Tî is 朿; but this is pronounced 3hze. Neither in form nor sound is there any similitude between it and Tî. An error, probably, has crept into the text. Dr. Chalmers, in his treatise on 'the Origin of the Chinese,' attempts (p. 12) to analyse the character into its constituent parts in the following way:—'The peculiar nature of the Chinese written language has done good service in stereotyping the primi-

but Tâi Thung gives the following account of its meaning:—'Tî is the honourable designation of lordship and rule,' adding, 'Therefore Heaven is called Shang Tî; the five Elementary Powers are called the five Tî; and the Son of Heaven[1]—that is, the Sovereign—is called Tî.' Here then is the name Heaven, by which the idea of Supreme Power in the absolute is vaguely expressed; and when the Chinese would speak of it by a personal name, they use the terms Tî and Shang Tî;—saying, I believe, what our early fathers did, when they began to use the word God. Tî is the name which has been employed in China for this concept for fully 5000 years. Our word God fits naturally into every passage where the character occurs in the old Chinese Classics, save those to which I referred above on p. xxiii. It never became with the people a proper name like the Zeus of the Greeks. I can no more translate Tî or Shang Tî by any other word but God than I can translate *zăn* (人) by anything else but man.

The preceding is a brief abstract of the reasoning by which I was determined to retain the term God for Tî and Shang Tî in this volume, excepting in the cases that have called for these observations. But in the account of Tî which I have adduced from Tâi Thung, it is said that 'the sovereign is also called Tî;' and most of my readers know that Hwang Tî (皇帝) is the title of the emperor of China. How did this application of the name arise? Was it in the first place a designation of the ruler or emperor; and was it then given to the Supreme Power, when the vague Heaven failed to satisfy the thinker and worshipper,

tive belief in one Supreme Tî (帝), who is 大 "great," over, and 丨, "ruling," heaven (⌒ = 一) and earth (冂).' This is ingenious, but not entirely satisfactory. The three last steps are so; but the finding 大 (great) in the top part of 帝 does not in the same way carry conviction to the mind.

[1] Thien Ȝze, 'the Son of Heaven,' is a common designation of the sovereign of China. Originally Ȝze performed in the expression the part of a verb, and Thien Ȝze was equivalent to 'he whom Heaven sons,' that is, considers and treats as its son. See the second line of the ode, p. 318.

and he wished to express his recognition of a personal Being who was to himself his almighty ruler? If these questions be answered in the affirmative, Tî would be a name applied to the Supreme Being, just as we rise from the paternal relation among ourselves and call him Father. Or, on the other hand, was Tî the designation of the Supreme Lord and Ruler, corresponding to our God, and was it subsequently applied to the earthly ruler, thereby deifying him, just as the title Divus was given to a Roman emperor? I believe that it was in this latter way that Tî came to be used of the sovereigns of China; and therefore in again publishing a translation of the Shû, I resolved, that where the appellation is given in it to Yâo and Shun, and it is only to them that it is given, I would retain the Chinese term instead of rendering it, as formerly, by 'emperor.'

The following are the reasons which weighed with me in coming to this resolution:

First, the first really historical sovereign of China who used the title of Hwang Tî was the founder of the *Kh*in dynasty; and he assumed it in B.C. 221, when he had subjugated all the sovereignties into which the feudal kingdom of *K*âu had become divided, and was instituting the despotic empire that has since subsisted.

The *K*âu dynasty had continued for 867 years, from B.C. 1122 to 256, and its rulers had been styled Wang or kings.

*K*âu superseded the dynasty of Shang or Yin, that had endured for 644 years, from B.C. 1766 to 1123; and its rulers had similarly been styled Wang or kings.

Shang superseded the dynasty of Hsiâ, which had lasted for 439 years, from B.C. 2205 to 1767, and its rulers had been styled Wang, or kings, and Hâu, or sovereigns.

Thus, from the great Yü, B.C. 2205 to B.C. 221, that is, for nearly 2000 years, there was no Tî or emperor in China. During all that time the people had on the whole been increasing in numbers, and the nation growing in territory;—how did it come to pass, that the higher title, if it had previously existed, gave place to an inferior one?

Prior to the dynasty of Hsiâ, with the exception of the period of Yâo and Shun, the accounts which we have of the history of China have been, and ought to be, pronounced 'fabulous' and 'legendary.' The oldest documents that purport to be historical are the books in the Shû about Yâo and Shun, and even they do not profess to be contemporaneous with those personages. The earlier accounts open with a Phan-kû, in whose time 'heaven and earth were first separated.' To him succeeded the period of the San Hwang, or Three August Lines, consisting of twelve Celestial, eleven Terrestrial, and nine Human Sovereigns, who ruled together about 50,000 years. After them come a host of different Lines, till we arrive at the Wû Tî, or Five Emperors. The first of these is commonly said to be Fû-hsî, while he and two others are sometimes put down as the San Hwang, in order to bring in Yâo and Shun as the last two of the Tîs.

I have entered into these details because of the account which we have of the king of *Kh*in's assuming the title of Hwang Tî. We are told:—'As soon as the king had brought the whole country into subjection, thinking that he united in himself the virtues of the three Hwangs, and that his merits exceeded those of the five Tîs, he changed his title into Hwang Tî.' The three Hwangs are entirely fabulous, and the five Tîs are, to say the least, legendary. That there were either Hwangs or Tîs ruling in China before the age of the Hsiâ dynasty cannot be admitted.

Second, it has been stated above, and is shown in the Introduction to the Shû, pp. 13–19, that the books in the Shû, previous to the Hsiâ dynasty, are not historical in the sense of their being contemporaneous documents of the times about which they speak. They profess to be compilations merely from older documents; and when they speak of Yâo and Shun as Tîs, the title Tî precedes the name or designation, instead of following it, as it ought to do, according to Chinese usage, if Tî is to be taken in the sense of emperor. Yâo Tî would be 'the emperor Yâo,' but we have Tî Yâo, where Tî performs the part of an adjective. King Wăn, the founder of the *K*âu dynasty, is invariably mentioned as Wăn Wang, 'Wăn the king.' To say Wang Wăn would be felt at once by every Chinese scholar to be inadmissible; and not less so is Tî Yâo for 'the emperor Yâo.' It was the perception of this violation of usage in Chinese composition, five years ago, that first showed me the error of translating Tî Yâo and Tî Shun by 'the emperor Yâo' and 'the emperor Shun.' It is true that in the early books of the Shû, we have Tî used alone, without the adjunct of Yâo or Shun, and referring to those personages. In those cases it does perform the part of a substantive, but its meaning depends on that which belonged to it as an adjective in the phrases Tî Yâo and Tî Shun. If it be ascertained that in these it means 'the Deified,' then when used singly as a noun, it will mean Divus, or the Divine One.

Third, the sovereigns of the Hsiâ, the Shang, and the *K*âu dynasties, it has been seen, were styled Wang and not Tî. Confucius speaks repeatedly in the Analects of Yâo and Shun, but he never calls either of them by the title of Tî. Mencius, however, uses it both of the one and the other, when he is quoting in substance from the accounts of them in the Shû. This confirms the view that the early books of the Shû were current after the middle of the *K*âu dynasty, very much in the form in which we now have them; and the question arises whether we can show how the application of the title Tî as given in them to Yâo and Shun arose. We can.

The fourth Book of the Lî *K*î is called Yüeh Ling, 'the Monthly Record of the Proceedings of Government.' In it certain sacrificial observances paid to the five Tîs are distributed through the four seasons. The Tîs are Fû-hsî, Shăn-năng, Yû-hsiung or Hsien-yüan, *K*in-thien, and Kâo-yang, who are styled Thâi Hâo (the Greatly Resplendent), Yen Tî (the Blazing Tî), Hwang Tî (the Yellow Tî), Shâo Hâo (the Less Resplendent), and *K*wan Hsü (the Solely Correct); with each Tî there is associated in the ceremony a personage of inferior rank, who is styled Shăn (神 = a Spirit). The language descriptive of the ceremony is the same in all the cases, with the exception of the names and months. Thus the first entry is:—'In the first month of spring, on such and such days, the Tî is Thâi Hâo, and the Shân is Kâu-mang.' Now this Kâu-mang was a son of Shâo Hâo, several hundreds of years later than Thâi Hâo, so that the associating them together in this ceremony could only have arisen in later times.

However we explain the ceremony thus curtly described; whether we see in it the growing prevalence of nature-worship, or an illustration of the practice of worshipping ancient heroes and worthies:—Tî appears in the account of it plainly used in the sense of God. In each of the five instances, we have a Tî and a Shăn, not an emperor and a spirit, but a God and a Spirit,—a Spirit standing in the same relation to the God, that *Kh*ăn (臣 = a subject or minister) stands in to a ruler. Thus it was that, by a process of deification, the title of Tî came to be given, in the time of the *K*âu dynasty, to the great names, fabulous and legendary, of antiquity; and thus it was that it was applied to the heroes Yâo and Shun. It may well be that the title Hwang Tî, used by a Chinese of the present emperor or of any emperor of the past, does not call up to his mind any other idea than that of a human sovereign; but being satisfied as to the proper signification of Tî as God, and as to the process by which the title came to be applied to the ancient Yâo and Shun, I could no longer render it, when used of them in the Shû, by emperor, and elected to leave it untranslated in the present volume.

To any unimportant changes of translation it is unnecessary to refer. The dates B.C. in the introductions and notes are all one year more than in the translations formerly published. They are thus brought into accordance with those of P. Gaubil and the useful Chinese Chronological Tables of the late Mr. Mayers.

The changes in the transliteration of Chinese names are very considerable. As foreigners are now resident in Peking, it seemed proper to adopt the pronunciation of the capital as given by Sir T. F. Wade in his Hsin Ching Lu and Tzŭ Erh Chî. At the same time, in order to secure as near an approach as possible to uniformity in all the volumes of the Sacred Books of the East, the letters employed were made to conform to those in Professor Max Müller's Scheme for the Transliteration of Oriental Alphabets. It was not easy at first to do this, for Chinese, having no alphabet, reluctated against being made to appear as if it had; but use has more than reconciled me to the method now employed. It was not possible to introduce into the table all the diphthongs in which Chinese speech is rich. The reader has to be informed that i before another vowel or a diphthong approximates to the sound of y, so that the whole utterance is still monosyllabic. The powers of *r* and ze must be heard before they can be appreciated.

To call the attention of the reader to passages in the Shû, embodying, more or less distinctly, religious ideas, an asterisk (*) will be found appended to them.

J. L.

Oxford,
18th April, 1879.

THE SHÛ KING

OR

BOOK OF HISTORICAL DOCUMENTS.

INTRODUCTION.

CHAPTER I.

THE NATURE AND HISTORY OF THE SHÛ.

1. The Shû is the most ancient of the Chinese classical books, and contains historical documents of various kinds, relating to the period from about B.C. 2357–627. The character Shû shows us by its composition that it denotes 'the pencil speaking,' and hence it is often used as a designation of the written characters of the language. This, indeed, was the earliest meaning of it, but from this the transition was easy to its employment in the sense of writings or books, applicable to any consecutive compositions; and we find it further specially employed by Confucius and others to designate the historical remains of antiquity, in distinction from the poems, the accounts of rites, and other monuments of former times. Not that those other monuments might not also be called by the general name of Shû. The peculiar significancy of the term, however, was well established, and is retained to the present day.

Meaning of the name Shû King.

The book has come down to us in a mutilated condition; but even as it is said to have existed in the time of Confucius, it did not profess to contain a history of China, and much less, to give the annals of that history. It was simply a collection of historical memorials, extending over a space of about 1700 years, but on no connected method, and with frequent and great gaps between them.

The name King (now in Pekinese *K*ing) was not added to Shû till the time of the Han dynasty (began B. C. 202). If Confucius applied it to any of the classical works, it was to the classic of Filial Piety, as will be seen in the Introduction to the translation of that work. The Han scholars, however, when engaged in collecting and digesting the ancient literary monuments of their country, found it convenient to distinguish the most valuable of them, that had been acknowledged by Confucius, as King, meaning what was canonical and of unchallengeable authority.

2. In the Confucian Analects, the sage and one of his disciples quote from the Shû by the simple formula—'The Shû says.' In the Great Learning, four different books or chapters of the classic, all in it as we have it now, are mentioned, each by its proper name. Mencius sometimes uses the same formula as Confucius, and at other times designates particular books. It is most natural for us to suppose that Confucius, when he spoke of the Shû, had in his mind's eye a collection of documents bearing that title.

The Shû was an existing collection of documents before Confucius.

One passage in Mencius seems to put it beyond a doubt that the Shû existed as such a collection in his time. Having said that 'it would be better to be without the Shû than to give entire credit to it,' he makes immediate reference to one of the books of our classic by name, and adds, 'In the Completion of the War I select two or three passages only, and believe them[1].' In Mo-ʒze, Hsün-ʒze, and other writers of the last two centuries of the *K*âu dynasty, the Shû is quoted in the same way, and also frequently with the specification of its parts or larger divisions,—'The Books of Yü,' 'of Hsiâ,' 'of Shang,' 'of *K*âu.' And, in fine, in many of the narratives of Ȝo *Kh*iû-ming's commentary on the Spring and Autumn, the Shû is quoted in the same way, even when the narratives are about men and events long anterior to the sage[2]. All these consi-

[1] Mencius, VII, ii, ch. 3.

[2] The first quotation of the Shû in Ȝo is under the sixth year of duke Yin, B. C. 717.

derations establish the thesis of this paragraph, that the Shû was an existing collection of historical documents before Confucius.

Confucius did not compile the Shû. The number of documents in it in his time. The Preface ascribed to him.

3. From the above paragraph it follows that Confucius did not compile the collection of documents that form the Shû. The earliest assertion that he did so we have from Khung An-kwo, his descendant in the eleventh generation, in the second century, B.C. Recounting the labours of his ancestor, An-kwo says, in the Preface to his edition of the Shû, that 'he examined and arranged the old literary monuments and records, deciding to commence with Yâo and Shun, and to come down to the times of *K*âu. Of those deserving to be handed down to other ages and to supply permanent lessons, he made in all one hundred books, consisting of canons, counsels, instructions, announcements, speeches, and charges.' The same thing is stated by Sze-mâ *Kh*ien in his Historical Records, completed about B.C. 100, but *Kh*ien's information was derived from An-kwo. Such a compilation would have been in harmony with the character which Confucius gave of himself, as 'a transmitter and not a maker, believing and loving the ancients[1],' and with what his grandson says of him in the Doctrine of the Mean, that 'he handed down (the lessons of) Yâo and Shun, as if they had been his ancestors, and elegantly displayed those of Wăn and Wû, whom he took for his model[2].'

We have seen, however, that the collection existed in his time and before it. Did it then, as An-kwo says, consist of a hundred books? His authority for saying so was a Preface, which was found along with the old tablets of the Shû that were discovered in his time and deciphered by him, as will be related farther on. He does not say, however, that it was the work of Confucius, though *Kh*ien does. It still exists,—a list of eighty-one documents in a hundred books. The prevailing opinion of scholars in China is now, that it was not written by the sage. I entirely

[1] Analects, VII, i.

[2] The Doctrine of the Mean, XXX, 1.

agree myself with the judgment of 3*h*âi *K*ăn, the disciple of *K*û Hsî, whose Collected Comments, first published A.D. 1210, are now the standard of orthodoxy in the interpretation of the Shû. He says of the document: 'It sheds light on nothing, and there are things in it at variance with the text of the classic. On the books that are lost it is specially servile and brief, affording us not the slightest help. That it is not the work of Confucius is exceedingly plain.'

The eighty-one documents mentioned in it, and more, may have been in the Shû of the time of Confucius. I think, however, that several of them must have been lost subsequently, before the rise of the tyrant of *Kh*in, who doomed the whole collection to the flames. Mencius complains that in his days the feudal princes destroyed many of the records of antiquity that they might the better perpetrate their own usurpations and innovations [1]. Other considerations, on the exhibition of which I need not enter, confirm me in this conclusion.

The sources of the Shû.

4. It will be well here to devote a paragraph to the sources of the Shû. Have we sufficient proofs of the composition in ancient times of such documents as it contains, and of their preservation, so that they could be collected in a sort of historical canon?

We have. Under the dynasty of *K*âu (B.C. 1122–256), at the royal court, and at the courts of the feudal princes on a smaller scale, there were officers styled Sze, which has been translated 'Recorders,' 'Annalists,' 'Historiographers,' and simply 'Clerks.' There were the Grand Recorder, the Assistant Recorder, the Recorder of the Interior, the Recorder of the Exterior, and the Recorder in Attendance on the Sovereign. Among the duties of the Recorder of the Interior were the following:—'In case of any charge given by the king to the prince of a state, or to any other dignitary, he writes it on tablets;' 'In case of any memorials on business coming in from the different quarters of the kingdom, he reads them (to the king);' 'It is his business

[1] Mencius, V, ii, ch. 2.

to write all charges of the king, and to do so in duplicate.' Of the duties of the Recorder of the Exterior it is said:—'He has charge of the histories of the states in all parts of the kingdom;' 'He has charge of the most ancient books;' 'It is his business to publish in all parts of the kingdom the books and the characters in them[1].'

These entries show that under the *K*âu dynasty there was provision made for the recording and preservation of royal charges and ordinances, of the operations of the general government, and of the histories of the different states; and, moreover, for the preservation and interpretation of documents come down from more ancient times. Confucius himself tells us that in his early days a recorder would leave a blank in his text, rather than enter anything of which he had not sufficient evidence[2]. Mencius also mentions three works, the Shăng of *K*in, the Thâo-wû of *Kh*û, and the *Kh*un *Kh*iû of Lû, which must have come from the recorders of those states.

Of the existence of a similar class of officers under the previous dynasties of Shang or Yin (B.C. 1766–1123) and Hsiâ (B.C. 2205–1765), we have not such abundant evidence. Chapter 2 in the 10th Book of the 5th Part of our classic, however, seems to speak of them in the time of the former. Wû-ting (B.C. 1324–1264), the twentieth sovereign of it, is described as communicating, in writing, a dream which he had had, to his ministers[3]; and fully four hundred years earlier, Î Yin, the chief minister, remonstrates, in writing, with his young and careless sovereign Thâi *K*iâ[4]. Going back to the dynasty of Hsiâ, we find the prince of Yin, during the reign of *K*ung Khang (B.C. 2159–2145), in addressing his troops, quotes the Statutes of Government in a manner which makes us conceive of him as referring to a well-known written compilation[5]. The grandsons of the great Yü, its founder (B.C. 2205–2196), likewise, make mention, in the Songs of the Five Sons, of his Lessons, in a style that suggests to us the formula that Mencius was

[1] See for all these statements the Ritual or Official Book of *K*âu, XXXI, 35-42.

[2] Analects, XV, xxv.

[3] Part IV, viii, section 1.

[4] Part IV, v, section 1.

[5] Part III, iv.

wont to employ when referring to the documents acknowledged to be of authority in his day[1].

Mâ Twan-lin, the encyclopedist, in his General Examination of Records and Scholars, first published A. D. 1321, says that 'the pencil of the recorders was busy from the time of Hwang Tî (B. C. 2697).' The compilers of the records of the Sui dynasty (A. D. 589–617) say that 'historical documents began immediately with the invention of written characters.' That invention I must place myself at an earlier date than the time assigned to Hwang Tî. When once the characters were invented, they would come in time to be employed in the writing of history. The early dates alleged for many of the documents in the Shû are no valid reason for rejecting them without further examination. We may rather be surprised that, when the compilation was made, it did not contain many more than a hundred documents.

5. The dynasty of *K*âu came to an end in B. C. 256, and after an anarchic interval of thirty-five years, the king of *Kh*in succeeded in uniting all the feudal states under his own sway, and proclaimed himself emperor. Up to this time the Shû had sustained no other damage than all human works are liable to in the course of time; but now it narrowly escaped an entire destruction. An edict went forth from the tyrant in B. C. 213, commanding that all the old classical books should be consigned to the flames, excepting those belonging to the great scholars in the service of the court, and the Yî. His rage was hottest against the Shû and the Shih (the Book of Poetry). Death was the doom of scholars who should be known to meet together and speak of these works, and all who should be discovered having copies of them in their possession, when thirty days had elapsed after the publication of the edict, were to be branded, and sent to labour for four years on the Great Wall, which was then building.

Destruction of the classical literature by the emperor of *Kh*in.

This is not the place to explain the reasons that led to

[1] Part III, iii.

this insane attempt to extinguish, with the exception of one work, the ancient literary monuments of China. The edict was ruthlessly enforced, and hundreds of scholars who refused obedience to the imperial command were buried alive. The Shû had nearly perished from off the earth.

6. The tyrant, however, died in B. C. 210, within four years from the issuing of his edict. The dynasty which he had sought to establish passed away in B. C. 206. That of Han dates from the year B. C. 202, and in 191 the edict against the ancient books was formally repealed. They had been under the ban for less than a quarter of a century. There would probably have been no difficulty in recovering copies of them, but for the sack of the capital in B. C. 206 by the most formidable opponent of the founder of the House of Han. Then the fires blazed, we are told, for three months among the palaces and public buildings, and proved as destructive to the copies that might have been preserved about the court as the edict of *Kh*in had been to those among the people.

Recovery of the Shû.

Among the scholars of *Kh*in, however, there had been one, of the surname Fû, who, when the edict was issued, hid his tablets of the Shû in a wall. Returning for them, after the rule of Han was established, he found that many were perished or gone. He recovered only twenty-nine of the documents, containing, according to the division of them that has long been followed, thirty-five books in all. About one of them there is some difficulty, on the discussion of which I need not enter. Fû commenced teaching them, and from all parts scholars resorted to him, and sat at his feet. The emperor Wăn (B. C. 179–155) heard of him, and sent one of the recorders of the court to visit him, and bring the recovered tablets themselves, or a copy of them, to the capital. They were in the form of the character that was prevalent at that time, different from that which had been used in previous centuries, and are known as 'the Shû of the modern text.' The Catalogue of the Imperial Library, prepared by Liû Hin for the emperor Âi (B. C. 6–1), contains an entry of 'the text of the Shû in twenty-nine portions,'—the same, no doubt, which was received from Fû. Fû himself commented on his Shû. The text was engraved on the stone tablets of the emperor Ling (A.D. 168–189). Very many scholars of the Han times laboured on this text, taught it to their disciples, and published their views on it. Not one of their writings, however, survived, in a complete form, the troubles which desolated the empire during the reign of the emperor Hwâi (A.D. 307–312) of the western dynasty of *K*in.

In the reign of the Han emperor Wû (B.C. 140–85) a discovery was made in the wall of the house of the Khung or Confucian family of the tablets of the Shû, the Spring and Autumn, the classic of Filial Piety, and the Lun-yü or Confucian Analects. How long they had lain there we do not know. It is commonly said that they had been hidden by some one of the Khung family to save them from the fires of *Kh*in. But they were in a form of the character that had long gone into disuse, and which hardly any one could decipher, and must have been deposited towards the beginning of the fifth century B.C. They were committed to the care of Khung An-kwo, who was then one of the 'great scholars' of the empire, and the chief of the Khung family. By means of the current text of Fû and other resources he made out all the tablets of the Shû that were in good preservation, and in addition to Fû's twenty-nine documents several others. He found also that Fû had in three cases incorporated two different documents under one name, and taken no note of the division of one other into three books or sections. Altogether there were now forty-six documents or different portions of the old Shû brought anew to light. They appear in Liû Hin's Catalogue as 'the text of the Shû in old characters in forty-six portions.'

When An-kwo had made out the tablets, he presented them to the emperor in B.C. 97, with a transcript of them in the current characters of the time, keeping a second transcript of them for himself; and he received an order to make a commentary on the whole. He did so, but when he was about to lay the result of his labours before the court, troubles had arisen which prevented for several years the paying attention to literary matters. It was owing to these that his commentary was neglected for a time, and the enlarged text which he had deciphered was not officially put in charge of the Board of 'Great Scholars,' to which the care of the five King, so far as they had been recovered, had been committed in B.C. 136.

An-kwo's commentary, however, was not lost; but before speaking of it, I must refer to a third recovery of a large portion of the Shû early in our first century. A scholar and officer, named Tû Lin, had been a fugitive, having many wonderful escapes, during the usurpation of Mang (A.D. 9–22). During his wanderings he discovered a portion of the Shû on 'lacquered' tablets, or perhaps on lacquered cloth, which he thenceforth guarded as his richest treasure, and kept near his person. When the empire was again settled by the first emperor of the eastern Han, he communicated his text to other scholars. Wei Hung published a commentary on it, and subsequently *K*iâ Khwei, Mâ Yung, and *K*ăng Khang-*kh*ăng (all, great names in Chinese literature) did the same. Tû Lin's 'lacquered' books were the same in number as An-kwo's, but they contained five documents in thirteen books, which were not in the text of the other, and wanted nine documents, also in thirteen books, which An-kwo's text had. The commentary of *K*ăng Khang-*kh*ăng continued till the Sui dynasty, after which we lose sight of it.

I return to the commentary of An-kwo, which, of course, contained his text. Its transmission from hand to hand down to the close of the western Han dynasty is clearly traced. Less distinctly, but surely, we can discover evidence of its preservation, till we come to the commencement of the eastern dynasty of *K*in, when Mei Ȝeh, a recorder of the Interior, having come into possession of a copy, presented it to the emperor Yüan (A.D. 317–322). The Canon of Shun was wanting in it, and was supplied from the commentary of Mâ Yung, based on the text of Tû Lin. From this time the text and commentary of An-kwo had their place assigned them in the Imperial College. They are mentioned in the Catalogue of the Imperial Library of Sui. The second emperor of the Thang dynasty gave orders for a grand edition of the Shû, under the superintendence of Khung Ying-tâ, assisted by others. They adopted the commentary of An-kwo, and enriched it with profuse annotations. In A.D. 654 their work was ordered to be printed, and happily remains to the present day. The text of the Shû, that is, of all of it that had been recovered by An-kwo, was still further secured, being engraved with that of all the other classics on the Thang tablets of stone which were completed in the year 837, and are still preserved at *Kh*ang-an, in Shen-hsî.

It is not necessary to trace the history of the Shû further on. The titles of more than 500 works, on the whole of it or on portions, from the dynasty of Thang to the present day, could easily be adduced. Under the Sung dynasty, indeed, there began the sceptical criticism, which, setting comparatively little store on external evidence, decides on the genuineness of documents principally from their style. The results of such criticism always vary according to the knowledge and the subjective character of the mind of its author. Many maintain that the commentary said to be that of An-kwo was not really from him, but was made by Mei 3eh, and palmed on the world under the name of the great Han scholar. Even if it were so, the work would remain, produced nearly 1600 years ago. And to the annotations of the Thang scholars upon it we are indebted for most of what we know of the earlier views of Mâ Yung, *K*ăng Khang-*kh*ăng, and other writers of the Han period. Whether its author were the true Khung or a false Khung, its value cannot be over-estimated. But I do not believe that it was a forgery. That An-kwo did write a commentary on his 'Shû in the ancient characters' is admitted by all. When did it perish? There is no evidence that it ever did so. On the contrary, its existence rises as a fact, here and there, at no great intervals of time, on the surface of the literary history of the empire, till we arrive at Mei 3eh, who received it, as Khung Ying-tâ proves, from a scholar named 3ang 3hâo.

Then as to the text of the Shû, there is no controversy about the documents which were recovered in the first place by Fû ; but the additional ones found by Khung An-kwo are so much more easily understood, that I do not wonder that the charge of not being genuine has been raised against him. But even they are not easy. They only appear to be so, when we come to one of them, after toiling through some of the more contorted portions common to both texts. And, moreover, the style of the different books differs according to their subjects. The 'Announcements' are the hardest to understand of all. The 'Charges,' 'Speeches,' and 'Instructions' are much simpler in their construction ; and the portions which we owe to An-kwo consist principally of these. In making out his obsolete characters he had, in the first place, to make use of the Books of Fû. That he did not servilely follow his text we conclude from the readings of Fû's followers, different from his in many passages which the industry of critics has gathered up. When he came, however, to new books, which were not in Fû's copy, he had to make out his tablets as he best could. His most valuable aid had ceased. We can conceive that, when he had managed to read the greater portion of a paragraph, and yet there were some stubborn characters that defied him, he completed it according to his understanding of the sense with characters of his own. That he was faithful and successful in the main we find by the many passages of his peculiar books that are found quoted in writings of the *K*âu dynasty. This is a fact worthy of the most attentive consideration. I do not think there is an important statement in his chapters that is not thus vouched for. The characteristics of his books which have exposed them to suspicion are not sufficient to overthrow their claims to be regarded as genuine transcripts of the tablets discovered in the wall of the house of the Khung family.

The conclusion to which I come, at the close of this chapter, is, that there is nothing seriously to shake our confidence in the portions of the Shû that we now possess, as being substantially the same as those which were in the collection of the *K*âu dynasty both before and after Confucius.

CHAPTER II.

THE CREDIBILITY OF THE RECORDS IN THE SHÛ.

Whether the records in the Shû are reliable or not.

1. Accepting the conclusion which I have stated immediately above, I now go on to enquire whether the documents in the Shû can be relied on as genuine narratives of the transactions which they profess to relate. And it may be said at once, in reference to the greater number of them, that there is no reasonable ground to call their credibility in question. Allowance must be made, indeed, for the colouring with which the founders of one dynasty set forth the misdeeds of the closing reigns of that which they were superseding, and for the way in which the failures of a favourite hero may be glossed over. But the documents of the Shû are quite as much entitled to credit as the memorials and edicts which are published at the present day in the Peking Gazette.

The more recent the documents are, the more, of course, are they to be relied on. And provision was made, we have seen, by the statutes of *K*âu, for the preservation of the records of previous dynasties. But it was not to be expected that many of those should not perish in the lapse of time, and others suffer mutilations and corruptions. And this, we find, was the case. Of the eighty-one documents that the Shû at one time contained, only one belonged to the period of Yâo; seven to the period of Shun; four to the dynasty of Hsiâ, much the larger one of which narrates what was done in the time of Yâo; thirty-one to the dynasty of Shang; and thirty-eight to the first 500 years of that of *K*âu. All this seems to bear on the surface of it the stamp of verisimilitude.

The Books of *K*âu.

2. The Books of *K*âu were contemporaneous with the events which they describe, and became public property not long after their composition. They are to be received without hesitation.

Nor are those of the previous dynasty of Shang open to suspicion. We ascend by means of them to Thang the Successful, its founder, with a confident step. The beginning of his rule is placed chronologically in B.C. 1766.

The Books of Shang.

Of the still earlier dynasty of Hsiâ, there are only four documents, and we have no evidence that there were any more when the collection of the Shû was made in the times of *K*âu. The first and longest of the four, though occupied with the great achievement of Yü, the founder of Hsiâ, whose chronological place is B.C. 2205–2196, really belongs to the reign of Yâo, and is out of place among the records of Hsiâ. The other three documents bring us down only to the reign of *K*ung Khang (B.C. 2159–2145), and I see no grounds for doubting their genuineness. In the last of them a celestial phenomenon is mentioned, which has always been understood to have been an eclipse of the sun in Fang, a space of about $5\frac{1}{2}°$ from π to σ of Scorpio, on the first day of the last month of autumn. P. Gaubil thought he had determined by calculation that such an eclipse really took place in the fifth year of *K*ung Khang, B.C. 2155. Doubts, however, have been cast, as will be seen in the next chapter, on the accuracy of his calculation, and therefore I do not avail myself of it here as a confirmation of the truth of the document.

The Books of Hsiâ.

3. We come to the earlier records,—those of the reigns of Yâo and Shun, with which must be classed the Tribute of Yü, the first of the documents of Hsiâ; and it must be admitted that there is not the same evidence that they existed originally in their present form.

The Books of Thang and Yü.

i. The Canon of Yâo and three of the four still existing books of the time of Yü, all commence with the words, 'Examining into antiquity, we find.' They are therefore, on their own showing, the compilations of a later age. The writer separates himself from the date of the events which he narrates, and while professing to draw from the records

They are professedly later compilations.

of 'antiquity,' yet writes himself from a modern standpoint. The Yî and *K*î, the last of the documents of the Shun period, formed one book with the preceding in the Shû of Fû, and came under the opening words of that, as being a result of 'the examination of antiquity.' I will draw separate attention farther on to the Tribute of Yü.

They are legendary.

ii. Much of what is related in the Canons of Yâo and Shun, as well as in the other documents, has more the air of legend than of history. When Yâo has been on the throne for seventy years, he proposes to resign in favour of his principal minister, who is styled the Four Mountains. That worthy declares himself unequal to the office. Yâo then asks him whom he can recommend for it; be the worthiest individual a noble or a poor man, he will appoint him to the dignity. This brings Shun upon the stage. All the officers about the court can recommend him,—Shun of Yü [1], an unmarried man among the lower people. His father, a blind man, was obstinately unprincipled; his mother, or stepmother, was insincere; his brother was arrogant; and yet Shun had been able by his filial piety to live harmoniously with them, and to bring them to a considerable measure of self-government and good conduct. Yâo is delighted. He had himself heard something of Shun. He resolved to give him a preliminary trial. And a strange trial it was. He gave him his own two daughters in marriage, and declared that he would test his fitness for the throne by seeing his behaviour with his two wives.

Shun must have stood the test. Yâo continued to employ him as General Regulator for three years, and then called him to ascend the throne. Shun refused to do so, but discharged the royal duties till the death of Yâo in 2257, becoming himself sole ruler in B.C. 2255. These

[1] 虞舜,—Yü is the dynastic designation of Shun. It is to be distinguished from Yü (禹), the name of Shun's successor, the founder of the dynasty of Hsiâ. Bunsen confounded the two appellations (Egypt's Place in Universal History, III, p. 399).

and other marvellous notices of Yâo and Shun are largely added to by Mencius and Sze-mâ *Kh*ien, but their accounts are of the same extraordinary character. I must believe that the oldest portions of the Shû do not give us the history of Yâo and Shun, but legendary tales about them.

Their compiler had ancient documents on which to base his representations.

At the same time it must be allowed that the compiler of these books in their present form had in his possession some documents as old as the time of Yâo. To my mind three things render this admission necessary. First, the titles of the high officers of Yâo and Shun are different from those of the corresponding dignitaries at a later age. The principal personage was called the Four Mountains; next to him was the General Regulator; and the Minister of Religion was the Arranger of the Ancestral Temple. It is more probable that the compiler received these and other peculiar designations from old documents than that he invented them himself. Second, the style of these early books is distinguished in several particulars from the style of those of Hsiâ, Shang, and *K*âu. I need only specify the exclamations, 'Alas!' 'Ah!' and 'Oh!' which are expressed by characters that we do not elsewhere find used in the same way. Third, the directions of Yâo to his astronomers, telling them how to determine the equinoxes and solstices, by means of the stars culminating at dusk in those seasons, could not be the inventions of a later age. The reader will find this subject discussed in the next chapter, where it is shown how those culminating stars may be employed to ascertain the era of Yâo. No compiler, ignorant of the precession of the equinoxes, which was not known in China till about the middle of our fourth century, could have framed Yâo's directions with such an adjustment to the time assigned to him in chronology.

When the Books of Thang and Yü received their present form, we cannot tell. Probably it was in the early period of the *K*âu dynasty, though I am not without a suspicion that some verbal changes were made in them under the short-lived dynasty of *Kh*in, which intervened between the dynasties of *K*âu and Han, and possibly some also when they were recovered under the latter.

4. It remains for us to consider the case of the Tribute of Yü, the first, as the books are now arranged, of those of Hsiâ, but belonging, as has been already said, to the period of Yâo, or at least to the period when Yâo and Shun were together on the throne. It thus appears out of its chronological order, and must share in the general uncertainty which attaches to the documents of the first two parts of our classic.

The Tribute of Yü.

Yâo, in what year of his reign we are not told, appears suddenly startled by the ravages of a terrible inundation. The waters were overtopping the hills, and threatening the heavens in their surging fury. The people everywhere were groaning and murmuring. Was there a capable man to whom he could assign the correction of the calamity? All the nobles recommend one Khwăn, to whom Yâo, against his own better judgment, delegates the difficult task, on which Khwăn labours without success for nine years. His son Yü then entered on the work. From beyond the western bounds of the present China proper he is represented as tracking the great rivers, here burning the woods, hewing the rocks, and cutting through the mountains that obstructed their progress, and there deepening their channels until their waters flow peacefully into the eastern sea. He forms lakes, and raises mighty embankments, till at length 'the grounds along the rivers were everywhere made habitable; the hills cleared of their superfluous wood; and access to the capital was secured for all within the four seas. A great order was effected in the six magazines (of material wealth); the different parts of the country were subjected to an exact comparison, so that contribution of revenue could be carefully adjusted according to their resources. The fields were all classified according to the three characters of the soil, and the revenues of the Middle Kingdom were established.' Of the devotion with which Yü pursued his work, he says himself in the Yî and *K*î:—'I mounted my four conveyances,'—carriages on the land, boats on the water, sledges in icy places, and shoes with spikes in them in ascending the hills,—'and all along the hills hewed down the woods, at the same time, along with Yî, showing the people how to get flesh to eat,'—that is, by capturing fish and birds and beasts. 'I opened passages for the streams throughout the nine provinces, and conducted them to the sea. I deepened the channels and canals, and conducted them to the streams, at the same time, along with *K*î, sowing grain, and showing the people how to procure the food of toil in addition to flesh meat. I urged them to exchange what they had for what they had not, and to dispose of their accumulated stores. In this way all the people got grain to eat, and the myriad regions began to come under good rule.' And again:—'When I married in Tû-shan, I remained with my wife only four days.' Mencius says that while engaged on his task, he thrice passed the door of his house, but did not enter it. His own words are:—'When *Kh*î (my son) was wailing and weeping, I did not regard him, but kept planning with all my might my labour on the land.'

Along with his operations to assuage the wide-spread inundation, Yü thus carried on other most important labours proper to an incipient civilization. We gather from the Shû that it did not take him many years to accomplish his mighty undertaking. It was successfully finished before the death of Yâo. All this is incredible. The younger Biot, in an article on the Tribute of Yü, published in the Journal Asiatique, in 1842, says:—'If we are to believe the commentators, Yü will become a supernatural being, who could lead the immense rivers of China as if he had been engaged in regulating the course of feeble streamlets.' There is no occasion to say, 'If we are to believe the commentators;'—if we are to believe the Shû, this is the judgment that we must form about Yü.

The general conclusion to which Biot came about the document under our notice was that we are to find in it only the progress of a great colony. Yü was the first explorer of the Chinese world. He established posts of colonists or planters in different parts of the territory. He caused the wood around those posts to be cut down, and commenced the cultivation of the soil. After Yü, the labours of draining the country and clearing the forests continued during some ages, and the result of all was attributed by Chinese tradition to the first chief. I have no doubt there is an inkling of the truth in this view of the French sinologue, but the idea of Yü's being the leader of a Chinese colony had better be abandoned. We recognise the primitive seat of the Chinese people, in the southern parts of the present Shan-hsî, with the Ho on the west and south of it. His son fought a battle with the Chief of Hû at a place in the present department of Hsî-an, in Shen-hsî, across the Ho, and his grandson was kept a sort of prisoner at large in the present province of Ho-nan, south of the river. The people or tribe extended itself westward, eastward, and southward, and still later northward, as it increased in numbers, and was able to subdue the earth.

The flood of Yâo was probably an inundation of the Ho, similar to many in subsequent times which have procured for that river the name of 'China's Sorrow,' and Yü distinguished himself in the assuaging of it, and the regulation of its course to the sea. The extent of the country came to be ascertained under the dynasties of Hsiâ and Shang, and its different parts were gradually occupied by the increasing numbers of the people, and contributed their various proportions of revenue to the central government. There were memorials of the toils which Yü had undergone, and of allotments of territory which he had made to the most distinguished among his followers. It occurred to some historiographer to form a theory as to the way in which the whole country might have been brought to order by the founder of the Hsiâ dynasty, and he proceeded to glorify Yü by ascribing so grand an achievement to him. About the same time, probably, the popular stories of Yü's self-denial had found their expression in the Yî and *K*î, prompting at once the conception of the Tribute of Yü, and obtaining for it a favourable reception. Yü entered well into association with Yâo and Shun, and formed a triad with them at the beginning of the Chinese monarchy. Their wisdom and benevolence appeared in him, combined with a practical devotion to the duties of his position, in which all sovereigns would have a model, to win them from indolence and self-indulgence, and stimulate them to a painstaking discharge of their responsibilities.

In the nineteenth of the Books of Part V, the duke of *K*âu counsels his young sovereign, king *Kh*ăng (B.C. 1115–1077), to have his armies in a good state of preparation, so that he might go forth 'beyond the footsteps of Yü,' and travel over all beneath the sky, everywhere meeting with submission. The duke's reference to 'the footsteps of Yü' does not prove that Yü really travelled and toiled as the Tribute of Yü reports, but only that such was the current belief at the commencement of the *K*âu dynasty, while it affords at the same time a presumption that our document was then among the archives of the kingdom. It may have been compiled before the end of the Hsiâ dynasty, or under that of Shang. From Shang it passed to *K*âu, and came under the care of the recorders of the Exterior. Then subsequently it was very properly incorporated in the collection of the Shû.

5. While we are thus unable to receive the six earliest documents in our classic as contemporaneous in their present form with the events which they relate, it is not meant to throw doubt on the existence of Yâo, Shun, and Yü as historical personages. More especially does Yü stand forth as the first sovereign of the dynasty of Hsiâ, the man who laid the foundation of the hereditary monarchy in China, its feudal sovereign who 'conferred surnames and lands.' The documents which follow the Tribute of Yü, commencing with the Speech at Kan, delivered in B.C. 2197 by Yü's son and successor, may all be received as veritable monuments of antiquity.

Yâo, Shun, and Yü are all historical personages.

CHAPTER III.

ON THE CHRONOLOGY OF CHINA, AND THE PRINCIPAL ERAS IN THE SHÛ.

1. I do not enter here on the subject of the chronology of China further than is necessary to show that there is no chronological difficulty in the way of our accepting the documents of the Shû, which I have just specified, as being possessed of the antiquity ascribed to them.

No detailed chronological system can be made out from the Shû.

The Shû itself does not supply the means of laying down any scheme of chronology for the long period of time which it covers. We learn from it that the dynasty of *K*âu succeeded to that of Shang (another name for which was Yin), and the dynasty of Shang to that of Hsiâ, and that prior to Yü, the founder of the Hsiâ, there were the reigns of Shun and Yâo. As P. Gaubil has observed, 'If we had only the Shû King, we should have but confused ideas of the time comprised in the different parts of the book.' There is nothing in this to awaken our surprise. The chronology of a nation comes to be cultivated as a science only when a necessity is felt to arrange the events of its history in regular series on the course of time.

Attempts at systematic chronology began in the Han period.

2. It was under the Han dynasty that it was first attempted to construct a chronological scheme of the history of the nation. For this purpose its scholars employed the well-known cycle of sixty years, in the fifteenth year of the seventy-sixth revolution of which I am now writing. It was assumed that this cycle was first devised by Tâ-nâo, an officer of Hwang Tî, in B. C. 2637, which is the first year of the first cycle. But all scholars in China, whether they call in question this origin of the cycle or not, now agree in saying that the use of the cyclic characters to chronicle years was not the ancient method, and did not begin earlier than the time of the usurper Mang (A. D. 9–22).

In the Shû itself the current cycle is used to chronicle

days, and days only. Years are specified according to their order in the reign of the sovereign to whom they are referred. Such specification of years in it, however, is rare.

Ancient method of determining the length of Chinese history.

Before the Han dynasty a list of sovereigns, and of the length of their several reigns, was the only method which the Chinese had of determining the duration of their national history. And it would still be a satisfactory method, if we had a list of sovereigns, and of the years that each reigned, that was complete and reliable. But we do not have this. Even in the early part of the Han dynasty, Sze-mâ *Kh*ien's father and himself, in their Historical Records, completed about B. C. 100, were obliged to content themselves with giving simply the names and order of most of the rulers of Shang and Hsiâ. It is right to state also that in A. D. 279, when the grave of king Hsiang of Wei (died in B. C. 295) was opened, there were found a number of bamboo tablets in it, written in the ancient seal characters, among which the most valuable portion was a book of annals, beginning with the reign of Hwang Tî, and coming down to the sixteenth year of the last king of *K*âu, B.C. 299. This work is still current under the name of the Annals of the Bamboo Books. The chronology derived from it is shorter than the received system by rather more than 200 years.

If in any of the classical books of the *K*âu dynasty we had a statement of the length of the national history from any given era to the time of the writer, the notice would be exceedingly valuable; or, if the length of the reigns of the sovereigns of Shang and Hsiâ, cursorily mentioned in it, were correctly given, we should be in a position to make an approximate computation for ourselves. But there are only two passages in all those books which are helpful to us in this point. The former of them is in a narrative in 3o *Kh*iû-ming's supplement to the Spring and Autumn, under the third year of duke Hsüan, where it is said that the dynasty of Shang possessed the throne for 600 years. The other passage is the last chapter of the works of Mencius, where that philosopher says that 'from Yâo and Shun to Thang'—a period including all the dynasty of Hsiâ—

'there were 500 years and more; from Thang to king Wăn'—the period of the Shang dynasty—'500 years and more; and from king Wăn to Confucius, 500 years and more.' We know that Confucius was born in B.C. 551. Adding 551 to the 1500 years 'and more,' given by Mencius, we have the era of Yâo and Shun at 2100 years 'and more' before our Christian era. And the received chronology places Yü's accession to the throne, as the successor of Shun, in B.C. 2205. Vague as the language of Mencius is, I do not think that with the most painstaking research, apart from conclusions based on astronomical considerations, we can determine anything more precise and definite concerning the length of Chinese history than it conveys.

The period of the *K*âu dynasty.

3. The Charge to the Marquis Wăn, which now forms the 28th Book of the 5th Part of the Shû, is understood to have been delivered by king Phing, the thirteenth of his line. His place in historical time is well ascertained. Confucius' chronicle of the Spring and Autumn commences in B.C. 722. The first of the thirty-six solar eclipses mentioned in it took place three years after, on the 14th February (N.S.) 719, and it is recorded that in the month after king Phing died. Here therefore is a point of time about which there can be no dispute. An earlier date in the *K*âu dynasty is known with the same certainty. The Book of Poetry mentions an eclipse of the sun which took place on the 29th August, B.C. 776, in the sixth year of king Yû, who preceded Phing. Yû reigned eleven years, and his predecessor, Hsüan, forty-six, whose reign consequently commenced B.C. 827. Up to this date Chinese chronologers agree. To the ten reigns before king Hsüan, the received chronology assigns 295 years, making the dynasty begin in B.C. 1122, which cannot be far from the truth.

The period of the Shang dynasty.

4. In the period of the Shang dynasty we cannot fix a single reign by means of astronomical facts. The received chronology assigns to it twenty-eight reigns, extending over 644 years, so that its commencement was in B.C. 1766. The scheme

derived from the bamboo books makes the sovereigns to be thirty, but the aggregate of their reigns is only 508. Mencius says that between Thang, the founder of the dynasty, and Wû-ting, the twentieth sovereign (in the common scheme), 'there had been six or seven worthy and sage rulers[1],'—leading to the conclusion that the number of twenty-eight sovereigns in all is not beyond the truth. In the fifteenth of the Books of *K*âu the names of three of the Shang rulers are given, and the duration of their reigns,—to show how Heaven is likely to crown a good king with length of sway. They are Thâi Mâu, who reigned seventy-five years; Wû-ting, who reigned fifty-nine; and Ȝû-*k*iâ, who reigned thirty-three. The two schemes agree in the length of those reigns and of five others. From the statement in the Ȝo-*k*wan, to which I have referred above, that the Shang dynasty possessed the throne for 600 years, and Mencius' language that it lasted 'for 500 years and more,' we may believe that the 644 years of the common scheme are more likely to be correct than the 508 of the shorter.

The period of Hsiâ.

5. The dynasty of Hsiâ lasted, according to the received chronology, 439 years, and according to the bamboo books, 431; so that the difference here between the two schemes is small. The former estimate carries us up to B.C. 2205, as the first year of Yü's reign.

I referred on page 13 to an eclipse of the sun, mentioned in the fourth of the Books of Hsiâ, as having occurred in the reign of *K*ung Khang, a grandson of Yü, and stated that P. Gaubil had found by calculation that on the day and month stated in the document, and in the quarter of the heavens given, an eclipse did occur in the fifth year of *K*ung Khang, that is, in B.C. 2156, and was visible at his capital at $6^h 49'$, A.M. In 1840, J. B. Biot submitted a copy of Gaubil's calculations to the younger Largeteau, a member, like himself, of the Institute of France, who went over them with the lunar tables of Damoiseau and the solar tables of Delambre, and brought out the result that

[1] Mencius, II, i, ch. 1.

there was indeed an eclipse on the day stated, but before the rising of the sun at the then capital of China[1]. My friend, the Rev. Dr. Chalmers of Canton, not knowing anything of the examination made by Largeteau, undertook to verify the eclipse in 1861, and found that while the year, the month, and the day, as given by Gaubil, were correct, the eclipse had taken place during the night, and could not have been seen by the Chinese astronomers. The eclipse mentioned in the document of the Shû cannot therefore be used at present to confirm the received chronology of China; but I am unwilling to give it up entirely. M. Biot says that, 'Notwithstanding the failure of the attempt of Largeteau to verify the eclipse, the hope of yet finding it in some one of the years of the twenty-second century before our era is not entirely lost. We ought to wait till the further perfecting of the lunar tables brings us new lights, by means of which we can form a surer judgment.'

6. We come to the earliest period of Chinese history of which the Shû makes more than a cursory mention,—that of Yâo and Shun. It says that Shun was thirty years on the throne with Yâo, and that, fifty years after, he died and went on high. We learn from it also that it was in the seventieth year of his reign that Yâo sought for another to relieve him of the toils of government. The period covered by the two therefore is 150 years, which both the schemes of chronology accept. Adding two years of mourning between Shun's death and Yü's accession to the throne, we have B.C. 2357 as the first year of Yâo.

The period of Yâo and Shun.

In the Canon of Yâo, when that personage is giving directions to his astronomers how to determine the equinoxes and solstices, he tells them that at the vernal equinox they would find the star in Niâo, and at the autumnal in Hsü; at the summer solstice, the star in Hwo, and at the winter in Mâo. It has always been assumed by Chinese scholars that when Yâo said, 'The star of mid-spring is in

[1] Etudes sur l'Astronomie Indienne et sur l'Astronomie Chinoise, pp. 376–382.

Niâo,' he meant the star culminating at dusk at that season, at the point of observation. And so of the other stars and seasons. A Chinese astronomer at the present day would similarly express himself.

Further, the most common, and what was the earliest division of the ecliptic in China, is that of the twenty-eight lunar mansions, forming what we may call the Chinese zodiac. These mansions are grouped together in four classes of seven each, assigned to the four quarters of the heavens[1]. Of the celestial spaces which Yâo specified, Niâo is the general name for the seven mansions or constellations belonging to the southern quarter; Hwo is an old name of what is now called Fang, the central constellation of the eastern quarter; Hsü and Mâo are the central constellations of the northern and southern quarters respectively. What Yâo meant therefore was, that his astronomers could determine the solstices and the autumnal equinox by the culmination of the stars in the mansions which he specified for those seasons. And we may assume that he directed them, for the star of the vernal equinox, to Hsing, the central mansion in the southern space Niâo. Now, Hsing corresponds to α (Alphard) Hydræ, and small stars near it, in our stellar nomenclature; Hwo, to β, δ in Scorpio; Hsü, to β Aquarii; and Mâo, to Pleiades. When we wish to make the directions of Yâo available for the purpose of chronological enquiry, the question that arises is this:—When did the above-named stars culminate at dusk in China at the equinoctial and solstitial seasons?

Bunsen tells us that Ideler, computing the places of the constellations backwards, fixed the accession of Yâo at B.C. 2163, and that Freret was of opinion that the observations left an uncertainty of 3°, leaving a margin of 210

[1] In the Official Book of *K*âu, a work of the twelfth century before our era, Book XXVI, par. 25, in the enumeration of the duties of the astronomer royal of that day, there is mentioned the determination of 'the places of the twenty-eight stars,' meaning 'the principal stars in the twenty-eight lunar mansions.' The names of the stars and their mansions are not mentioned;—surely a sufficient indication that they were even then well known. See Biot's Etudes sur l'Astronomie Indienne, &c., pp. 112, 113.

years [1]. On the other hand, J. B. Biot found in the directions a sufficient confirmation of the received date for Yâo's accession,—B. C. 2357 [2]. Appended to this Introduction is a chart of the stars as they were visible in China in B. C. 2300, which the Rev. C. Pritchard, Savilian Professor of Astronomy in the University of Oxford, kindly prepared for me. An inspection of it, in the manner directed by him, will show that the phenomena indicated by Yâo to his astronomers were all apparent at that date. This fact must be accepted as a strong proof of the approximate correctness of the chronology, which places Yâo in the twenty-fourth century B. C. The precession of the equinoxes, it has already been observed, was not known in China till more than 2500 years after the time assigned to Yâo, so that the culminating stars at the equinoxes and solstices of his remote period could not have been computed back scientifically in the time of the *K*âu dynasty, during which the collection of the Shû existed. The form in which the directions are given, and other things in the Canon, savour, indeed, of legend, and I have not claimed for it that in its present form it be received as a document contemporaneous with the reign of Yâo. I have argued, however, that the compiler of it had before him ancient documents, and one of them must have contained the facts about the culminating of the stars, which I have now endeavoured to set in a clear light.

The mention of these culminating stars does seem to fix Yâo's place in chronology in the twenty-fourth century B. C., and to show that at that remote era it was the custom to make and to record astronomical observations of the heavenly bodies. Having respect to these things, my claim to have the documents of the Shû from the Speech at Kan, nearly two centuries later than Yâo, downwards, regarded as contemporaneous with the events which they describe, cannot be considered extravagant.

7. In the 27th Book of the 5th Part, the Marquis of

[1] Egypt's Place in Universal History, III, pp. 400, 401.
[2] Études sur l'Astronomie Indienne, &c., pp. 361–366.

Lü on Punishments, there is a historical reference which would carry us back four centuries beyond the time of Yâo. It is said that, 'According to the teachings of antiquity, *Kh*ih Yû was the first to create disorder.' There is no intimation, however, of the time when this rebel disturbed the happy order and innocence which had previously prevailed; and the very same sentence brings the review of antiquity down to the time of Shun. But the chronologers place him in the reign of Hwang Tî, towards the end of the twenty-seventh century B. C. Other writers describe the struggle between him and Hwang Tî, in which dragons, mists, and the invention of the compass play conspicuous parts. It is to the credit of the Shû, and an evidence of its being a genuine collection of historical memorials, that this cursory reference to *Kh*ih Yû is the only mention in it of any name older than that of Yâo.

The Use of the Chart.

This chart is intended to represent approximately the aspect of the principal zodiacal stars as seen above the horizon of any place in central China, at any hour of any day, about the year B.C. 2300.

In order to apply the chart to a practical purpose, the reader is advised to cut out a sheet of paper (cardboard is preferable) with its upper edge exactly fitting the curved line A B O C D, and to draw, near to the bottom of the paper, a line coinciding with 'the hour-line' on the chart.

This being done, if it be asked what will be the aspect of the heavens when the Sun sets at the Vernal Equinox, the reader is to move the line at the bottom of the cardboard along the horizontal 'hour-line' of the chart until the place of the Sun in the Ecliptic at the Vernal Equinox O just touches the curved top of the paper; then all the stars not covered over are above the horizon at the time of that sunset, viz. in this case Aldebaran, Sirius, Spica, &c.; the Pleiades are just setting, Regulus and α Hydræ are very near the meridian, β Centauri is on the point of rising, and α Serpentis is well up above the horizon. This exactly corresponds with that state of the heavens which Yâo, (alleged in the Chinese records to have flourished about B.C. 2300,) indicated to his astronomers (Hsî and Ho) would be the case, viz. that he would find the star (or the stellar division) Shun Hwo (corresponding, it is said, to α Hydræ) culminating at the time of sunset at the Vernal Equinox [1].

Again, if it be required to find what constellation is culminating at the time of sunset at the Summer Solstice, the cardboard must be moved, as before, towards the right hand until the position of the Sun at the Summer Solstice, viz. G, just touches the horizon curve, when it will be seen that α Serpentis and Antares are then culminating, Regulus and β Centauri are just setting, while the constellations of Aquila and Aquarius are rising; Vega is a conspicuous object above the eastern horizon. This again corresponds to the indications given by Yâo to his astronomers, viz. that they would find the constellation Scorpio culminating at the time.

Thirdly, to find what constellation is culminating at sunset at the Winter Solstice, the cardboard horizon is to be moved, as before, until the Sun at F falls upon it, when the constellations Aries and Taurus with the Pleiades will be seen near to their culmination. This is a third correspondence with the indications of the astronomical sovereign.

Lastly, at sunset of the Autumnal Equinox the movable horizon is to be shifted to the left until the point A falls upon it, where it will be seen in this position that the stars in Aquarius are culminating at the time. It is scarcely possible that all these indications of the positions of the stars at these several times of the year could be simultaneously correct at any other epoch than somewhere about B.C. 2300 or a very small number of centuries before or after.

The reader may easily make for himself many other interesting applications of the chart. A general notion of the effects of precession on the positions of the stars may be seen at once by observing the three positions of the Pleiades, at the three epochs B.C. 2300, A.D. 1, and A.D. 1878, marked in the chart by the letters K, L, M; and as the approximate effect of precession is to cause all stars to move parallel to the Ecliptic and through the same arc, if the reader will imagine every star to be shifted parallel to the Ecliptic through spaces equal respectively to K L, L M, he will get the aspect of the heavens at the epochs A.D. 1 and A.D. 1878.

The following table has been calculated for the apparent positions of the principal stars in the years B.C. 2300, B.C. 1500, A.D. 1, and A.D. 1000; except in one instance it will be found to confirm a similar calculation made by Biot for the earliest of these dates.

[1] See an excellent memoir by Mr. Williams, the late Assistant Secretary of the Royal Astronomical Society, on Chinese Comets, procurable at the apartments of the Royal Astronomical Society, Burlington House, London.

Name of Star.	For the year B.C. 2300. R. A.	For the year B.C. 2300. N. P. D.	For the year B.C. 1500. R. A.	For the year B.C. 1500. N. P. D.	For the year A.D. 1. R. A.	For the year A.D. 1. N. P. D.	For the year A.D. 1000. R. A.	For the year A.D. 1000. N. P. D.	For the year A.D. 1878. R. A.	For the year A.D. 1878. N. P. D.
	h. m. s.	° ′	h. m. s.	° ′	h. m. s.	° ′	h. m. s.	° ′	h. m. s.	° ′
α Andromedæ	20 33 18	82 1·7	21 13 18	79 1·3	22 27 33	71 49·4	23 18 4	66 28·4	0 2 5	61 35·0
γ Pegasi	20 28 50	96 1·1	21 12 0	92 58·9	22 30 26	85 45·9	23 22 23	80 23·8	0 6 57	75 29·7
β Ceti	20 40 23	129 55·3	21 32 5	126 40·1	22 59 27	119 2·8	23 53 7	113 33·4	0 37 28	108 39·4
α Arietis	22 18 8	89 27·4	22 59 59	85 16·6	0 18 20	76 57·2	1 12 25	71 36·3	2 0 18	67 6·9
η Tauri	23 49 0	86 8·3	0 31 15	81 42·1	1 52 20	73 52·4	2 49 17	69 31·6	3 40 14	66 16·4
Aldebaran	0 40 10	90 54·6	1 22 25	86 38·2	2 43 20	79 37·0	3 39 17	76 7·5	4 28 55	73 44·3
Capella	0 43 7	60 13·1	1 22 14	55 56·4	2 55 15	49 3·0	4 4 9	45 54·0	5 7 41	44 7·7
Rigel	1 47 31	111 43·8	2 26 12	107 58·3	3 38 7	102 21·2	4 26 41	99 52·2	5 8 40	98 20·7
α Orionis	2 5 7	93 37·4	2 46 56	90 4·8	4 6 40	85 9·1	5 1 10	83 22·1	5 48 34	82 37·1
Sirius	3 16 27	112 9·0	4 2 2	108 57·4	5 14 27	106 24·3	6 0 31	106 6·5	6 39 46	106 33·0
Castor	2 54 18	62 4·9	3 44 10	59 14·8	5 22 33	56 27·0	6 29 36	56 35·9	7 26 49	57 50·7
Procyon	3 44 27	85 4·8	4 28 20	83 50·0	5 50 36	82 18·3	6 45 52	82 59·1	7 32 55	84 27·8
α Hydræ	5 45 32	88 32·7	6 28 6	88 43·5	7 46 41	91 25·9	8 38 14	94 39·4	9 21 35	98 7·8
Regulus	5 55 10	65 40·6	6 45 15	66 6·8	8 16 11	69 36·6	9 14 2	74 25·8	10 1 52	77 26·2
β Leonis	7 39 12	55 54·2	8 31 25	58 6·5	10 1 9	64 43·8	10 56 54	69 54·5	11 42 50	74 44·8
Spica	9 37 49	78 15·6	10 37 29	82 7·8	11 40 35	90 15·5	12 33 13	95 45·2	13 18 46	100 31·4
β Centauri	10 16 8	127 25·1	10 46 42	131 31·7	12 1 16	139 48·1	12 59 23	145 11·8	13 55 14	149 47·0
Arcturus	10 36 18	47 58·2	11 22 12	52 16·1	12 39 47	60 40·3	13 28 52	65 48·7	14 10 6	70 10·9
α Serpentis	12 10 58	63 47·2	12 51 58	68 11·0	14 6 6	75 46·5	14 55 30	79 58·8	15 38 16	83 11·4
Antares	12 24 0	98 16·5	13 6 50	102 37·4	14 30 11	109 53·9	15 29 8	113 36·6	16 21 56	116 9·6
α Lyræ	16 8 29	48 3·6	16 36 28	49 51·2	17 28 24	51 38·0	18 3 18	51 43·1	18 32 48	51 19·7
α Aquilæ	16 17 0	82 12·2	16 57 6	83 44·0	18 12 14	84 21·1	19 2 19	83 12·7	19 44 50	81 27·2
α Aquarii	18 19 16	103 8·6	18 55 26	102 28·3	20 19 41	98 45·1	21 14 2	94 53·9	21 59 31	90 54·7
Fomalhaut	18 16 30	134 54·0	19 15 43	133 57·8	20 58 57	129 17·4	22 1 5	124 46·9	22 50 54	120 16·1
α Pegasi	19 24 1	92 34·4	20 6 35	90 33·5	21 24 14	84 49·4	22 15 19	80 2·6	22 58 41	75 27·0

THE SHÛ KING.

PART I. THE BOOK OF THANG.

THE CANON OF YÂO.

SHÛ KING, the name of the whole work, has been sufficiently explained in the Introduction. The name of this Part, the first of the five into which the whole is divided, is the Book of Thang, Thang being taken as the dynastic designation of Yâo, who before his elevation to the throne had been marquis of the small state of Thang, the name of which is supposed to be still retained in Thang, one of the districts of the department Pâo-ting, in *K*ih-lî. It is said that after his elevation he established his capital in Phing-yang, lat. 36° 06′, long. 111° 33′, in Shan-hsî. But all this is very uncertain. See on Part III, Book iii, ch. 2. The one Book, forming this Part, is called the Canon of Yâo. The character which we translate 'Canon' means a document of the most exalted nature, the contents of which are entitled to the greatest regard. The name is given expressly only to one other Book in the Shû. The Canons are the first of the six classes of documents which the Shû contains.

Yâo is the subject of the Book:—In ch. 1, in his personal character and the general results of his government; in ch. 2, in his special care for the regulation of the calendar and the labours of agriculture; in ch. 3, in his anxiety to find one who could cope with the ravages of a terrible inundation, and take his place on the throne. The third chapter introduces to our notice Shun, the successor of Yâo.

1. Examining into antiquity, (we find that) the Tî Yâo [1] was styled Fang-hsün [2]. He was reverential, intelligent, accomplished, and thoughtful,—naturally and without effort. He was sincerely courteous, and capable of (all) complaisance. The bright (influence of these qualities) was felt through the four quarters (of the land), and reached to (heaven) above and (earth) beneath.

He made the able and virtuous distinguished, and thence proceeded to the love of (all in) the nine classes of his kindred, who (thus) became harmonious. He (also) regulated and polished the people (of his domain), who all became brightly intelligent. (Finally), he united and harmonized the myriad states; and so the black-haired people were transformed. The result was (universal) concord.

2. He commanded the Hsîs and Hos [3], in reverent accordance with (their observation of) the wide heavens, to calculate and delineate (the movements and appearances of) the sun, the moon, the stars, and the zodiacal spaces, and so to deliver respectfully the seasons to be observed by the people.

---

[1] Yâo is to us now the name of the ancient ruler so denominated. The character means 'high,' 'lofty and grand.' It may originally have been an epithet, 'the Exalted One.' On the meaning of Tî in Tî Yâo, see what has been said in the Preface.

[2] The Han scholars held that Fang-hsün was the name of Yâo. Those of Sung, taking the characters as an epithet, make them signify 'the Highly Meritorious.'

[3] The Hsîs and Hos seem to have been brothers of two families, on whom devolved the care of the calendar, principally with a view to regulate the seasons of agriculture. See Parts III, iv, and V, xxvii. On Yâo's directions to them, see the Introduction, pp. 24–28.

He separately commanded the second brother Hsî to reside at Yü-î[1], in what was called the Bright Valley, and (there) respectfully to receive as a guest the rising sun, and to adjust and arrange the labours of the spring. 'The day,' (said he), 'is of the medium length, and the star is in Niâo;—you may thus exactly determine mid-spring. The people are dispersed (in the fields), and birds and beasts breed and copulate.'

He further commanded the third brother Hsî to reside at Nan-*k*iâo[2], (in what was called the Brilliant Capital), to adjust and arrange the transformations of the summer, and respectfully to observe the exact limit (of the shadow). 'The day,' (said he), 'is at its longest, and the star is in Hwo;—you may thus exactly determine mid-summer. The people are more dispersed; and birds and beasts have their feathers and hair thin, and change their coats.'

He separately commanded the second brother Ho to reside at the west, in what was called the Dark Valley, and (there) respectfully to convoy the setting sun, and to adjust and arrange the completing labours of the autumn. 'The night,' (said he), 'is of the medium length, and the star is in Hsü;—you may thus exactly determine mid-autumn. The people feel at ease, and birds and beasts have their coats in good condition.'

He further commanded the third brother Ho to

---

[1] Yü-î is by some identified with Tăng-*k*âu, in Shan-tung, lat. 37° 48′, long. 121° 4′; by others, it is sought in Corea.

[2] Nan-*k*iâo was south, it is said, on the border of An-nan or Cochin-China. The characters for 'in what was called the Brilliant Capital' are supposed to have dropt out of the text.

reside in the northern region, in what was called the Sombre Capital, and (there) to adjust and examine the changes of the winter. 'The day,' (said he), 'is at its shortest, and the star is in Mâo;—you may thus exactly determine mid-winter. The people keep in their houses, and the coats of birds and beasts are downy and thick.'

The Tî said, 'Ah! you, Hsîs and Hos, a round year consists of three hundred, sixty, and six days. Do you, by means of the intercalary month, fix the four seasons, and complete (the period of) the year. (Thereafter), the various officers being regulated in accordance with this, all the works (of the year) will be fully performed.'

3. The Tî said, 'Who will search out (for me) a man according to the times, whom I can raise and employ?' Fang-*kh*î said, '(Your) heir-son *K*û[1] is highly intelligent.' The Tî said, 'Alas! he is insincere and quarrelsome:—can he do?'

The Tî said, 'Who will search out (for me) a man equal to the exigency of my affairs?' Hwan-tâu[2] said, 'Oh! the merits of the Minister of Works have just been displayed on a wide scale.' The Tî said, 'Alas! when all is quiet, he talks; but when employed, his actions turn out differently. He is respectful (only) in appearance. See! the floods assail the heavens!'

The Tî said, 'Ho! (President of) the Four

---

[1] In Part II, iv, 2, Yü speaks of this son of Yâo as 'the haughty *K*û of Tan,' Tan probably being the name of a state, over which, according to tradition, he had been appointed.

[2] Hwan-tâu and the Minister of Works, whom he recommends, appear in the next Book as great criminals.

Mountains[1], destructive in their overflow are the waters of the inundation. In their vast extent they embrace the hills and overtop the great heights, threatening the heavens with their floods, so that the lower people groan and murmur! Is there a capable man to whom I can assign the correction (of this calamity)?' All (in the court) said, 'Ah! is there not Khwăn[2]?' The Tî said, 'Alas! how perverse is he! He is disobedient to orders, and tries to injure his peers.' (The President of) the Mountains said, 'Well but—. Try if he can (accomplish the work).' (Khwăn) was employed accordingly. The Tî said (to him), 'Go; and be reverent!' For nine years he laboured, but the work was unaccomplished.

The Tî said, 'Ho! (President of) the Four Mountains, I have been on the throne seventy years. You can carry out my commands;—I will resign my place to you.' The Chief said, 'I have not the virtue;—I should disgrace your place.' (The Tî) said, 'Show me some one among the illustrious, or set forth one from among the poor and mean.' All (then) said to the Tî, 'There is an unmarried man among the lower people, called Shun of Yü[3].' The Tî

[1] (President of) the Four Mountains, or simply Four Mountains, appears to have been the title of the chief minister of Yâo. The four mountains were—mount Thâi in the east; Hwâ in the west, in Shan-hsî; Hăng in the south, in Hû-nan; and Hăng in the north, in *K*ih-lî. These, probably, were the limits of the country, so far as known, and all within these points were the care of the chief minister.

[2] Khwăn is believed to have been the father of Yü, who afterwards coped successfully with the inundation. We are told that he was earl of *Kh*ung, corresponding to the present district of Hû, in Shen-hsî.

[3] See on the title of next Book.

said, 'Yes, I have heard of him. What have you to say about him?' The Chief said, 'He is the son of a blind man. His father was obstinately unprincipled; his (step-)mother was insincere; his (half-) brother Hsiang was arrogant. He has been able, (however), by his filial piety to live in harmony with them, and to lead them gradually to self-government, so that they (no longer) proceed to great wickedness.' The Tî said, 'I will try him; I will wive him, and thereby see his behaviour with my two daughters.' (Accordingly) he arranged and sent down his two daughters to the north of the Kwei[1], to be wives in (the family of) Yü. The Tî said to them, 'Be reverent!'

---

[1] The Kwei is a small stream in Shan-hsî, which flows into the Ho.

PART II. THE BOOKS OF YÜ.

BOOK I. THE CANON OF SHUN.

THE Books of Yü is the name of this Part of the Shû, Yü being the dynastic designation of Shun, as Thang was that of Yâo. It does not appear so clearly, however, how it came to be so. Yü must be the name of a state, and is commonly identified with the present district of An-yî, in *K*ieh *K*âu, Shan-hsî. Some think that Yâo, after marrying his two daughters to Shun, appointed him lord of this state; but in the first mention of him to Yâo in the last Book, he is called Shun of Yü. It is generally said that Shun's ancestors had been lords of the principality of Yü up to the time of his father, who lost his patrimony and was reduced to the rank of a private man. But after what has been said, in the Introduction, on the Books in the first two Parts of the Shû, it will not be thought surprising that much in the accounts about Yâo and Shun should be open to suspicion. According to Mencius, IV, Part ii, ch. 1, Shun was from the country of the wild tribes on the east. Sze-mâ *Kh*ien makes him to have been descended from Hwang-Tî, in which case he and his wives, the daughters of Yâo, would have had the same ancestor. Nothing more injurious to the fame of Yâo and Shun, according to Chinese notions of propriety, could be alleged against them.

Shun is the subject of this Canon, as Yâo was of the former. As it now stands, we may divide it into six chapters:—the first, describing Shun's virtues and gradual advancement; the second, Yâo's satisfaction with his administration of affairs, and associating of Shun with himself on the throne; the third, the acts of Shun in that position; the fourth, the demise of Yâo, and Shun's accession as sole monarch; the fifth, his choice of ministers and complete organization of his government; and the sixth, his death.

1. Examining into antiquity, (we find that) the Tî Shun[1] was styled *Kh*ung-hwâ[2]. His character was entirely conformed to (that of) the (former) Tî; he was profound, wise, accomplished, and intelligent. He was mild and courteous, and truly sincere. The report of his mysterious virtue was heard on high, and he was appointed to office.

2. (Shun) carefully set forth the beauty of the five cardinal duties, and they came to be (universally) observed. Being appointed to be General Regulator, the affairs of every (official) department were arranged in their proper seasons. (Being charged) to receive (the princes) from the four quarters of the land, they were all docilely submissive. Being sent to the great plains at the foot of the mountains, notwithstanding the tempests of wind, thunder, and rain, he did not go astray.

The Tî said, 'Come, you Shun. I have consulted you on (all) affairs, and examined your words, and found that they can be carried into practice;—(now) for three years. Do you ascend the seat of the Tî.' Shun wished to decline in favour of some one more virtuous, and not to consent to be (Yâo's) successor. On the first day of the first month, (however), he received (Yâo's) retirement (from his duties) in the temple of the Accomplished Ancestor[3].*

3. He examined the pearl-adorned turning sphere,

---

[1] If Shun be taken as an epithet, it will mean 'the Benevolent and Sage.'

[2] *Kh*ung-hwâ, the name of Shun according to the Han scholars, may mean 'the Glorious (Yâo) repeated.'

[3] The Accomplished Ancestor would be, probably, the individual in some distant time to whom Yâo traced his possession of the throne.

with its transverse tube of jade, and reduced to a harmonious system (the movements of) the Seven Directors[1].

Thereafter, he sacrificed specially, but with the ordinary forms, to God; sacrificed with reverent purity to the Six Honoured Ones; offered their appropriate sacrifices to the hills and rivers; and extended his worship to the host of spirits[2].*

He called in (all) the five jade-symbols of rank; and when the month was over, he gave daily audience to (the President of) the Four Mountains, and all the Pastors[3], (finally) returning their symbols to the various princes.

In the second month of the year he made a tour of inspection eastwards, as far as Thâi-ʒung[4], where he presented a burnt-offering to Heaven, and sacrificed in order to the hills and rivers.* Thereafter he gave audience to the princes of the east. He set in accord their seasons and months, and regulated the days; he made uniform the standard-tubes, with the measures of length and of capacity, and the steelyards; he regulated the five (classes of) ceremonies, with (the various) articles of introduction,—the five

---

[1] Probably the seven stars of the Great Bear.

[2] Who the Six Honoured Ones were cannot be determined with certainty. An-kwo thought they were, 'the seasons, cold and heat, the sun, the moon, the stars, and drought,' that is, certain spirits, supposed to rule over these phenomena and things, and residing probably in different stars. The whole paragraph describes Shun's exercise of the prerogative of the sovereign, so far as religious worship was concerned.

[3] The princes of the various states, whose official chief was the President of the Four Mountains, all 'shepherds of men.'

[4] Thâi-ʒung is mount Thâi, in Shan-tung. See note on the President of the Four Mountains, p. 35.

symbols of jade, the three kinds of silk, the two living (animals) and the one dead one. As to the five instruments of rank, when all was over, he returned them. In the fifth month he made a similar tour southwards, as far as the mountain of the south[1], where he observed the same ceremonies as at Thâi. In the eighth month he made a tour westwards, as far as the mountain of the west[1], where he did as before. In the eleventh month he made a tour northwards, as far as the mountain of the north[1], where he observed the same ceremonies as in the west. He (then) returned (to the capital), went to (the temple of) the Cultivated Ancestor[2], and sacrificed a single bull.*

In five years there was one tour of inspection, and there were four appearances of the princes at court. They gave a report (of their government) in words, which was clearly tested by their works. They received chariots and robes according to their merits.

He instituted the division (of the land) into twelve provinces[3], raising altars upon twelve hills in them.* He (also) deepened the rivers.

He exhibited (to the people) the statutory punishments, enacting banishment as a mitigation of the five (great) inflictions[4]; with the whip to be employed in the magistrates' courts, the stick to be

---

[1] See note on the President of the Four Mountains, p. 35.

[2] Probably the same as the Accomplished Ancestor on p. 38.

[3] As Yü, according to Part III, i, divided the land into nine provinces, this division of it into twelve must have been subsequent to the completion of Yü's work. See on the Tribute of Yü.

[4] Those five great inflictions were—branding on the forehead; cutting off the nose; cutting off the feet; castration; and death, inflicted in various ways.

employed in schools[1], and money to be received for redeemable offences. Inadvertent offences and those which could be ascribed to misfortune were to be pardoned, but those who transgressed presumptuously and repeatedly were to be punished with death. 'Let me be reverent! Let me be reverent!' (he said to himself.) 'Let compassion rule in punishment!'

He banished the Minister of Works to Yû island; confined Hwan-tâu on mount *Kh*ung; drove (the chief of) San-miâo (and his people) into San-wei, and kept them there; and held Khwăn a prisoner till death on mount Yü. These four criminals being thus dealt with, all under heaven acknowledged the justice (of Shun's administration)[2].

4. After twenty-eight years the Tî deceased, when the people mourned for him as for a parent for three years. Within the four seas all the eight kinds of instruments of music were stopped and hushed. On the first day of the first month (of the) next year, Shun went to (the temple of) the Accomplished Ancestor.*

---

[1] This punishment was for officers in training; not for boys at school.

[2] The Minister of Works, Hwan-tâu, and Khwăn are mentioned in the former Canon. Yû island, or Yû *K*âu, was in the extreme north of the present district of Mî-yun, department Shun-thien, *K*ih-lî.

Mount *Kh*ung was in the district of Yung-ting, Lî *K*âu, Hû-nan. San-miâo was the name of a territory, embracing the present departments of Wû-*kh*ang in Hû-pei, Yo-*k*âu in Hû-nan, and *K*iû-*k*iang in *K*iang-hsî. San-wei was a tract of country round a mountain of the same name in the present department of An-hsî, Kan-sû. Mount Yü was in the present district of Than-*kh*ăng, Shan-tung.

5. He deliberated with (the President of) the Four Mountains how to throw open the doors (of communication between himself and the) four (quarters of the land), and how he could see with the eyes, and hear with the ears of all.

He consulted with the twelve Pastors[1], and said to them, 'The food!—it depends on observing the seasons. Be kind to the distant, and cultivate the ability of the near. Give honour to the virtuous, and your confidence to the good, while you discountenance the artful;—so shall the barbarous tribes lead on one another to make their submission.'

Shun said, 'Ho! (President of) the Four Mountains, is there any one who can with vigorous service attend to all the affairs of the Tî, whom I may appoint to be General Regulator, to assist me in (all) affairs, managing each department according to its nature?' All (in the court) replied, 'There is Po-yü[2], the Minister of Works.' The Tî said, 'Yes. Ho! Yü, you have regulated the water and the land. In this (new office) exert yourself.' Yü did obeisance with his head to the ground, and wished to decline in favour of the Minister of Agriculture, or Hsieh, or Kâo-yâo. The Tî said, 'Yes, but do you go (and undertake the duties).'

The Tî said, '*Kh*î[3], the black-haired people are (still) suffering from famine. Do you, O prince, as

---

[1] These were the twelve princes holding the chief sway and superintendence in his twelve provinces.

[2] Po-yü is the great Yü, the founder of the Hsiâ dynasty. Po denotes, probably, his order as the eldest among his brothers.

[3] *Kh*î was the name of the Minister of Agriculture, better known in the Shih and other books as Hâu-*k*î, the progenitor of the kings of *K*âu. See the legend about him in the Shih, Part III, ii, Ode 1.

Minister of Agriculture, (continue to) sow (for them) the various kinds of grain.'

The Tî said, 'Hsieh[1], the people are (still) wanting in affection for one another, and do not docilely observe the five orders of relationship. It is yours, as the Minister of Instruction, reverently to set forth the lessons of duty belonging to those five orders. Do so with gentleness.'

The Tî said, 'Kâo-yâo[2], the barbarous tribes trouble our great land. There are (also) robbers, murderers, insurgents, and traitors. It is yours, as the Minister of Crime, to use the five punishments to deal with their offences. For the infliction of these there are the three appointed places. There are the five cases in which banishment in the appropriate places is to be resorted to, to which places, though five, three localities are assigned. Perform your duties with intelligence, and you will secure a sincere (submission).'

The Tî said, 'Who can superintend my works, as they severally require?' All (in the court) replied, 'Is there not *Z*ui[3]?' The Tî said, 'Yes. Ho! *Z*ui, you must be Minister of Works.' *Z*ui did obeisance with his head to the ground, and wished to decline in favour of Shû, *Kh*iang, or Po-yü. The

---

[1] Hsieh was honoured by the kings of the Shang dynasty as their progenitor. See the Shih, Part IV, iii, Odes 3 and 4.

[2] See the preliminary note to Book iii.

[3] *Z*ui was not claimed by any great family as its progenitor, but he was handed down by tradition as a great artificer. See a reference to him in Part V, xxii, 2. Shû and *Kh*iang must have been named from their skill in making halberds and axes. The Yü (quite different from the name of the great Yü) in Po-yü gives us no indication of the skill of that individual.

Tî said, 'Yes, but do you go (and undertake the duties). Effect a harmony (in all the departments).'

The Tî said, 'Who can superintend, as the nature of the charge requires, the grass and trees, with the birds and beasts on my hills and in my marshes?' All (in the court) replied, 'Is there not Yî[1]?' The Tî said, 'Yes. Ho! Yî, do you be my Forester.' Yî did obeisance with his head to the ground, and wished to decline in favour of *K*û, Hû, Hsiung, or Pî[1]. The Tî said, 'Yes, but do you go (and undertake the duties). You must manage them harmoniously.'

The Tî said, 'Ho! (President of the) Four Mountains, is there any one able to direct my three (religious) ceremonies[2]?' All (in the court) answered, 'Is there not Po-î[3]?' The Tî said, 'Yes. Ho! Po, you must be the Arranger in the Ancestral Temple. Morning and night be reverent. Be upright, be pure.' Po did obeisance with his head to the ground, and wished to decline in favour of Khwei or Lung. The Tî said, 'Yes, but do you go (and undertake the duties). Be reverential!'*

The Tî said, 'Khwei[4], I appoint you to be Director of Music, and to teach our sons, so that the straightforward shall yet be mild; the gentle, dignified; the strong, not tyrannical; and the impetuous,

---

[1] For Yî, see the preliminary note to Book iv. He wishes here to decline his appointment in favour of *K*û ('The Cedar'), Hû ('The Tiger'), Hsiung ('The Bear'), or Pî ('The Grisly Bear').

[2] The three ceremonies were the observances in the worship of the Spirits of Heaven, the Spirits of Earth, and the Spirits of Men.

[3] Po-î was the progenitor of the great family of *K*iang, members of which ruled in *Kh*î and other states.

[4] Of Khwei we know nothing more than what is here told us. The character denotes a monstrous animal, 'a dragon with one leg.'

not arrogant. Poetry is the expression of earnest thought; singing is the prolonged utterance of that expression; the notes accompany that utterance, and they are harmonized themselves by the standard-tubes. (In this way) the eight different kinds of musical instruments can be adjusted so that one shall not take from or interfere with another; and spirits and men are brought into harmony.' Khwei said, 'I smite the (sounding-) stone, I gently strike it, and the various animals lead on one another to dance.'

The Tî said, 'Lung[1], I abominate slanderous speakers and destroyers of the (right) ways, who agitate and alarm my people. I appoint you to be the Minister of Communication. Early and late give forth my orders and report to me, seeing that everything is true.'

The Tî said, 'Ho! you, twenty and two men, be reverent; so shall you be helpful to the business (entrusted to me by) Heaven.'*

Every three years there was an examination of merits, and after three examinations the undeserving were degraded, and the deserving advanced. (By this arrangement) the duties of all the departments were fully discharged; the (people of) San-miâo (also) were discriminated and separated.

6. In the thirtieth year of his age, Shun was called to employment. Thirty years he was on the throne (with Yâo). Fifty years afterwards he went on high and died[2].*

---

[1] We are in ignorance of Lung, as we are of Khwei. The character denotes 'the dragon.'

[2] The Chinese text is here difficult to construe. *K*û Hsî says that the term 'went on high' is appropriate to the death of the Son of Heaven; and that the meaning is that Shun went to heaven.

Book II. The Counsels of the Great Yü.

Of the six classes of documents in the Shû, 'Counsels' are the second, containing the wise remarks and suggestions of high officers on the subject of government.

This Book may be divided into three chapters:—the first, containing counsels of Yü and Yî on principles and methods of government; the second, occupied with Shun's resignation of the administration to Yü, and containing also many sage observations and maxims; and the third, describing Yü's operations against the people of Miâo, and counsels addressed to him by Yî. The style differs from that of the Canons; being more sententious, and falling occasionally into rhyme.

1. Examining into antiquity, (we find that) the Great Yü[1] was styled Wăn-ming[2]. Having arranged and divided (the land), all to the four seas, in reverent response to the Tî, he said, 'If the sovereign can realize the difficulty of his sovereignship, and the minister the difficulty of his ministry, the government will be well ordered, and the black-haired people will sedulously seek to be virtuous.'

The Tî said, 'Yes; let this really be the case, and good words will nowhere lie hidden; no men of virtue and talents will be left neglected, away from court, and the myriad states will all enjoy repose. (But) to obtain the views of all; to give up one's opinion and follow that of others; to keep from oppressing the helpless, and not to neglect the

---

[1] The name Yü, taken as an epithet, would mean 'the Unconstrained.' As an epithet after death, it has the meaning of 'Receiving the Resignation and Perfecting the Merit;' but this is evidently based on the commonly received history of Yü.

[2] Wăn-ming may be translated, 'the Accomplished and the Issuer of Commands.

straitened and poor;—it was only the (former) Tî who could attain to this.'

Yî said, 'Oh! your virtue, O Tî, is vast and incessant. It is sagely, spirit-like, awe-inspiring, and adorned with all accomplishments. Great Heaven regarded you with its favour, and bestowed on you its appointment. Suddenly you possessed all within the four seas, and became ruler of all under heaven.'*

Yü said, 'Accordance with the right leads to good fortune; following what is opposed to it, to bad;—the shadow and the echo.' Yî said, 'Alas! be cautious! Admonish yourself to caution, when there seems to be no occasion for anxiety. Do not fail to observe the laws and ordinances. Do not find your enjoyment in idleness. Do not go to excess in pleasure. In your employment of men of worth, let none come between you and them. Put away evil without hesitation. Do not carry out plans, of (the wisdom of) which you have doubts. Study that all your purposes may be with the light of reason. Do not go against what is right, to get the praise of the people. Do not oppose the people's (wishes), to follow your own desires. (Attend to these things) without idleness or omission, and the barbarous tribes all around will come and acknowledge your sovereignty.'

Yü said, 'Oh! think (of these things), O Tî. The virtue (of the ruler) is seen in (his) good government, and that government in the nourishing of the people. There are water, fire, metal, wood, the earth, and grain,—these must be duly regulated; there are the rectification of (the people's) virtue, (the tools and other things) that supply the conveniences of life, and the securing abundant means of sustentation,—these must be harmoniously attended to. When the nine services (thus indicated) have been orderly accomplished, that accomplishment will be hailed by (the people's) songs. Caution them with gentle (words), correct them with the majesty (of law), stimulate them with the songs on those nine subjects,—in order that (your success) may not suffer diminution.' The Tî said, 'The earth has been reduced to order, and the (influences of) heaven produce their complete effect; those six magazines and three departments of (governmental) action are all truly regulated, and may be depended on for a myriad generations:—this is your merit.'

2. The Tî said, 'Come, you Yü. I have occupied my place for thirty and three years. I am between ninety and a hundred years old, and the laborious duties weary me. Do you, eschewing all indolence, take the leading of my people.' Yü replied, 'My virtue is not equal (to the position), and the people will not repose in me. (But there is) Kâo-yâo with vigorous activity sowing abroad his virtue, which has descended on the black-haired people, till they cherish him in their hearts. O Tî, think of him! When I think of him, (my mind) rests on him (as the man fit for this place); when I would put him out of my thoughts, (my mind still) rests on him; when I name and speak of him, (my mind) rests on him (for this); the sincere outgoing of my thoughts about him is that he is the man. O Tî, think of his merits.'

The Tî said, 'Kâo-yâo, that of these my ministers and all (my people) hardly one is found to offend against the regulations of the government is owing to your being Minister of Crime, and intelligent in the use of the five punishments, thereby assisting (the inculcation of) the five cardinal duties, with a view to the perfection of my government, and that through punishment there may come to be no punishments, but the people accord with (the path of) the Mean. (Continue to) be strenuous.' Kâo-yâo replied, 'Your virtue, O Tî, is faultless. You condescend to your ministers with a kindly ease; you preside over the multitudes with a generous forbearance. Punishments do not extend to (the criminal's) heirs, while rewards reach to (succeeding) generations. You pardon inadvertent faults, however great, and punish purposed crimes, however small. In cases of doubtful crimes, you deal with them lightly; in cases of doubtful merit, you prefer the high estimation. Rather than put an innocent person to death, you will run the risk of irregularity and error. This life-loving virtue has penetrated the minds of the people, and this is why they do not render themselves liable to be punished by your officers.' The Tî said, 'That I am able to follow and obtain what I desire in my government, the people responding everywhere as if moved by the wind,—this is your excellence.'

The Tî said, 'Come Yü. The inundating waters filled me with dread, when you accomplished truly (all that you had represented), and completed your service;—thus showing your superiority to other men. Full of toilsome earnestness in the service of the country, and sparing in your expenditure on your family, and this without being full of yourself and elated,—you (again) show your superiority to other men. You are without any prideful assumption, but no one under heaven can contest with you the palm of ability; you make no boasting, but no one under heaven can contest with you the palm of merit. I see how great is your virtue, how admirable your vast achievements. The determinate appointment of Heaven rests on your person; you must eventually ascend (the throne) of the great sovereign.* The mind of man is restless, prone (to err); its affinity to what is right is small. Be discriminating, be uniform (in the pursuit of what is right), that you may sincerely hold fast the Mean. Do not listen to unsubstantiated words; do not follow plans about which you have not sought counsel. Of all who are to be loved, is not the ruler the chief? Of all who are to be feared, are not the people the chief? If the multitude were without their sovereign Head, whom should they sustain aloft? If the sovereign had not the multitude, there would be none to guard the country for him. Be reverential! Carefully maintain the throne which you are to occupy, cultivating (the virtues) that are to be desired in you. If within the four seas there be distress and poverty, your Heaven-conferred revenues will come to a perpetual end. It is the mouth which sends forth what is good, and raises up war. I will not alter my words.'

Yü said, 'Submit the meritorious ministers one by one to the trial of divination[1], and let the favouring indication be followed.' The Tî replied, '(According to the rules for) the regulation of divination, one should first make up his mind, and afterwards refer (his judgment) to the great tortoise-shell. My mind (in this matter) was determined in the first place; I consulted and deliberated with all (my

[1] On Divination, see Part V, iv.

ministers and people), and they were of one accord with me. The spirits signified their assent, and the tortoise-shell and divining stalks concurred. Divination, when fortunate, should not be repeated.'* Yü did obeisance with his head to the ground, and firmly declined (the place). The Tî said, 'You must not do so. It is you who can suitably (occupy my place).' On the first morning of the first month, (Yü) received the appointment in the temple (dedicated by Shun) to the spirits of his ancestors [1], and took the leading of all the officers, as had been done by the Tî at the commencement (of his government).*

3. The Tî said, 'Alas! O Yü, there is only the lord of Miâo [2] who refuses obedience; do you go and correct him.' Yü on this assembled all the princes, and made a speech to the host, saying, 'Ye multitudes here arrayed, listen all of you to my orders. Stupid is this lord of Miâo, ignorant, erring, and disrespectful. Despiteful and insolent to others, he thinks that all ability and virtue are with himself. A rebel to the right, he destroys (all the obligations of) virtue. Superior men are kept by him in obscurity, and mean men fill (all) the offices. The people reject him and will not protect him. Heaven

[1] Many contend that this was the ancestral temple of Yâo But we learn from Confucius, in the seventeenth chapter of the Doctrine of the Mean, that Shun had established such a temple for his own ancestors, which must be that intended here.

[2] The lord of Miâo against whom Yü proceeded would not be the one whom Shun banished to San-wei, as related in the former Book, but some chieftain of the whole or a portion of the people, who had been left in their native seat. That Yâo, Shun, and Yü were all obliged to take active measures against the people of Miâo, shows the difficulty with which the Chinese sway was established over the country.

is sending down calamities upon him.* I therefore, along with you, my multitude of gallant men, bear the instructions (of the Tî) to punish his crimes. Do you proceed with united heart and strength, so shall our enterprize be crowned with success.'

At the end of three decades, the people of Miâo continued rebellious against the commands (issued to them), when Yî came to the help of Yü, saying, 'It is virtue that moves Heaven; there is no distance to which it does not reach. Pride brings loss, and humility receives increase;—this is the way of Heaven.* In the early time of the Tî, when he was living by mount Lî[1], he went into the fields, and daily cried with tears to compassionate Heaven, and to his parents, taking to himself all guilt, and charging himself with (their) wickedness.* (At the same time) with respectful service he appeared before Kû-sâu, looking grave and awe-struck, till Kû also became transformed by his example. Entire sincerity moves spiritual beings,—how much more will it move this lord of Miâo!'* Yü did homage to the excellent words, and said, 'Yes.' (Thereupon) he led back his army, having drawn off the troops. The Tî set about diffusing on a grand scale the virtuous influences of peace;—with shields and feathers they danced between the two staircases (in his courtyard). In seventy days, the lord of Miâo came (and made his submission).

---

[1] Mount Lî is found in a hill near Phû *K*âu, department of Phing-yang, Shan-hsî. It is difficult to reconcile what Yî says here of Shun 'in his early life' and his father Kû-sâu with the account of it as happening when Shun was fifty years old; see Mencius V, Part i, ch. 5. The whole is legendary, and there were, no doubt, more forms of the legend than one.

BOOK III. THE COUNSELS OF KÂO-YÂO.

KÂO-YÂO was Minister of Crime to Shun, and is still celebrated in China as the model for all administrators of justice. There are few or no reliable details of his history. Sze-mâ *Kh*ien says that Yü, on his accession to the throne, made Kâo-yâo his chief minister, with the view of his ultimately succeeding him, but that the design was frustrated by Kâo-yâo's death. But if there had been such a tradition in the time of Mencius, he would probably have mentioned it, when defending Yü from the charge of being inferior to Yâo and Shun, who resigned the throne to the worthiest, whereas he transmitted it to his son. Kâo-yâo's surname was Yen, but an end was made of his representatives, when the principality belonging to them was extinguished in the dynasty of *K*âu by the ambitious state of *Kh*û. There is still a family in China with the surname Kâo, claiming to be descended from this ancient worthy; but Kâo and Yâo are to be taken together in the Shû as his name.

The 'Counsels' in the Book do not appear as addressed directly to Shun, but are found in a conversation between Yü and Kâo-yâo, the latter being the chief speaker. The whole may be divided into four chapters:—the first, enunciating the principle that in government the great thing is for the ruler to pursue the course of his virtue, which will be seen in his knowledge and choice of men for office, thereby securing the repose of the people; the second, illustrating how men may be known; the third, treating of the repose of the people; in the fourth, the speaker asserts the reasonableness of his sentiments, and humbly expresses his own desire to be helpful to the sovereign.

1. Examining into antiquity, (we find that) Kâo-yâo said, 'If (the sovereign) sincerely pursues the course of his virtue, the counsels (offered to him) will be intelligent, and the aids (of admonition that he receives) will be harmonious.' Yü said, 'Yes, but explain yourself.' Kâo-yâo said, 'Oh! let him be careful about his personal cultivation, with thoughts that are far-reaching, and thus he will

produce a generous kindness and nice observance of distinctions among the nine branches of his kindred. All the intelligent (also) will exert themselves in his service; and in this way from what is near he will reach to what is distant.' Yü did homage to the excellent words, and said, 'Yes.' Kâo-yâo continued, 'Oh! it lies in knowing men, and giving repose to the people.' Yü said, 'Alas! to attain to both these things might well be a difficulty even to the Tî. When (the sovereign) knows men, he is wise, and can put every one into the office for which he is fit. When he gives repose to the people, his kindness is felt, and the black-haired race cherish him in their hearts. When he can be (thus) wise and kind, what occasion will he have for anxiety about a Hwan-tâu? what to be removing a lord of Miâo? what to fear any one of fair words, insinuating appearance, and great artfulness?'

2. Kâo-yâo said, 'Oh! there are in all nine virtues to be discovered in conduct, and when we say that a man possesses (any) virtue, that is as much as to say he does such and such things.' Yü asked, 'What (are the nine virtues)?' Kâo-yâo replied, 'Affability combined with dignity; mildness combined with firmness; bluntness combined with respectfulness; aptness for government combined with reverent caution; docility combined with boldness; straightforwardness combined with gentleness; an easy negligence combined with discrimination; boldness combined with sincerity; and valour combined with righteousness. (When these qualities are) displayed, and that continuously, have we not the good (officer)? When there is a daily

display of three (of these) virtues, their possessor could early and late regulate and brighten the clan (of which he was made chief). When there is a daily severe and reverent cultivation of six of them, their possessor could brilliantly conduct the affairs of the state (with which he was invested). When (such men) are all received and advanced, the possessors of those nine virtues will be employed in (the public) service. The men of a thousand and men of a hundred will be in their offices; the various ministers will emulate one another; all the officers will accomplish their duties at the proper times, observant of the five seasons (as the several elements predominate in them),—and thus their various duties will be fully accomplished. Let not (the Son of Heaven) set to the holders of states the example of indolence or dissoluteness. Let him be wary and fearful, (remembering that) in one day or two days there may occur ten thousand springs of things. Let him not have his various officers cumberers of their places. The work is Heaven's; men must act for it!' *

3. 'From Heaven are the (social) relationships with their several duties; we are charged with (the enforcement of) those five duties;—and lo! we have the five courses of honourable conduct[1]. From Heaven are the (social) distinctions with their several ceremonies; from us come the observances of those five ceremonies;—and lo! they appear in

[1] The five duties are those belonging to the five relationships, which are the constituents of society;—those between husband and wife, father and son, ruler and subject, elder brother and younger, friend and friend.

regular practice[1]. When (sovereign and ministers show) a common reverence and united respect for these, lo! the moral nature (of the people) is made harmonious. Heaven graciously distinguishes the virtuous;—are there not the five habiliments, five decorations of them[2]? Heaven punishes the guilty;—are there not the five punishments, to be severally used for that purpose? The business of government!—ought we not to be earnest in it? ought we not to be earnest in it? *

'Heaven hears and sees as our people hear and see; Heaven brightly approves and displays its terrors as our people brightly approve and would awe;—such connexion is there between the upper and lower (worlds). How reverent ought the masters of territories to be!' *

4. Kâo-yâo said, 'My words are in accordance with reason, and may be put in practice.' Yü said, 'Yes, your words may be put in practice, and crowned with success.' Kâo-yâo added, '(As to that) I do not know, but I wish daily to be helpful. May (the government) be perfected!'

BOOK IV. THE YÎ AND *K*Î.

Yî and *K*î, the names of Shun's Forester and Minister of Agriculture, both of whom receive their appointments in Book i, occur near the commencement of this Book, and occasion is thence taken to give its title to the whole. But without good reason; for these worthies do not appear at all as interlocutors

---

[1] The five ceremonies are here those belonging to the distinctions of rank in connexion with the five constituent relations of society.

[2] See in next Book, ch. 1.

in it. Yü is the principal speaker; the Book belongs to the class of 'Counsels.'

To Yî there is, of course, assigned an ancient and illustrious descent; what is of more importance, is that the lords of *Kh*in, who finally superseded the kings of *K*âu, traced their lineage to him. *Kh*î was the name of *K*î, the character for the latter term meaning 'Millet,' and *Kh*î was so styled from his labours in teaching the people to sow and reap, so that *K*î became equivalent to 'Minister of Agriculture.'

The contents of the Book have been divided into three chapters. The first gives a conversation between Shun and Yü. Yü relates his own diligence and achievements as a model to Shun, and gives him various admonitions, while Shun insists on what his ministers should be, and wherein he wished them to help him. In the second chapter, Khwei, the Minister of Music, makes his appearance; it has no apparent connexion with the former. In the third, Shun and Kâo-yâo sing to each other on the mutual relation of the sovereign and his ministers.

1. The Tî said, 'Come Yü, you also must have excellent words (to bring before me).' Yü did obeisance, and said, 'Oh! what can I say, O Tî, (after Kâo-yâo)? I can (only) think of maintaining a daily assiduity.' Kâo-yâo said, 'Alas! will you describe it?' Yü replied, 'The inundating waters seemed to assail the heavens, and in their vast extent embraced the hills and overtopped the great mounds, so that the people were bewildered and overwhelmed. I mounted my four conveyances[1], and all along the hills hewed down the trees, at the same time, along with Yî, showing the multitudes how to get flesh to eat. I (also) opened passages for the streams (throughout the) nine (provinces), and conducted them to the four seas. I deepened (moreover) the channels and canals, and conducted them to the streams, sowing (grain), at the same time,

[1] See the Introduction, pp. 16, 17.

along with *K*î, and showing the multitudes how to procure the food of toil, (in addition to) the flesh meat. I urged them (further) to exchange what they had for what they had not, and to dispose of their accumulated stores. (In this way) all the people got grain to eat, and the myriad regions began to come under good rule.' Kâo-yâo said, 'Yes, we ought to model ourselves after your excellent words.'

Yü said, 'Oh! carefully maintain, O Tî, the throne which you occupy.' The Tî replied, 'Yes;' and Yü went on, 'Find your repose in your (proper) resting-point. Attend to the springs of things; study stability; and let your assistants be the upright:—then shall your movements be grandly responded to, (as if the people only) waited for your will. Thus you will brightly receive (the favour of) God;—will not Heaven renew its appointment of you, and give you blessing?' *

The Tî said, 'Alas! what are ministers?—are they not (my) associates? What are associates?—are they not (my) ministers?' Yü replied, 'Yes;' and the Tî went on, 'My ministers constitute my legs and arms, my ears and eyes. I wish to help and support my people;—you give effect to my wishes. I wish to spread the influence (of my government) through the four quarters;—you act as my agents. I wish to see the emblematic figures of the ancients,—the sun, the moon, the stars, the mountain, the dragons, and the flowery fowl (= the pheasant), which are depicted (on the upper garment); the temple cups, the pondweed, the flames, the grains of rice, the hatchet, and the symbol of distinction, which are embroidered (on the lower garment),—(I wish to see all these) fully displayed in the five colours, so as to form the (ceremonial) robes;—it is yours to see them clearly (for me). I wish to hear the six pitch-tubes, the five notes (determined by them), and the eight kinds of musical instruments (regulated again by these), examining thereby the virtues and defects of government, according as (the odes that) go forth (from the court, set to music), and come in (from the people), are ordered by those five notes;—it is yours to hear them (for me). When I am doing wrong, it is yours to correct me;—do not follow me to my face, and, when you have retired, have other remarks to make. Be reverent, ye associates, who are before and behind and on each side of me! As to all the obstinately stupid and calumniating talkers, who are found not to be doing what is right, are there not—the target to exhibit (their true character)[1], the scourge to make them recollect, and the book of remembrance[2]? Do we not wish them to live along with us? There are also the masters (of music) to receive their compositions, (set them to music), and continually publish them (as corrected by themselves). If they become reformed they are to be received and employed; if they do not, let the terrors (of punishment) overtake them.'

---

[1] Archery was anciently made much of in China, and supposed to be a test of character. Unworthy men would not be found hitting frequently, and observing the various rules of the exercise. Confucius more than once spoke of archery as a discipline of virtue; see Analects, III, xvi.

[2] In the Official Book of *K*âu, the heads of districts are required to keep a register of the characters of the people. Shun's Book of Remembrance would be a record on wood or cloth. The reference implies the use of writing.

Yü said, 'So far good! But let your light shine, O Tî, all under heaven, even to every grassy corner of the sea-shore, and throughout the myriad regions the most worthy of the people will all (wish) to be your ministers. Then, O Tî, you may advance them to office. They will set forth, and you will receive, their reports; you will make proof of them according to their merits; you will confer chariots and robes according to their services. Who will then dare not to cultivate a humble virtue? who will dare not to respond to you with reverence? If you, O Tî, do not act thus, all (your ministers) together will daily proceed to a meritless character.'

'Be not haughty like *K*û of Tan[1], who found his pleasure only in indolence and dissipation, and pursued a proud oppressive course. Day and night without ceasing he was thus. He would make boats go where there was no water. He introduced licentious associates into his family. The consequence was that he brought the prosperity of his house to an end. I took warning from his course. When I married in Thû-shan[2], (I remained with my wife only the days) hsin, *z*ăn, kwei, and *k*iâ. When (my son) *Kh*î was wailing and weeping, I did not regard him, but kept planning with all my might my labour on the land. (Then) I assisted in completing the five Tenures[3], extending over 5000 lî[4]; (in appointing) in the provinces twelve Tutors, and in establishing

[1] This was the son of Yâo. He must have been made lord of some principality, called Tan.

[2] Yü married the daughter of the lord of Thû-shan, a principality in the present department of Făng-yung, An-hui.

[3] See in the Tribute of Yü, Part II.

[4] The lî is what is called the Chinese mile, generally reckoned to be 360 paces.

in the regions beyond, reaching to the four seas, five Presidents. These all pursue the right path, and are meritorious; but there are still (the people of) Miâo, who obstinately refuse to render their service. Think of this, O Tî.' The Tî said, 'That my virtue is followed is the result of your meritorious services so orderly displayed. And now Kâo-yâo, entering respectfully into your arrangements, is on every hand displaying the (various) punishments, as represented, with entire intelligence.'

2. Khwei said, 'When the sounding-stone is tapped or struck with force, and the lutes are strongly swept or gently touched, to accompany the singing, the progenitors (of the Tî) come (to the service),* the guest of Yü [1] is in his place, and all the princes show their virtue in giving place to one another. (In the court) below (the hall) there are the flutes and hand-drums, which join in at the sound of the rattle, and cease at that of the stopper, when the organ and bells take their place. (This makes) birds and beasts fall moving. When the nine parts of the service, as arranged by the Tî, have all been performed, the male and female phœnix come with their measured gambolings (into the court).'

Khwei said, 'Oh! when I smite the (sounding-) stone, or gently strike it, the various animals lead on one another to dance [2], and all the chiefs of the official departments become truly harmonious.'

---

[1] *K*û of Tan.

[2] These last words of Khwei have already appeared in Book i, ch. 5. They are more in place here, though this second chapter has no apparent connexion with what precedes. 'The stone' is the sonorous stone formed, often in the shape of a carpenter's square, into a musical instrument, still seen everywhere in China.

3. The Tî on this made a song, saying, 'We must deal cautiously with the favouring appointment of Heaven, at every moment and in the smallest particular.'* He then sang,

'When the members (work) joyfully,
The head rises (grandly);
And the duties of all the offices are fully discharged!'

Kâo-yâo did obeisance with his head to his hands and then to the ground, and with a loud and rapid voice said, 'Think (O Tî). It is yours to lead on and originate things. Pay careful attention to your laws (in doing so). Be reverential! and often examine what has been accomplished (by your officers). Be reverential!' With this he continued the song,

'When the head is intelligent,
The members are good;
And all affairs will be happily performed!'

Again he continued the song,

'When the head is vexatious,
The members are idle;
And all affairs will go to ruin!'

The Tî said, 'Yes, go and be reverently (attentive to your duties).'

PART III. THE BOOKS OF HSIÂ.

Book I. The Tribute of Yü.

Hsiâ is the dynastic designation under which Yü and his descendants held the throne for 439 years (B.C. 2205–1767). On the conclusion of his labours, according to what was the universally accepted tradition in the *K*âu period, Yü was appointed by Yâo to be earl of Hsiâ, a small principality in Ho-nan, identified with the present Yü-*k*âu, department Khâi-făng, which thus still retains the name of Yü.

It has been repeatedly said in the Introduction that the Tribute of Yü describes what was done before the death of Yâo. The reason why it got its place as the first of the Books of Hsiâ was, no doubt, because the merit set forth in it was the ground of Yü's advancement to the throne.

Altogether the Books of Hsiâ are properly no more than three;—a fact which shows that in so early a period the duty of the recorder was little exercised, or that the destruction of its monuments in the course of time was nearly complete. We may assume that it was in consequence of both of these things that, when the collection of the Shû was made, only three documents of Hsiâ were found, to go into it.

The word 'Tribute' in the name of this first Book is not to be understood only in the sense of a contribution paid by one nation to another in acknowledgment of subjection, but also as the contribution of revenue paid by subjects to their proper ruler. The term, moreover, gives a very inadequate idea of the contents, which describe generally the labours of Yü in remedying the disasters occasioned by the inundation with which he had to cope, and how he then defined the boundaries of the different provinces, made other important territorial divisions, and determined the quality of the soil in each province, and the proportion of revenue it should pay, with other particulars. The Book, if we could fully credit it, would be a sort of domesday book of China in the twenty-third century

B.C., in the compass of a few pages. In the classification of the Books of the Shû, according to their subject-matter, this is rightly considered as a Canon. The first section of it is divided into one short introductory chapter, and nine others, each containing the account of one province.

Section 1.

1. Yü divided the land. Following the course of the hills, he cut down the trees. He determined the highest hills and largest rivers (in the several regions).

2. With respect to *K*î *K*âu[1], he did his work at Hû-khâu, and took effective measures at (the mountains) Liang and *Kh*î. Having repaired the works on Thâi-yüan, he proceeded on to the south of (mount) Yo. He was successful with his labours on Tan-hwâi, and went on to the cross-flowing stream of *K*ang.

The soil of this province was whitish and mellow. Its contribution of revenue was the highest of the highest class, with some proportion of the second. Its fields were the average of the middle class.

---

[1] *K*î *K*âu embraced the present provinces of Shan-hsî, *K*ih-lî, the three most northern departments of Ho-nan, and the western portion of Liâo-tung. It had the Ho—what we call the Yellow river—on three sides of it. On the west was all that part of the Ho which forms the dividing line between Shen-hsî and Shan-hsî. At the south-western corner of Shan-hsî, the Ho turns to the east: and in Yü's time it flowed eastwards to about the place where *K*ih-lî, Shan-tung, and Ho-nan all touch, forming the southern boundary of *K*î *K*âu. Thence it ran north and east, till its waters entered the present gulph of *K*ih-lî, forming, so far, the eastern boundary of the province. The northern boundary must be left undefined.

It would be foreign to the object of the present publication of the Shû, and take too much space, to give notes on the details of Yü's operations in *K*î *K*âu and the other provinces.

The (waters of the) Hăng and Wei were brought to their proper channels, and Tâ-lü was made capable of cultivation.

The wild people of the islands (brought) dresses of skins (i. e. fur dresses); keeping close on the right to the rocks of *K*ieh, they entered the Ho.

3. Between the *K*î and the Ho was Yen *K*âu [1].

The nine branches of the Ho were made to keep their proper channels. Lêi-hsiâ was made a marsh, in which (the waters of) the Yung and the Ʒü were united. The mulberry grounds were made fit for silkworms, and then (the people) came down from the heights, and occupied the grounds (below).

The soil of this province was blackish and rich; the grass in it was luxuriant, and the trees grew high. Its fields were the lowest of the middle class. Its contribution of revenue was fixed at what would just be deemed the correct amount; but it was not required from it, as from the other provinces, till after it had been cultivated for thirteen years. Its articles of tribute were varnish and silk, and, in baskets, woven ornamental fabrics.

They floated along the *K*î and Thâ, and so reached the Ho.

4. The sea and (mount) Tâi were the boundaries of *Kh*ing *K*âu [2].

---

[1] Yen *K*âu was a small province, having the Ho on the north, the *K*î on the south, the gulph of *K*ih-lî on the east, and Yü *K*âu, Yü's seventh province, on the west. It embraced the department of Tâ-ming, with portions of those of Ho-*k*ien and Thien-*k*ing, in *K*ih-lî, and the department of Tung-*kh*ang, with portions of those of *K*î-nan and Yen-*k*âu, in Shan-tung.

[2] *Kh*ing *K*âu, having mount Tâi and Hsü *K*âu (the next province) on the west and south, Yen *K*âu and the sea on the north-west and the north, and the sea on the east and south,

(The territory of) Yü-î was defined; and the Wei- and Ʒze were made to keep their (old) channels.

Its soil was whitish and rich. Along the shore of the sea were wide tracts of salt land. Its fields were the lowest of the first class, and its contribution of revenue the highest of the second. Its articles of tribute were salt, fine cloth of dolichos fibre, productions of the sea of various kinds; with silk, hemp, lead, pine trees, and strange stones, from the valleys of Tâi. The wild people of Lâi were taught tillage and pasturage, and brought in their baskets the silk from the mountain mulberry tree.

They floated along the Wăn, and so reached the *K*î.

5. The sea, mount Tâi, and the Hwâi were (the boundaries of) Hsü *K*âu [1].

The Hwâi and the Î (rivers) were regulated. The (hills) Măng and Yü were made fit for cultivation. (The waters of) Tâ-yeh were confined (so as to form

would be still smaller than Yen *K*âu, and contain the three departments of *Kh*ing-*k*âu, Lâi-*k*âu, and Têng-*k*âu, with the western portion of that of *K*î-nan, in Shan-tung. From the text we should never suppose that it passed across the sea which washes the north and east of Shan-tung, and extended indefinitely into Liâo-tung and Corla. This, however, is the view of many Chinese geographers.

[1] The western boundary of Hsü *K*âu, which is not given in the text, was Yü *K*âu, and part of *Kh*ing *K*âu. It embraced the present department of Hsü-*k*âu, the six districts—Thâo-yüan, *Kh*ing-ho, An-tung, Hsü-*kh*ien, Sui-ning, and Kan-yü, department of Hwâi-an, with Phei *K*âu and Hâi *K*âu,—all in *K*iang-sû; the whole of Yen-*k*âu department, Tung-phing *K*âu and the south of Phing-yin district in the department of Thâi-an, the department of Î-*k*âu, and portions of those of *K*î-nan and *Kh*ing-*k*âu,—all in Shan-tung; with the four districts Hwâi-yüan, Wû-ho, Hung, and Ling-pî, department of Făng-yang, with Sze *K*âu and Hsü *K*âu,—all in An-hui.

a marsh); and (the tract of) Tung-yüan was successfully brought under management.

The soil of this province was red, clayey, and rich. Its grass and trees grew more and more bushy. Its fields were the second of the highest class; its contribution of revenue was the average of the second. Its articles of tribute were—earth of five different colours, variegated pheasants from the valleys of mount Yü, the solitary dryandra from the south of mount Yî, and the sounding-stones that (seemed to) float on the (banks of the) Sze. The wild tribes about the Hwâi brought oyster-pearls and fish, and their baskets full of deep azure and other silken fabrics, chequered and pure white.

They floated along the Hwâi and the Sze, and so reached the Ho.

6. The Hwâi and the sea formed (the boundaries of) Yang *K*âu [1].

The (lake of) Phăng-lî was confined to its proper limits, and the sun-birds (= the wild geese) had places

---

[1] The Hwâi was the boundary of Yang *K*âu on the north, and we naturally suppose that the other boundary mentioned, the sea, should be referred to the south of the province. If it were really so, Yang *K*âu must have extended along the coast as far as Cochin-China, and not a few Chinese scholars argue that it did so. But that no southern boundary of the province is mentioned may rather be taken as proving that when this Book was compiled, the country south of the *K*iang—the present Yang-ȝze—was unknown.

Along the greater part of its course, the province was conterminous on the west with *K*ing *K*âu, and in the north-west with Yü *K*âu. We may safely assign to it the greater portion of An-hui, and a part of the department of Hwang-*k*âu, in Hû-pei. All this would be the northern portion of the province. How far it extended southwards into *K*ê-*k*iang and *K*iang-hsî, it is impossible to say.

to settle on. The three *K*iang were led to enter the sea, and it became possible to still the marsh of *K*ăn. The bamboos, small and large, then spread about; the grass grew thin and long, and the trees rose high; the soil was miry.

The fields of this province were the lowest of the lowest class; its contribution of revenue was the highest of the lowest class, with a proportion of the class above. Its articles of tribute were gold, silver, and copper; yâo and khwăn stones; bamboos, small and large; (elephants') teeth, hides, feathers, hair, and timber. The wild people of the islands brought garments of grass, with silks woven in shell-patterns in their baskets. Their bundles contained small oranges and pummeloes,—rendered when specially required.

They followed the course of the *K*iang and the sea, and so reached the Hwâi and the Sze.

7. (Mount) *K*ing and the south of (mount) Hăng formed (the boundaries of) *K*ing *K*âu [1].

The *K*iang and the Han pursued their (common) course to the sea, as if they were hastening to court. The nine *K*iang were brought into complete order. The Tho and *Kh*ien (streams) were conducted by

---

[1] Mount *K*ing, which bounded *K*ing *K*âu on the north, is in the department of Hsiang-yang, Hû-pei, and is called the southern *K*ing, to distinguish it from another mountain of the same name farther north in Yung *K*âu. Mount Hăng, its southern boundary, is 'the southern mountain' of the Canon of Shun in Hăng-*k*âu department, Hû-nan. Yang *K*âu was on the east, and the country on the west was almost unknown. *K*ing *K*âu contained the greater portion of the present provinces of Hû-pei and Hû-nan, and parts also of Kwei-*k*âu and Sze-*kh*üan. Some geographers also extend it on the south into Kwang-tung and Kwang-hsî, which is very unlikely.

their proper channels. The land in (the marsh of) Yün (became visible), and (the marsh of) Măng was made capable of cultivation.

The soil of this province was miry. Its fields were the average of the middle class; and its contribution of revenue was the lowest of the highest class. Its articles of tribute were feathers, hair, (elephants') teeth, and hides; gold, silver, and copper; *kh*un trees, wood for bows, cedars, and cypresses; grindstones, whetstones, flint stones to make arrow-heads, and cinnabar; and the *kh*ün and lû bamboos, with the hû tree, (all good for making arrows)—of which the Three Regions were able to contribute the best specimens. The three-ribbed rush was sent in bundles, put into cases. The baskets were filled with silken fabrics, azure and deep purple, and with strings of pearls that were not quite round. From the (country of the) nine *K*iang, the great tortoise was presented when specially required (and found).

They floated down the *K*iang, the Tho, the *Kh*ien, and the Han, and crossed (the country) to the Lo, whence they reached the most southern part of the Ho.

8. The *K*ing (mountain) and the Ho were (the boundaries of) Yü *K*âu[1].

The Î, the Lo, the *Kh*an, and the *K*ien were conducted to the Ho. The (marsh of) Yung-po was

[1] Yü *K*âu was the central one of Yü's nine divisions of the country, and was conterminous, for a greater or less distance, with all of them, excepting *Kh*ing *K*âu, which lay off in the east by itself. It embraced most of the present Ho-nan, stretching also into the east and south, so as to comprehend parts of Shan-tung and Hû-pei.

confined within its proper limits. The (waters of that of) Ko were led to (the marsh of) Măng-*k*û.

The soil of this province was mellow; in the lower parts it was (in some places) rich, and (in others) dark and thin. Its fields were the highest of the middle class; and its contribution of revenue was the average of the highest class, with a proportion of the very highest. Its articles of tribute were varnish, hemp, fine cloth of dolichos fibre, and the bœhmerea. The baskets were full of chequered silks, and of fine floss silk. Stones for polishing sounding-stones were rendered when required.

They floated along the Lo, and so reached the Ho.

9. The south of (mount) Hwâ and the Black-water were (the boundaries of) Liang *K*âu [1].

The (hills) Min and Po were made capable of cultivation. The Tho and *Kh*ien streams were conducted by their proper channels. Sacrifices were offered to (the hills) ȝhâi and Mâng on the regulation (of the country about them).* (The country of) the wild tribes about the Ho was successfully operated on.

---

[1] Liang *K*âu was an extensive province, and it is a remarkable fact that neither the dominions of the Shang nor the *K*âu dynasty, which followed Hsiâ, included it. Portions of it were embraced in the Yü and Yung provinces of *K*âu, but the greater part was considered as wild, savage territory, beyond the limits of the Middle Kingdom. It is difficult to believe that the great Yü operated upon it, as this chapter would seem to indicate. The Hwâ at its north-eastern corner is the western mountain of Shun. The Black-water, or 'the *K*iang of the Golden Sands,' is identified with the present Lû. The province extended over most of the present Sze-*kh*üan, with parts of Shen-hsî and Kan-sû. I can hardly believe, as many do, that it extended far into Yün-nan and Kwei-*k*âu.

The soil of this province was greenish and light. Its fields were the highest of the lowest class; and its contribution of revenue was the average of the lowest class, with proportions of the rates immediately above and below. Its articles of tribute were —the best gold, iron, silver, steel, flint stones to make arrow-heads, and sounding-stones; with the skins of bears, foxes, and jackals, and (nets) woven of their hair.

From (the hill of) Hsî-*kh*ing they came by the course of the Hwan; floated along the *Kh*ien, and then crossed (the country) to the Mien; passed to the Wei, and (finally) ferried across the Ho.

10. The Black-water and western Ho were (the boundaries of) Yung *K*âu [1].

The Weak-water was conducted westwards. The *K*ing was led to mingle its waters with those of the Wei. The *Kh*î and the *Kh*ü were next led in a similar way (to the Wei), and the waters of the Fêng found the same receptacle.

(The mountains) *K*ing and *Kh*î were sacrificed to.* (Those of) *K*ung-nan and *Kh*un-wû (were also regulated), and (all the way) on to Niâo-shû. Successful measures could now be taken with the plains and swamps, even to (the marsh of) *K*û-yeh. (The country of) San-wei was made habitable, and the (affairs of the) people of San-miâo were greatly arranged.

[1] The Black-water, which was the western boundary of Yung *K*âu, was a different river from that which, with the same name, ran along the south of Liang *K*âu. Yung *K*âu was probably the largest of Yü's provinces, embracing nearly all the present provinces of Shen-hsî and Kan-sû, and extending indefinitely northwards to the Desert.

The soil of the province was yellow and mellow. Its fields were the highest of the highest class, and its contribution of revenue the lowest of the second. Its articles of tribute were the *kh*iû jade and the lin, and (the stones called) lang-kan.

Past *K*î-shih they floated on to Lung-măn on the western Ho. They then met on the north of the Wei (with the tribute-bearers from other quarters).

Hair-cloth and skins (were brought from) Khwăn-lun, Hsî-*k*ih, and *Kh*ü-sâu;—the wild tribes of the west (all) coming to (submit to Yü's) arrangements.

Section 2.

The division of the Book into two sections is a convenient arrangement, but modern, and not always followed. The former section gives a view of Yü's labours in each particular province. This gives a general view of the mountain ranges of the country, and of the principal streams; going on to other labours, subsequently, as was seen in the Introduction, ascribed to Yü,—his conferring lands and surnames, and dividing the whole territory into five domains. The contents are divided into five chapters:—the first, describing the mountains; the second, describing the rivers; the third, containing a summary of all the labours of Yü thus far mentioned; the fourth, relating his other labours; and the fifth, celebrating Yü's fame, and the completion of his work.

1. (Yü) surveyed and described (the hills), beginning with *Kh*ien and *Kh*î and proceeding to mount *K*ing; then, crossing the Ho, Hû-khâu, and Lêi-shâu, going on to Thâi-yo. (After these came) Tî-*k*û and Hsî-*kh*ăng, from which he went on to Wang-wû; (then there were) Thâi-hang and mount Hăng, from which he proceeded to the rocks of *K*ieh, where he reached the sea.

(South of the Ho, he surveyed) Hsî-*kh*ing, *K*û-yü,

and Niâo-shû, going on to Thâi-hwâ; (then) Hsiung-*r*, Wâi-fang, and Thung-pâi, from which he proceeded to Pei-wei.

He surveyed and described Po-*kh*ung, going on to (the other) mount *K*ing; and Nêi-fang, from which he went on to Tâ-pieh.

(He did the same with) the south of mount Min, and went on to mount Hăng. Then crossing the nine *K*iang, he proceeded to the plain of Fû-*kh*ien.

2. He traced the Weak-water as far as the Ho-lî (mountains), from which its superfluous waters went away among the moving sands.

He traced the Black-water as far as San-wei, from which it (went away to) enter the southern sea.

He traced the Ho from *K*î-shih as far as Lung-măn; and thence, southwards, to the north of (mount) Hwâ; eastward then to Tî-*kh*û; eastward (again) to the ford of Măng; eastward (still) to the junction of the Lo; and then on to Tâ-pei. (From this the course was) northwards, past the *K*iang-water, on to Tâ-lü; north from which the river was divided, and became the nine Ho, which united again, and formed the Meeting Ho, when they entered the sea.

From Po-*kh*ung he traced the Yang, which, flowing eastwards, became the Han. Farther east it became the water of Ȝhang-lang; and after passing the three Dykes, it went on to Tâ-pieh, southwards from which it entered the *K*iang. Eastward still, and whirling on, it formed the marsh of Phăng-lî; and from that its eastern flow was the northern *K*iang, as which it entered the sea.

From mount Min he traced the *K*iang, which, branching off to the east, formed the Tho; eastward again, it reached the Lî, passed the nine *K*iang, and went on to Tung-ling; then flowing east, and winding to the north, it joined (the Han) with its eddying movements. From that its eastern flow was the middle *K*iang, as which it entered the sea.

He traced the Yen water, which, flowing eastward, became the *K*î, and entered the Ho. (Thereafter) it flowed out, and became the Yung (marsh). Eastward, it issued forth on the north of Thâo-*kh*iû, and flowed farther east to (the marsh of) Ko; then it went north-east, and united with the Wăn; thence it went north, and (finally) entered the sea on the east.

He traced the Hwâi from the hill of Thung-pâi. Flowing east, it united with the Sze and the Î, and (still) with an eastward course entered the sea.

He traced the Wei from (the hill) Niâo-shû-thung-hsüeh. Flowing eastward, it united with the Fêng, and eastwards again with the *K*ing. Farther east still, it passed the *Kh*î and the *Kh*ü, and entered the Ho.

He traced the Lo from (the hill) Hsiung-*r*. Flowing to the north-east, it united with the *K*ien and the *Kh*an, and eastwards still with the Î. Then on the north-east it entered the Ho.

3. (Thus), throughout the nine provinces a similar order was effected:—the grounds along the waters were everywhere made habitable; the hills were cleared of their superfluous wood and sacrificed to;* the sources of the rivers were cleared; the marshes were well banked; and access to the capital was secured for all within the four seas.

The six magazines (of material wealth) were fully attended to; the different parts of the country were subjected to an exact comparison, so that contribution of revenue could be carefully adjusted according to their resources. (The fields) were all classified with reference to the three characters of the soil; and the revenues for the Middle Region were established.

4. He conferred lands and surnames. (He said), 'Let me set the example of a reverent attention to my virtue, and none will act contrary to my conduct.'

Five hundred lî formed the Domain of the Sovereign. From the first hundred they brought as revenue the whole plant of the grain; from the second, the ears, with a portion of the stalk; from the third, the straw, but the people had to perform various services; from the fourth, the grain in the husk; and from the fifth, the grain cleaned.

Five hundred lî (beyond) constituted the Domain of the Nobles. The first hundred lî was occupied by the cities and lands of the (sovereign's) high ministers and great officers; the second, by the principalities of the barons; and the (other) three hundred, by the various other princes.

Five hundred lî (still beyond) formed the Peace-securing Domain. In the first three hundred, they cultivated the lessons of learning and moral duties; in the other two, they showed the energies of war and defence.

Five hundred lî (remoter still) formed the Domain of Restraint. The (first) three hundred were occupied by the tribes of the Î; the (other) two hundred, by criminals undergoing the lesser banishment.

Five hundred lî (the most remote) constituted the Wild Domain. The (first) three hundred were occupied by the tribes of the Man; the (other) two hundred, by criminals undergoing the greater banishment.

5. On the east, reaching to the sea; on the west, extending to the moving sands; to the utmost limits of the north and south:—his fame and influence filled up (all within) the four seas. Yü presented the dark-coloured symbol of his rank, and announced the completion of his work.

Book II. The Speech at Kan.

With this Book there commence the documents of the Shû that may be regarded, as I have said in the Introduction, as contemporaneous with the events which they describe. It is the first of the 'Speeches,' which form one class of the documents of the classic.

The text does not say who the king mentioned in it was, but the prevalent tradition has always been that he was *Kh*î, the son and successor of Yü. Its place between the Tribute of Yü and the next Book belonging to the reign of Thâi Khang, *Kh*î's son, corroborates this view.

Kan is taken as the name of a place in the southern border of the principality of Hû, with the lord of which *Kh*î fought. The name of Hû itself still remains in the district so called of the department Hsî-an, in Shen-hsî.

The king, about to engage in battle with a rebellious vassal, assembles his generals and troops, and addresses them. He declares obscurely the grounds of the expedition which he had undertaken, and concludes by stimulating the soldiers to the display of courage and observance of order by promises of reward and threats of punishment.

There was a great battle at Kan. (Previous to it), the king called together the six nobles, (the leaders of his six hosts), and said, 'Ah! all ye who are engaged in my six hosts, I have a solemn announcement to make to you.

'The lord of Hû wildly wastes and despises the five elements (that regulate the seasons), and has idly abandoned the three acknowledged commencements of the year[1]. On this account Heaven is about to destroy him, and bring to an end his appointment (to Hû); and I am now reverently executing the punishment appointed by Heaven.*

'If you, (the archers) on the left[2], do not do your work on the left, it will be a disregard of my orders. If you, (the spearmen) on the right[2], do not do your work on the right, it will be a disregard of my orders. If you, charioteers[2], do not observe the rules for the management of your horses, it will be a disregard of my orders. You who obey my orders, shall be rewarded before (the spirits of) my ancestors; and you who disobey my orders, shall be put to death before the altar of the spirits of the land, and I will also put to death your children.'*

---

[1] The crimes of the lord of Hû are here very obscurely stated. With regard to the second of them, we know that Hsiâ commenced its year with the first month of spring, Shang a month earlier, and *K*âu about mid-winter. It was understood that every dynasty should fix a new month for the beginning of the year, and the dynasty of *Kh*in actually carried its first month back into our November. If the lord of Hû claimed to begin the year with another month than that which Yü had fixed, he was refusing submission to the new dynasty. No doubt, the object of the expedition was to put down a dangerous rival.

[2] The chariots were the principal part of an ancient Chinese army; it is long before we read of cavalry. A war-chariot generally carried three. The driver was in the centre; on his left was an archer, and a spearman occupied the place on his right. They all wore mail.

Book III. The Songs of the Five Sons.

This Book ranks in that class of the documents of the Shû which goes by the name of 'Instructions.' Though the form of it be poetical, the subject-matter is derived from the Lessons left by Yü for the guidance of his posterity.

Thâi Khang succeeded to his father in B.C. 2188, and his reign continues in chronology to 2160. His character is given here in the introductory chapter. *Kh*iung, the principality of Î who took the field against him, is identified with the sub-department of Tê-*K*âu, department *K*î-nan, Shan-tung. There is a tradition that Î, at an early period of his life, was lord of a state in the present Ho-nan. This would make his movement against Thâi Khang, 'south of the Ho,' more easy for him. The name of Thâi Khang remains in the district so called of the department *Kh*ăn-*k*âu, Ho-nan. There, it is said, he died, having never been able to recross the Ho.

In his song the king's first brother deplores how he had lost the affections of the people; the second speaks of his dissolute extravagance; the third mourns his loss of the throne; the fourth deplores his departure from the principles of Yü, and its disastrous consequences; and the fifth is a wail over the miserable condition of them all.

1. Thâi Khang occupied the throne like a personator of the dead [1]. By idleness and dissipation he extinguished his virtue, till the black-haired people all wavered in their allegiance. He, however, pursued his pleasure and wanderings without any

[1] The character that here as a verb governs the character signifying 'throne' means properly 'a corpse,' and is often used for the personator of the dead, in the sacrificial services to the dead which formed a large part of the religious ceremonies of the ancient Chinese. A common definition of it is 'the semblance of the spirit,'=the image into which the spirit entered. Thâi Khang was but a personator on the throne, no better than a sham sovereign.

self-restraint. He went out to hunt beyond the Lo, and a hundred days elapsed without his returning. (On this) Î, the prince of *Kh*iung, taking advantage of the discontent of the people, resisted (his return) on (the south of) the Ho. The (king's) five brothers had attended their mother in following him, and were waiting for him on the north of the Lo; and (when they heard of Î's movement), all full of dissatisfaction, they related the Cautions of the great Yü in the form of songs.

2. The first said,

'It was the lesson of our great ancestor:—
The people should be cherished,
And not looked down upon.
The people are the root of a country;
The root firm, the country is tranquil.
When I look at all under heaven,
Of the simple men and simple women,
Any one may surpass me.
If the One man err repeatedly [1],
Should dissatisfaction be waited for till it appears?
Before it is seen, it should be guarded against.
In my dealing with the millions of the people,
I should feel as much anxiety as if I were driving six horses with rotten reins.
The ruler of men—
How should he be but reverent (of his duties)?'

The second said,

'It is in the Lessons:—
When the palace is a wild of lust,
And the country is a wild for hunting;

[1] Any king, in the person of Yü, may be understood to be the speaker.

When spirits are liked, and music is the delight;
When there are lofty roofs and carved walls;—
The existence of any one of these things
Has never been but the prelude to ruin.'

The third said,
'There was the lord of Thâo and Thang[1],
Who possessed this region of *K*î.
Now we have fallen from his ways,
And thrown into confusion his rules and laws;—
The consequence is extinction and ruin.'

The fourth said,
'Brightly intelligent was our ancestor,
Sovereign of the myriad regions.
He had canons, he had patterns,
Which he transmitted to his posterity.
The standard stone and the equalizing quarter
Were in the royal treasury.
Wildly have we dropt the clue he gave us,
Overturning our temple, and extinguishing our sacrifices.'*

The fifth said,
'Oh! whither shall we turn?
The thoughts in my breast make me sad.
All the people are hostile to us;
On whom can we rely?
Anxieties crowd together in our hearts;
Thick as are our faces, they are covered with blushes.
We have not been careful of our virtue;
And though we repent, we cannot overtake the past.'

[1] The lord of Thâo and Thang is Yâo, who was lord of the principalities of Thâo and Thang, but of which first and which last is uncertain, before his accession to the throne. *K*î is the *K*î *K*âu of the Tribute of Yü.

BOOK IV. THE PUNITIVE EXPEDITION OF YIN.

THIS Book is another of the 'Speeches' of the Shû, belonging to the reign of *K*ung Khang, a brother of Thâi Khang, the fourth of the kings of Shang (B.C. 2159–2147).

Hsî and Ho, the principal ministers of the Board of Astronomy, descended from those of the same name in the time of Yâo, had given themselves over to licentious indulgence in their private cities, and grossly neglected their duties. Especially had they been unobservant of an eclipse of the sun in autumn. The king considered them worthy of death, and commissioned the marquis of Yin to execute on them the sentence of his justice. Where Yin was is not now known.

The principal part of the Book consists of the speech made by the marquis to his troops.

1. When *K*ung Khang commenced his reign over all within the four seas, the marquis of Yin was commissioned to take charge of the (king's) six hosts. (At this time) the Hsî and Ho had neglected the duties of their office, and were abandoned to drink in their (private) cities; and the marquis of Yin received the king's charge to go and punish them.

2. He made an announcement to his hosts, saying, 'Ah! ye, all my men, there are the well-counselled instructions of the sage (founder of our dynasty), clearly verified in their power to give stability and security:—"The former kings were carefully attentive to the warnings of Heaven[1],* and their ministers observed the regular laws (of their offices). All the officers (moreover) watchfully did their duty to

[1] That is, here, such warnings as were supposed to be conveyed by eclipses and other unusual celestial phenomena.

assist (the government), and their sovereign became entirely intelligent." Every year, in the first month of spring, the herald, with his wooden-tongued bell, goes along the roads[1], (proclaiming), "Ye officers able to instruct, be prepared with your admonitions. Ye workmen engaged in mechanical affairs, remonstrate on the subjects of your employments. If any of you do not attend with respect (to this requirement), the country has regular punishments for you."

'Now here are the Hsî and Ho. They have allowed their virtue to be subverted, and are besotted by drink. They have violated the duties of their office, and left their posts. They have been the first to let the regulating of the heavenly (bodies) get into disorder, putting far from them their proper business. On the first day of the last month of autumn, the sun and moon did not meet harmoniously in Fang[2]. The blind musicians beat their drums; the inferior officers galloped, and the common people (employed about the public offices) ran about[3]. The Hsî and the Ho, however, as if they were (mere) personators of the dead in their offices, heard nothing and knew nothing;—so stupidly went they astray (from their duties) in the matter of the heavenly appearances, and rendered themselves liable to the death appointed by the former kings. The statutes of government say, "When they anticipate the time, let them be put to death without mercy; when (their

[1] A similar practice existed in the *K*âu dynasty.

[2] See the Introduction, p. 13.

[3] Similar observances are still practised on occasion of an eclipse of the sun. See Biot's Etudes sur l'Astronomie Indienne et Chinoise, pp. 357–360.

reckoning) is behind the time, let them be put to death without mercy."

'Now I, with you all, am entrusted with the execution of the punishment appointed by Heaven.* Unite your strength, all of you warriors, for the royal House. Give me your help, I pray you, reverently to carry out the dread charge of the Son of Heaven.

'When the fire blazes over the ridge of Khwăn[1], gems and stones are burned together; but if a minister of Heaven exceed in doing his duty, the consequences will be fiercer than blazing fire. While I destroy, (therefore), the chief criminals, I will not punish those who have been forced to follow them; and those who have long been stained by their filthy manners will be allowed to renovate themselves.

'Oh! when sternness overcomes compassion, things are surely conducted to a successful issue. When compassion overcomes sternness, no merit can be achieved. All ye, my warriors, exert yourselves, and take warning, (and obey my orders)!'

---

[1] Khwăn is perhaps a part of the Khwăn-lun mountain in the west of the Ko-ko-nor, where the Ho has its sources. The speaker evidently thought of it as volcanic.

PART IV. THE BOOKS OF SHANG.

Book I. The Speech of Thang.

Shang was the name under which the dynasty that superseded Hsiâ (B.C. 1766) held the kingdom for fully 300 years. Yin then began to be used as well as Shang, and the dynasty was called indifferently Shang or Yin, and sometimes Yin-Shang by a combination of the two names. The ruling House traced its origin into the remote times of antiquity, through Hsieh, whose appointment by Shun to be Minister of Instruction is related in the Canon of Shun. For his services Hsieh was invested with the principality of Shang, corresponding to the present small department of the same name in Shen-hsî. From Hsieh to Thang, the founder of the dynasty, there are reckoned fourteen generations, and we find Thang, when he first becomes prominent in history, a long way from the ancestral fief, in 'the southern Po,' corresponding to the present district of Shang-*kh*iû, department Kwei-teh, Ho-nan. The title of the dynasty, however, was derived from the original Shang.

There were in the Shû, when the collection was formed, thirty-one documents of Shang in forty Books, of which only eleven remain in seventeen Books, two of them containing each three parts or sections. The Speech of Thang, that is now the first Book in the Part, was originally only the sixth. Thang was the designation of the hero, whose surname, dating from Hsieh, was 3ze, and name Lî. Thang may be translated, 'the Glorious One.' His common style in history is as *Kh*ăng Thang, 'Thang the Completer,' or 'Thang the Successful.'

He had summoned his people to take the field with him against *K*ieh, the cruel and doomed sovereign of Hsiâ, and finding them backward to the enterprise, he sets forth in this Book his reasons for attacking the tyrant, argues against their reluctance, using in the end both promises and threats to induce them to obey his orders.

The king said, 'Come, ye multitudes of the people, listen all to my words. It is not I, the little child[1], who dare to undertake a rebellious enterprise; but for the many crimes of the sovereign of Hsiâ, Heaven has given the charge to destroy him.*

'Now, ye multitudes, you are saying, "Our prince does not compassionate us, but (is calling us) away from our husbandry to attack and punish Hsiâ." I have indeed heard (these) words of you all; (but) the sovereign of Hsiâ is guilty, and, as I fear God, I dare not but punish him.*

'Now you are saying, "What are the crimes of Hsiâ to us?" The king of Hsiâ in every way exhausts the strength of his people, and exercises oppression in the cities of Hsiâ. His multitudes are become entirely indifferent (to his service), and feel no bond of union (to him). They are saying, "When wilt thou, O sun, expire? We will all perish with thee[2]." Such is the course of (the sovereign) of Hsiâ, and now I must go (and punish him).

'Assist, I pray you, me, the One man, to carry out the punishment appointed by Heaven. I will greatly reward you. On no account disbelieve me;—I will not eat my words. If you do not obey the words which I have thus spoken to you, I will put

---

[1] 'The little child' is a designation used humbly of themselves by the kings of Shang and *K*âu. It is given also to them and others by such great ministers as Î Yin and the duke of *K*âu.

[2] *K*ieh, it is said, had on one occasion, when told of the danger he was incurring by his cruelties, pointed to the sun, and said that as surely as the sun was in the heavens, so firm was he on the throne.

your children to death with you;—you shall find no forgiveness.'

Book II. The Announcement of *K*ung-hui.

This Book is the first of the 'Announcements,' which form a large class of the documents in the Shû. They are distinguished from the Speeches, as being made in a general assembly, or published, for the information of all, whereas the Speeches were made to an army.

*K*ung-hui, of an old family, whose surname was *Z*ăn, with its seat in the territory of Hsieh, corresponding to the present district of Thang, department Yen-*k*âu, Shan-tung, was a minister of Thang. Thang has been successful against *K*ieh, and dethroned him, but is haunted by some feeling of remorse, and afraid that what he has done may be appealed to in future ages as an apology for rebellion. This gives occasion to the Announcement, in which *K*ung-hui vindicates the proceeding of the king, showing, first, that he had only obeyed the guidance of Heaven, and, then, that men consented with Heaven in the matter. He concludes with various counsels addressed to the king.

1. When Thang the Successful was keeping *K*ieh in banishment in Nan-*kh*âo[1], he had a feeling of shame on account of his conduct, and said, 'I am afraid that in future ages men will fill their mouths with me, (as an apology for their rebellious proceedings.)'

2. On this *K*ung-hui made the following announcement: 'Oh! Heaven gives birth to the people with (such) desires, that without a ruler they must fall into all disorders; and Heaven again gives birth

[1] Nan-*kh*âo is identified with the present district of *Kh*âo, department Lû-*k*âu, An-hui.

to the man of intelligence to regulate them.* The sovereign of Hsiâ had his virtue all-obscured, and the people were (as if they had fallen) amid mire and (burning) charcoal. Heaven hereupon gifted (our) king with valour and prudence, to serve as a sign and director to the myriad regions, and to continue the old ways of Yü. You are now (only) following the proper course, honouring and obeying the appointment of Heaven. The king of Hsiâ was an offender, falsely and calumniously alleging the sanction of supreme Heaven, to spread abroad his commands among the people. On this account God viewed him with disapprobation, caused our Shang to receive his appointment, and employed (you) to enlighten the multitudes (of the people).' *

3. 'Contemners of the worthy and parasites of the powerful,—many such followers he had indeed; (but) from the first our country was to the sovereign of Hsiâ like weeds among the springing corn, and blasted grains among the good. (Our people), great and small, were in constant apprehension, fearful though they were guilty of no crime. How much more was this the case, when our (prince's) virtues became a theme (eagerly) listened to! Our king did not approach to (dissolute) music and women; he did not seek to accumulate property and wealth. To great virtue he gave great offices, and to great merit great rewards. He employed others as if (their excellences) were his own; he was not slow to change his errors. Rightly indulgent and rightly benevolent, from the display (of such virtue), confidence was reposed in him by the millions of the people.

'When the earl of Ko[1] showed his enmity to the provision-carriers, the work of punishment began with Ko. When it went on in the east, the wild tribes of the west murmured; when it went on in the south, those of the north murmured:—they said, "Why does he make us alone the last?" To whatever people he went, they congratulated one another in their families, saying, "We have waited for our prince; our prince is come, and we revive." The people's honouring our Shang is a thing of long existence.'

4. 'Show favour to the able and right-principled (among the princes), and aid the virtuous; distinguish the loyal, and let the good have free course. Absorb the weak, and punish the wilfully blind; take their states from the disorderly, and deal summarily with those going to ruin. When you (thus) accelerate the end of what is (of itself) ready to perish, and strengthen what is itself strong to live, how will the states all flourish! When (a sovereign's) virtue is daily being renewed, he is cherished throughout the myriad regions; when his mind is full (only) of himself, he is abandoned by the nine branches of his kindred. Exert yourself, O king, to make your virtue (still more) illustrious, and set up (the standard of) the Mean before the people. Order your affairs

[1] Ko was a principality corresponding to the present district of Ning-ling, department of Kwei-teh, Ho-nan. It was thus near the southern Po, which belonged to Thang. Mencius tells us (III, ii, ch. 3) that Thang sent a multitude of his people to assist the farmers of Ko, about the poor produce of which their chief had lamented to him. That chief, however, instead of showing any gratitude, surprised and robbed those who were carrying provisions from Po to the labourers in the field, and committed various atrocities upon them. This aroused Thang's indignation, and he made him the first object of his punitive justice.

by righteousness; order your heart by propriety;—so shall you transmit a grand example to posterity. I have heard the saying, "He who finds instructors for himself, comes to the supreme dominion; he who says that others are not equal to himself, comes to ruin. He who likes to put questions, becomes enlarged; he who uses only his own views, becomes smaller (than he was)." Oh! he who would take care for the end must be attentive to the beginning. There is establishment for the observers of propriety, and overthrow for the blinded and wantonly indifferent. To revere and honour the path prescribed by Heaven is the way ever to preserve the favouring appointment of Heaven.' *

Book III. The Announcement of Thang.

Thang had made an end of the dynasty of Hsiâ, and returned to Po, when he issued this Announcement, which may be considered as a solemn inauguration of the new dynasty. He shows how he had taken possession of the throne in reverent submission to the will of Heaven, what appreciation he had of the duties devolving on him, and the spirit in which he would discharge them. In the end he calls on the princes and the people to sympathize and co-operate with him.

1. When the king returned from vanquishing Hsiâ and came to Po, he made a grand announcement to the myriad regions.

2. The king said, 'Ah! ye multitudes of the myriad regions, listen clearly to the announcement of me, the One man [1]. The great God has conferred

[1] 'The One man' has occurred before, in the Songs of the Five Sons, as a designation of the sovereign. It continues to be so to the present day.

(even) on the inferior people a moral sense, compliance with which would show their nature invariably right.* To make them tranquilly pursue the course which it would indicate is the work of the sovereign.

'The king of Hsiâ extinguished his virtue, and played the tyrant, extending his oppression over you, the people of the myriad regions. Suffering from his cruel injuries, and unable to endure the wormwood and poison, you protested with one accord your innocence to the spirits of heaven and earth.* The way of Heaven is to bless the good, and make the bad miserable. It sent down calamities on (the House of) Hsiâ, to make manifest its guilt. Therefore I, the little child, charged with the decree of Heaven and its bright terrors, did not dare to forgive (the criminal). I presumed to use a dark-coloured victim-bull, and, making clear announcement to the Spiritual Sovereign in the high heavens [1], requested leave to deal with the ruler of Hsiâ as a criminal.* Then I sought for the great Sage [2], with whom I might unite my strength, to request the favour (of Heaven) for you, my multitudes. High Heaven truly showed its favour to the inferior people, and the criminal has been degraded and subjected. What Heaven appoints is without error;—brilliantly (now), like the blossoming of plants and trees, the millions of the people show a true reviving.'*

3. 'It is given to me, the One man, to secure the

[1] For 'the Spiritual Sovereign in the high heavens,' we have in the Confucian Analects, XX, 1, professing to quote this passage, 'the most great and Sovereign God.'

[2] 'The great Sage' must be Î Yin, Thang's chief adviser and minister, who appears prominently in the next Book.

harmony and tranquillity of your states and clans; and now I know not whether I may not offend against (the Powers) above and below.* I am fearful and trembling, as if I were in danger of falling into a deep abyss. Throughout all the regions that enter on a new life under me, do not, (ye princes), follow lawless ways; make no approach to insolence and dissoluteness; let every one be careful to keep his statutes;—that so we may receive the favour of Heaven.* The good in you I will not dare to keep concealed; and for the evil in me I will not dare to forgive myself. I will examine these things in harmony with the mind of God.* When guilt is found anywhere in you who occupy the myriad regions, let it rest on me, the One man[1]. When guilt is found in me, the One man, it shall not attach to you who occupy the myriad regions.

'Oh! let us attain to be sincere in these things, and so we shall likewise have a (happy) consummation.'

---

[1] There was a tradition in the *K*âu dynasty, given with variations by Hsün-ʒze, Sze-mâ *Kh*ien, and others, which may be quoted to illustrate these noble sentiments of Thang. For seven years after his accession to the throne, B.C. 1766–1760, there was a great drought and famine. It was suggested at last that some human being should be offered in sacrifice to Heaven, and prayer made for rain. Thang said, 'If a man must be the victim, I will be he.' He fasted, cut off his hair and nails, and in a plain carriage, drawn by white horses, clad in rushes, in the guise of a sacrificial victim, he proceeded to a forest of mulberry trees, and there prayed, asking to what error or crime of his the calamity was owing. He had not done speaking when a copious rain fell.

Book IV. The Instructions of Î.

Thang died in B.C. 1754 or 1753, and was succeeded, so far as the evidence of the Shû goes, by his grandson, known as Thâi *K*iâ. The chief minister of Thang had been Î Yin, who delivers these Instructions to his young sovereign soon after his accession. Î was a great and wise man, 'a great sage,' as Thang calls him in the last Book, and is classed by Mencius among other celebrated ministers as 'the one most inclined to take office.' He reasons thus:—'Heaven's plan with mankind is that they who are first informed should instruct those who are later in being informed, and they who first apprehend principles should instruct those who are later in doing so.' He thought he was one of the former class, and a fire burned within him, impelling him to seek for office with a view to benefit the ignorant and erring. There were many legends about him in the times of *K*âu. He was surnamed Î, from having been born near the river of that name, an affluent of the Ho. His name is said to have been *K*ih, and also Â-hăng (see the beginning of next Book). Yin was his designation. Thang had, probably, entrusted to him the guardianship of his grandson, and so he now went over the history of the kingdom from Yü, till it was transferred from the line of Hsiâ to that of Shang, celebrated the virtues of Thang and his government, and warned the young king of the fate that he must incur, if he neglected the instructions given to him.

1. In the twelfth month of the first year, on (the day) Yî-*kh*âu, Î Yin sacrificed to the former king, and presented the heir-king reverently before (the shrine of) his grandfather.* All the princes from the domain of the nobles and the royal domain were present; all the officers (also), each continuing to discharge his particular duties, were there to receive the orders of the chief minister. Î Yin then clearly described the complete virtue of the Meritorious Ancestor for the instruction of the (young) king.

2. He said, 'Oh! of old the former kings of Hsiâ cultivated earnestly their virtue, and then there were no calamities from Heaven. The spirits of the hills and rivers likewise were all in tranquillity; and the birds and beasts, the fishes and tortoises, all enjoyed their existence according to their nature.* But their descendant did not follow (their example), and great Heaven sent down calamities, employing the agency of our (ruler) who was in possession of its favouring appointment.* The attack (on Hsiâ) may be traced to (the orgies in) Ming-thiâo[1], but our (rise) began in Po. Our king of Shang brilliantly displayed his sagely prowess; for oppression he substituted his generous gentleness; and the millions of the people gave him their hearts. Now your Majesty is entering on the inheritance of his virtue;—all depends on (how) you commence your reign. To set up love, it is for you to love (your relations); to set up respect, it is for you to respect (your elders). The commencement is in the family and the state; the consummation is in (all within) the four seas.'

3. 'Oh! the former king began with careful attention to the bonds that hold men together. He listened to expostulation, and did not seek to resist it; he conformed to (the wisdom of) the ancients; occupying the highest position, he displayed intelligence; occupying an inferior position, he displayed his loyalty; he allowed (the good qualities of) the men (whom he employed), and did

[1] Ming-thiâo was a place not far from the capital of *K*ieh (in the present district of An-yî, Hâi *K*âu, Shan-hsî). He had a palace there, where the vilest orgies were celebrated that alienated the minds of the people from him.

not seek that they should have every talent; in the government of himself, he seemed to think that he could never (sufficiently) attain. It was thus he arrived at the possession of the myriad regions.—How painstaking was he in these things!

'He extensively sought out wise men, who should be helpful to you, his descendant and heir. He laid down the punishments for officers, and warned those who were in authority, saying, "If you dare to have constant dancing in your palaces, and drunken singing in your chambers,—that is called the fashion of sorcerers; if you dare to set your hearts on wealth and women, and abandon yourselves to wandering about or to the chase,—that is called the fashion of extravagance; if you dare to despise sage words, to resist the loyal and upright, to put far from you the aged and virtuous, and to seek the company of procacious youths,—that is called the fashion of disorder. Now if a high noble or officer be addicted to one of these three fashions with their ten evil ways[1], his family will surely come to ruin; if the prince of a country be so addicted, his state will surely come to ruin. The minister who does not (try to) correct (such vices in the sovereign) shall be punished with branding." These rules were minutely inculcated (also) on the sons of officers and nobles in their lessons.'

4. 'Oh! do you, who now succeed to the throne, revere (these warnings) in your person. Think of

---

[1] The 'ten evil ways' are those mentioned in connexion with the three evil fashions;—two under the sorcerers' fashion, and four under each of the other two fashions.

them!—sacred counsels of vast importance, admirable words forcibly set forth! (The ways) of God are not invariable:—on the good-doer he sends down all blessings, and on the evil-doer he sends down all miseries.* Do you but be virtuous, be it in small things (or in large), and the myriad regions will have cause for rejoicing. If you be not virtuous, be it in large things (or in small), it will bring the ruin of your ancestral temple.'

Book V. The Thâi *K*iâ.

This Book also belongs to the class of 'Lessons or Instructions,' and is called 'the Thâi *K*iâ,' because the Instructions were addressed to the young monarch so named. It is divided into three sections or parts. Î Yin finds the young sovereign disobedient to his counsels, and proceeds to a high-handed measure. He removes him from his palace and companions, and keeps him in a sort of easy confinement, near the grave of his grandfather, all the period of mourning; and Thâi *K*iâ becomes sincerely penitent and virtuous. This is related in the first section. In the second, Î Yin brings the king back with honour to Po, to undertake the duties of the government, and congratulates him on his reformation. The king responds suitably, and asks the minister to continue to afford him his counsels, which the other at once proceeds to do. The third section is all occupied with further and important counsels.

Section 1.

1. The king, on succeeding to the throne, did not follow (the advice of) Â-hăng[1]. (Â-hăng or) Î Yin

[1] Â-hăng, it is said by Sze-mâ *Kh*ien, was the name of Î. Others make it the title of the chief minister under the dynasty of Shang, = 'the Support and Steelyard,' 'the Buttress and Director.'

then made the following writing[1]:—'The former king kept his eye continually on the bright requirements of Heaven, and so he maintained the worship of the spirits of heaven and earth, of those presiding over the land and the grain, and of those of the ancestral temple;—all with a sincere reverence.* Heaven took notice of his virtue, and caused its great appointment to light on him, that he should soothe and tranquillize the myriad regions.* I, Yin, then gave my assistance to my sovereign in the settlement of the people; and thus it is that you, O heir-king, have received the great inheritance. I have seen it myself in Hsiâ with its western capital[2], that when its rulers went through a prosperous course to the end, their ministers also did the same, and afterwards, when their successors could not attain to such a consummation, neither did their ministers. Take warning, O heir-king. Reverently use your sovereignty. If you do not play the sovereign, as the name requires, you will disgrace your grandfather.'

2. The king would not think (of these words), nor listen to them. On this Î Yin said, 'The former king, before it was light, sought to have large and clear views, and then sat waiting for the dawn (to carry them into practice). He (also) sought on every side for men of ability and virtue, to instruct and guide his posterity. Do not frustrate his charge (to me), and bring on yourself your own overthrow. Be careful to strive after the virtue

---

[1] This is the first direct statement in the Shû of a communication made in writing.

[2] An-yî, the capital of Hsiâ, might be described as 'western,' from the standpoint of Po.

of self-restraint, and cherish far-reaching plans. Be like the forester, who, when he has adjusted the spring, goes to examine the end of the arrow, whether it be placed according to rule, and then lets go; reverently determine your aim, and follow the ways of your grandfather. Thus I shall be delighted, and be able to show to all ages that I have discharged my trust.'

3. The king was not yet able to change (his course). Î Yin said (to himself), 'This is (real) unrighteousness, and is becoming by practice (a second) nature. I cannot bear to be near (so) disobedient (a person). I will build (a place) in the palace at Thung[1], where he can be in silence near (the grave of) the former king. This will be a lesson which will keep him from going astray all his life.' The king went (accordingly) to the palace at Thung, and dwelt during the period of mourning. In the end he became sincerely virtuous.

Section 2.

1. On the first day of the twelfth month of his third year, Î Yin escorted the young king in the royal cap and robes back to Po. (At the same time) he made the following writing:—

'Without the sovereign, the people cannot have that guidance which is necessary to (the comfort of) their lives; without the people, the sovereign would have no sway over the four quarters (of the kingdom).

[1] Thung was the place where Thang's tomb was; probably in the present district of Yung-ho, department of Phû-*k*âu, Shan-hsî. The site or supposed site of the grave there was washed away in an overflow of the Fân river under the Yüan dynasty, and a stone coffin was removed to another position, near which a royal tomb has been built.

Great Heaven has graciously favoured the House of Shang, and granted to you, O young king, at last to become virtuous.* This is indeed a blessing that will extend without limit to ten thousand generations.'

2. The king did obeisance with his face to his hands and his head to the ground, saying, 'I, the little child, was without understanding of what was virtuous, and was making myself one of the unworthy. By my desires I was setting at nought all rules of conduct, and violating by my self-indulgence all rules of propriety, and the result must have been speedy ruin to my person. Calamities sent by Heaven may be avoided, but from calamities brought on by one's self there is no escape.* Heretofore I turned my back on the instructions of you, my tutor and guardian;—my beginning has been marked by incompetency. Let me still rely on your correcting and preserving virtue, keeping this in view that my end may be good!'

3. Î Yin did obeisance with his face to his hands and his head on the ground, and said, 'To cultivate his person, and by being sincerely virtuous, bring (all) below to harmonious concord with him;—this is the work of the intelligent sovereign. The former king was kind to the distressed and suffering, as if they were his children, and the people submitted to his commands,—all with sincere delight. Even in the states of the neighbouring princes, (the people) said, "We are waiting for our sovereign; when our sovereign comes, we shall not suffer the punishments (that we now do)."

'O king, zealously cultivate your virtue. Regard (the example of) your meritorious grandfather. At no time allow yourself in pleasure and idleness. In worshipping your ancestors, think how you can prove your filial piety; * in receiving your ministers, think how you can show yourself respectful; in looking to what is distant, try to get clear views; have your ears ever open to lessons of virtue;—then shall I acknowledge (and respond to) the excellence of your majesty with an untiring (devotion to your service).'

Section 3.

1. Î Yin again made an announcement to the king, saying, 'Oh! Heaven has no (partial) affection;—only to those who are reverent does it show affection.* The people are not constant to those whom they cherish;—they cherish (only) him who is benevolent. The spirits do not always accept the sacrifices that are offered to them;—they accept only the sacrifices of the sincere.* A place of difficulty is the Heaven-(conferred) seat. When there are (those) virtues, good government is realized; when they are not, disorder comes. To maintain the same principles as those who secured good government will surely lead to prosperity; to pursue the courses of disorder will surely lead to ruin. He who at last, as at first, is careful as to whom and what he follows is a truly intelligent sovereign. The former king was always zealous in the reverent cultivation of his virtue, so that he was the fellow of God[1].* Now, O king, you have entered on the inheritance of his excellent line;—fix your inspection on him.'

2. '(Your course must be) as when in ascending

[1] This phrase is used, as here, with reference to the virtue of a sovereign, making him as it were the mate of God, ruling on earth as He rules above; and with reference to the honours paid to a departed sovereign, when he is associated with God in the great sacrificial services.

high you begin from where it is low, and when in travelling far you begin from where it is near. Do not slight the occupations of the people;—think of their difficulties. Do not yield to a feeling of repose on your throne;—think of its perils. Be careful for the end at the beginning. When you hear words that are distasteful to your mind, you must enquire whether they be not right; when you hear words that accord with your own views, you must enquire whether they be not contrary to what is right. Oh! what attainment can be made without anxious thought? what achievement can be made without earnest effort? Let the One man be greatly good, and the myriad regions will be rectified by him.'

3. 'When the sovereign does not with disputatious words throw the old rules of government into confusion, and the minister does not, for favour and gain, continue in an office whose work is done,—then the country will lastingly and surely enjoy happiness.'

Book VI.

The Common Possession of Pure Virtue.

This is the last of the 'Instructions' of Î Yin;—addressed, like those of the last two Books, to Thâi *K*iâ, but at a later period when the great minister wished to retire from the toils of administration. He now disappears from the stage of history, though according to Sze-mâ *Kh*ien, and a notice in the Preface to the Shû, he lived on to B.C. 1713, the eighth year of Thâi *K*iâ's son and successor.

In this Book, his subject is 'Pure or Single-eyed Virtue,' and the importance of it to the ruler of the kingdom. He dwells on the fall of *K*ieh through his want of this virtue, and the elevation of Thang through his possession of it; treats generally on its nature and results; and urges the cultivation of it on Thâi *K*iâ:

1. Î Yin, having returned the government into

the hands of his sovereign, and being about to announce his retirement, set forth admonitions on the subject of virtue.

2. He said, 'Oh! it is difficult to rely on Heaven;—its appointments are not constant.* (But if the sovereign see to it that) his virtue be constant, he will preserve his throne; if his virtue be not constant, the nine provinces will be lost by him. The king of Hsiâ could not maintain the virtue (of his ancestors) unchanged, but contemned the spirits and oppressed the people. Great Heaven no (longer) extended its protection to him. It looked out among the myriad regions to give its guidance to one who should receive its favouring appointment, fondly seeking (a possessor of) pure virtue, whom it might make lord of all the spirits.* Then there were I, Yin, and Thang, both possessed of pure virtue, and able to satisfy the mind of Heaven. He received (in consequence) the bright favour of Heaven, so as to become possessor of the multitudes of the nine provinces, and proceeded to change Hsiâ's commencement of the year. It was not that Heaven had any private partiality for the lord of Shang;—it simply gave its favour to pure virtue.* It was not that Shang sought (the allegiance of) the lower people;—the people simply turned to pure virtue. Where (the sovereign's) virtue is pure, his enterprizes are all fortunate; where his virtue is wavering and uncertain, his enterprizes are all unfortunate. Good and evil do not wrongly befal men, but Heaven sends down misery or happiness according to their conduct.' *

3. 'Now, O young king, you are newly entering on your (great) appointment,—you should be seeking to

make new your virtue. At last, as at first, have this as your one object, so shall you make a daily renovation. Let the officers whom you employ be men of virtue and ability, and let the ministers about you be the right men. The minister, in relation to (his sovereign) above him, has to promote his virtue, and, in relation to the (people) beneath him, has to seek their good. How hard must it be (to find the proper man)! what careful attention must be required! (Thereafter) there must be harmony (cultivated with him), and a oneness (of confidence placed in him).

'There is no invariable model of virtue;—a supreme regard to what is good gives the model of it. There is no invariable characteristic of what is good that is to be supremely regarded;—it is found where there is a conformity to the uniform consciousness (in regard to what is good). (Such virtue) will make the people with their myriad surnames all say, "How great are the words of the king!" and also, "How single and pure is the king's heart!" It will avail to maintain in tranquillity the rich possession of the former king, and to secure for ever the (happy) life of the multitudes of the people.'

4. 'Oh! (to retain a place) in the seven-shrined temple[1] of ancestors is a sufficient witness of virtue.* To be acknowledged as chief by the myriad heads of families is a sufficient evidence of one's government.

[1] It is beyond a doubt that the ancestral temple of the kings of *K*âu contained seven shrines or seven small temples, for the occupancy of which, by the spirit-tablets of such and such kings, there were definite rules, as the line of sovereigns increased. It would appear from the text that a similar practice prevailed in the time of the Shang dynasty.

The sovereign without the people has none whom he can employ; and the people without the sovereign have none whom they can serve. Do not think yourself so large as to deem others small. If ordinary men and women do not find the opportunity to give full development to their ability, the people's lord will be without the proper aids to complete his merit.'

Book VII. The Pan-kăng.

Pan-kăng was the seventeenth sovereign in the line of Thang. From Thâi *K*iâ to him, therefore, there was a space of 321 years, which are a gap in the history of the Shang dynasty, so far as the existing documents of the Shû are concerned. When the collection was complete, there were seven other documents between 'the Common Possession of Pure Virtue' and 'the Pan-kăng,' but the latest of them belonged to the reign of Ȝû-yî, B.C. 1525–1507.

The reign of Pan-kăng extended from B.C. 1401 to 1374, and is remarkable as that in which the dynasty began to be called Yin, instead of Shang. The Book belongs to the class of 'Announcements,' and is divided into three sections.

The contents centre round the removal of the capital from the north of the Ho to Yin on the south of it. The king saw that the removal was necessary, but had to contend with the unwillingness of the people to adopt such a step, and the opposition of the great families. The first section relates how he endeavoured to vindicate the measure, and contains two addresses, to the people and to those in high places, respectively, designed to secure their cordial co-operation. The second section brings before us the removal in progress, but there continue to be dissatisfactions, which the king endeavours to remove by a long and earnest defence of his course. The third section opens with the removal accomplished. The new city has been founded, and the plan of it laid out. The king makes a fresh appeal to the people and chiefs, to forget all their heart-burnings, and join with him in building up in the new capital a great destiny for the dynasty.

Section 1.

1. Pan-kăng wished to remove (the capital) to Yin[1], but the people would not go to dwell there. He therefore appealed to all the discontented, and made the following protestations. 'Our king, (Ȝû-yî), came, and fixed on this (Kăng for his capital). He did so from a deep concern for our people, and not because he would have them all die, where they cannot (now) help one another to preserve their lives. I have consulted the tortoise-shell, and obtained the reply—"This is no place for us." When the former kings had any (important) business, they gave reverent heed to the commands of Heaven.* In a case like this especially they did not indulge (the wish for) constant repose,—they did not abide ever in the same city. Up to this time (the capital has been) in five regions[2]. If we do not follow (the example) of these old times, we shall be refusing to acknowledge that Heaven is making an end of our dynasty (here);—how little can it be said of us that we are following the meritorious course of the former kings! As from the stump of a felled tree there are sprouts and shoots, Heaven will perpetuate its decree in our favour in this new city;—the great inheritance of the former kings will be continued and renewed, and tranquillity will be secured to the four quarters (of the kingdom).' *

---

[1] The removal was probably necessitated by an inundation of the Ho. Kăng had been fixed on by Ȝû-yî for his capital. The Yin to which Pan-kăng removed was in the present district of Yen-sze, department Ho-nan, Ho-nan.

[2] This fact—the frequent change of capital—does not give us a great idea of the stability and resources of the Shang dynasty.

2. Pan-kăng, in making the people aware of his views, began with those who were in (high) places, and took the constantly-recurring circumstances of former times to lay down the right law and measure (for the present emergency), saying, 'Let none of you dare to suppress the remonstrances of the poor people.' The king commanded all to come to him in the courtyard (of his palace).

The king spoke to this effect:—'Come, all of you; I will announce to you my instructions. Take counsel how to put away your (selfish) thoughts. Do not with haughty (disregard of me) follow after your own ease. Of old, our former kings planned like me how to employ the men of old families to share in (the labours of) government. When they wished to proclaim and announce what was to be attended to, these did not conceal the royal views; and on this account the kings greatly respected them. They did not exceed the truth (in their communications with the people), and on this account the people became greatly changed (in their views). Now, (however), you keep clamouring, and get the confidence (of the people) by alarming and shallow speeches;— I do not know what you are wrangling about. (In this movement) I am not myself abandoning my proper virtue, but you conceal the goodness of my intentions, and do not stand in awe of me, the One man. I see you as clearly as one sees a fire; but I, likewise, by my undecided plans, have produced your error.

'When the net has its line, there is order and not confusion; and when the husbandman labours upon his fields, and reaps with all his might, there is the (abundant) harvest. If you can put away your (selfish) thoughts, and bestow real good upon the people, reaching (also) to your own relatives and friends, you may boldly venture to make your words great, and say that you have accumulated merit. But you do not fear the great evils which (through our not removing) are extending far and near; (you are like) idle husbandmen, who yield themselves to ease, and are not strong to toil and labour on their acres, so that they cannot get their crop of millets. You do not speak in a spirit of harmony and goodness to the people, and are only giving birth to bitter evils for yourselves. You play the part of destroyers and authors of calamity, of villains and traitors, to bring down misery on your own persons. You set the example of evil, and must feel its smart;—what will it avail you (then) to repent? Look at the poor people;—they are still able to look to one another and give expression to their remonstrances, but when they begin to speak, you are ready with your extravagant talk;—how much more ought you to have me before your eyes, with whom it is to make your lives long or short! Why do you not report (their words) to me, but go about to excite one another by empty speeches, frightening and involving the multitudes in misery? When a fire is blazing in the flames so that it cannot be approached, can it still be beaten out? So, it will not be I who will be to blame, that you all cause dispeace in this way, (and must suffer the consequences.)

'*Kh*ih Zăn[1] has said, "In men we seek those of old families; in vessels, we do not seek old ones,

[1] Who *Kh*ih Zăn was is not known. The general opinion is, that he was an ancient historiographer. A *K*âu Zăn is introduced in a similar way in the Confucian Analects, XVI, 1.

but new." Of old, the kings, my predecessors, and your forefathers and fathers shared together the ease and labours (of the government);—how should I dare to lay undeserved afflictions on you? For generations the toils of your (fathers) have been approved, and I will not conceal your goodness. Now when I offer the great sacrifices to my predecessors, your forefathers are present to share in them.* (They all observe) the happiness I confer and the sufferings I inflict, and I cannot dare to reward virtue that does not exist.

'I have announced to you the difficulties (of the intended movement), being bent on it, like an archer (whose only thought is to hit). Do not you despise the old and experienced, and do not make little of the helpless and young. Seek every one long continuance in this (new city), which is to be your abode; exert yourselves and put out your strength (in furthering the removal), and listen to the plans of me, the One man. I will make no distinction between men as being more distantly or more nearly related to me;—the criminal (in this matter) shall die the death, and the good-doer shall have his virtue distinguished. The prosperity of the country (ought to) come from you all. If it fail of prosperity, that must arise from me, the One man, erring in the application of punishment. Be sure, all of you, to make known this announcement. From this time forward, attend respectfully to your business; have (the duties of) your offices regularly adjusted; bring your tongues under the rule of law:—lest punishment come upon you, when repentance will be of no avail.'

Section 2.

1. Pan-kăng arose, and (was about to) cross the Ho with the people, moving (to the new capital). Accordingly, he addressed himself to those of them who were (still) dissatisfied, and made a full announcement to their multitudes, to induce a sincere acquiescence (in the measure). They all attended, and (being charged) to take no liberties in the royal courtyard, he called them near, and said, 'Listen clearly to my words, and do not disregard my commands.

'Oh! of old time my royal predecessors cherished, every one and above every other thing, a respectful care of the people, who (again) upheld their sovereign with a mutual sympathy. Seldom was it that they were not superior to any (calamitous) time sent by Heaven. When great calamities came down on Yin, the former kings did not fondly remain in their place. What they did was with a view to the people's advantage, and therefore they moved (their capitals). Why do you not reflect that I, according to what I have heard of the ancient sovereigns, in my care of you and actings towards you, am only wishing to rejoice with you in a common repose? It is not that any guilt attaches to you, so that (this movement) should be like a punishment. If I call upon you to cherish this new city, it is simply on your account, and as an act of great accordance with your wishes. My present undertaking to remove with you, is to give repose and stability to the country. You, (however), have no sympathy with the anxieties of my mind; but you all keep a great reserve in declaring your minds, (when you might) respectfully think by your sincerity to move me, the One man. You only exhaust and distress yourselves. The case is like that of sailing in a boat;—if you do not cross the stream (at the proper time), you will destroy all the cargo. Your sincerity does not respond to mine, and we are in danger of going together to destruction. You, notwithstanding, will not examine the matter;—though you anger yourselves, what cure will that bring?

'You do not consult for a distant day, nor think of the calamity that must befal you (from not removing). You greatly encourage one another in what must prove to your sorrow. Now you have the present, but you will not have the future;—what prolongation of life can you look for from above? My measures are forecast to prolong your (lease of) life from Heaven;—do I force you by the terrors of my power? My object is to support and nourish you all. I think of my ancestors, (who are now) the spiritual sovereigns;* when they made your forefathers toil (on similar occasions it was only for their good), and I would be enabled in the same way greatly to nourish you and cherish you.'

2. 'Were I to err in my government, and remain long here, my high sovereign, (the founder of our dynasty), would send down on me great punishment for my crime, and say, "Why do you oppress my people?"* If you, the myriads of the people, do not attend to the perpetuation of your lives, and cherish one mind with me, the One man, in my plans, the former kings will send down on you great punishment for your crime, and say, "Why do you not agree with our young grandson, but go on to forfeit

your virtue?" When they punish you from above, you will have no way of escape.* Of old, my royal predecessors made your ancestors and fathers toil (only for their good). You are equally the people whom I (wish to) cherish. But your conduct is injurious;—it is cherished in your hearts. Whereas my royal predecessors made your ancestors and fathers happy, they, your ancestors and fathers, will (now) cut you off and abandon you, and not save you from death.* Here are those ministers of my government, who share with me in the offices (of the kingdom);—and yet they (only think of hoarding up) cowries and gems. Their ancestors and fathers earnestly represent (their course) to my high sovereign, saying, "Execute great punishments on our descendants." So do they advise my high sovereign to send down great calamities (on those men).' *

3. 'Oh! I have now told you my unchangeable purpose;—do you perpetually respect (my) great anxiety; let us not get alienated and removed from one another; share in my plans and thoughts, and think (only) of following me; let every one of you set up the true rule of conduct in his heart. If there be bad and unprincipled men, precipitously or carelessly disrespectful (to my orders), and taking advantage of this brief season to play the part of villains or traitors, I will cut off their noses, or utterly exterminate them. I will leave none of their children. I will not let them perpetuate their seed in this new city.

'Go! preserve and continue your lives. I will now transfer you (to the new capital), and (there) establish your families for ever.'

Section 3.

1. Pan-kăng having completed the removal, and settled the places of residence, proceeded to adjust the several positions (of all classes at an assembly); and then he soothed and comforted the multitudes, saying to them, 'Do not play nor be idle, but exert yourselves to build (here) a great destiny (for us).

'Now I have disclosed my heart and belly, my reins and bowels, and fully declared to you, my people, all my mind. I will not treat any of you as offenders; and do not you (any more) help one another to be angry, and form parties to defame me, the One man.

'Of old, my royal predecessor, (Thang), that his merit might exceed that of those who were before him, proceeded to the hill-site[1]. Thereby he removed our evils, and accomplished admirable good for our country. Now you, my people, were by (your position) dissipated and separated, so that you had no abiding place. (And yet) you asked why I was troubling your myriads and requiring you to remove. But God, being about to renew the virtuous service of my high ancestor, and secure the good order of our kingdom, I, with the sincere and respectful (of my ministers), felt a reverent care for the lives of the people, and have made a lasting settlement in (this) new city.*

'I, a youth, did not neglect your counsels;— I (only) used the best of them. Nor did any of

[1] It is supposed that this 'hill-site' of Thang was the same as that which Pan-kăng had fixed on, but this does not clearly appear in the text.

you presumptuously oppose the decision of the tortoise-shell;—so we are here to enlarge our great inheritance.'*

2. 'Oh! ye chiefs of regions, ye heads of departments, all ye, the hundreds of officers, would that ye had a sympathy (with my people)! I will exert myself in the choice and guiding of you;—do ye think reverently of my multitudes. I will not employ those who are fond of enriching themselves; but will use and revere those who are vigorously, yet reverently, labouring for the lives and increase of the people, nourishing them and planning for their enduring settlement.

'I have now brought forward and announced to you my mind, whom I approve and whom I disallow;—let none of you but reverence (my will). Do not seek to accumulate wealth and precious things, but in fostering the life of the people, seek to find your merit. Reverently display your virtue in behalf of the people. For ever maintain this one purpose in your hearts.'

Book VIII. The Charge to Yüeh.

After Pan-kăng came the reigns of Hsiâo-hsin and Hsiâo-yî, of which we have no accounts in the Shû. Hsiâo-yî was followed by Wû-ting (B.C. 1324–1264), to the commencement of whose reign this Book, in three sections, belongs. His name is not in it, but that he is the king intended appears from the prefatory notice, and the Confucian Analects, XIV, xliii. The Book is the first of the 'Charges' of the Shû. They relate the designation by the king of some officer to a particular charge or to some fief, with the address delivered by him on the occasion. Here the charge is to Yüeh, in the first section, on his appointment to be chief minister. In the other two sections Yüeh is the principal speaker, and not the king. They partake more of the nature of the 'Counsels.' Yüeh had been a recluse, living in obscurity. The king's attention was drawn to him in the manner related in the Book, and he was discovered in Fû-yen, or amidst 'the Crags of Fû,' from which he was afterwards called Fû Yüeh, as if Fû had been his surname.

The first section tells us how the king met with Yüeh, and appointed him to be his chief minister, and how Yüeh responded to the charge that he received. In the second section, Yüeh counsels the king on a variety of points, and the king responds admiringly. In the third, the king introduces himself as a pupil at the feet of Yüeh, and is lectured on the subject of enlarging his knowledge. In the end the king says that he looks to Yüeh as another Î Yin, to make him another Thang.

Section 1.

1. The king passed the season of sorrow in the mourning shed for three years[1], and when the period of mourning was over, he (still) did not speak (to give any commands). All the ministers remonstrated with him, saying, 'Oh! him who is (the first) to apprehend we pronounce intelligent, and the intelligent man is the model for others. The Son of Heaven rules over the myriad regions, and all the officers look up to and reverence him. They are the king's words which form the commands (for them). If he do not speak, the ministers have no way to receive their orders.' On this the king made a writing, for their information, to the following effect:—'As it is mine to serve as the

[1] A young king, mourning for his father, had to 'afflict' himself in various ways for twenty-five months, nominally for three years. Among other privations, he had to exchange the comforts of a palace for a rough shed in one of the courtyards. During the time of mourning, the direction of affairs was left to the chief minister.

director for the four quarters (of the kingdom), I have been afraid that my virtue is not equal to (that of my predecessors), and therefore have not spoken. (But) while I was reverently and silently thinking of the (right) way, I dreamt that God gave me a good assistant who should speak for me.' * He then minutely recalled the appearance (of the person whom he had seen), and caused search to be made for him everywhere by means of a picture. Yüeh, a builder in the wild country of Fû-yen, was found like to it.

2. On this the king raised and made (Yüeh) his prime minister, keeping him (also) at his side.

He charged him, saying, 'Morning and evening present your instructions to aid my virtue. Suppose me a weapon of steel;—I will use you for a whetstone. Suppose me crossing a great stream;—I will use you for a boat with its oars. Suppose me in a year of great drought;—I will use you as a copious rain. Open your mind, and enrich my mind. (Be you) like medicine, which must distress the patient, in order to cure his sickness. (Think of me) as one walking barefoot, whose feet are sure to be wounded, if he do not see the ground.

'Do you and your companions all cherish the same mind to assist your sovereign, that I may follow my royal predecessors, and tread in the steps of my high ancestor, to give repose to the millions of the people. Oh! respect this charge of mine;—so shall you bring your work to a (good) end.'

3. Yüeh replied to the king, saying, 'Wood by the use of the line is made straight, and the sovereign who follows reproof is made sage. When the sovereign can (thus) make himself sage, his ministers,

without being specially commanded, anticipate his orders;—who would dare not to act in respectful compliance with this excellent charge of your Majesty?'

Section 2.

1. Yüeh having received his charge, and taken the presidency of all the officers, he presented himself before the king, and said, 'Oh! intelligent kings act in reverent accordance with the ways of Heaven. The founding of states and the setting up of capitals, the appointing of sovereign kings, of dukes and other nobles, with their great officers and heads of departments, were not designed to minister to the idleness and pleasures (of one), but for the good government of the people. It is Heaven which is all-intelligent and observing;—let the sage (king) take it as his pattern.* Then his ministers will reverently accord with him, and the people consequently will be well governed.

'It is the mouth that gives occasion for shame; they are the coat of mail and helmet that give occasion to war. The upper robes and lower garments (for reward should not be lightly taken from) their chests; before spear and shield are used, one should examine himself. If your Majesty will be cautious in regard to these things, and, believing this about them, attain to the intelligent use of them, (your government) will in everything be excellent. Good government and bad depend on the various officers. Offices should not be given to men because they are favourites, but only to men of ability. Dignities should not be conferred on men of evil practices, but only on men of worth.

'Anxious thought about what will be best should precede your movements, which also should be taken at the time proper for them. Indulging the consciousness of being good is the way to lose that goodness; being vain of one's ability is the way to lose the merit it might produce.

'For all affairs let there be adequate preparation;—with preparation there will be no calamitous issue. Do not open the door for favourites, from whom you will receive contempt. Do not be ashamed of mistakes, and (go on to) make them crimes. Let your mind rest in its proper objects, and the affairs of your government will be pure. Officiousness in sacrificing is called irreverence; * and multiplying ceremonies leads to disorder. To serve the spirits acceptably (in this way) is difficult.' *

2. The king said, 'Excellent! your words, O Yüeh, should indeed be put in practice (by me). If you were not so good in counsel, I should not have heard these rules for my conduct.' Yüeh did obeisance with his head to the ground, and said, 'It is not the knowing that is difficult, but the doing. (But) since your Majesty truly knows this, there will not be the difficulty, and you will become really equal in complete virtue to our first king. Wherein I, Yüeh, refrain from speaking (what I ought to speak), the blame will rest with me.'

Section 3.

1. The king said, 'Come, O Yüeh. I, the little one, first learned with Kan Pan [1]. Afterwards I lived

[1] From Part V, xvi, 2, we learn that Kan Pan was a great minister of Wû-ting. It is supposed that he had been minister to Wû-ting's father, and died during the king's period of mourning.

concealed among the rude countrymen, and then I went to (the country) inside the Ho, and lived there [1]. From the Ho I went to Po;—and the result has been that I am unenlightened. Do you teach me what should be my aims. Be to me as the yeast and the malt in making sweet spirits, as the salt and the prunes in making agreeable soup. Use various methods to cultivate me; do not cast me away;—so shall I attain to practise your instructions.'

Yüeh said, 'O king, a ruler should seek to learn much (from his ministers), with a view to establish his affairs; but to learn the lessons of the ancients is the way to attain this. That the affairs of one, not making the ancients his masters, can be perpetuated for generations, is what I have not heard.

'In learning there should be a humble mind and the maintenance of a constant earnestness;—in such a case (the learner's) improvement will surely come. He who sincerely cherishes these things will find all truth accumulating in his person. Teaching is the half of learning; when a man's thoughts from first to last are constantly fixed on learning, his virtuous cultivation comes unperceived.

'Survey the perfect pattern of our first king;—so shall you for ever be preserved from error. Then shall I be able reverently to meet your views, and on every side to look out for men of eminence to place in the various offices.'

2. The king said, 'Oh! Yüeh, that all within the four

---

[1] We do not know the events of Wû-ting's early life sufficiently to explain his language here. His living concealed among the rude people of the country, and then crossing to the north of the Ho, was owing probably to troubles in the kingdom.

seas look up to my virtue is owing to you. As his legs and arms form the man, so does a good minister form the sage (king). Formerly, there was the first premier of our dynasty, Pâo-hăng[1], who raised up and formed its royal founder. He said, "If I cannot make my sovereign like Yâo or Shun, I shall feel ashamed in my heart, as if I were beaten in the market-place." If any common man did not get (all he should desire), he said, "It is my fault." (Thus) he assisted my meritorious ancestor, so that he became equal to great Heaven.* Do you give your intelligent and preserving aid to me, and let not Â-hăng engross all the good service to the House of Shang.

'The sovereign should share his government with none but worthy officers. The worthy officer should accept his support from none but the proper sovereign. May you now succeed in making your sovereign a (true) successor of the founder of his line, and in securing the lasting happiness of the people!'

Yüeh did obeisance with his head to the ground, and said, 'I will venture to respond to, and display abroad, your Majesty's excellent charge.'

Book IX. The Day of the Supplementary Sacrifice to Kâo Ȝung.

Kâo Ȝung was the title given to Wû-ting, after his death, in the ancestral temple. A supplementary sacrifice was offered on the day following the regular and more solemn service. What special idea was connected with it, it would be difficult to say;

[1] Styled Â-hăng in the beginning of 'the Thâi-*k*iâ.' Pâo-hăng = 'the Protector and Steelyard.'

but at the close of it, the representatives or personators of the dead in the sacrifice of the preceding day were all feasted.

The title of this short Book leaves it uncertain whether the sacrifice was offered to Wû-ting or by him. The prefatory notice proceeds on the former view. Many critics of great intelligence decide for the latter, which a renewed consideration of the text has induced me to adopt. The king then is Ȝû-kăng, Wû-ting's son. Something irregular or excessive in his sacrificing to his father was the thing which his monitor Ȝû *K*î wished to censure, taking occasion to do so from the incident mentioned in the first sentence.

On the day of the supplementary sacrifice of Kâo Ȝung, there appeared a crowing pheasant [1]. Ȝû *K*î said, 'To rectify this affair, the king must first be corrected.' He delivered accordingly a lesson to the king, saying, 'In its inspection of men below, Heaven's first consideration is of their righteousness, and it bestows on them (accordingly) length of years or the contrary.* It is not Heaven that cuts short men's lives; they bring them to an end themselves. Some men who have not complied with virtue will yet not acknowledge their offences, and when Heaven has by evident tokens charged them to correct their conduct, they still say, "What are these things to us?"

'Oh! your Majesty's business is to care reverently for the people. And all (your ancestors) were the heirs of (the kingdom by the gift of) Heaven;—in attending to the sacrifices (to them), be not so excessive in those to your father.' *

[1] Sze-mâ *Kh*ien, after the prefatory notice, says that the pheasant sat on the ear—one of the handles—of a tripod.

Book X.

The Chief of the West's Conquest of Lî.

The reigns of seven more kings of Yin or Shang have passed, and this Book brings us to the time of *K*âu-hsin or Shâu, its last sovereign, B.C. 1154–1123. The House of *K*âu begins to come to the front, for 'the Chief of the West' was one of the acknowledged founders of the *K*âu dynasty;—whether *Kh*ang, known as king Wăn, or his son Fâ, known as king Wû, is uncertain. *Kh*ang's father, the duke of *K*âu in the present department of Făng-hsiang, Shen-hsî, had been appointed Chief of the West, that is, of all the western portion of the kingdom, embracing Yü's provinces of Yung, Liang, and *K*ing. The same jurisdiction descended to his son and grandson. The state of Lî, the conquest of which is mentioned, was in the present department of Lû-an, Shan-hsî, within the royal domain, so that the Chief of the West was no longer confining himself to the west, but threatening the king himself.

Ȝû Î, a loyal officer, hears of the conquest of Lî, and hurries away to inform the king and warn him of the danger threatening the dynasty through his evil conduct. The king gives no heed to his remonstrances, and Ȝû Î retires, sighing over the ruin, which he sees is not to be averted.

The Book is classed, it would be hard to tell why, among the 'Announcements.'

The Chief of the West having subdued Lî, Ȝû Î was afraid, and hastened to report it to the king.

He said, 'Son of Heaven, Heaven is bringing to an end the dynasty of Yin; * the wisest men and the shell of the great tortoise do not presume to know anything fortunate for it.* It is not that the former kings do not aid us, the men of this later time;* but by your dissoluteness and sport you are bringing on the end yourself. On this account Heaven has cast us off, and there are no good harvests to supply us with food.* Men have no regard to their heavenly nature, and pay no obedience to the statutes (of the kingdom). (Yea), our people now all wish (the dynasty) to perish, saying, "Why does not Heaven send down its indignation? Why does not (some one with) its great appointment make his appearance? What has the present king to do with us?"'

The king said, 'Oh! was not my birth in accordance with the appointment of Heaven (in favour of my House)?' (On this) 3û Î returned (to his own city), and said, 'Your crimes, which are many, are registered above, and can you still appeal to the appointment of Heaven in your favour? * Yin will perish very shortly. As to all your deeds, can they but bring ruin on your country?'

Book XI. The Count of Wei.

The conversation recorded here—called, like the last Book, and with as little reason, an 'Announcement'—is referred to B.C. 1123, the year in which the dynasty of Shang perished.

Wei was a principality in the royal domain, corresponding to the present district of Lû-*kh*ăng, department Lû-an, Shan-hsî, the lords of which were counts. The count who appears here was, most probably, an elder brother of the king, and by the same mother, who was, however, only a concubine when the count was born, but raised to be queen before the birth of *K*âu-hsin. Saddened with the thought of the impending ruin of the dynasty, the count seeks the counsel of two other high nobles, and asks them to tell him what was to be done. One of them replies to him in still stronger language about the condition and prospects of the kingdom, and concludes by advising the count to make his escape, and declaring that he himself would remain at his post, and share in the unavoidable ruin.

1. The Count of Wei spoke to the following effect:—'Grand-Master and Junior-Master[1], (the House of) Yin, we may conclude, can no longer exercise rule over the four quarters (of the kingdom). The great deeds of our founder were displayed in former ages, but by our maddened indulgence in spirits, we have destroyed (the effects of) his virtue in these after-times. (The people of) Yin, small and great, are given to highway robberies, villainies, and treachery. The nobles and officers imitate one another in violating the laws, and there is no certainty that criminals will be apprehended. The smaller people (consequently) rise up, and commit violent outrages on one another. Yin is now sinking in ruin;—its condition is like that of one crossing a stream, who can find neither ford nor bank. That Yin should be hurrying to ruin at the present pace!'

He added, 'Grand-Master and Junior-Master, we are manifesting insanity. The most venerable members of our families are withdrawn to the wilds; and you indicate no course (to be taken), but (only) tell me of the impending ruin;—what is to be done?'

2. The Grand-Master made about the following reply:—'O son of our (former) king, Heaven in anger is sending down calamities, and wasting the country of Yin.* Hence has arisen that mad indulgence in spirits. (The king) has no reverence

---

[1] For high ministers with these titles under the *K*âu dynasty, see next Part, Book xx. The individuals whom the count of Wei consulted were probably the count of *K*î and Pî-kan, who are classed with him in the Confucian Analects, XVIII, 1.

for things which he ought to reverence, but does despite to the venerable aged, the men who have long been in office. The people of Yin will now steal even the pure and perfect victims devoted to the spirits of heaven and earth; * and their conduct is connived at, and though they proceed to eat the victims, they suffer no punishment. (On the other hand), when I look down and survey the people of Yin, the methods by which they are governed are hateful exactions, which call forth outrages and hatred;—and this without ceasing. Such crimes equally belong to all in authority, and multitudes are starving with none to whom to appeal. Now is the time of Shang's calamity;—I will arise and share in its ruin. When ruin overtakes Shang, I will not be the servant (of another House). (But) I tell you, O king's son, to go away, as being the course (for you). Formerly I injured you by what I said; if you do not (now) go away, our (sacrifices) will entirely perish. Let us rest quietly (in our several parts), and each present himself to the former kings[1] (as having done so).* I do not think of making my escape.'

---

[1] It is understood that the former king, the father of both *Kh*î and *K*âu-hsin, had wished to leave the throne to *Kh*î, and that the Grand-Master had advocated such a measure;—thereby injuring *Kh*î when it did not take effect, through making *K*âu-hsin jealous of him.

PART V. THE BOOKS OF *K*ÂU.

BOOK I. THE GREAT DECLARATION.

*K*ÂU is the dynastic designation under which king Wû and his descendants possessed the throne from B.C. 1122 to 256, a period of 867 years. They traced their lineage up to *Kh*î, who was Minister of Agriculture under Shun. He was invested with the principality of Thâi, the present district of Fû-făng, department of Făng-hsiang, Shen-hsî. Long afterwards Than-fû, claiming to be one of his descendants, appears in B.C. 1326, founding the state of *K*âu, near mount *Kh*î, in the same department of Făng-hsiang. This Than-fû was the great-grandfather of king Wû. The family surname was *K*î.

When the collection of the Shû was complete, it contained thirty-eight different documents of the *K*âu dynasty, of which twenty-eight remain, twenty of them being of undisputed genuineness.

This first Book, 'the Great Declaration,' is one of the contested portions; and there is another form of it, that takes the place of this in some editions. It has appeared in the Introduction that the received text of the Shû was formed with care, and that everything of importance in the challenged Books is to be found in quotations from them, while the collection was complete, that have been gathered up by the industry of scholars.

King Wû, having at last taken the field against *K*âu-hsin, the tyrant of Shang, made three speeches to his officers and men, setting forth the reasons for his enterprise, and urging them to exert themselves with him in the cause of humanity and Heaven. They are brought together, and constitute 'the Great Declaration.'

'In the first Part,' says a Chinese critic, 'king Wû addresses himself to the princes and nobles of inferior rank; in the second, to their hosts; and in the third, to his officers. The ruling idea in the first is the duty of the sovereign,—what he ought to be and to do; with this it begins and ends. There is not the same continuity of thought in the second, but the will and purpose of Heaven is the principal thing insisted on. The last Part shows the difference between the good sovereign and the bad, and touches on the consent that there is between Heaven and men. There is throughout an unsparing exhibition of the wickedness of *K*âu-hsin.'

Section 1.

In the spring of the thirteenth year[1] there was a great assembly at Mâng-*k*ing[2]. The king said, 'Ah! ye hereditary rulers of my friendly states, and all ye my officers, managers of my affairs, hearken clearly to my declaration.

'Heaven and earth is the parent of all creatures; and of all creatures man is the most highly endowed.* The sincerely intelligent (among men) becomes the great sovereign; and the great sovereign is the parent of the people. But now, Shâu, the king of Shang, does not reverence Heaven above, and inflicts calamities on the people below.* Abandoned to drunkenness and reckless in lust, he has dared to exercise cruel oppression. He has extended the punishment of offenders to all their relatives. He has put men into offices on the hereditary principle. He has made it his pursuit to have palaces, towers, pavilions, embankments, ponds, and all other extravagances, to the most painful injury of you, the myriads of the people. He has burned and roasted the loyal and good. He has ripped up pregnant

---

[1] The thirteenth year is reckoned from king Wû's succeeding to his father as 'the Chief of the West.'

[2] Mâng-*k*ing, or 'the Ford of Mâng,' is still the name of a district in the department of Ho-nan, Ho-nan.

women. Great Heaven was moved with indignation, and charged my deceased father Wăn to display its terrors; but (he died) before the work was completed.*

'On this account, I, Fâ, the little child, have by means of you, the hereditary rulers of my friendly states, contemplated the government of Shang; but Shâu has no repentant heart. He sits squatting on his heels, not serving God nor the spirits of heaven and earth, neglecting also the temple of his ancestors, and not sacrificing in it.* The victims and the vessels of millet all become the prey of wicked robbers, and still he says, "The people are mine; the (heavenly) appointment is mine," never trying to correct his contemptuous mind.*

'Heaven, for the help of the inferior people, made for them rulers, and made for them instructors, that they might be able to be aiding to God, and secure the tranquillity of the four quarters (of the kingdom). In regard to who are criminals and who are not, how dare I give any allowance to my own wishes? *

'"Where the strength is the same, measure the virtue of the parties; where the virtue is the same, measure their righteousness." Shâu has hundreds of thousands and myriads of officers, but they have hundreds of thousands and myriads of minds; I have (but) three thousand officers, but they have one mind. The iniquity of Shang is full. Heaven gives command to destroy it. If I did not obey Heaven, my iniquity would be as great.*

'I, the little child, early and late am filled with apprehensions. I have received the command of my deceased father Wăn; I have offered special sacrifice to God; I have performed the due services to the great earth; and I lead the multitude of you to execute the punishment appointed by Heaven.* Heaven compassionates the people. What the people desire, Heaven will be found to give effect to.* Do you aid me, the One man, to cleanse for ever (all within) the four seas. Now is the time!—It should not be lost.'

Section 2.

On (the day) Wû-wû[1], the king halted on the north of the Ho. When all the princes with their hosts were assembled, the king reviewed the hosts, and made the following declaration:—'Oh! ye multitudes of the west, hearken all to my words.

'I have heard that the good man, doing good, finds the day insufficient; and that the evil man, doing evil, also finds the day insufficient. Now Shâu, the king of Shang, with strength pursues his lawless way. He has driven away the time-worn sires, and cultivates intimacies with wicked men. Dissolute, intemperate, reckless, oppressive, his ministers have become assimilated to him; and they form combinations and contract animosities, and depend on their power to exterminate one another. The innocent cry to Heaven. The odour of such a state is felt on high.*

'Heaven loves the people, and the sovereign should reverently carry out (this mind of) Heaven. *K*ieh, the sovereign of Hsiâ, would not follow the

[1] In Book iii we are told that Wû commenced his march to attack *K*âu-hsin, on Kwei-*k*î, the 2nd day of the moon. Calculating on to the day Wû-wû, we find that it was the 28th day of the same moon.

example of Heaven, but sent forth his poisonous injuries through the states of the kingdom :—Heaven therefore gave its aid to Thang the Successful, and charged him to make an end of the appointment of Hsiâ.* But the crimes of Shâu exceed those of *K*ieh. He has degraded from office the greatly good man[1]; he has behaved with cruel tyranny to his reprover and helper[2]. He says that with him is the appointment of Heaven; he says that a reverent care of his conduct is not worth observing; he says that sacrifice is of no use; he says that tyranny is no harm.* The beacon for him to look to was not far off;—it was that king of Hsiâ. It would seem that Heaven is going by means of me to rule the people. My dreams coincide with my divinations; the auspicious omen is double.* My attack on Shang must succeed.

'Shâu has hundreds of thousands and millions of ordinary men, divided in heart and divided in practice;—I have of ministers, able to govern, ten men[3], one in heart and one in practice. Though he has his nearest relatives with him, they are not like my virtuous men. Heaven sees as my people see; Heaven hears as my people hear.* The people are blaming me, the One man, for my delay;—I must now go forward. My military prowess is displayed, and I enter his territories to take the wicked tyrant. My punishment (of evil) will be great, and more glorious than that executed by Thang. Rouse ye,

---

1 The count of Wei. 2 Pî-kan.

3 Confucius tells us, in the Analects, VIII, xx, that one of these ten was a woman; but whether the lady was Wû's wife or mother is disputed.

my heroes! Do not think that he is not to be feared;—better think that he cannot be withstood. (His) people stand in trembling awe of him, as if the horns were falling from their heads. Oh! unite your energies, unite your hearts;—so shall you forthwith surely accomplish the work, to last for all ages!'

Section 3.

The time was on the morrow, when the king went round his six hosts in state, and made a clear declaration to all his officers. He said, 'Oh! my valiant men of the west, from Heaven are the illustrious courses of duty, of which the (several) requirements are quite plain. And now Shâu the king of Shang, treats with contemptuous slight the five regular (virtues), and abandons himself to wild idleness and irreverence. He has cut himself off from Heaven, and brought enmity between himself and the people.*

'He cut through the leg-bones of those who were wading in the morning [1]; he cut out the heart of the worthy man [2]. By the use of his power, killing and murdering, he has poisoned and sickened all within the four seas. His honours and confidence are given to the villainous and bad. He has driven from him his instructors and guardians. He has thrown to the winds the statutes and penal laws. He has imprisoned and enslaved the upright officer [3]. He neglects the sacrifices to heaven and earth. He

[1] This was in winter. Observing some people then wading through a stream, *K*âu-hsin caused their legs to be cut through at the shank-bone, that he might see their marrow.

[2] Pî-kan.

[3] The count of *Kh*î; see Book iv.

has discontinued the offerings in the ancestral temple. He makes contrivances of wonderful device and extraordinary cunning to please his wife[1].—God will no longer indulge him, but with a curse is sending down on him this ruin.* Do ye with untiring zeal support me, the One man, reverently to execute the punishment appointed by Heaven. The ancients have said, "He who soothes us is our sovereign; he who oppresses us is our enemy." This solitary fellow Shâu, having exercised great tyranny, is your perpetual enemy. (It is said again), "In planting (a man's) virtue, strive to make it great; in putting away (a man's) wickedness, strive to do it from the roots." Here I, the little child, by the powerful help of you, all my officers, will utterly exterminate your enemy. Do you, all my officers, march forward with determined boldness to sustain your prince. Where there is much merit, there shall be large reward; where you do not so advance, there shall be conspicuous disgrace.

'Oh! (the virtue of) my deceased father Wăn was like the shining of the sun and moon. His brightness extended over the four quarters of the land, and shone signally in the western region. Hence it is that our *K*âu has received (the allegiance of) many states. If I subdue Shâu, it will not be from my prowess, but from the faultless (virtue of) my deceased father Wăn. If Shâu subdue me, it will not be from any fault of my deceased father Wăn, but because I, the little child, am not good.'

---

[1] The notorious Tâ-*k*î, the accounts of whose shameless wickedness and atrocious cruelties almost exceed belief.

BOOK II. THE SPEECH AT MÛ.

IT is the morning of the day of battle, for which the king has prepared his host by the three speeches of the last Book. Once more he addresses his confederate princes, his officers, and his men. He sets forth more briefly the intolerable wickedness of Shâu, and instructs and warns his troops how they are to behave in the fight.

Mû was in the south of the present district of *Kh*î, department Wei-hui, Ho-nan, a tract of open country stretching into the district of *K*î, and at no great distance from the capital of Shâu.

1. The time was the grey dawn of the day *K*iâ-ȝze. On that morning the king came to the open country of Mû, in the borders of Shang, and addressed his army. In his left hand he carried a battle-axe, yellow with gold, and in his right he held a white ensign, which he waved, saying, 'Far are ye come, ye men of the western regions!' He added, 'Ah! ye hereditary rulers of my friendly states; ye managers of affairs,—the Ministers of Instruction, of War, and of Works; the great officers subordinate to these, and the many other officers; the master of my body-guards; the captains of thousands and captains of hundreds; and ye, O men of Yung, Shû, *K*iang, Mâo, Wei, Lû, Phang, and Pho[1], lift up your lances, join your shields, raise your spears:—I have a speech to make.'

[1] These are the names of eight different tribes or confederations of tribes of the south and west. We are to look for their sites in Sze-*kh*üan, Yün-nan, and Hû-pei. They were, no doubt, an important portion of Wû's army, but only as auxiliaries. It is too much to ascribe, as some have done, the overthrow of Shang to an irruption of barbarous people from the west.

2. The king (then) said, 'The ancients have said, "The hen does not announce the morning. The crowing of a hen in the morning (indicates) the subversion of the family." Now Shâu, the king of Shang, follows only the words of his wife. In his blindness he has neglected the sacrifices which he ought to offer, and makes no response (for the favours that he has received); * he has also cast off his paternal and maternal relations, not treating them properly. They are only the vagabonds from all quarters, loaded with crimes, whom he honours and exalts, whom he employs and trusts, making them great officers and high nobles, so that they can tyrannize over the people, and exercise their villainies in the cities of Shang.

'Now, I, Fâ, am simply executing respectfully the punishment appointed by Heaven.* In to-day's business do not advance more than six or seven steps, and then stop and adjust your ranks;—my brave men, be energetic! Do not exceed four blows, five blows, six blows, or seven blows, and then stop and adjust your ranks;—my brave men, be energetic! Display a martial bearing. Be like tigers and panthers, like bears and grisly bears,—(here) in the borders of Shang. Do not rush on those who fly (to us in submission), but receive them to serve our western land;—my brave men, be energetic! If you be not energetic (in all these matters), you will bring destruction on yourselves.'

BOOK III.

THE SUCCESSFUL COMPLETION OF THE WAR.

I HAVE divided this Book into three chapters:—one, consisting of brief historical notes of the commencement and close of Wû's expedition; a second, giving the address (or a part of it) delivered by Wû to his nobles and officers on occasion, we may suppose, of their recognition of him as king, and his confirming some of them in their old states or appointments, and giving new ones to others; the third again historical, and relating several incidents of the battle between Wû and Shâu, and going on to subsequent events and important governmental measures of the new dynasty.

Most Chinese critics hold that portions of the Book are lost, and that the paragraphs of it are, besides, erroneously arranged. In what division of the documents of the Shû it should be classified, it is not easy to say. It is more like a 'Canon' than anything else.

1. In the first month, the day *Z*ăn-*kh*ăn immediately followed the end of the moon's waning. The next day was Kwei-*k*î, when the king, in the morning, marched from *K*âu[1] to attack and punish Shang. In the fourth month, at the first appearance of the moon, the king came from Shang to Făng[2], when he hushed all the movements of war, and proceeded to cultivate the arts of peace. He sent back his horses to the south of mount Hwâ,

---

[1] *K*âu is, probably, Wû's capital, called Hâo, about ten miles south of the present district city of *Kh*ang-an, and not quite so far from his father's capital of Făng. The river Făng ran between them.

[2] In Făng there was the ancestral temple of the lords of *K*âu, and thither from the capital of Shang, Wû now repaired for the purpose of sacrificing.

and let loose his oxen in the open country of Thâo-lin[1], showing to all under heaven that he would not use them (again).

On the day Ting-wei, he sacrificed in the ancestral temple of *K*âu, when (the princes) of the royal domain, and of the Tien, Hâu, and Wei domains, all hurried about, carrying the dishes.* The third day after was Kăng-hsü, when he presented a burnt-offering to Heaven, and worshipped towards the hills and rivers, solemnly announcing the successful completion of the war.*

After the moon began to wane, the hereditary princes of the various states, and all the officers, received their appointments from *K*âu[2].

2. The king spoke to the following effect:—'Oh! ye host of princes, the first of our kings[3] founded his state, and commenced (the enlargement of) its territory. Kung Liû[4] was able to consolidate the services of his predecessor. But it was the king Thâi who laid the foundations of the royal inheritance. The king *K*î was diligent for the royal House; and my deceased father, king Wăn, completed his merit, and grandly received the appoint-

[1] The country about the hill of Mû-niû or Khwâ-fû, in the south-east of the present department of Thung-*k*âu. Thâo-lin may be translated 'Peach-forest.'

[2] The new dynasty of *K*âu was now fully inaugurated.

[3] By 'the first of our kings,' we must understand *Kh*î, Shun's Minister of Agriculture; and his state was that of Thâi.

[4] Kung Liû, perhaps 'duke Liû,' appears in Pin, the present Pin *K*âu of Shen-hsî, about the beginning of the eighteenth century B.C., reviving the fallen fortunes of the House of *Kh*î. History is then silent about the family for more than four centuries, when we find Than-fû, called here 'king Thâi,' founding the state of *K*âu.

ment of Heaven, to soothe the regions of our great land.* The great states feared his strength; the small states thought fondly of his virtue. In nine years, however, the whole kingdom was not united under his rule, and it fell to me, the little child, to carry out his will.

'Detesting the crimes of Shang, I announced to great Heaven and the sovereign Earth, to the famous hill [1] and the great river [1] by which I passed, saying, "I, Fâ, the principled, king of *K*âu by a long descent, am about to administer a great correction to Shang. Shâu, the present king of Shang, is without principle, cruel and destructive to the creatures of Heaven, injurious and tyrannical to the multitudes of the people, lord of all the vagabonds under heaven, who collect about him as fish in the deep, and beasts in the prairie. I, the little child, having obtained (the help of) virtuous men, presume reverently to comply with (the will of) God, and make an end of his disorderly ways.* Our flowery and great land, and the tribes of the south and north, equally follow and consent with me. Reverently obeying the determinate counsel of Heaven, I pursue my punitive work to the east, to give tranquillity to its men and women. They meet me with their baskets full of dark-coloured and yellow silks, thereby showing (the virtues) of us, the kings of *K*âu. Heaven's favours stir them up, so that they come with their allegiance to our great state of *K*âu. And now, ye spirits, grant me your aid, that I may relieve the millions of the people, and nothing turn out to your shame."' *

---

[1] Probably mount Hwâ and the Ho.

3. On the day Wû-wû, the army crossed the ford of Mâng, and on Kwei-hâi it was drawn up in array in the borders of Shang, waiting for the gracious decision of Heaven. On *K*iâ-ȝze, at early dawn, Shâu led forward his troops, (looking) like a forest, and assembled them in the wild of Mû. But they offered no opposition to our army. Those in the front inverted their spears, and attacked those behind them, till they fled; and the blood flowed till it floated the pestles of the mortars. Thus did (king Wû) once don his armour, and the kingdom was grandly settled. He overturned the (existing) rule of Shang, and made government resume its old course. He delivered the count of *Kh*î from prison, and raised a mound over the grave of Pî-kan. He bowed forward to the cross-bar of his carriage at the gate of Shang Yung's village [1]. He dispersed the treasures of the Stag Tower [2], and distributed the grain of *K*ü-*kh*iâo [3], thus conferring great gifts on all within the four seas, so that the people joyfully submitted to him.

He arranged the nobles in five orders [4], assigning the territories to them according to a threefold

---

[1] Shang Yung must have been some worthy in disgrace with Shâu, and living in the retirement of his village.

[2] The Stag Tower was the name of a place in the present department of Wei-hui, Ho-nan, where Shâu had accumulated great treasures. He fled to it after his defeat, and burned himself to death; but it would appear he had not succeeded in consuming at the same time all his wealth.

[3] *K*ü-*kh*iâo was in the present district of *Kh*ü-*k*âu, department Kwang-phing, *K*ih-lî, where Shâu had collected great stores of grain.

[4] Dukes, marquises, earls, counts, and barons.

scale[1]. He gave offices only to the worthy, and employments only to the able. He attached great importance to the people's being taught the duties of the five relations of society, and to measures for ensuring a sufficient supply of food, attention to the rites of mourning, and to sacrifices.* He showed the reality of his truthfulness, and proved clearly his righteousness. He honoured virtue, and rewarded merit. Then he had only to let his robes fall down, and fold his hands, and the kingdom was orderly ruled.

Book IV. The Great Plan.

The Great Plan, ordinarily classed among the 'Counsels' or among the 'Instructions' of the Shû, might as well have a place among the 'Canons.' It is a remarkable production, and though it appears among the documents of the *K*âu dynasty, there is claimed for the substance of it a much greater antiquity. According to the introductory sentences, king Wû, the founder of *K*âu, obtained it from the count of *Kh*î in the same year, the thirteenth of his dignity as Chief of the West, that he took the field against the tyrant of Shang. The count of *Kh*î, it is understood, was the Grand-Master at the court of Shang, who appears in the concluding Book of the last Part. He says there, that, when ruin overtook the House of Shang, he would not be the servant of another dynasty. Accordingly, he refused to acknowledge the sovereignty of king Wû, who had delivered him from the prison in which he had been confined by *K*âu-hsin, and fled—or purposed perhaps to flee—to Corea. Wû respected and admired his fidelity to the fallen dynasty, and invested him with that territory. He then, it is said, felt constrained to appear at the court of *K*âu, when the king consulted

[1] Dukes and marquises had the same amount of territory assigned to them, and counts and barons also.

him on the principles of government; and the result was that he communicated to him this Great Plan, with its nine divisions. When we read the Book, we see that it belonged originally to the time of Hsiâ, and that the larger portion of it should be ascribed to the Great Yü, and was as old, indeed, as the reign of Yâo. How it had come into the possession of the count of *Kh*î we cannot tell. Nor does it appear how far the language of it should be ascribed to him. That the larger portion of it had come down from the times of Hsiâ is not improbable. The use of the number nine and other numbers, and the naming of the various divisions of the Plan, are in harmony with Yü's style and practice in his Counsels in the second Part of our Classic, and in the second Part also of the Tribute of Yü. We are told in the introductory sentences, that Heaven or God gave the Plan with its divisions to Yü. To explain the way in which the gift was made, there is a tradition about a mysterious tortoise that appeared in the waters of the Lo, bearing well-defined marks on its back from one to nine, and that thereupon Yü determined the meaning of those marks and of their numbers, and completed the nine divisions of the Plan. Of this legend, however, it is not necessary to speak in connexion with the Shû, which does not mention it; it will come up in connexion with the translation of the Yî King.

The Great Plan means the great model for the government of the nation,—the method by which the people may be rendered happy and tranquil, in harmony with their condition, through the perfect character of the king, and his perfect administration of government.

P. Gaubil says that the Book is a treatise at once of physics, astrology, divination, morals, politics, and religion, and that it has a sufficiently close resemblance to the work of Ocellus the Lucanian. There is a shadowy resemblance between the Great Plan and the curious specimen of Pythagorean doctrine which we have in the treatise on the Universe; but the dissimilarities are still greater and more numerous. More especially are the differences between the Greek mind, speculative, and the Chinese mind, practical, apparent in the two works. Where the Chinese writer loses himself in the sheerest follies of his imagining, he yet gropes about for a rule to be of use in the conduct of human affairs.

The whole of the treatise is divided into three chapters. The first is introductory, and relates how the Great Plan with its nine divisions was at first made known to Yü, and came at this time to be communicated to king Wû; the second contains the names of the nine divisions of the Plan; and in the third we have a description of the several divisions. 'The whole,' says a Chinese writer, 'exhibits the great model for the government of the nation.' The fifth or middle division on royal perfection is the central one of the whole, about which the Book revolves. The four divisions that precede it show how this royal perfection is to be accomplished, and the four that follow show how it is to be maintained.

1. In the thirteenth year[1], the king went to enquire of the count of *Kh*î, and said to him, 'Oh! count of *Kh*î, Heaven, (working) unseen, secures the tranquillity of the lower people, aiding them to be in harmony with their condition[2]. I do not know how the unvarying principles (of its method in doing so) should be set forth in due order.'

The count of *Kh*î thereupon replied, 'I have heard that in old time Khwăn dammed up the inundating waters, and thereby threw into disorder the arrangement of the five elements. God was consequently roused to anger, and did not give him the Great Plan with its nine divisions, and thus the unvarying principles (of Heaven's method) were allowed to go to ruin.* Khwăn was therefore

[1] See the commencement of Book i.

[2] Khung Ying-tâ of the Thang dynasty says on this:—'The people have been produced by supreme Heaven, and both body and soul are Heaven's gift. Men have thus the material body and the knowing mind, and Heaven further assists them, helping them to harmonize their lives. The right and the wrong of their language, the correctness and errors of their conduct, their enjoyment of clothing and food, the rightness of their various movements;—all these things are to be harmonized by what they are endowed with by Heaven.'

kept a prisoner till his death, and his son Yü rose up (and entered on the same undertaking). To him Heaven gave the Great Plan with its nine divisions, and the unvarying principles (of its method) were set forth in their due order.' *

2. '(Of those divisions) the first is called "the five elements;" the second, "reverent attention to the five (personal) matters;" the third, "earnest devotion to the eight (objects of) government;" the fourth, "the harmonious use of the five dividers of time;" the fifth, "the establishment and use of royal perfection;" the sixth, "the discriminating use of the three virtues;" the seventh, "the intelligent use of (the means for) the examination of doubts;" the eighth, "the thoughtful use of the various verifications;" the ninth, "the hortatory use of the five (sources of) happiness, and the awing use of the six (occasions of) suffering."'

3. i. 'First, of the five elements[1].—The first is

[1] Gaubil gives here 'les cinq hing,' without translating the Chinese term. English sinologists have got into the habit of rendering it by 'elements,' but it hardly seems possible to determine what the Chinese mean by it. We intend by 'elements' 'the first principles or ingredients of which all things are composed.' The Pythagoreans, by their four elements of earth, water, air, and fire, did not intend so much the nature or essence of material substances, as the forms under which matter is actually presented to us. The character hsing, meaning 'to move,' 'to be in action,' shows that the original conception of the Chinese is of a different nature; and it is said in the Khang-hsî Dictionary, 'The five hsing move and revolve between heaven and earth, without ever ceasing, and hence they are named.' The editors of the latest imperial edition of the Shû say, 'Distributed through the four seasons, they make "the five dividers of time;" exhibited in prognostications, they give rise to divination by the tortoise-shell and the reeds; having lodgment in the human body, they produce "the five personal matters;" moved by good fortune and bad, they

water; the second is fire; the third, wood; the fourth, metal; and the fifth, earth. (The nature of) water is to soak and descend; of fire, to blaze and ascend; of wood, to be crooked and straight; of metal, to yield and change; while (that of) earth is seen in seed-sowing and in-gathering. That which soaks and descends becomes salt; that which blazes and ascends becomes bitter; that which is crooked and straight becomes sour; that which yields and changes becomes acrid; and from seed-sowing and in-gathering comes sweetness.'

ii. 'Second, of the five (personal) matters [1].—The first is the bodily demeanour; the second, speech; the third, seeing; the fourth, hearing; the fifth, thinking. (The virtue of) the bodily appearance is respectfulness; of speech, accordance (with reason); of seeing, clearness; of hearing, distinctness; of thinking, perspicaciousness. The respectfulness becomes manifest in gravity; accordance (with reason), in orderliness; the clearness, in wisdom; the distinctness, in deliberation; and the perspicaciousness, in sageness.'

iii. 'Third, of the eight (objects of) government [2].—

produce "the various verifications;" communicated to organisms, they produce the different natures, hard and soft, good and evil; working out their results in the changes of those organisms, they necessitate—here benevolence and there meanness, here longevity and there early death:—all these things are from the operation of the five hsing. But if we speak of them in their simplest and most important character, they are what man's life depends on, what the people cannot do without.' After all this, I should still be sorry to be required to say what the five hsing are.

[1] These five 'matters' are represented as being in the human person what the five hsing are in nature. Demeanour is the human correspondency of water, speech that of fire, &c.

[2] Medhurst calls the eight (objects of) government 'the eight

The first is food; the second, wealth and articles of convenience; the third, sacrifices; the fourth, (the business of) the Minister of Works; the fifth, (that of) the Minister of Instruction; the sixth, (that of) the Minister of Crime; the seventh, the observances to be paid to guests; the eighth, the army.'

iv. 'Fourth, of the five dividers of time [1].—The first is the year (or the planet Jupiter); the second, the moon; the third, the sun; the fourth, the stars and planets, and the zodiacal spaces; and the fifth, the calendaric calculations.'

v. 'Fifth, of royal perfection [2].—The sovereign, having established (in himself) the highest degree and pattern of excellence, concentrates in his own person the five (sources of) happiness, and proceeds to diffuse them, and give them to the multitudes of the people. Then they, on their part, embodying your perfection, will give it (back) to you, and secure the preservation of it. Among all the multitudes of the people there will be no unlawful confederacies, and among men (in office) there will be no bad and selfish combinations;—let the sovereign

---

regulators,' and Gaubil calls them 'les huit règles du gouvernement.' The phrase means the eight things to be attended to in government,—its objects and departments.

[1] 'The five dividers of time' are with Medhurst 'the five arrangers,' and with Gaubil 'les cinq périodes.' This division of the Great Plan is substantially the same as Yâo's instructions to his astronomers.

[2] By 'royal perfection' we are to understand the sovereign when he is, or has made himself, all that he ought to be. 'Perfection' is 'the utmost point,' the extreme of excellence, realized in the person of the sovereign, guiding his administrative measures, and serving as an example and attractive influence to all below, both ministers and people.

establish in (himself) the highest degree and pattern of excellence.

'Among all the multitudes of the people there will be those who have ability to plan and to act, and who keep themselves (from evil):—do you keep such in mind; and there will be those who, not coming up to the highest point of excellence, yet do not involve themselves in evil:—let the sovereign receive such. And when a placid satisfaction appears in their countenances, and they say, "Our love is fixed on virtue," do you then confer favours on them;—those men will in this way advance to the perfection of the sovereign. Do not let him oppress the friendless and childless, nor let him fear the high and distinguished. When men (in office) have ability and administrative power, let them be made still more to cultivate their conduct; and the prosperity of the country will be promoted. All (such) right men, having a competency, will go on in goodness. If you cannot cause them to have what they love in their families, they will forthwith proceed to be guilty of crime. As to those who have not the love of virtue, although you confer favours (and emoluments) on them, they will (only) involve you in the guilt of employing the evil.

'Without deflection, without unevenness,
Pursue the royal righteousness.
Without selfish likings,
Pursue the royal way.
Without selfish dislikings,
Pursue the royal path.
Avoid deflection, avoid partiality;—
Broad and long is the royal way.

Avoid partiality, avoid deflection;—
Level and easy is the royal way.
Avoid perversity, avoid one-sidedness;—
Correct and straight is the royal way.
(Ever) seek for this perfect excellence,
(Ever) turn to this perfect excellence.'

He went on to say, 'This amplification of the royal perfection contains the unchanging (rule), and is the (great) lesson;—yea, it is the lesson of God.* All the multitudes of the people, instructed in this amplification of the perfect excellence, and carrying it into practice, will thereby approximate to the glory of the Son of Heaven, and say, "The Son of Heaven is the parent of the people, and so becomes the sovereign of all under the sky."'

vi. 'Sixth, of the three virtues[1].—The first is correctness and straightforwardness; the second, strong rule; and the third, mild rule. In peace and tranquillity, correctness and straightforwardness (must sway); in violence and disorder, strong rule; in harmony and order, mild rule. For the reserved and retiring there should be (the stimulus of) the strong rule; for the high(-minded) and distinguished, (the restraint of) the mild rule.

'It belongs only to the sovereign to confer dignities and rewards, to display the terrors of majesty, and to receive the revenues (of the kingdom). There should be no such thing as a minister's conferring dignities or rewards, displaying the terrors of majesty, or receiving the revenues. Such

[1] 'The three virtues' are not personal attributes of the sovereign, but characteristics of his rule, the varied manifestations of the perfection described in the preceding division.

a thing is injurious to the clans, and fatal to the states (of the kingdom); smaller affairs are thereby managed in a one-sided and perverse manner, and the people fall into assumptions and excesses.'

vii. 'Seventh, of the (means for the) examination of doubts[1].—Officers having been chosen and appointed for divining by the tortoise-shell and the

---

[1] The practice of divination for the satisfaction of doubts was thus used in China from the earliest times. In the Counsels of Yü, p. 50, that sage proposes to Shun to submit the question of who should be his successor on the throne to divination, and Shun replies that he had already done so. Gaubil says that according to the Great Plan divination was only used in doubtful cases; but if such was the practice of the sages, diviners and soothsayers must have formed, as they do now, a considerable and influential class in society. The old methods of divination have fallen into disuse, and we do not know how far other methods are employed and sanctioned by the government. Those old methods were by means of the tortoise-shell, and the stalks of the *Khî* plant. 'The tortoise,' says *Kû* Hsî, 'after great length of years becomes intelligent; and the *Khî* plant will yield, when a hundred years old, a hundred stalks from one root, and is also a spiritual and intelligent thing. The two divinations were in reality a questioning of spiritual beings, the plant and the shell being employed, because of their mysterious intelligence, to indicate their intimations. The way of divination by the shell was by the application of fire to scorch it till the indications appeared on it; and that by the stalks of the plant was to manipulate in a prescribed way forty-nine of them, eighteen different times, till the diagrams were formed.'

The outer shell of the tortoise was removed, leaving the inner portion on which were the marks of the lines of the muscles of the creature. This was smeared with a black pigment, and, fire being applied beneath, the pigment was examined, and according as it had been variously dried by the heat, presented the indications mentioned in the text. The *Khî* plant was probably the Achillea millefolium. It is cultivated largely on the mound over the grave of Confucius. I brought from that two bundles of the dried stalks in 1873.

stalks of the Achillea, they are to be charged (on occasion) to execute their duties. (In doing this), they will find (the appearances of) rain, of clearing up, of cloudiness, of want of connexion, and of crossing; and the inner and outer diagrams. In all (the indications) are seven;—five given by the shell, and two by the stalks; and (by means) of these any errors (in the mind) may be traced out. These officers having been appointed, when the divination is proceeded with, three men are to interpret the indications, and the (consenting) words of two of them are to be followed.*

'When you have doubts about any great matter, consult with your own mind; consult with your high ministers and officers; consult with the common people; consult the tortoise-shell and divining stalks. If you, the shell, the stalks, the ministers and officers, and the common people, all agree about a course, this is what is called a great concord, and the result will be the welfare of your person and good fortune to your descendants. If you, the shell, and the stalks agree, while the ministers, and officers, and the common people oppose, the result will be fortunate. If the ministers and officers, with the shell and stalks, agree, while you and the common people oppose, the result will be fortunate. If the common people, the shell, and the stalks agree, while you, with the ministers and officers, oppose, the result will be fortunate. If you and the shell agree, while the stalks, with the ministers and officers, and the common people, oppose, internal operations will be fortunate, and external undertakings unlucky. When the shell and stalks are both opposed to the views of men, there will be good fortune in being still, and active operations will be unlucky.' *

viii. 'Eighth, of the various verifications[1].—They are rain, sunshine, heat, cold, wind, and seasonableness. When the five come, all complete, and each in its proper order, (even) the various plants will be richly luxuriant. Should any one of them be either excessively abundant or excessively deficient, there will be evil.*

'There are the favourable verifications[2]:—namely,

---

[1] P. Gaubil renders by 'les apparences' the characters which I have translated 'the various verifications,' observing that he could not find any word which would cover the whole extent of the meaning. He says, 'In the present case, the character signifies meteors, phenomena, appearances, but in such sort that these have relation to some other things with which they are connected;—the meteor or phenomenon indicates some good or some evil. It is a kind of correspondency which is supposed, it appears, to exist between the ordinary events of the life of men and the constitution of the air, according to the different seasons;—what is here said supposes—I know not what physical speculation of those times. It is needless to bring to bear on the text the interpretation of the later Chinese, for they are full of false ideas on the subject of physics. It may be also that the count of *Kh*î wanted to play the physicist on points which he did not know.' There seems to underlie the words of the count that feeling of the harmony between the natural and spiritual worlds, which occurs at times to most men, and strongly affects minds under deep religious thought or on the wings of poetic rapture, but the way in which he endeavours to give the subject a practical application can only be characterised as grotesque.

[2] Compare with this what is said above on the second division of the Plan, 'the five (personal) matters.' It is observed here by Ʒhâi *Kh*ăn, the disciple of *K*û Hsî, and whose commentary on the Shû has, of all others, the greatest authority:—'To say that on occasion of such and such a personal matter being realized, there will be the favourable verification corresponding to it, or that, on occasion of the failure of such realization, there will be the corresponding

of gravity, which is emblemed by seasonable rain; of orderliness, emblemed by seasonable sunshine; of wisdom, emblemed by seasonable heat; of deliberation, emblemed by seasonable cold; and of sageness, emblemed by seasonable wind. There are (also) the unfavourable verifications:—namely, of recklessness, emblemed by constant rain; of assumption, emblemed by constant sunshine; of indolence, emblemed by constant heat; of hastiness, emblemed by constant cold; and of stupidity, emblemed by constant wind.' *

He went on to say, 'The king should examine the (character of the whole) year; the high ministers and officers (that of) the month; and the inferior officers (that of) the day. If, throughout the year, the month, the day, there be an unchanging seasonableness, all the grains will be matured; the measures of government will be wise; heroic men will stand forth distinguished; and in the families (of the people) there will be peace and prosperity. If, throughout the year, the month, the day, the seasonableness be interrupted, the various kinds of grain will not be matured; the measures of government will be dark and unwise; heroic men will be kept in

unfavourable verification, would betray a pertinacious obtuseness, and show that the speaker was not a man to be talked with on the mysterious operations of nature. It is not easy to describe the reciprocal meeting of Heaven and men. The hidden springs touched by failure and success, and the minute influences that respond to them:—who can know these but the man that has apprehended all truth?' This is in effect admitting that the statements in the text can be of no practical use. And the same thing is admitted by the latest imperial editors of the Shû on the use which the text goes on to make of the thoughtful use of the verifications by the king and others.

obscurity; and in the families (of the people) there will be an absence of repose.

'By the common people the stars should be examined. Some stars love wind, and some love rain. The courses of the sun and moon give winter and summer. The way in which the moon follows the stars gives wind and rain.'

ix. 'Ninth, of the five (sources of) happiness[1].—The first is long life; the second, riches; the third, soundness of body and serenity of mind; the fourth, the love of virtue; and the fifth, fulfilling to the end the will (of Heaven).* Of the six extreme evils, the first is misfortune shortening the life; the second, sickness; the third, distress of mind; the fourth, poverty; the fifth, wickedness; the sixth, weakness[2].'

Book V. The Hounds of Lü.

Lü was the name of one of the rude tribes of the west, lying beyond the provinces of *K*âu. Its situation cannot be more exactly defined. Its people, in compliment to king Wû, and impressed by a sense of his growing power, sent to him some of their hounds, and he having received them, or intimated that he would do so, the Grand-Guardian remonstrated with him, showing that to receive such animals would be contrary to precedent, dangerous to the virtue of the sovereign, and was not the way to deal with outlying tribes and nations. The Grand-Guardian, it is supposed, was the duke of Shâo, author of the Announcement which forms the twelfth Book of this Part. The Book is one of the 'Instructions' of the Shû.

---

[1] It is hardly possible to see how this division enters into the scheme of the Great Plan.

[2] 'Wickedness' is, probably, boldness in what is evil, and 'weakness,' feebleness of will in what is good.

1. After the conquest of Shang, the way being open to the nine tribes of the Î[1] and the eight of the Man[1], the western tribe of Lü sent as tribute some of its hounds, on which the Grand-Guardian made 'the Hounds of Lü,' by way of instruction to the king.

2. He said, 'Oh! the intelligent kings paid careful attention to their virtue, and the wild tribes on every side acknowledged subjection to them. The nearer and the more remote all presented the productions of their countries,—in robes, food, and vessels for use. The kings then displayed the things thus drawn forth by their virtue, (distributing them) to the (princes of the) states of different surnames from their own, (to encourage them) not to neglect their duties. The (more) precious things and pieces of jade they distributed among their uncles in charge of states, thereby increasing their attachment (to the throne). The recipients did not despise the things, but saw in them the power of virtue.

'Complete virtue allows no contemptuous familiarity. When (a ruler) treats superior men with such familiarity, he cannot get them to give him all their hearts; when he so treats inferior men, he cannot get them to put forth for him all their strength. Let him keep from being in bondage to his ears and eyes, and strive to be correct in all his measures. By trifling intercourse with men, he ruins his virtue; by finding his amusement in things (of mere pleasure),

[1] By 'the nine Î and eight Man' we are to understand generally the barbarous tribes lying round the China of *K*âu. Those tribes are variously enumerated in the ancient books. Generally the Î are assigned to the east, the *Z*ung to the west, the Tî to the north, and the Man to the south.

he ruins his aims. His aims should repose in what is right; he should listen to words (also) in their relation to what is right.

'When he does not do what is unprofitable to the injury of what is profitable, his merit can be completed. When he does not value strange things to the contemning things that are useful, his people will be able to supply (all that he needs). (Even) dogs and horses that are not native to his country he will not keep. Fine birds and strange animals he will not nourish in his state. When he does not look on foreign things as precious, foreigners will come to him; when it is real worth that is precious to him, (his own) people near at hand will be in a state of repose.

'Oh! early and late never be but earnest. If you do not attend jealously to your small actions, the result will be to affect your virtue in great matters; —in raising a mound of nine fathoms, the work may be unfinished for want of one basket (of earth). If you really pursue this course (which I indicate), the people will preserve their possessions, and the throne will descend from generation to generation.'

BOOK VI. THE METAL-BOUND COFFER.

A CERTAIN chest or coffer, that was fastened with bands of metal, and in which important state documents were deposited, plays an important part among the incidents of the Book, which is therefore called 'the Metal-bound Coffer.' To what class among the documents of the Shû it should be assigned is doubtful.

King Wû is very ill, and his death seems imminent. His brother, the duke of *K*âu, apprehensive of the disasters which such an event would occasion to their infant dynasty, conceives the idea of dying in his stead, and prays to 'the three kings,' their immediate progenitors, that he might be taken and king Wû left. Having done so, and divined that he was heard, he deposits the prayer in the metal-bound coffer. The king gets well, and the duke is also spared; but five years later, Wû does die, and is succeeded by his son, a boy only thirteen years old. Rumours are spread abroad that the duke has designs on the throne, and he withdraws for a time from the court. At length, in the third year of the young king, Heaven interposes. He has occasion to open the coffer, and the prayer of the duke is found. His devotion to his brother and to the interests of their family is brought to light. The boy-monarch weeps because of the unjust suspicions he had harboured, and welcomes the duke back to court, amid unmistakeable demonstrations of the approval of Heaven.

The whole narrative is a very pleasing episode in the history of the times. It divides itself naturally into two chapters:—the first, ending with the placing the prayer in the coffer; and the second, detailing how it was brought to light, and the consequences of the discovery.

It is in this Book that we first meet in the Shû with the duke of *K*âu, a name in Chinese history only second to that of Confucius. He was the legislator and consolidator of the dynasty of *K*âu, equally mighty in words and in deeds,—a man of counsel and of action. Confucius regarded his memory with reverence, and spoke of it as a sign of his own failing powers, that the duke of *K*âu no longer appeared to him in his dreams. He was the fourth son of king Wăn; his name was Tan, and he had for his appanage the territory of *K*âu, where Than-fû, canonized by him as king Thâi, first placed the seat of his family in B.C. 1327, and hence he is commonly called 'the duke of *K*âu.'

1. Two years after the conquest of Shang[1], the king fell ill, and was quite disconsolate. The two (other great) dukes[2] said, 'Let us reverently consult

[1] B.C. 1121.

[2] These were the duke of Shâo, to whom the preceding Book is ascribed, and Thâi-kung, who became the first of the lords of *Kh*î.

the tortoise-shell about the king;' but the duke of *K*âu said, 'You must not so distress our former kings [1].' He then took the business on himself, and reared three altars of earth on the same cleared space; and having made another altar on the south of these, and facing the north, he took there his own position. Having put a round symbol of jade (on each of the three altars), and holding in his hands the lengthened symbol (of his own rank), he addressed the kings Thâi, *K*î, and Wăn.*

The (grand) historiographer had written on tablets his prayer, which was to this effect:—'A. B., your great descendant, is suffering from a severe and violent disease;—if you three kings have in heaven the charge of (watching over) him, (Heaven's) great son, let me Tan be a substitute for his person [2]. I was lovingly obedient to my father; I am possessed of many abilities and arts, which fit me to serve spiritual beings. Your great descendant, on the other hand, has not so many abilities and arts as I, and is not so capable of serving spiritual beings. And moreover he was appointed in the hall of God to extend his aid all over the kingdom, so that he might establish your descendants in this lower earth. The people of the four quarters all stand in reverent

---

[1] He negatives their proposal, having determined to take the whole thing on himself.

[2] Two things are here plain:—first, that the duke of *K*âu offered himself to die in the room of his brother; and second, that he thought that his offer might somehow be accepted through the intervention of the great kings, their progenitors. He proceeds to give his reasons for making such an offer, which are sufficiently interesting. It was hardly necessary for Chinese scholars to take the pains they have done to free the duke from the charge of boasting in them.

awe of him. Oh! do not let that precious Heaven-conferred appointment fall to the ground, and (all the long line of) our former kings will also have one in whom they can ever rest at our sacrifices.* I will now seek for your determination (in this matter) from the great tortoise-shell. If you grant me (my request), I will take these symbols and this mace, and return and wait for your orders. If you do not grant it, I will put them by [1].'*

The duke then divined with the three tortoise-shells, and all were favourable. He opened with a key the place where the (oracular) responses were kept, and looked at them, and they also were favourable. He said, 'According to the form (of the prognostic) the king will take no injury. I, the little child, have got the renewal of his appointment from the three kings, by whom a long futurity has been consulted for. I have now to wait for the issue. They can provide for our One man.'*

When the duke returned, he placed the tablets (of the prayer) in a metal-bound coffer [2], and next day the king got better.

2. (Afterwards), upon the death of king Wû, (the duke's) elder brother, he of Kwan, and his younger brothers, spread a baseless report through the king-

---

[1] I suppose that the divination took place before the altars, and that a different shell was used to ascertain the mind of each king. The oracular responses would be a few lines, kept apart by themselves, and consulted, on occasion, according to certain rules which have not come down to the present day.

[2] Many scholars think that it was this coffer which contained the oracles of divination mentioned above. It may have been so; but I rather suppose it to have been different, and a special chest in which important archives of the dynasty, to be referred to on great emergencies, were kept.

dom, to the effect that the duke would do no good to the (king's) young son. On this the duke said to the two (other great) dukes, 'If I do not take the law (to these men), I shall not be able to make my report to the former kings[1].'*

He resided (accordingly) in the east for two years[2], when the criminals were taken (and brought to justice). Afterwards he made a poem to present to the king, and called it 'the Owl[3].' The king on his part did not dare to blame the duke.

In the autumn, when the grain was abundant and ripe, but before it was reaped, Heaven sent a great storm of thunder and lightning, along with wind, by which the grain was all broken down, and great trees torn up. The people were greatly terrified; and the king and great officers, all in their caps of state, proceeded to open the metal-bound coffer and examine the writings in it, where they found the words of the duke when he took on himself the business of being a substitute for king Wû. The two (great) dukes and the king asked the historiographer and all the other officers (acquainted with the transaction) about the thing, and they replied, 'It was really thus; but ah! the duke charged us that we

[1] Wû died in B.C. 1116, and was succeeded by his son Sung, who is known in history as king *Kh*ăng, or 'the Completer.' He was at the time only thirteen years old, and his uncle, the duke of *K*âu, acted as regent. The jealousy of his elder brother Hsien, 'lord of Kwan,' and two younger brothers, was excited, and they spread the rumour which is referred to, and entered into a conspiracy with the son of the tyrant of Shang, to overthrow the new dynasty.

[2] These two years were spent in military operations against the revolters.

[3] See the Book of Poetry, Part I, xv, Ode 2.

should not presume to speak about it.' The king held the writing in his hand, and wept, saying, 'We need not (now) go on reverently to divine. Formerly the duke was thus earnest for the royal House, but I, being a child, did not know it. Now Heaven has moved its terrors to display his virtue. That I, the little child, (now) go with my new views and feelings to meet him, is what the rules of propriety of our kingdom require.'*

The king then went out to the borders (to meet the duke), when Heaven sent down rain, and, by virtue of a contrary wind, the grain all rose up. The two (great) dukes gave orders to the people to take up the trees that had fallen and replace them. The year then turned out very fruitful.*

Book VII. The Great Announcement.

This 'Great Announcement' was called forth by the emergency referred to in the second chapter of the last Book. The prefatory notice says, 'When king Wû had deceased, the three overseers and the wild tribes of the Hwâi rebelled. The duke of *K*âu acted as minister for king *Kh*ăng, and having purposed to make an end of the House of Yin (or Shang), he made 'the Great Announcement.' Such was the occasion on which the Book was composed. The young king speaks in it the words and sentiments of the duke of *K*âu; and hence the style in which it commences, 'The king speaks to the following effect.'

The young sovereign speaks of the responsibility lying on him to maintain the kingdom gained by the virtues and prowess of his father, and of the senseless movements of the House of Shang to regain its supremacy. He complains of the reluctance of many of the princes and high officers to second him in putting down revolt, and proclaims with painful reiteration the support and assurances of success which he has received from the divining shell. His traitorous uncles, who were confederate with the son of the tyrant of Shang, are only alluded to.

1. The king speaks to the following effect:—'Ho! I make a great announcement to you, (the princes of) the many states, and to you, the managers of my affairs.—We are unpitied, and Heaven sends down calamities on our House, without the least intermission [1].* It greatly occupies my thoughts that I, so very young, have inherited this illimitable patrimony with its destinies and domains. I cannot display wisdom and lead the people to prosperity; and how much less should I be able to reach the knowledge of the decree of Heaven!* Yes, I who am but a little child am in the position of one who has to go through a deep water;—I must go and seek where I can cross over. I must diffuse the elegant institutions of my predecessor and display the appointment which he received (from Heaven);—so shall I not be forgetful of his great work. Nor shall I dare to restrain the majesty of Heaven in sending down its inflictions (on the criminals) [2].'*

2. 'The Tranquillizing king [3] left to me the great precious tortoise-shell, to bring into connexion with me the intelligence of Heaven. I divined by it, and it told me that there would be great trouble in the region of the west [4], and that the western people would not be still [4].* Accordingly we have these senseless movements. Small and reduced as Yin

[1] With reference, probably, to the early death of his father, and the revolt that followed quickly upon it.

[2] The duke had made up his mind that he would deal stern justice even on his own brothers.

[3] King Wû.

[4] The troubles arose in the east, and not in the west. We do not know the facts in the state of the kingdom sufficiently to explain every difficulty in these Books. Perhaps the oracular response had been purposely ambiguous.

now is, (its prince) greatly dares to take in hand its (broken) line. Though Heaven sent down its terrors (on his House), yet knowing of the evils in our kingdom, and that the people are not tranquil, he says, "I will recover (my patrimony);" and so (he wishes to) make our *K*âu a border territory again.

'One day there was a senseless movement, and the day after, ten men of worth appeared among the people, to help me to go forward to restore tranquillity and perpetuate the plans (of my father)[1]. The great business I am engaging in will (thus) have a successful issue. I have divined (also) by the tortoise-shell, and always got a favourable response.* Therefore I tell you, the princes of my friendly states, and you, the directors of departments, my officers, and the managers of my affairs,—I have obtained a favourable reply to my divinations. I will go forward with you from all the states, and punish those vagabond and transported ministers of Yin.'

3. '(But) you the princes of the various states, and you the various officers and managers of my affairs, all retort on me, saying, "The hardships will be great, and that the people are not quiet has its source really in the king's palace and in the mansions of the princes in that (rebellious) state[2]. We little ones, and the old and reverend men as well, think the expedition ill-advised;—why does your Majesty not go contrary to the divinations?" I, in my youth, (also) think continually of these hardships, and say,

---

[1] Who these 'ten men of worth' were, we do not know, nor the circumstances in which they came forward to help the government.

[2] Here is an allusion, as plain as the duke could permit himself to make, to the complicity of his brothers in the existing troubles.

Alas! these senseless movements will deplorably afflict the wifeless men and widows! But I am the servant of Heaven, which has assigned me this great task, and laid the hard duty on my person.* I therefore, the young one, do not pity myself; and it would be right in you, the many officers, the directors of departments, and the managers of my affairs, to comfort me, saying, "Do not be distressed with sorrow. We shall surely complete the plans of your Tranquillizing father."

'Yes, I, the little child, dare not disregard the charge of God[1].* Heaven, favourable to the Tranquillizing king, gave such prosperity to our small country of *K*âu. The Tranquillizing king divined and acted accordingly, and so he calmly received his (great) appointment. Now when Heaven is (evidently) aiding the people, how much more should we follow the indications of the shell! Oh! the clearly intimated will of Heaven is to be feared:—it is to help my great inheritance!' *

4. The king says, 'You, who are the old ministers, are fully able to remember the past; you know how great was the toil of the Tranquillizing king. Where Heaven (now) shuts up (our path) and distresses us, is the place where I must accomplish my work;—I dare not but do my utmost to complete the plans of the Tranquillizing king. It is on this account that I use such efforts to remove the doubts and carry forward the inclinations of the princes of my friendly states. And Heaven assists me with sincere expressions of (sympathy), which I have ascertained among

[1] Probably the charge understood to be conveyed by the result of the divinations spoken of above.

the people;—how dare I but aim at the completion of the work formerly begun by the Tranquillizer? Heaven, moreover, is thus toiling and distressing the people;—it is as if they were suffering from disease; how dare I allow (the appointment) which my predecessor, the Tranquillizer, received, to be without its happy fulfilment?' *

The king says, 'Formerly, at the initiation of this expedition, I spoke of its difficulties, and thought of them daily. But when a deceased father, (wishing) to build a house, had laid out the plan, if his son be unwilling to raise up the hall, how much less will he be willing to complete the roof! Or if the father had broken up the ground, and his son be unwilling to sow the seed, how much less will he be willing to reap the crop! In such a case could the father, (who had himself) been so reverently attentive (to his objects), have been willing to say, "I have a son who will not abandon his patrimony?"—How dare I therefore but use all my powers to give a happy settlement to the great charge entrusted to the Tranquillizing king? If among the friends of an elder brother or a deceased father there be those who attack his son, will the elders of the people encourage (the attack), and not (come to the) rescue?'

5. The king says, 'Oh! take heart, ye princes of the various states, and ye managers of my affairs. The enlightening of the country was from the wise, even from the ten men[1] who obeyed and knew the

[1] 'The ten men' here can hardly be the 'ten men of worth' above in the second chapter. We must find them rather in the 'ten virtuous men, one in heart and one in practice, capable of good,' mentioned by king Wû, in the second Part of the Great Declaration.

charge of God,* and the real assistance given by Heaven. At that time none of you presumed to change the rules (prescribed by the Tranquillizing king). And now when Heaven is sending down calamity on the country of *K*âu, and the authors of these great distresses (make it appear on a grand scale as if) the inmates of a house were mutually to attack one another, you are without any knowledge that the decree of Heaven is not to be changed! *

'I ever think and say, Heaven in destroying Yin was doing husbandman's work[1];—how dare I but complete the work on my fields? Heaven will thereby show its favour to my predecessor, the Tranquillizer. How should I be all for the oracle of divination, and presume not to follow (your advice)? * I am following the Tranquillizer, whose purpose embraced all within the limits of the land. How much more must I proceed, when the divinations are all favourable! It is on these accounts that I make this expedition in force to the east. There is no mistake about the decree of Heaven. The indications given by the tortoise-shell are all to the same effect.' *

Book VIII. The Charge to the Count of Wei.

The count of Wei was the principal character in the eleventh Book of the last Part, from which it appeared that he was a brother of the tyrant *K*âu-hsin. We saw how his friends advised him to withdraw from the court of Shang, and save

[1] That is, thorough work,—clearing the ground of weeds, and not letting their roots remain.

himself from the destruction that was impending over their House. He had done so, and king Wû had probably continued him in the possession of his appanage of Wei, while Wû-kăng, the son of the tyrant, had been spared, and entrusted with the duty of continuing the sacrifices to the great Thang and the other sovereigns of the House of Shang. Now that Wû-kăng has been punished with death for his rebellion, the duke of *K*âu summons the count of Wei to court, and in the name of king *Kh*ăng invests him with the dukedom of Sung, corresponding to the present department of Kwei-teh, Ho-nan, there to be the representative of the line of the departed kings of Shang.

The king speaks to the following effect:—'Ho! eldest son of the king of Yin, examining into antiquity, (I find) that the honouring of the virtuous (belongs to their descendants) who resemble them in worth, and (I appoint) you to continue the line of the kings your ancestors, observing their ceremonies and taking care of their various relics. Come (also) as a guest to our royal House[1], and enjoy the prosperity of our kingdom, for ever and ever without end.

'Oh! your ancestor, Thang the Successful, was reverent and sage, (with a virtue) vast and deep. The favour and help of great Heaven lighted upon him, and he grandly received its appointment, to soothe the people by his gentleness, and remove the wicked oppressions from which they were suffering.* His achievements affected his age, and his virtue was transmitted to his posterity. And you are the one who pursue and cultivate his plans;—this praise

[1] Under the dynasty of *K*âu, the representatives of the two previous dynasties of Shang and Hsiâ were distinguished above the other princes of the kingdom, and denominated 'guests' of the sovereign, coming to his court and assisting in the services in his ancestral temple, nearly on a footing of equality with him.

has belonged to you for long. Reverently and carefully have you discharged your filial duties; gravely and respectfully you behave to spirits and to men.* I admire your virtue, and pronounce it great and not to be forgotten. God will always enjoy your offerings; the people will be reverently harmonious (under your sway).* I raise you therefore to the rank of high duke, to rule this eastern part of our great land[1].

'Be reverent. Go and diffuse abroad your instructions. Be carefully observant of your robes and (other accompaniments of) your appointment[2]; follow and observe the proper statutes;—so as to prove a bulwark to the royal House. Enlarge (the fame of) your meritorious ancestor; be a law to your people;—so as for ever to preserve your dignity. (So also) shall you be a help to me, the One man; future ages will enjoy (the benefit of) your virtue; all the states will take you for a pattern;—and thus you will make our dynasty of *K*âu never weary of you.

'Oh! go, and be prosperous. Do not disregard my charge.'

---

[1] Sung lay east from Făng and Hâo, the capitals of Wăn and Wû, which were in the present department of Hsî-an, Shen-hsî.

[2] Meaning probably that he was to bear in mind that, however illustrious his descent, he was still a subject of the king of *K*âu.

BOOK IX.

THE ANNOUNCEMENT TO THE PRINCE OF KHANG.

OF the ten sons of king Wăn, the ninth was called Fâng, and is generally spoken of as Khang Shû, or 'the uncle, (the prince of) Khang.' We must conclude that Khang was the name of Făng's appanage, somewhere in the royal domain. This Book contains the charge given to him on his appointment to be marquis of Wei (the Chinese name is quite different from that of the appanage of the count of Wei), the chief city of which was *K*âo-ko, that had been the capital of *K*âu-hsin. It extended westward from the present Khâi *K*âu, department Tâ-ming, *K*ih-lî, to the borders of the departments of Wei-hui and Hwâi-*kh*ing, Ho-nan.

The Book is called an 'Announcement,' whereas it properly belongs to the class of 'Charges.' Whether the king who speaks in it, and gives the charge be Wû, or his son king *Kh*ăng, is a point on which there is much difference of opinion among Chinese critics. The older view that the appointment of Făng to be marquis of Wei, and ruler of that part of the people who might be expected to cling most tenaciously to the memory of the Shang dynasty, took place after the death of Wû-kăng, the son of the tyrant, and was made by the duke of *K*âu, in the name of king *Kh*ăng, is on the whole attended with the fewer difficulties.

The first paragraph, which appears within brackets, does not really belong to this Book, but to the thirteenth, where it will be found again. How it got removed from its proper place, and prefixed to the charge to the prince of Khang, is a question on which it is not necessary to enter. The key-note of the whole charge is in what is said, at the commencement of the first of the five chapters into which I have divided it, about king Wăn, that 'he was able to illustrate his virtue and be careful in the use of punishments.' The first chapter celebrates the exhibition of these two things given by Wăn, whereby he laid the foundations of the great destiny of his House, and set an example to his descendants. The second inculcates on Făng how he should illustrate his virtue, as the basis of his good government of the people entrusted to him. The third inculcates on him how he should be careful in the use of punishments, and sets forth the happy effects of his being so. The fourth insists on the influence of virtue, as being superior in government to that of punishment, and how punishments should all be regulated by the ruler's virtue. The last chapter winds the subject up with a reference to the uncertainty of the appointments of Heaven, and their dependance for permanence on the discharge of the duties connected with them by those on whom they have lighted.

[On the third month, when the moon began to wane, the duke of *K*âu commenced the foundations, and proceeded to build the new great city of Lo, of the eastern states. The people from every quarter assembled in great harmony. From the Hâu, Tien, Nan, 3hâi, and Wei domains, the various officers stimulated this harmony of the people, and introduced them to the business there was to be done for *K*âu. The duke encouraged all to diligence, and made a great announcement about the performance (of the works).]

1. The king speaks to this effect:—'Head of the princes[1], and my younger brother[2], little one[2], Făng, it was your greatly distinguished father, the king Wăn, who was able to illustrate his virtue and be careful in the use of punishments. He did not dare to treat with contempt (even) wifeless men and widows. He employed the employable, and revered the reverend; he was terrible to those who needed to be awed:—so getting distinction among the people. It was thus he laid the foundations of (the sway of) our small portion of the kingdom[3], and the one

[1] Făng had, no doubt, been made chief or leader of all the feudal lords in one of the *K*âu or provinces of the kingdom.

[2] The duke of *K*âu, though speaking in the name of king *Kh*ăng, yet addresses Făng from the standpoint of his own relation to him.

[3] Referring to the original principality of *K*âu.

or two (neighbouring) regions were brought under his improving influence, until throughout our western land all placed in him their reliance. The fame of him ascended up to the high God, and God approved. Heaven accordingly gave a grand charge to king Wăn, to exterminate the great (dynasty of) Yin, and grandly receive its appointment, so that the various countries belonging to it and their peoples were brought to an orderly condition.* Then your unworthy elder brother[1] exerted himself; and thus it is that you Făng, the little one, are here in this eastern region.'

2. The king says, 'Oh! Făng, bear these things in mind. Now (your success in the management of) the people will depend on your reverently following your father Wăn;—do you carry out his virtuous words which you have heard, and clothe yourself with them. (Moreover), where you go, seek out among (the traces of) the former wise kings of Yin what you may use in protecting and regulating their people. (Again), you must in the remote distance study the (ways of) the old accomplished men of Shang, that you may establish your heart, and know how to instruct (the people). (Further still), you must search out besides what is to be learned of the wise kings of antiquity, and employ it in tranquillizing and protecting the people. (Finally), enlarge (your thoughts) to (the comprehension of all) heavenly (principles), and virtue will be richly displayed in your person, so that you will not render nugatory the king's charge.'

---

[1] Is it strange that the duke should thus speak of king Wû? Should we not think the better of him for it?

The king says, 'Oh! Făng, the little one, be respectfully careful, as if you were suffering from a disease. Awful though Heaven be, it yet helps the sincere.* The feelings of the people can for the most part be discerned; but it is difficult to preserve (the attachment of) the lower classes. Where you go, employ all your heart. Do not seek repose, nor be fond of ease and pleasure. I have read the saying,—"Dissatisfaction is caused not so much by great things, or by small things, as by (a ruler's) observance of principle or the reverse, and by his energy of conduct or the reverse." Yes, it is yours, O little one,—it is your business to enlarge the royal (influence), and to protect the people of Yin in harmony with their feelings. Thus also shall you assist the king, consolidating the appointment of Heaven, and renovating the people.' *

3. The king says, 'Oh! Făng, deal reverently and intelligently in your infliction of punishments. When men commit small crimes, which are not mischances, but purposed, they of themselves doing what is contrary to the laws intentionally, though their crimes be but small, you may not but put them to death. But in the case of great crimes, which were not purposed, but from mischance and misfortune, accidental, if the transgressors confess their guilt without reserve, you must not put them to death.'

The king says, 'Oh! Făng, there must be the orderly regulation (of this matter). When you show a great discrimination, subduing (men's hearts), the people will admonish one another, and strive to be obedient. (Deal firmly yet tenderly with evil), as if it were a disease in your own person, and the people will entirely put away their faults. (Deal with them) as if you were protecting your own infants, and the people will be tranquil and orderly. It is not you, O Făng, who (can presume to) inflict a (severe) punishment or death upon a man;—do not, to please yourself, so punish a man or put him to death.' Moreover, he says, 'It is not you, O Făng, who (can presume to inflict a lighter punishment), cutting off a man's nose or ears;—do not, to please yourself, cause a man's nose or ears to be cut off.'

The king says, 'In things beyond (your immediate supervision), have laws set forth which the officers may observe, and these should be the penal laws of Yin which were rightly ordered.' He also says, 'In examining the evidence in (criminal) cases, reflect upon it for five or six days, yea, for ten days or three months. You may then boldly come to a decision in such cases [1].'

The king says, 'In setting forth the business of the laws, the punishments will be determined by (what were) the regular laws of Yin. But you must see that those punishments, and (especially) the penalty of death, be righteous. And you must not let them be warped to agree with your own inclinations, O Făng. Then shall they be entirely accordant with right, and you may say, "They are properly ordered;" yet you must say (at the same time), "Perhaps they are not yet entirely accordant with right." Yes, though you are the little one, who has a heart like you, O Făng? My heart and my virtue are also known to you.

[1] This is supposed to refer to a case where guilt would involve death, so that there could be no remedying a wrong decision.

'All who of themselves commit crimes, robbing, stealing, practising villainy and treachery, and who kill men or violently assault them to take their property, being reckless and fearless of death;—these are abhorred by all.'

The king says, 'O Făng, such great criminals are greatly abhorred, and how much more (detestable) are the unfilial and unbrotherly!—as the son who does not reverently discharge his duty to his father, but greatly wounds his father's heart, and the father who can (no longer) love his son, but hates him; as the younger brother who does not think of the manifest will of Heaven, and refuses to respect his elder brother, and the elder brother who does not think of the toil of their parents in bringing up their children, and is very unfriendly to his junior. If we who are charged with government do not treat parties who proceed to such wickedness as offenders, the laws (of our nature) given by Heaven to our people will be thrown into great disorder and destroyed. You must resolve to deal speedily with such according to the penal laws of king Wăn, punishing them severely and not pardoning.

'Those who are disobedient (to natural principles) are to be thus subjected to the laws;—how much more the officers employed in your state as the instructors of the youth, the heads of the official departments, and the smaller officers charged with their several commissions, when they propagate other lessons, seeking the praise of the people, not thinking (of their duty), nor using (the rules for their offices), but distressing their ruler! These lead on (the people) to wickedness, and are an abomination to me. Shall they be let alone? Do you speedily, according to what is right, put them to death.

'And you will be yourself ruler and president;—if you cannot manage your own household, with your smaller officers, and the heads of departments in the state, but use only terror and violence, you will greatly set aside the royal charge, and be trying to regulate your state contrary to virtue. You must in everything reverence the statutes, and proceed by them to the happy rule of the people. There were the reverence of king Wăn and his caution;—in proceeding by them to the happy rule of the people, say, "If I could only attain to them—." So will you make me, the One man, to rejoice.'

4. The king says, 'O Făng, when I think clearly of the people, I see that they should be led (by example) to happiness and tranquillity. I think of the virtue of the former wise kings of Yin, whereby they tranquillized and regulated the people, and rouse myself to make it my own. Moreover, the people now are sure to follow a leader. If one do not lead them, he cannot be said to exercise a government in their state.'

The king says, 'O Făng, I cannot dispense with the inspection (of the ancients), and I make this declaration to you about virtue in the use of punishments. Now the people are not quiet; they have not yet stilled their minds; notwithstanding my leading of them, they have not come to accord (with my government). I clearly consider that severe as are the inflictions of Heaven on me, I dare not murmur. The crimes (of the people), though they were not great or many, (would all be chargeable on me), and how much more shall this be said when the report of them goes up so manifestly to heaven!'

The king says, 'Oh! Făng, be reverent! Do not what will cause murmurings; and do not use bad counsels and uncommon ways. With the determination of sincerity, give yourself to imitate the active virtue (of the ancients). Hereby give repose to your mind, examine your virtue, send far forward your plans; and thus by your generous forbearance you will make the people repose in what is good, and I shall not have to blame you or cast you off.'

5. The king says, 'Oh! you, Făng, the little one, (Heaven's) appointments are not unchanging.* Think of this, and do not make me deprive you of your dignity. Make illustrious the charge which you have received; exalt (the instructions) which you have heard, and tranquillize and regulate the people accordingly.'

The king speaks to this effect: 'Go, Făng. Do not disregard the statutes you should reverence; hearken to what I have told you;—so shall you among the people of Yin enjoy (your dignity), and hand it down to your posterity.'

BOOK X.

THE ANNOUNCEMENT ABOUT DRUNKENNESS.

THIS Announcement was, like the last, made to Făng, the prince of Khang, about the time when he was invested with the principality of Wei. Mention has often been made in previous documents of the Shû of the drunken debauchery of *K*ieh as the chief cause of the downfal of the dynasty of Hsiâ, and of the same vice in *K*âu-hsin, the last of the kings of

Shang. The people of Shang had followed the example of their sovereign, and drunkenness, with its attendant immoralities, characterised both the highest and lowest classes of society. One of Făng's most difficult tasks in his administration would be, to correct this evil habit, and he is called in this Book to the undertaking. He is instructed in the proper use and the allowable uses of spirits ; the disastrous consequences of drunkenness are set forth ; and he is summoned to roll back the flood of its desolation from his officers and people.

I have divided the Book into two chapters :—the one preliminary, showing the original use and the permissible uses of ardent spirits ; the other, showing how drunkenness had proved the ruin of the Shang dynasty, and how they of *K*âu, and particularly Făng in Wei, should turn the lesson to account.

The title might be translated—'The Announcement about Spirits,' but the cursory reader would most readily suppose that the discourse was about Spiritual Beings. The Chinese term *K*iû, that is here employed, is often translated by wine, but it denotes, it seems to me, ardent spirits. As Gaubil says, 'We have here to do with le vin du riz, the art of which was discovered, according to most writers, in the time of Yü, the founder of the first dynasty. The grape was not introduced to China till that of the first Han.'

[Since the above sentences were in manuscript, the Rev. Dr. Edkins of Pekin has stated at a meeting of the North-China branch of the Royal Asiatic Society, and in a letter to myself (April 24th), that he has lately investigated the question whether the *K*iû of the ancient Chinese was spirits or not, and found that distillation was first known in China in the Mongol or Yüan dynasty (A.D. 1280–1367), so that the Arabs must have the credit of the invention ; that the process in making *K*iû was brewing, or nearly so, but, as the term beer is inadmissible in a translation of the classics, he would prefer to use the term wine ; and that *K*iû with Shâo ('fired,' 'ardent') before it, means spirits, but without Shâo, it means wine.

If the whole process of Dr. Edkins' investigation were before me, I should be glad to consider it, and not hesitate to alter my own view, if I saw reason to do so. Meanwhile, what he says makes me glad that I adopted 'the Announcement about Drunkenness' as the title of this chapter. It is drunkenness, by whatever liquor occasioned, that the king of *K*âu condemns and denounces.

What we commonly understand by wine is never intended by *K*iû in the Chinese classics, and therefore I cannot use that term. After searching as extensively as I could do in this country, since I received Dr. Edkins' letter, I have found nothing to make me think that the Chinese term is not properly translated by 'spirits.'

Dr. Williams, in his Syllabic Dictionary of the Chinese Language (Shanghai, 1874), gives this account of *K*iû :—'Liquor; it includes spirits, wine, beer, and other drinks. The Chinese make no wine, and chiefly distil their liquors, and say that Tû Khang, a woman of the Tî tribes, first made it.' This account is to a considerable extent correct. The Chinese distil their liquors. I never saw beer or porter of native production among them, though according to Dr. Edkins they had been brewing 'or nearly so' for more than 3000 years. Among his examples of the use of *K*iû, Williams gives the combinations of 'red *K*iû' for claret, 'white *K*iû' for sherry, and 'pî (simply phonetical) *K*iû' for beer, adding that they 'are all terms of foreign origin.' What he says about the traditional account of the first maker of *K*iû is not correct. It is said certainly that this was Tû Khang, but who he was, or when he lived, I have never been able to discover. Some identify him with Î-tî, said by Williams to have been 'a woman of the Tî tribes.' The attributing of the invention to Î-tî is probably an independent tradition. We find it in the 'Plans of the Warring States' (ch. xiv, art. 10), a work covering about four centuries from the death of Confucius :—'Anciently, the daughter of the Tî ordered Î-tî to make *K*iû. She admired it, and presented some to Yü, who drank it, and found it pleasant. He then discarded Î-tî, and denounced the use of such generous *K*iû, saying, "In future ages there are sure to be those who by *K*iû will lose their states."' According to this tradition intoxicating *K*iû was known in the time of Yü—in the twenty-third century B.C. The daughter of the Tî would be Yü's wife, and Î-tî would probably be their cook. It does not appear as the name of a woman, or one from the wild Tî tribes.

With regard to the phrase Shâo *K*iû, said to be the proper term for ardent spirits, and unknown in China till the Yüan dynasty, a reference to the Khang-hsî Tonic Thesaurus of the language will show instances of its use as early at least as the Thang dynasty (A.D. 618–906).]

1. The king speaks to the following effect :—'Do

you clearly make known my great commands in the country of Mei[1].

'When your reverent father, the king Wăn, laid the foundations of our kingdom in the western region, he delivered announcements and cautions to (the princes of) the various regions, and to all his (high) officers, with their assistants, and the managers of affairs, saying, morning and evening, "At sacrifices spirits should be employed." * When Heaven was sending down its favouring decree, and laying the foundations of (the eminence of) our people, (spirits) were used only at the great sacrifices. When Heaven sends down its terrors, and our people are thereby greatly disorganized and lose their virtue, this may be traced invariably to their indulgence in spirits; yea, the ruin of states, small and great, (by these terrors), has been caused invariably by their guilt in the use of spirits[2].

---

[1] There is a place called 'the village of Mei,' in the north of the present district of *Kh*î, department Wei-hui, Ho-nan;—a relic of the ancient name of the whole territory. The royal domain of Shang, north from the capital, was all called Mei. Făng's principality of Wei must have embraced most of it.

[2] Kû Hsî says upon the meaning of the expressions 'Heaven was sending down its favouring decree' (its order to make *K*iû, as he understood the language), and 'when Heaven sends down its terrors,' in this paragraph:—'*K*ang Nan-hsien has brought out the meaning of these two statements much better than any of the critics who went before him, to the following effect:—*K*iû is a thing intended to be used in offering sacrifices and in entertaining guests;—such employment of it is what Heaven has prescribed. But men by their abuse of *K*iû come to lose their virtue, and destroy their persons;—such employment of it is what Heaven has annexed its terrors to. The Buddhists, hating the use of things where Heaven sends down its terrors, put away as well the use of them which Heaven has prescribed. It is not so with us of the learned (i. e. the Confucian or orthodox) school;—we only put

'King Wăn admonished and instructed the young nobles, who were charged with office or in any employment, that they should not ordinarily use spirits; and throughout all the states, he required that such should drink spirits only on occasion of sacrifices, and that then virtue should preside so that there might be no drunkenness [1].'

He said, 'Let my people teach their young men that they are to love only the productions of the soil, for so will their hearts be good. Let the young also hearken wisely to the constant instructions of their fathers; and let them look at all virtuous actions, whether great or small, in the same light (with watchful heed).

'(Ye people of) the land of Mei, if you can employ your limbs, largely cultivating your millets, and hastening about in the service of your fathers and elders; and if, with your carts and oxen, you traffic diligently to a distance, that you may thereby filially minister to your parents; then, when your parents are happy, you may set forth your spirits clear and strong, and use them [2].

'Hearken constantly to my instructions, all ye my (high) officers and ye heads of departments, all ye, my noble chiefs;—when ye have largely done your

---

away the use of things to which Heaven has annexed its terrors, and the use of them, of which it approves, remains as a matter of course.'

[1] In sacrificing, the fragrant odour of spirits was supposed to be acceptable to the Beings worshipped. Here the use of spirits seems to be permitted in moderation to the worshippers after the sacrifices. Observe how king Wăn wished to guard the young from acquiring the habit of drinking spirits.

[2] Here is another permissible use of spirits;—at family feasts, with a view especially to the comfort of the aged.

duty in ministering to your aged, and serving your ruler, ye may eat and drink freely and to satiety. And to speak of greater things:—when you can maintain a constant, watchful examination of yourselves, and your conduct is in accordance with correct virtue, then may you present the offerings of sacrifice,* and at the same time indulge yourselves in festivity. In such case you will indeed be ministers doing right service to your king, and Heaven likewise will approve your great virtue, so that you shall never be forgotten in the royal House.' *

2. The king says, 'O Făng, in our western region, the princes of states, and the young (nobles), sons of the managers of affairs, who in former days assisted king Wăn, were all able to obey his lessons, and abstain from excess in the use of spirits; and so it is that I have now received the appointment which belonged to Yin.'

The king says, 'O Făng, I have heard it said, that formerly the first wise king of Yin manifested a reverential awe of the bright principles of Heaven and of the lower people, acting accordingly, steadfast in his virtue, and holding fast his wisdom.* From him, Thang the Successful, down to Tî-yî[1], all completed their royal virtue and revered their chief ministers, so that their managers of affairs respectfully discharged their helping duties, and dared not to allow themselves in idleness and pleasure;—how much less would they dare to indulge themselves in drinking! Moreover, in the exterior domains, (the princes of) the Hâu, Tien,

[1] Tî-yî was the father of *K*âu-hsin, the twenty-seventh Shang sovereign. The sovereigns between Thang and him had not all been good, but the duke of *K*âu chooses here to say so.

Nan, and Wei (states)[1], with their presiding chiefs; and in the interior domain, all the various officers, the directors of the several departments, the inferior officers and employés, the heads of great houses, and the men of distinguished name living in retirement, all eschewed indulgence in spirits. Not only did they not dare to indulge in them, but they had not leisure to do so, being occupied with helping to complete the sovereign's virtue and make it more illustrious, and helping the directors of affairs reverently to attend to his service.

'I have heard it said likewise, that the last successor of those kings was addicted to drink, so that no charges came from him brightly before the people, and he was (as if) reverently and unchangingly bent on doing and cherishing what provoked resentment. Greatly abandoned to extraordinary lewdness and dissipation, for pleasure's sake he sacrificed all his majesty. The people were all sorely grieved and wounded in heart; but he gave himself wildly up to drink, not thinking of restraining himself, but continuing his excess, till his mind was frenzied, and he had no fear of death. His crimes (accumulated) in the capital of Shang; and though the extinction of the dynasty (was imminent), this gave him no concern, and he wrought not that any sacrifices of fragrant virtue might ascend to Heaven.* The rank odour of the people's resentments, and the drunkenness of his herd of creatures, went loudly up on high, so that Heaven sent down ruin on Yin,

[1] These were the first, second, third, and fifth domains or territorial divisions of the land under *K*âu, counting back from the royal domain. It appears here that an arrangement akin to that of *K*âu had been made in the time of Shang.

and showed no love for it,—because of such excesses. There is not any cruel oppression of Heaven; people themselves accelerate their guilt, (and its punishment.)' *

The king says, 'O Făng, I make you this long announcement, not (for the pleasure of doing so); but the ancients have said, "Let not men look into water; let them look into the glass of other people." Now that Yin has lost its appointment, ought we not to look much to it as our glass, (and learn) how to secure the repose of our time? I say to you,—Strenuously warn the worthy ministers of Yin, and (the princes) in the Hâu, the Tien, the Nan, and the Wei domains; and still more your friends, the great Recorder and the Recorder of the Interior, and all your worthy ministers, the heads of great Houses; and still more those whom you serve, with whom you calmly discuss matters, and who carry out your measures; and still more those who are, as it were, your mates,—your Minister of War who deals with the rebellious, your Minister of Instruction who is like a protector to the people, and your Minister of Works who settles the boundaries; and above all, do you strictly keep yourself from drink.

'If you are informed that there are companies that drink together, do not fail to apprehend them all, and send them here to *K*âu, where I may put them to death. As to the ministers and officers of Yin who were led to it and became addicted to drink, it is not necessary to put them to death (at once);—let them be taught for a time. If they follow these (lessons of mine), I will give them bright distinction. If they disregard my lessons, then I, the One man, will show them no pity. As they cannot change their way, they shall be classed with those who are to be put to death.'

The king says, 'O Făng, give constant heed to my admonitions. If you do not rightly manage the officers, the people will continue lost in drunkenness.'

Book XI. The Timber of the Rottlera.

'The wood of the 3ze tree'—the Rottlera Japonica, according to Dr. Williams—is mentioned in the Book, and was adopted as the name for it. The 3ze was esteemed a very valuable tree for making articles of furniture and for the carver's art. The title perhaps intimates that the administrator of government ought to go about his duties carefully and skilfully, as the cabinet-maker and carver deal with their materials.

The Book is wanting in unity. Divided into two chapters, the first may be taken as a charge to 'the prince of Khang.' He is admonished of his duty to promote a good understanding between the different classes in his state, and between them all and the sovereign; and that, in order to this, his rule must be gentle, eschewing the use of punishments. The second chapter is of a different character, containing not the charges of a sovereign, but the admonitions or counsels of a minister, loyally cautioning him, and praying for the prosperity of his reign. We might suppose them the response of Făng to the previous charge, but the text does not indicate the introduction of a new speaker.

1. The king says, 'O Făng, to secure a good understanding between the multitudes of his people and his ministers (on the one hand), and the great families (on the other); and (again) to secure the same between all the subjects under his charge, and the sovereign:—is the part of the ruler of a state.

'If you regularly, in giving out your orders, say, "My instructors whom I am to follow, my Minister of Instruction, my Minister of War, and my Minister of Works; my heads of departments, and all ye, my officers, I will on no account put any to death oppressively[1]"—. Let the ruler also set the example of respecting and encouraging (the people), and these will (also) proceed to respect and encourage them. Then let him go on, in dealing with villainy and treachery, with murderers and harbourers of criminals, to exercise clemency (where it can be done), and these will likewise do the same with those who have assaulted others and injured their property. When sovereigns appointed overseers (of states), they did so in order to the government of the people, and said to them, "Do not give way to violence or oppression, but go on to show reverent regard for the friendless, and find helping connexions for (destitute) women[2]." Deal with all according to this method, and cherish them. And when sovereigns gave their injunctions to the rulers of states, and their managers of affairs, what was their charge? It was that they should lead (the people) to the enjoyment of plenty and peace. Such was the way of the kings from of old. An overseer is to eschew the use of punishments.'

(The king) says, 'As in the management of a field, when the soil has been all laboriously turned up, they have to proceed by orderly arrangements to make its boundaries and water-courses; as in building a house, after all the toil on its walls, they have to plaster and thatch it; as in working with the wood of the rottlera, when the toil of the coarser and finer operations has been completed, they have

[1] The sentence here is incomplete. Many of the critics confess that the text is unintelligible to them.

[2] It is difficult to say what the exact meaning here is.

to apply the paint of red and other colours;—(so do you finish for me the work which I have begun in the state of Wei.)'

2. Now let your majesty say, 'The former kings diligently employed their illustrious virtue, and produced such attachment by their cherishing (of the princes), that from all the states they brought offerings, and came with brotherly affection from all quarters, and likewise showed their virtue illustrious. Do you, O sovereign, use their methods to attach (the princes), and all the states will largely come with offerings. Great Heaven having given this Middle Kingdom with its people and territories to the former kings, do you, our present sovereign, display your virtue, effecting a gentle harmony among the deluded people, leading and urging them on;—so (also) will you comfort the former kings, who received the appointment (from Heaven).*

'Yes, make these things your study. I say so simply from my wish that (your dynasty) may continue for myriads of years, and your descendants always be the protectors of the people.'

BOOK XII.

THE ANNOUNCEMENT OF THE DUKE OF SHÂO.

SHÂO was the name of a territory within the royal domain, corresponding to the present district of Hwan-*kh*ü, *K*iang *K*âu, Shan-hsî. It was the appanage of Shih, one of the ablest of the men who lent their aid to the establishment of the dynasty of *K*âu. He appears in this book as the Grand-Guardian at the court of king *Kh*ăng, and we have met with him before in the Hounds of Lü and the Metal-bound Coffer. He is introduced here in connexion with one of the most important enterprises of the duke of *K*âu, the building of the city of Lo, not very far from the present city of Lo-yang, in Ho-nan, as a new and central capital of the kingdom. King Wû had conceived the idea of such a city; but it was not carried into effect till the reign of his son, and is commonly assigned to *Kh*ăng's seventh year, in B.C. 1109.

Shih belonged to the royal House, and of course had the surname *K*î. He is styled the duke of Shâo, as being one of the 'three dukes,' or three highest officers of the court, and also the chief of Shâo, all the country west of Shen being under him, as all the east of it was under the duke of *K*âu. He was invested by Wû with the principality of 'the Northern Yen,' corresponding to the present department of Shun-thien, *K*ih-lî, which was held by his descendants fully nine hundred years. It was in Lo—while the building of it was proceeding—that he composed this Book, and sent it by the hands of the duke of *K*âu to their young sovereign.

The whole may be divided into three chapters. The first contains various information about the arrangements for the building of Lo, first by the duke of Shâo, and then by the duke of *K*âu; and about the particular occasion when the former recited the counsels which he had composed, that they might be made known to the king. These form the second chapter. First, it sets forth the uncertainty of the favour of Heaven, and urges the king to cultivate the 'virtue of reverence,' in order to secure its permanence, and that he should not neglect his aged and experienced ministers. It speaks next of the importance and difficulty of the royal duties, and enforces the same virtue of reverence by reference to the rise and fall of the previous dynasties. Lastly, it sets forth the importance, at this early period of his reign, of the king's at once setting about the reverence which was thus described. There is a concluding chapter, where the duke gives expression to his loyal and personal feelings for the king, and the purpose to be served by the offerings, which he was then sending to the court.

The burden of the Announcement is 'the virtue of reverence.' Let the king only feel how much depended on his attending reverently to his duties, and all would be well. The people would love and support the dynasty of *K*âu, and Heaven would smile upon and sustain it.

1. In the second month, on the day Yî-wei, six days after full moon, the king proceeded in the morning from *K*âu to Făng[1]. (Thence) the Grand-Guardian went before the duke of *K*âu to survey the locality (of the new capital); and in the third month, on the day Wû-shăn, the third day after the first appearance of the moon on Ping-wû, he came in the morning to Lo. He divined by the tortoise-shell about the (several) localities, and having obtained favourable indications, he set about laying out the plan (of the city).* On Kăng-hsü, the third day after, he led the people of Yin to prepare the various sites on the north of the Lo; and this work was completed on *K*iâ-yin, the fifth day after.

On Yî-mâo, the day following, the duke of *K*âu came in the morning to Lo, and thoroughly inspected the plan of the new city. On Ting-sze, the third day after, he offered two bulls as victims in the (northern and southern) suburbs[2]; and on the morrow, Wû-wû, at the altar to the spirit of the land in the new city, he sacrificed a bull, a ram, and a boar.* After seven days, on *K*iâ-ȝze, in the morning, from his written (specifications) he gave their several orders to the people of Yin, and to the presiding chiefs of the princes from the Hâu, Tien, and Nan domains. When the people of Yin had thus received their orders, they arose and entered with vigour on their work.

(When the work was drawing to a completion),

---

[1] That is, from Wû's capital of Hâo to king Wăn's at Făng.

[2] By the addition to the text here of 'northern and southern,' I intimate my opinion that the duke of *K*âu offered two sacrifices, one to Heaven at the altar in the southern suburb, and one to Earth in the northern suburb.

the Grand-Guardian went out with the hereditary princes of the various states to bring their offerings (for the king)[1]; and when he entered again, he gave them to the duke of *K*âu, saying, 'With my hands to my head and my head to the ground, I present these to his Majesty and your Grace[2]. Announcements for the information of the multitudes of Yin must come from you, with whom is the management of affairs.'

2. 'Oh! God (dwelling in) the great heavens has changed his decree respecting his great son and the great dynasty of Yin. Our king has received that decree. Unbounded is the happiness connected with it, and unbounded is the anxiety:—Oh! how can he be other than reverent?*

'When Heaven rejected and made an end of the decree in favour of the great dynasty of Yin, there were many of its former wise kings in heaven.* The king, however, who had succeeded to them, the last of his race, from the time of his entering into their appointment, proceeded in such a way as at last to keep the wise in obscurity and the vicious in office. The poor people in such a case, carrying their children and leading their wives, made their moan to Heaven. They even fled away, but were apprehended again. Oh! Heaven had compassion on the people of the four quarters; its favouring

---

[1] These 'offerings' were the 'presents of introduction,' which the feudal princes brought with them to court, when they were to have audience of the king. This has led many critics to think that the king was now in Lo, which was not the case.

[2] The original text here is difficult and remarkable;—intended probably to indicate that the king's majesty was revered in the person of the duke of *K*âu, who was regent.

decree lighted on our earnest (founders). Let the king sedulously cultivate the virtue of reverence.*

'Examining the men of antiquity, there was the (founder of the) Hsiâ dynasty. Heaven guided (his mind), allowed his descendants (to succeed him), and protected them.* He acquainted himself with Heaven, and was obedient to it. But in process of time the decree in his favour fell to the ground.* So also is it now when we examine the case of Yin. There was the same guiding (of its founder), who corrected (the errors of Hsiâ), and (whose descendants) enjoyed the protection (of Heaven). He (also) acquainted himself with Heaven, and was obedient to it.* But now the decree in favour of him has fallen to the ground. Our king has now come to the throne in his youth;—let him not slight the aged and experienced, for it may be said of them that they have studied the virtuous conduct of the ancients, and have matured their counsels in the sight of Heaven.

'Oh! although the king is young, yet he is the great son (of God).* Let him effect a great harmony with the lower people, and that will be the blessing of the present time. Let not the king presume to be remiss in this, but continually regard and stand in awe of the perilous (uncertainty) of the people's (attachment).

'Let the king come here as the vice-gerent of God, and undertake (the duties of government) in this centre of the land.* Tan[1] said, "Now that this great city has been built, from henceforth he may

[1] Tan was the name of the duke of *K*âu, and his brother duke here refers to him by it, in accordance with the rule that 'ministers

be the mate of great Heaven, and reverently sacrifice to (the spirits) above and beneath; from henceforth he may from this central spot administer successful government." Thus shall the king enjoy the favouring regard (of Heaven) all-complete, and the government of the people will now be prosperous.*

'Let the king first subdue to himself those who were the managers of affairs under Yin, associating them with the managers of affairs for our *K*âu. This will regulate their (perverse) natures, and they will make daily advancement. Let the king make reverence the resting-place (of his mind);—he must maintain the virtue of reverence.

'We should by all means survey the dynasties of Hsiâ and Yin. I do not presume to know and say, "The dynasty of Hsiâ was to enjoy the favouring decree of Heaven just for (so many) years," nor do I presume to know and say, "It could not continue longer." * The fact simply was, that, for want of the virtue of reverence, the decree in its favour prematurely fell to the ground. (Similarly), I do not presume to know and say, "The dynasty of Yin was to enjoy the favouring decree of Heaven just for (so many) years," nor do I presume to know and say, "It could not continue longer." * The fact simply was, that, for want of the virtue of reverence, the decree in its favour fell prematurely to the ground. The king has now inherited the decree,—the same decree, I consider, which belonged to those two dynasties. Let him seek to inherit (the virtues

should be called by their names in the presence of the sovereign.' King *Kh*ăng, indeed, was not now really present in Lo, but he was represented by his uncle, the regent.

of) their meritorious (sovereigns);—(let him do this especially) at this commencement of his duties.

'Oh! it is as on the birth of a son, when all depends on (the training of) his early life, through which he may secure his wisdom in the future, as if it were decreed to him. Now Heaven may have decreed wisdom (to the king); it may have decreed good fortune or bad; it may have decreed a (long) course of years;—we only know that now is with him the commencement of his duties. Dwelling in this new city, let the king now sedulously cultivate the virtue of reverence. When he is all-devoted to this virtue, he may pray to Heaven for a long-abiding decree in his favour.*

'In the position of king, let him not, because of the excesses of the people in violation of the laws, presume also to rule by the violent infliction of death;—when the people are regulated gently, the merit (of government) is seen. It is for him who is in the position of king to overtop all with his virtue. In this case the people will imitate him throughout the kingdom, and he will become still more illustrious.

'Let the king and his ministers labour with a mutual sympathy, saying, "We have received the decree of Heaven, and it shall be great as the long-continued years of Hsiâ;—yea, it shall not fail of the long-continued years of Yin." I wish the king, through (the attachment of) the lower people, to receive the long-abiding decree of Heaven.'*

3. (The duke of Shâo) then did obeisance with his hands to his head and his head to the ground, and said, 'I, a small minister, presume, with the king's (heretofore) hostile people and all their officers, and

with his (loyal) friendly people, to maintain and receive his majesty's dread command and brilliant virtue. That the king should finally obtain the decree all-complete, and that he should become illustrious,—this I do not presume to labour for. I only bring respectfully these offerings to present to his majesty, to be used in his prayers to Heaven for its long-abiding decree.' *

Book XIII. The Announcement concerning Lo.

The matters recorded in this Book are all connected, more or less nearly, with Lo, the new capital, the arrangements for the building of which are related at the commencement of the last Book. According to the summary of the contents given by the commentator 3hâi *Kh*ăn, 'The arrangements for the building having been made, the duke of *K*âu sent a messenger to inform the king of the result of his divinations. The historiographer recorded this as the Announcement about Lo, and at the same time related a dialogue between the king and his minister, and how the king charged the duke to remain at Lo, and conduct the government of it.' Passing over the commencing paragraph, which I have repeated here from the ninth Book, 3hâi divides all the rest into seven chapters. Ch. 1 contains the duke's message concerning his divinations; and the next gives the king's reply. Ch. 3 is occupied with instructions to the king about the measures which he should pursue on taking up his residence at Lo. In ch. 4, the king charges the duke to remain at Lo, and undertake its government. In ch. 5, the duke responds, and accepts the charge, dwelling on the duties which the king and himself would have to perform. Ch. 6 relates the action of the duke in reference to a message and gift from the king intended for his special honour. In ch. 7, the historiographer writes of sacrifices offered by the king in Lo, and a proclamation that he issued, and tells how long the duke continued in his government;—showing how the duke began the city and completed it, and how king *Kh*ăng, after offering the sacrifices and inaugurating the government, returned to Hâo, and did not, after all, make his capital at Lo.

Many critics make much to do about the want of historical order in the Book, and suppose that portions have been lost, and other portions transposed; but the Book may be explained without resorting to so violent a supposition.

[In the third month, when the moon began to wane, the duke of *K*âu commenced the foundations and proceeded to build the new great city of Lo of the eastern states. The people from every quarter assembled in great harmony. From the Hâu, Tien, Nan, ʒhâi, and Wei domains, the various officers stimulated this harmony of the people, and introduced them to the business that was to be done for *K*âu. The duke encouraged all to diligence, and made a great announcement about the performance (of the works)[1].]

1. The duke of *K*âu did obeisance with his hands to his head and his head to the ground[2], saying, 'Herewith I report (the execution of my commission) to my son, my intelligent sovereign. The king appeared as if he would not presume to be present at Heaven's founding here the appointment (of our dynasty), and fixing it, whereupon I followed the (Grand-)Guardian, and made a great survey of this eastern region, hoping to found the place where he should become the intelligent sovereign of the people. On the day Yî-mâo, I came in the morning to this capital of Lo. I (first) divined by the shell concerning (the ground about) the Lî-water on the north of the Ho. I then divined concerning the east of the *K*ien-water, and the west of the *Kh*an, when the (ground near the) Lo was indicated. Again

[1] See the introductory note to Book ix.

[2] In sending his message to the king, the duke does obeisance as if he were in the presence of his majesty. The king responds with a similar ceremony.

I divined concerning the east of the *Kh*an-water, when the (ground near the) Lo was also indicated. I (now) send a messenger with a map, and to present the (result of the) divinations.' *

2. The king did obeisance with his hands to his head and his head to the ground, saying, 'The duke did not presume not to acknowledge reverently the favour of Heaven, and has surveyed the locality where our *K*âu may respond to that favour. Having settled the locality, he has sent his messenger to show me the divinations, favourable and always auspicious. We two must together sustain the responsibility. He has made provision for me (and my successors), for myriads and tens of myriads of years, there reverently to acknowledge the favour of Heaven.* With my hands to my head and my head to the ground, (I receive) his instructive words.'

3. The duke of *K*âu said[1], 'Let the king at first employ the ceremonies of Yin, and sacrifice in the new city,* doing everything in an orderly way, but without display. I will marshal all the officers to attend you from *K*âu, merely saying that probably there will be business to be done (in sacrificing). Let the king instantly issue an order to the effect that the most meritorious (ministers) shall have the first place in the sacrifices; and let him also say in an order, "You, in whose behalf the above order is issued, must give me your assistance with sincere earnestness." Truly display the record of merits, for

[1] We must suppose that the duke of *K*âu, after receiving the reply to his message, had himself returned to Hâo, to urge upon the king the importance of his repairing in person to Lo, and solemnly inaugurating the new city as the capital of the kingdom.

it is you who must in everything teach the officers. My young son, can you indulge partiality? Eschew it, my young son. (If you do not), the consequence hereafter will be like a fire, which, a spark at first, blazes up, and by and by cannot be extinguished. Let your observance of the constant rules of right, and your soothing measures be like mine. Take only the officers that are in *K*âu with you to the new city, and make them there join their (old) associates, with intelligent vigour establishing their merit, and with a generous largeness (of soul) completing (the public manners);—so shall you obtain an endless fame.'

The duke said, 'Yes, young as you are, be it yours to complete (the work of your predecessors). Cultivate (the spirit of) reverence, and you will know who among the princes (sincerely) present their offerings to you, and who do not. In connexion with those offerings there are many observances. If the observances are not equal to the articles, it must be held that there is no offering. When there is no service of the will in the offerings (of the princes), all the people will then say, "We need not (be troubled about) our offerings," and affairs will be disturbed by errors and usurpations.

'Do you, my young son, manifest everywhere my unwearied diligence, and listen to my instructions to you how to help the people to observe the constant rules of right. If you do not bestir yourself in these things, you will not be of long continuance. If you sincerely and fully carry out the course of your Directing father, and follow exactly my example, there will be no venturing to disregard your orders. Go, and be reverent. Henceforth I will study husbandry [1]. There do you generously rule our people, and there is no distance from which they will not come to you.'

4. The king spoke to this effect [2], 'O duke, you are the enlightener and sustainer of my youth. You have set forth the great and illustrious virtues, that I, notwithstanding my youth, may display a brilliant merit like that of Wăn and Wû, reverently responding to the favouring decree of Heaven; and harmonize and long preserve the people of all the regions, settling the multitudes (in Lo); and that I may give due honour to the great ceremony (of recording) the most distinguished (for their merits), regulating the order for the first places at the sacrifices, and doing everything in an orderly manner without display.

'But your virtue, O duke, shines brightly above and beneath, and is displayed actively throughout the four quarters. On every hand appears the deep reverence (of your virtue) in securing the establishment of order, so that you fail in nothing of the earnest lessons of Wăn and Wû. It is for me, the youth, (only) to attend reverently, early and late, to the sacrifices.' *

The king said, 'Great, O duke, has been your merit in helping and guiding me;—let it ever continue so.'

---

[1] By this expression the duke indicates his wish and intention now to retire from public life, and leave the government and especially the affairs of Lo in the king's hands.

[2] From the words of the king in this chapter, we receive the impression that they were spoken in Lo. He must have gone there with the duke from Hâo. He deprecates the duke's intention to retire into private life; intimates his own resolution to return to Hâo; and wishes the duke to remain in Lo, accomplishing all that was still necessary to the establishment of their dynasty.

The king said, 'O duke, let me, the little child, return to my sovereignty in *K*âu, and I charge you, O duke, to remain behind (here). Order has been initiated throughout the four quarters of the kingdom, but the ceremonies to be honoured (by general observance) have not yet been settled, and I cannot look on your service as completed. Commence on a great scale what is to be done by your remaining here, setting an example to my officers and greatly preserving the people whom Wăn and Wû received; —by your good government you will be a help to the whole kingdom.'

The king said, 'Remain, O duke. I will certainly go. Your services are devoutly acknowledged and reverently rejoiced in. Do not, O duke, occasion me this difficulty. I on my part will not be weary in seeking the tranquillity (of the people);—do not let the example which you have afforded me be intermitted. So shall the kingdom enjoy for generations (the benefit of your virtue).'

5. The duke of *K*âu did obeisance with his hands to his head and his head to the ground, saying, 'You have charged me, O king, to come here. I undertake (the charge), and will protect the people whom your accomplished grandfather, and your glorious and meritorious father, king Wû, received by the decree (of Heaven). I will enlarge the reverence which I cherish for you. (But), my son, come (frequently), and inspect this settlement. Pay great honour to (old) statutes, and to the good and wise men of Yin. Good government (here) will make you (indeed) the new sovereign of the kingdom, and an example of (royal) respectfulness to all your successors of *K*âu.'

(The duke) proceeded to say, 'From this time, by the government administered in this central spot, all the states will be conducted to repose; and this will be the completion of your merit, O king.

'I, Tan, with the numerous officers and managers of affairs, will consolidate the achievements of our predecessors, in response to (the hopes of) the people. I will afford an example of sincerity to (future ministers of) *K*âu, seeking to render complete the pattern intended for the enlightenment of you, my son, and thus to carry fully out the virtue of your accomplished grandfather.'

6. (Afterwards, on the arrival of a message and gifts from the king, the duke said[1]), '(The king) has sent messengers to admonish (the people of) Yin, and with a soothing charge to me, along with two flagons of the black-millet herb-flavoured spirits, saying, "Here is a pure sacrificial gift, which with my hands to my head and my head to the ground I offer for you to enjoy its excellence!" * I dare not keep this by me, but offer it in sacrifice to king Wăn and king Wû.' (In doing so, he prayed), 'May he be obedient to, and observant of your course! Let him not bring on himself any evil or illness! Let him satisfy his descendants for myriads of years with your virtue! Let (the people of) Yin enjoy prolonged (prosperity)!'* (He also said to the messengers), 'The king has sent you to Yin,

[1] We must suppose that the king had returned to Hâo, and now sends a message to the duke with an extraordinary gift, doing honour to him as if he were a departed spirit, continuing in heaven the guardianship of the dynasty which he had so long efficiently discharged on earth. This gives occasion for the duke to exhibit anew his humility, piety, and loyalty.

and we have received his well-ordered charges, (sufficient to direct us) for myriads of years, but let (the people) ever (be able to) observe the virtue cherished by my son.'

7. On the day Wû-*kh*ăn, the king, being in the new city[1], performed the annual winter sacrifice, offering (moreover) one red bull to king Wăn and another to king Wû.* He then ordered a declaration to be prepared, which was done by Yî[2] in the form of a prayer, and it simply announced the remaining behind of the duke of *K*âu. The king's guests[3], on occasion of the killing of the victims and offering the sacrifice, were all present. The king entered the grand apartment, and poured out the libation.* He gave a charge to the duke of *K*âu to remain, and Yî, the preparer of the document, made the announcement;—in the twelfth month. (Thus) the duke of *K*âu grandly sustained the decree which Wăn and Wû had received through the space of seven years[4].

---

[1] The duke had asked the king to come frequently to the new city; he is there now accordingly.

[2] Yî was the name of the Recorder who officiated on the occasion.

[3] All the princes present and assisting at the sacrifices; and especially the representatives of the previous dynasties.

[4] These seven years are to be calculated from the seventh year of king *Kh*ăng, after the duke had served as administrator of the government seven years from the death of king Wû. Many think, however, that the 'seven years' are only those of the duke's regency.

Book XIV. The Numerous Officers.

We have in this Book another 'Announcement,' addressed to the people of Yin or Shang, and especially to the higher classes among them,—'the numerous officers,'—to reconcile them to their lot as subjects of the new dynasty. From the preceding two Books it appears that many of the people of Yin had been removed to the country about the Lo, before the dukes of Shâo and *K*âu commenced the building of the new city. Now that the city was completed, another and larger migration of them, we may suppose, was ordered, and the duke of *K*âu took occasion to issue the announcement that is here preserved.

I have divided it into four chapters. The first vindicates the kings of *K*âu for superseding the line of Shang, not from ambition, but in obedience to the will of God. The second unfolds the causes why the dynasty of Yin or Shang had been set aside. The third shows how it had been necessary to remove them to Lo, and with what good intention the new capital had been built. The fourth tells how comfort and prosperity were open to their attainment at Lo, while by perseverance in disaffection they would only bring misery and ruin upon themselves.

1. In the third month, at the commencement (of the government) of the duke of *K*âu in the new city of Lo, he announced (the royal will) to the officers of the Shang dynasty, saying, 'The king speaks to this effect:—"Ye numerous officers who remain from the dynasty of Yin, great ruin came down on Yin from the cessation of forbearance in compassionate Heaven, and we, the lords of *K*âu, received its favouring decree.* We felt charged with its bright terrors, carried out the punishments which kings inflict, rightly disposed of the appointment of Yin, and finished (the work of) God.* Now, ye numerous officers, it was not our small state that dared to aim at the appointment belonging to Yin. But Heaven was not with (Yin), for indeed it would not

strengthen its misrule. It (therefore) helped us;—did we dare to seek the throne of ourselves? God was not for (Yin), as appeared from the mind and conduct of our inferior people, in which there is the brilliant dreadfulness of Heaven."' *

2. 'I have heard the saying, "God leads men to tranquil security," * but the sovereign of Hsiâ would not move to such security, whereupon God sent down corrections, indicating his mind to him. (*K*ieh), however, would not be warned by God, but proceeded to greater dissoluteness and sloth and excuses for himself. Then Heaven no longer regarded nor heard him, but disallowed his great appointment, and inflicted extreme punishment. Then it charged your founder, Thang the Successful, to set Hsiâ aside, and by means of able men to rule the kingdom. From Thang the Successful down to Tî-yî, every sovereign sought to make his virtue illustrious, and duly attended to the sacrifices.* And thus it was that, while Heaven exerted a great establishing influence, preserving and regulating the House of Yin, its sovereigns on their part were humbly careful not to lose (the favour of) God, and strove to manifest a good-doing corresponding to that of Heaven.* But in these times, their successor showed himself greatly ignorant of (the ways of) Heaven, and much less could it be expected of him that he would be regardful of the earnest labours of his fathers for the country. Greatly abandoned to dissolute idleness, he gave no thought to the bright principles of Heaven, and the awfulness of the people.* On this account God no longer protected him, but sent down the great ruin which we have witnessed. Heaven was not with him, because he

did not make his virtue illustrious.* (Indeed), with regard to the overthrow of all states, great and small, throughout the four quarters of the kingdom, in every case reasons can be given for their punishment.'

'The king speaks to this effect:—"Ye numerous officers of Yin, the case now is this, that the kings of our *K*âu, from their great goodness, were charged with the work of God. There was the charge to them, 'Cut off Yin.' (They proceeded to perform it), and announced the execution of their service to God. In our affairs we have followed no double aims;—ye of the royal House (of Yin) must (now simply) follow us."' *

3. '"May I not say that you have been very lawless? I did not (want to) remove you. The thing came from your own city[1]. When I consider also how Heaven has drawn near to Yin with so great tribulations, it must be that there was (there) what was not right."

'The king says, "Ho! I declare to you, ye numerous officers, it is simply on account of these things that I have removed you and settled you here in the west[2];—it was not that I, the One man, considered it a part of my virtue to interfere with your tranquillity. The thing was from Heaven; do not offer resistance; I shall not presume to have any subsequent (charge concerning you); do not murmur against me. Ye know that your fathers of the Yin dynasty had their archives and statutes, (showing

[1] That is, your conduct in your own city.

[2] Lo is often called 'the eastern capital,' as being east from Hâo, the capital of king Wû; but it was west from *K*âo-ko, the capital of Yin.

how) Yin superseded the appointment of Hsiâ. Now, indeed, ye say further, '(The officers of) Hsiâ were chosen and employed in the royal court (of Shang), and had their duties among the mass of its officers.' (But) I, the One man, listen only to the virtuous, and employ them; and it was with this view that I ventured to seek you in your capital of Shang (once sanctioned by) Heaven, (and removed you here to Lo.) I thereby follow (the ancient example), and have pity on you. (Your present non-employment) is no fault of mine;—it is by the decree of Heaven." *

'The king says, "Ye numerous officers, formerly, when I came from Yen [1], I greatly mitigated the penalty and spared the lives of the people of your four states [2]. At the same time I made evident the punishment appointed by Heaven, and removed you to this distant abode, that you might be near the ministers who had served in our honoured (capital) [3], and (learn) their much obedience."

'The king says, "I declare to you, ye numerous officers of Yin, now I have not put you to death, and therefore I reiterate the declaration of my charge [4]. I have now built this great city here in

[1] Yen was the name of a territory, corresponding to the present district of *Kh*ü-fâu, in Shan-tung. The wild tribe inhabiting it, had joined with Wû-kăng and the king's uncles a few years before; and the crushing of the Yen had been the last act in the suppression of their rebellion.

[2] The royal domain of Yin, which had been allotted to Wû-kăng and the king's three uncles.

[3] Hâo. There were, no doubt, at this time many ministers and officers from Hâo in Lo; but the duke had intended that they should in the mass remove from the old to the new capital.

[4] The charge which had been delivered on the first removal of many of them to the neighbourhood of Lo.

Lo, considering that there was no (central) place in which to receive my guests from the four quarters, and also that you, ye numerous officers, might here with zealous activity perform the part of ministers to us, with the entire obedience (ye would learn). Ye have still here, I may say, your grounds, and may still rest in your duties and dwellings. If you can reverently obey, Heaven will favour and compassionate you. If you do not reverently obey, you shall not only not have your lands, but I will also carry to the utmost Heaven's inflictions on your persons. Now you may here dwell in your villages, and perpetuate your families; you may pursue your occupations and enjoy your years in this Lo; your children also will prosper;—(all) from your being removed here."

'The king says—[1]; and again he says, "Whatever I may now have spoken is on account of (my anxiety about) your residence here."'

Book XV. Against Luxurious Ease.

The name of this Book is taken from two characters in the first sentence of it, which are the key-note of the whole. It is classified among the 'Instructions' of the Shû, and was addressed to king *Kh*ăng by the duke of *K*âu soon after he had resigned the administration of the government into his hands.

There are six pauses in the course of the address, which is resumed always with 'The duke of *K*âu said, "Oh."' This suggests a division into seven chapters.

In the first, the duke suggests to the king to find a rule for himself in the laborious toils that devolve on the husbandman. In the second, he refers to the long reigns of three of the Yin sovereigns,

---

[1] There are probably some sentences lost here.

and the short reigns of others, as illustrating how the blessing of Heaven rests on the diligent monarch. In the third, the example of their own kings, Thâi, *K*î, and Wăn, is adduced with the same object. In the fourth, the duke addresses the king directly, and exhorts him to follow the pattern of king Wăn, and flee from that of *K*âu-hsin. In the fifth, he stimulates him, by reference to ancient precedents, to adopt his counsels, and shows the evil effects that will follow if he refuse to do so. In the sixth, he shows him, by the cases of the good kings of Yin and of king Wăn, how he should have regard to the opinions of the common people, and gird himself to diligence. The seventh chapter is a single admonition that the king should lay what had been said to heart.

1. The duke of *K*âu said, 'Oh! the superior man rests in this,—that he will indulge in no luxurious ease. He first understands how the painful toil of sowing and reaping conducts to ease, and thus he understands how the lower people depend on this toil (for their support). I have observed among the lower people, that where the parents have diligently laboured in sowing and reaping, their sons (often) do not understand this painful toil, but abandon themselves to ease, and to village slang, and become quite disorderly. Or where they do not do so, they (still) throw contempt on their parents, saying, "Those old people have heard nothing and know nothing."'

2. The duke of *K*âu said, 'Oh! I have heard that aforetime *K*ung 3ung, one of the kings of Yin [1], was grave, humble, reverential, and timorously cautious. He measured himself with reference to the decree of Heaven, and cherished a reverent apprehension in governing the people, not daring

[1] *K*ung 3ung was the sacrificial title of Thâi-wû, the seventh of the kings of Shang or Yin, who reigned B.C. 1637–1563.

to indulge in useless ease.* It was thus that he enjoyed the throne seventy and five years. If we come to the time of Kâo Ʒung[1], he toiled at first away from the court, and was among the lower people[2]. When he came to the throne, and occupied the mourning shed, it may be said that he did not speak for three years. (Afterwards) he was (still inclined) not to speak; but when he did speak, his words were full of harmonious (wisdom). He did not dare to indulge in useless ease, but admirably and tranquilly presided over the regions of Yin, till throughout them all, small and great, there was not a single murmur. It was thus that he enjoyed the throne fifty and nine years. In the case of Ʒû-*k*iâ[3], he refused to be king unrighteously, and was at first one of the lower people. When he came to the throne, he knew on what they must depend (for their support), and was able to exercise a protecting kindness towards their masses, and did not dare to treat with contempt the wifeless men and widows. Thus it was that he enjoyed the throne thirty and three years. The kings that arose after these, from their birth enjoyed ease. Enjoying ease from their birth, they did not know the painful toil of sowing and reaping, and had not heard of the hard labours of the lower people. They sought for nothing but excessive pleasure; and so not one of them had long life. They (reigned) for ten years,

[1] Kâo Ʒung was the sacrificial title of Wû-ting, the nineteenth sovereign of the Yin line, who reigned B.C. 1324–1266. He has already appeared in the 8th and 9th Books of Part IV.

[2] Compare Part IV, viii, sect. 3, ch. 1.

[3] Ʒû-*k*iâ was the twenty-first of the Yin sovereigns, and reigned B.C. 1258–1226.

for seven or eight, for five or six, or perhaps (only) for three or four.'

3. The duke of *K*âu said, 'Oh! there likewise were king Thâi and king *K*î of our own *K*âu, who were humble and reverentially cautious. King Wăn dressed meanly, and gave himself to the work of tranquillization and to that of husbandry. Admirably mild and beautifully humble, he cherished and protected the inferior people, and showed a fostering kindness to the wifeless men and widows. From morning to mid-day, and from mid-day to sundown, he did not allow himself leisure to eat;—thus seeking to secure the happy harmony of the myriads of the people. King Wăn did not dare to go to excess in his excursions or his hunting, and from the various states he would receive only the correct amount of contribution. The appointment (of Heaven) came to him in the middle of his life[1], and he enjoyed the throne for fifty years.' *

4. The duke of *K*âu said, 'Oh! from this time forward, do you who have succeeded to the throne imitate Wăn's avoiding of excess in his sight-seeing, his indulgence in ease, his excursions, his hunting; and from the myriads of the people receive only the correct amount of contribution. Do not allow yourself the leisure to say, "To-day I will indulge in pleasure." This would not be holding out a lesson to the people, nor the way to secure the favour of Heaven. Men will on the contrary be prompt to imitate you and practise evil. Become not like

[1] This can only be understood of Wăn's succeeding to his father as duke of *K*âu and chief of the West in B.C. 1185. He died in 1135, leaving it to his son Wû to overthrow the dynasty of Shang.

Shâu the king of Yin, who went quite astray, and became abandoned to drunkenness.'

5. The duke of *K*âu said, 'Oh! I have heard it said that, in the case of the ancients, (their ministers) warned and admonished them, protected and loved them, taught and instructed them; and among the people there was hardly one who would impose on them by extravagant language or deceiving tricks. If you will not listen to this (and profit by it), your ministers will imitate you, and so the correct laws of the former kings, both small and great, will be changed and disordered. The people, blaming you, will disobey and rebel in their hearts;—yea, they will curse you with their mouths.'

6. The duke of *K*âu said, 'Oh! those kings of Yin,—*K*ung Ʒung, Kâo Ʒung, and Ʒû-*k*iâ, with king Wăn of our *K*âu,—these four men carried their knowledge into practice. If it was told them, "The lower people murmur against you and revile you," then they paid great and reverent attention to their conduct; and with reference to the faults imputed to them they said, "Our faults are really so," thus not simply shrinking from the cherishing of anger. If you will not listen to this (and profit by it), when men with extravagant language and deceptive tricks say to you, "The lower people are murmuring against you and reviling you," you will believe them. Doing this, you will not be always thinking of your princely duties, and will not cultivate a large and generous heart. You will confusedly punish the guiltless, and put the innocent to death. There will be a general murmuring, which will be concentrated upon your person.'

7. The duke of *K*âu said, 'Oh! let the king, who has succeeded to the throne, make a study of these things.'

Book XVI. The Prince Shih.

The words 'Prince Shih' occur at the commencement of the Book, and are taken as its title. Shih was the name of the duke of Shâo, the author of Book xii. To him the address or announcement here preserved was delivered, and his name is not an inappropriate title for it.

The common view of Chinese critics is that the duke of Shâo had announced his purpose to withdraw from office on account of his age, when the duke of *K*âu persuaded him to remain at his post, and that the reasons which he set before him were recorded in this Book. It may have been so, but the language is far from clearly indicating it. A few expressions, indeed, may be taken as intimating a wish that Shih should continue at court, but some violence has to be put upon them.

I have divided the whole into four chapters, but the two principal ideas in the address are these:—that the favour of Heaven can be permanently secured for a dynasty only by the virtue of its sovereigns; and that that virtue is secured mainly by the counsels and help of virtuous ministers. The ablest sovereigns of Shang are mentioned, and the ministers by whose aid it was, in a great measure, that they became what they were. The cases of Wăn and Wû of their own dynasty, similarly aided by able men, are adduced in the same way; and the speaker adverts to the services which they—the two dukes—had already rendered to their sovereign, and insists that they must go on to the end, and accomplish still greater things.

1. The duke of *K*âu spoke to the following effect:—'Prince Shih, Heaven, unpitying, sent down ruin on Yin. Yin has lost its appointment (to the throne), which our House of *K*âu has received. I do not dare, however, to say, as if I knew

it, "The foundation will ever truly abide in prosperity. If Heaven aid sincerity,"—[1].* Nor do I dare to say, as if I knew it, "The end will issue in our misfortunes." Oh! you have said, O prince, "It depends on ourselves." I also do not dare to rest in the favour of God, not forecasting at a distance the terrors of Heaven in the present time, when there is no murmuring or disobedience among the people;*—(the issue) is with men. Should our present successor to his fathers prove greatly unable to reverence (Heaven) above and (the people) below, and so bring to an end the glory of his predecessors, could we in (the retirement of) our families be ignorant of it? The favour of Heaven is not easily preserved; Heaven is difficult to be depended on. Men lose its favouring appointment, because they cannot pursue and carry out the reverence and brilliant virtue of their forefathers.* Now I, Tan, the little child, am not able to make (the king) correct. I would simply conduct him to the glory of his fathers, and make him, who is my young charge, partaker of that.' He also said, 'Heaven is not to be trusted. Our course is only to seek the prolongation of the virtue of the Tranquillizing king, that Heaven may not find occasion to remove its favouring decree which king Wăn received.'*

2. The duke said, 'Prince Shih, I have heard that aforetime, when Thang the Successful had received the appointment (to the throne), he had with him Î Yin, making (his virtue) like that of great Heaven;* that Thâi *K*iâ had (the same

[1] The text is here defective; or perhaps the speaker purposely left his meaning only half expressed.

Î Yin), the Pâo-hăng[1]; that Thâi-wû[2] had Î *K*ih[2] and *Kh*ăn Hû[2], through whom (his virtue) was made to affect God,* and Wû Hsien[3] who regulated the royal House; that Ʒû-yî[3] had Wû Hsien's son; and that Wû-ting had Kan Phan[4]. (These ministers) carried out (their principles), and displayed (their merit), preserving and regulating the dynasty of Yin, so that, while its ceremonies lasted, (those sovereigns), when deceased, were assessors to Heaven[5],* and its duration extended over many years. Heaven thus determinately maintained its favouring appointment, and Shang was replenished with men. The various heads of great surnames and members of the royal House, holding employments, all held fast their virtue, and showed an anxious solicitude (for the kingdom). The smaller ministers, and the guardian princes in the Hâu and Tien domains, hurried about on their services. Thus did they all exert their virtue and aid their sovereign, so that whatever affairs he, the One man, had in hand, throughout the land, an entire faith was reposed in their justice as in the indications of the shell or the divining stalks.' *

The duke said, 'Prince Shih, Heaven gives length of days to the just and the intelligent; (it was thus

---

[1] See Part IV, v, sect. 1, ch. 1, where Î Yin is called Â-hăng, nearly = Pâo-hăng.

[2] Thâi-wû is the *K*ung Ʒung of last Book. Î *K*ih would be a son or grandson of Î Yin. Of *Kh*ăn Hû we know only what is stated here.

[3] Ʒû-yî was the eleventh Yin sovereign, reigning B.C. 1525–1507. We know of Wû Hsien only that he was Ʒû-yî's minister.

[4] See Part IV, viii, sect. 3, ch. 1.

[5] That is, they were associated with Heaven in the sacrifices to it.

that those ministers) maintained and regulated the dynasty of Yin.* He who came last to the throne granted by Heaven was extinguished by its terrors. Do you think of the distant future, and we shall have the decree (in favour of *K*âu) made sure, and its good government will be brilliantly exhibited in our newly-founded state.'

3. The duke said, 'Prince Shih, aforetime when God was inflicting calamity (on Yin), he encouraged anew the virtue of the Tranquillizing king, till at last the great favouring decree was concentrated in his person. (But) that king Wăn was able to conciliate and unite the portion of the great kingdom which we came to possess, was owing to his having (such ministers) as his brother of Kwo, Hung Yâo, San Î-shăng, Thâi Tien, and Nan-kung Kwo.'

He said further, 'But for the ability of those men to go and come in his affairs, developing his constant lessons, there would have been no benefits descending from king Wăn on the people. And it also was from the determinate favour of Heaven that there were these men of firm virtue, and acting according to their knowledge of the dread majesty of Heaven, to give themselves to enlighten king Wăn, and lead him forward to his high distinction and universal rule, till his fame reached the ears of God, and he received the appointment that had been Yin's.* There were still four of those men who led on king Wû to the possession of the revenues of the kingdom, and afterwards, along with him, in great reverence of the majesty of Heaven, slew all his enemies.* These four men, moreover, made king Wû so illustrious that his glory overspread the kingdom, and (the people) universally and greatly proclaimed his virtue. Now with me Tan, the little child, it is as if I were floating on a great stream;—with you, O Shih, let me from this time endeavour to cross it. Our young sovereign is (powerless), as if he had not yet ascended the throne. You must by no means lay the whole burden on me; and if you draw yourself up without an effort to supply my deficiencies, no good will flow to the people from our age and experience. We shall not hear the voices of the phœnixes[1], and how much less can it be thought that we shall be able to make (the king's virtue) equal (to Heaven)!' *

The duke said, 'Oh! consider well these things, O prince. We have received the appointment to which belongs an unlimited amount of blessing, but having great difficulties attached to it. What I announce to you are counsels of a generous largeness.—I cannot allow the successor of our kings to go astray.'

4. The duke said, 'The former king laid bare his heart, and gave full charge to you, constituting you one of the guides and patterns for the people, saying, "Do you with intelligence and energy second and help the king; do you with sincerity support and convey forward the great decree. Think of the virtue of king Wăn, and enter greatly into his boundless anxieties."'

The duke said, 'What I tell you, O prince, are my sincere thoughts. O Shih, the Grand-Protector, if you can but reverently survey with me the decay and great disorders of Yin, and thence consider the

[1] As a token of the goodness of the government and the general prosperity. See Part II, iv, ch. 3.

dread majesty of Heaven (which warns) us!—Am I not to be believed that I must reiterate my words? I simply say, "The establishment (of our dynasty) rests with us two." Do you agree with me? Then you (also) will say, "It rests with us two." And the favour of Heaven has come to us so largely:—it should be ours to feel as if we could not sufficiently respond to it. If you can but reverently cultivate your virtue (now), and bring to light our men of eminent ability, then when you resign (your position) to some successor in a time of established security, (I will interpose no objection.)

'Oh! it is by the earnest service of us two that we have come to the prosperity of the present day. We must both go on, abjuring all idleness, to complete the work of king Wăn, till it has grandly overspread the kingdom, and from the corners of the sea, and the sunrising, there shall not be one who is disobedient to the rule (of *K*âu).'

The duke said, 'O prince, have I not spoken in accordance with reason in these many declarations? I am only influenced by anxiety about (the appointment of) Heaven, and about the people.'

The duke said, 'Oh! you know, O prince, the ways of the people, how at the beginning they can be (all we could desire); but it is the end (that is to be thought of). Act in careful accordance with this fact. Go and reverently exercise the duties of your office.'

BOOK XVII. THE CHARGE TO *K*UNG OF 3HÂI.

3HÂI was the name of the small state or territory, which had been conferred on Tû, the next younger brother of the duke of *K*âu. The name still remains in the district of Shang-3hâi, department *Z*û-ning, Ho-nan. Tû was deprived of his state because of his complicity in the rebellion of Wû-*k*ăng; but it was subsequently restored to his son Hû by this charge. Hû is here called *K*ung, that term simply denoting his place in the roll of his brothers or cousins. King *Kh*ăng and Hû were cousins,—'brothers' according to Chinese usage of terms, and Hû being the younger of the two, was called 3hâi *K*ung, 'the second or younger brother,—of 3hâi.'

The Book consists of two chapters. The former is of the nature of a preface, giving the details necessary to explain the appointment of Hû. The second contains the king's charge, delivered in his name by the duke of *K*âu, directing Hû how to conduct himself, so that he might blot out the memory of his father's misdeeds, and win the praise of the king.

1. When the duke of *K*âu was in the place of prime minister and directed all the officers, the (king's) uncles spread abroad an (evil) report, in consequence of which (the duke) put to death the prince of Kwan in Shang[1]; confined the prince of 3hâi in Kwo-lin[2], with an attendance of seven chariots; and reduced the prince of Hwo[3] to be a private man, causing his name to be erased from the registers for three years. The son of the prince

[1] The prince of Kwan—corresponding to the present *Kh*ăng *K*âu, department Khâi-făng, Ho-nan—was the third of the sons of king Wăn, and older than the duke of *K*âu. The Shang where he was put to death was probably what had been the capital of the Shang kings.

[2] We do not know where Kwo-lin was.

[3] The name of Hwo remains in Hwo *K*âu, department Phing-yang, Shan-hsî. The prince of Hwo was the eighth of Wăn's sons.

of Ȝhâi having displayed a reverent virtue, the duke of *K*âu made him a high minister, and when his father died, requested a decree from the king, investing him with the country of Ȝhâi.

2. 'The king speaks to this effect:—"My little child, Hû, you follow the virtue (of our ancestors), and have changed from the conduct (of your father); you are able to take heed to your ways;—I therefore appoint you to be a marquis in the east. Go to your fief, and be reverent!

"In order that you may cover the faults of your father, be loyal, be filial[1]. Urge on your steps in your own way, diligent and never idle, and so shall you hand down an example to your descendants. Follow the constant lessons of your grandfather king Wăn, and be not, like your father, disobedient to the royal orders.

"Great Heaven has no partial affections;—it helps only the virtuous.* The people's hearts have no unchanging attachment;—they cherish only the kind. Acts of goodness are different, but they contribute in common to good order. Acts of evil are different, but they contribute in common to disorder. Be cautious!

"In giving heed to the beginning think of the end;—the end will then be without distress. If you do not think of the end, it will be full of distress, even of the greatest.

"Exert yourself to achieve your proper merit. Seek to be in harmony with all your neighbours.

[1] Hû's father had not been filial. When he is told to be filial, there underlies the words the idea of the solidarity of the family. His copying the example of his grandfather would be the best service he could render to his father.

Be a fence to the royal House. Live in amity with your brethren. Tranquillize and help the lower people.

"Follow the course of the Mean, and do not by aiming to be intelligent throw old statutes into confusion. Watch over what you see and hear, and do not for one-sided words deviate from the right rule. Then I, the One man, will praise you."

'The king says, "Oh! my little child, Hû, go, and do not idly throw away my charge."'

Book XVIII. The Numerous Regions.

The king has returned to his capital in triumph, having put down rebellion in the east, and specially extinguished the state or tribe of Yen. The third chapter of Book xiv contained a reference to an expedition against Yen. Critics are divided on the point of whether the expedition mentioned in this Book was the same as that, or another; and our sources of information are not sufficient to enable us to pronounce positively in the case. If we may credit what Mencius says, the Records of the Shû do not tell us a tithe of the wars carried on by the duke of *K*âu to establish the new dynasty:—'He smote Yen, and after three years put its ruler to death. He drove Fei-lien to a corner by the sea, and slew him. The states which he extinguished amounted to fifty' (Mencius, III, ii, ch. 9).

However this point be settled, on the occasion when the announcement in this Book was delivered, a great assembly of princes and nobles—the old officers of Yin or Shang, and chiefs from many regions—was met together. They are all supposed to have been secretly, if not openly, in sympathy with the rebellion which has been trampled out, and to grudge to yield submission to the rule of *K*âu. The king, by the duke of *K*âu, reasons and expostulates with them. He insists on the leniency with which they had been treated in the past; and whereas they might be saying that *K*âu's overthrow of the Yin dynasty was a usurpation, he shows that it was from the will of Heaven.

The history of the nation is then reviewed, and it is made to appear that king Wû had displaced the kings of Yin or Shang, just as Thang, the founder of the Shang dynasty, had displaced those of Hsiâ. It was their duty therefore to submit to *K*âu. If they did not avail themselves of its leniency, they should be dealt with in another way.

Having thus spoken, the duke turns, in the fourth of the five chapters into which I have divided the Book, and addresses the many officers of the states, and especially those of Yin, who had been removed to Lo, speaking to them, as 'the Numerous Officers,' after the style of Book xiv. Finally, he admonishes them all that it is time to begin a new course. If they do well, it will be well with them; if they continue perverse, they will have to blame themselves for the consequences.

1. In the fifth month, on the day Ting-hâi, the king arrived from Yen, and came to (Hâo), the honoured (capital of) *K*âu. The duke of *K*âu said, 'The king speaks to the following effect: "Ho! I make an announcement to you of the four states, and the numerous (other) regions. Ye who were the officers and people of the prince of Yin, I have dealt very leniently as regards your lives, as ye all know. You kept reckoning greatly on (some) decree of Heaven, and did not keep with perpetual awe before your thoughts (the preservation of) your sacrifices[1].*

'"God sent down correction on Hsiâ, but the sovereign (only) increased his luxury and sloth, and would not speak kindly to the people. He showed himself dissolute and dark, and would not yield for a single day to the leadings of God:—this is what you have heard.* He kept reckoning on the

[1] The extinction of the sacrifices of a state was its utter overthrow. None were left—or if some might be left, none of them were permitted—to continue the sacrifices to its founder and his descendants.

decree of God (in his favour), and did not cultivate the means for the people's support.* By great inflictions of punishment also he increased the disorder of the states of Hsiâ. The first cause (of his evil course) was the internal misrule[1], which made him unfit to deal well with the multitudes. Nor did he endeavour to find and employ men whom he could respect, and who might display a generous kindness to the people; but where any of the people of Hsiâ were covetous and fierce, he daily honoured them, and they practised cruel tortures in the cities. Heaven on this sought a (true) lord for the people, and made its distinguished and favouring decree light on Thang the Successful, who punished and destroyed the sovereign of Hsiâ.* Heaven's refusal of its favour (to Hsiâ) was decided. The righteous men of your numerous regions were not permitted to continue long in their posts of enjoyment, and the many officers whom Hsiâ's (last sovereign) honoured were unable intelligently to maintain the people in the enjoyment (of their lives), but, on the contrary, aided one another in oppressing them, till of the hundred ways of securing (prosperity) they could not promote (one).

'"In the case indeed of Thang the Successful, it was because he was the choice of your numerous regions that he superseded Hsiâ, and became the lord of the people. He paid careful attention to the essential virtue (of a sovereign)[2], in order to stimulate the people, and they on their part imitated him

---

[1] The vile debaucheries of which *K*ieh was guilty through his connexion with the notorious Mei-hsî.

[2] That is, to benevolence or the love of the people.

and were stimulated. From him down to Tî-yî, the sovereigns all made their virtue illustrious, and were cautious in the use of punishments;—thus also exercising a stimulating influence (over the people). When they, having examined the evidence in criminal cases, put to death those chargeable with many crimes, they exercised the same influence; and they did so also when they liberated those who were not purposely guilty. But when the throne came to your (last) sovereign, he could not with (the good will of) your numerous regions continue in the enjoyment of the favouring decree of Heaven."' *

2. 'Oh! the king speaks to the following effect:—"I announce and declare to you of the numerous regions, that Heaven had no set purpose to do away with the sovereign of Hsiâ or with the sovereign of Yin. But it was the case that your (last) ruler, being in possession of your numerous regions, abandoned himself to great excess, and reckoned on the favouring decree of Heaven, making trifling excuses for his conduct. And so in the case of the (last) sovereign of Hsiâ; his plans of government were not of a tendency to secure his enjoyment (of the kingdom), and Heaven sent down ruin on him, and the chief of the territory (of Shang) put an end (to the line of Hsiâ). In truth, the last sovereign of your Shang was luxurious to the extreme of luxury, while his plans of government showed neither purity nor progress, and thus Heaven sent down such ruin on him[1].*

[1] There must have been something remarkable in the closing period of *K*âu-hsin's history, to which the duke alludes in the subsequent specification of five years. We do not know the events of the times sufficiently to say what it was.

'"The wise, through not thinking, become foolish, and the foolish, by thinking, become wise. Heaven for five years waited kindly, and forbore with the descendant (of Thang), to see if he would indeed prove himself the ruler of the people; but there was nothing in him deserving to be regarded. Heaven then sought among your numerous regions, making a great impression by its terrors to stir up some one who would look (reverently) to it, but in all your regions there was not one deserving of its favouring regard. But there were the kings of our *K*âu, who treated well the multitudes of the people, and were able to sustain the burden of virtuous (government). They could preside over (all services to) spirits and to Heaven.* Heaven thereupon instructed us, and increased our excellence, made choice of us, and gave us the decree of Yin, to rule over your numerous regions."'*

3. '"Why do I now presume to make (these) many declarations? I have dealt very leniently as regards the lives of you, the people of these four states. Why do you not show a sincere and generous obedience in your numerous regions? Why do you not aid and co-operate with the kings of our *K*âu, to secure the enjoyment of Heaven's favouring decree? You now still dwell in your dwellings, and cultivate your fields;—why do you not obey our kings, and consolidate the decree of Heaven? The paths which you tread are continually those of disquietude;—have you in your hearts no love for yourselves? do you refuse so greatly to acquiesce in the ordinance of Heaven? do you triflingly reject that decree? do you of yourselves pursue unlawful courses, scheming (by your alleged reasons) for the

approval of upright men? I simply instructed you, and published my announcement[1]; with trembling awe I secured and confined (the chief criminals):—I have done so twice and for three times. But if you do not take advantage of the leniency with which I have spared your lives, I will proceed to severe punishments, and put you to death. It is not that we, the sovereigns of *K*âu, hold it virtuous to make you untranquil, but it is you yourselves who accelerate your crimes (and sufferings)."'

4. 'The king says, "Oh! ho! I tell you, ye many officers of the various regions, and you, ye many officers of Yin, now have ye been hurrying about, doing service to my overseers for five years. There are among you the inferior assistants, the chiefs, and the numerous directors, small and great;—see that ye all attain to the discharge of your duties. Want of harmony (in the life) rises from (the want of it in) one's (inner) self;—strive to be harmonious. Want of concord in your families (arises from the want of it in your conduct);—strive to be harmonious. When intelligence rules in your cities, then will you be proved to be attentive to your duties. Do not be afraid, I pray you, of the evil ways (of the people); and moreover, by occupying your offices with a reverent harmony, you will find it possible to select from your cities individuals on whose assistance you can calculate. You may thus long continue in this city of Lo[2], cultivating your fields. Heaven will favour and compassionate you, and we,

[1] Referring probably to 'the Great Announcement' in Book vii.

[2] It would almost seem from this that the announcement was made in Lo; and some critics have argued that Lo was 'the honoured capital' in the first sentence.

the sovereigns of *K*âu, will greatly help you, and confer rewards, selecting you to stand in our royal court. Only be attentive to your duties, and you may rank among our great officers."

'The king says, "Oh! ye numerous officers, if you cannot exhort one another to pay a sincere regard to my charges, it will further show that you are unable to honour your sovereign; and all the people will (also) say, 'We will not honour him.' Thus will ye be proved slothful and perverse, greatly disobedient to the royal charges. Throughout your numerous regions you will bring on yourselves the terrors of Heaven, and I will then inflict on you its punishments, removing you far from your country."'

5. 'The king says, "I do not (wish to) make these many declarations, but it is in a spirit of awe that I lay my commands before you." He further says, "You may now make a (new) beginning. If you cannot reverently realize the harmony (which I enjoin), do not (hereafter) murmur against me."'

Book XIX. The Establishment of Government.

The phrase, 'the Establishment of Government,' occurs several times in the course of the Book, and is thence taken to denominate it,—appropriately enough. The subject treated of throughout, is how good government may be established.

Some Chinese critics maintain that the text as it stands is very confused, 'head and tail in disorder, and without connexion,' and various re-arrangements of it have been proposed, for which, however, there is no manuscript authority. Keeping to the received text, and dividing it into six chapters, we may adopt a summary of its contents approved by the editors of the Shû, which was published in the Yung-*k*ăng reign of the present dynasty.—In government there is nothing more important than the employment of proper men; and when such men are being sought, the first care should be for those to occupy the three highest positions. When these are properly filled, all the other offices will get their right men, and royal government will be established. The appointment of the officers of business, of pastoral oversight, and of the law, is the great theme of the whole Book, and the concluding words of chapter 1 are its pulse,—may be felt throbbing everywhere in all the sentiments. Chapters 2 and 3 illustrate the subject from the history of the dynasties of Hsiâ and Shang; and in chapter 4 it is shown how kings Wăn and Wû selected their officers, and initiated the happy state which was still continuing. In chapter 5 there is set forth the duty of the king to put away from him men of artful tongues; to employ the good, distinguished by their habits of virtue; to be always well prepared for war; and to be very careful of his conduct in the matter of litigations. Chapter 6 seems to have hardly any connexion with the rest of the Book, and is probably a fragment of one of the lost Books of the Shû, that has got tacked on to this.

The Book belongs to the class of 'Instructions,' and was made, I suppose, after the duke of *K*âu had retired from his regency.

1. The duke of *K*âu spoke to the following effect:—'With our hands to our heads and our heads to the ground, we make our declarations to the Son of Heaven, the king who has inherited the throne.' In such manner accordingly all (the other ministers) cautioned the king, saying, 'In close attendance on your majesty there are the regular presidents [1], the regular ministers [2], and the officers of justice;—the keepers of the robes (also), and the guards.' The duke of *K*âu said, 'Oh! admirable are these (officers). Few, however, know to be sufficiently anxious about them.'

---

[1] We must understand by these the chiefs or presidents who had a certain jurisdiction over several states and their princes.

[2] The high ministers of Instruction, War, Works, &c.

2. 'Among the ancients who exemplified (this anxiety) there was the founder of the Hsiâ dynasty. When his House was in its greatest strength, he sought for able men who should honour God (in the discharge of their duties).* (His advisers), when they knew of men thoroughly proved and trustworthy in the practice of the nine virtues[1], would then presume to inform and instruct their sovereign, saying, "With our hands to our heads and our heads to the ground, O sovereign, we would say, Let (such an one) occupy one of your high offices: Let (such an one) be one of your pastors: Let (such an one) be one of your officers of justice. By such appointments you will fulfil your duty as sovereign. If you judge by the face only, and therefrom deem men well schooled in virtue, and appoint them, then those three positions will all be occupied by unrighteous individuals." The way of *K*ieh, however, was not to observe this precedent. Those whom he employed were cruel men;—and he left no successor.'

3. 'After this there was Thang the Successful, who, rising to the throne, grandly administered the bright ordinances of God.* He employed, to fill the three (high) positions, those who were equal to them; and those who were called possessors of the three kinds of ability[2] would display that ability.

---

[1] See chapter 2 of 'the Counsels of Kâo-yâo' in Part II.

[2] Some suppose that men are intended here who possessed 'the three virtues' of 'the Great Plan.' I think rather that men are intended who had talents and virtue which would make them eligible to the three highest positions. Thang had his notice fixed on such men, and was prepared to call them to office at the proper time.

He then studied them severely, and greatly imitated them, making the utmost of them in their three positions and with their three kinds of ability. The people in the cities of Shang[1] were thereby all brought to harmony, and those in the four quarters of the kingdom were brought greatly under the influence of the virtue thus displayed. Oh! when the throne came to Shâu, his character was all violence. He preferred men of severity, and who deemed cruelty a virtue, to share with him in the government of his states; and at the same time, the host of his associates, men who counted idleness a virtue, shared the offices of his court. God then sovereignly punished him, and caused us to possess the great land, enjoy the favouring decree which Shâu had (afore) received, and govern all the people in their myriad realms.' *

4. 'Then subsequently there were king Wăn and king Wû, who knew well the minds of those whom they put in the three positions, and saw clearly the minds of those who had the three grades of ability. Thus they could employ them to serve God with reverence, and appointed them as presidents and chiefs of the people. In establishing their government, the three things which principally concerned them were to find the men for (high) offices, the officers of justice, and the pastors. (They had also) the guards; the keepers of the robes; their equerries; their heads of small departments; their personal attendants; their various overseers; and their treasurers. They had their governors of the larger and smaller cities assigned in the royal domain to the

[1] That is, within the royal domain.

nobles; their men of arts[1]; their overseers whose offices were beyond the court; their grand historiographers; and their heads of departments;—all good men of constant virtue.

'(In the external states) there were the Minister of Instruction, the Minister of War, and the Minister of Works, with the many officers subordinate to them. Among the wild tribes, such as the Wei, the Lû, and the *Kh*ăng[2], in the three Po, and at the dangerous passes, they had wardens.

'King Wăn was able to make the minds of those in the (three high) positions his own, and so it was that he established those regular officers and superintending pastors, so that they were men of ability and virtue. He would not appear himself in the various notifications, in litigations, and in precautionary measures. There were the officers and pastors (to attend to them), whom he (simply) taught to be obedient (to his wishes), and not to be disobedient. (Yea), as to litigations and precautionary measures, he (would seem as if he) did not presume to know about them. He was followed by king Wû, who carried out his work of settlement, and did not presume to supersede his righteous and virtuous men, but entered into his plans, and employed, as before, those men. Thus it was that they unitedly received this vast inheritance.'

---

[1] All who employed their arts in the service of the government;—officers of prayer, clerks, archers, charioteers, doctors, diviners, and the practisers of the various mechanical arts, &c.

[2] Compare what is said in 'the Speech at Mû,' ch. 1. The *Kh*ăng are not mentioned there. It would seem to be the name of a wild tribe. The three Po had all been capitals of the Shang kings, and their people required the special attention of the sovereigns of *K*âu.

5. 'Oh! young son, the king, from this time forth be it ours to establish the government, appointing the (high) officers, the officers of the laws, and the pastors;—be it ours clearly to know what courses are natural to these men, and then fully to employ them in the government, that they may aid us in the management of the people whom we have received, and harmoniously conduct all litigations and precautionary measures. And let us never allow others to come between us and them. (Yea), in our every word and speech, let us be thinking of (these) officers of complete virtue, to regulate the people that we have received.

'Oh! I, Tan, have received these excellent words of others[1], and tell them all to you, young son, the king. From this time forth, O accomplished son (of Wû), accomplished grandson (of Wăn), do not err in regard to the litigations and precautionary measures;—let the proper officers manage them. From of old to the founder of Shang, and downwards to king Wăn of our *K*âu, in establishing government, when they appointed (high) officers, pastors, and officers of the laws, they settled them in their positions, and allowed them to unfold their talents;—thus giving the regulation of affairs into their hands. In the kingdom, never has there been the establishment of government by the employment of artful-tongued men; (with such men), unlessoned in virtue, never can a government be distinguished in the world. From this time forth, in establishing government, make no use of artful-tongued men,

[1] Probably all the other officers or ministers referred to in ch. 1. They are there prepared to speak their views, when the duke of *K*âu takes all the discoursing on himself.

but (seek for) good officers, and get them to use all their powers in aiding the government of our country. Now, O accomplished son (of Wû), accomplished grandson (of Wăn), young son, the king, do not err in the matter of litigations;—there are the officers and pastors (to attend to them).

'Have well arranged (also) your military accoutrements and weapons, so that you may go forth beyond the steps of Yü, and traverse all under the sky, even to beyond the seas, everywhere meeting with submission:—so shall you display the bright glory of king Wăn, and render more illustrious the great achievements of king Wû[1].

'Oh! from this time forth, may (our) future kings, in establishing the government, be able to employ men of constant virtue!'

6. The duke of *K*âu spoke to the following effect:—'O grand historiographer, the duke of Sû, the Minister of Crime, dealt reverently with all the criminal matters that came before him, and thereby perpetuated the fortunes of our kingdom. Here was an example of anxious solicitude (for future ministers), whereby they may rank with him in the ordering of the appropriate punishments[2].'

---

[1] At the close of his address to prince Shih, Book xvi, the duke of *K*âu breaks all at once into a warlike mood, as he does here.

[2] I have said in the introductory note that this chapter does not seem to have any connexion with the rest of the Book. From a passage in the Ȝo *K*wan, under the eleventh year of duke *Kh*ăng, we learn that a Sû Făn-shăng, or Făn-shăng of Sû, was Minister of Crime to king Wû. It is probably to him that the duke here alludes.

Book XX. The Officers of *K*âu.

'The Officers of *K*âu' contains a general outline of the official system of the *K*âu dynasty, detailing the names and functions of the principal ministers about the court and others, to whom, moreover, various counsels are addressed by the king who speaks in it,—no doubt, king *Kh*ăng. Chinese critics class it with the 'Instructions' of the Shû, but it belongs rather to the 'Announcements.'

There is no mention in it of the duke of *K*âu; and its date must therefore be in some year after he had retired from the regency, and resigned the government into the king's own hands.

The Book has a beginning, middle, and end, more distinctly marked than they are in many of the documents in the Shû. The whole is divided into five chapters. The first is introductory, and describes the condition of the kingdom, when the arrangements of the official system were announced. In the second, the king refers to the arrangements of former dynasties. In the third, he sets forth the principal offices of state, the ministers of which had their residence at court, and goes on to the arrangements for the administration of the provinces. The two other chapters contain many excellent advices to the ministers and officers to discharge their duties so that the fortunes of the dynasty might be consolidated, and no dissatisfaction arise among the myriad states.

1. The king of *K*âu brought the myriad regions (of the kingdom) to tranquillity; he made a tour of inspection through the Hâu and Tien tenures; he punished on all sides the chiefs who had refused to appear at court; thus securing the repose of the millions of the people, and all the (princes in the) six tenures acknowledging his virtue. He then returned to the honoured capital of *K*âu, and strictly regulated the officers of the administration.

2. The king said, 'It was the grand method of former times to regulate the government while there

was no confusion, and to secure the country while there was no danger.' He said, 'Yâo and Shun, having studied antiquity[1], established a hundred officers. At court, there were the General Regulator and (the President of) the Four Mountains; abroad, there were the pastors of the provinces and the princes of states. Thus the various departments of government went on harmoniously, and the myriad states all enjoyed repose. Under the dynasties of Hsiâ and Shang, the number of officers was doubled, and they were able still to secure good government. (Those early) intelligent kings, in establishing their government, cared not so much about the number of the offices as about the men (to occupy them). Now I, the little child, cultivate with reverence my virtue, concerned day and night about my deficiencies; I look up to (those) former dynasties, and seek to conform to them, while I instruct and direct you, my officers.'

3. 'I appoint the Grand-Master, the Grand-Assistant, and the Grand-Guardian. These are the three Kung[2]. They discourse about the principles

---

[1] It is the same phrase here, which occurs at the beginning of the Canons of Yâo and Shun, and of some other Books. It may be inferred, as P. Gaubil says, that Yâo and Shun had certain sources of knowledge, that is to say, some history of the times anterior to their own.

[2] That is, 'the three dukes;' but the term is here a name of office, more than of nobility, as is evident from the name of the three Kû, who were next to them. Kû was not used as a term expressing any order of nobility. It would seem to indicate that, while the men holding the office were assistant to the Kung, they yet had a distinct standing of their own. The offices of Grand-Master &c. had existed under the Shang dynasty; see Book xi, Part IV.

of reason[1] and adjust the states, harmonizing (also) and regulating the operations (in nature) of heaven and earth[2]. These offices need not (always) be filled; there must (first) be the men for them.

'(I appoint) the Junior Master, the Junior Assistant, and the Junior Guardian. These are called the three Kû[3]. They assist the Kung to diffuse widely the transforming influences, and display brightly with reverence (the powers of) heaven and earth,—assisting me, the One man.

'(I appoint) the Prime Minister, who presides over the ruling of the (various) regions, has the general management of all the other officers, and secures uniformity within the four seas; the Minister of Instruction, who presides over the education in the states, diffuses a knowledge of the duties belonging to the five relations of society, and trains the millions of the people to obedience; the Minister of Religion, who presides over the (sacred) ceremonies of the country, regulates the services rendered to the spirits and manes, and makes a harmony between high and low[4];* the Minister of War, who presides over the (military) administration of the

---

[1] Meaning, I suppose, the courses or ways, which it was right for the king, according to reason, to pursue.

[2] That is, probably, securing the material prosperity of the kingdom, in good seasons, &c.

[3] See note 2 on the preceding page.

[4] The name here for 'the Minister of Religion' is the same as that in the Canon of Shun. 'The spirits and manes' are 'the spirits of heaven, earth, and deceased men.' All festive, funeral, and other ceremonies, as well as those of sacrifices, came under the department of the Minister of Religion, who had therefore to define the order of rank and precedence. This seems to be what is meant by his 'making a harmony between high and low.'

country, commands the six hosts, and secures the tranquillity of all the regions; the Minister of Crime, who presides over the prohibitions of the country, searches out the villainous and secretly wicked, and punishes oppressors and disturbers of the peace; and the Minister of Works, who presides over the land of the country, settles the four classes of the people, and secures at the proper seasons the produce of the ground[1].

'These six ministers with their different duties lead on their several subordinates, and set an example to the nine pastors of the provinces, enriching and perfecting the condition of the millions of the people. In six years (the lords of) the five tenures appear once at the royal court; and after a second six years, the king makes a tour of inspection in the four seasons, and examines the (various) regulations and measures at the four mountains. The princes appear before him each at the mountain of his quarter; and promotions and degradations are awarded with great intelligence.'

4. The king said, 'Oh! all ye men of virtue, my occupiers of office, pay reverent attention to your charges. Be careful in the commands you issue; for, once issued, they must be carried into effect, and cannot be retracted. Extinguish all selfish aims by your public feeling, and the people will have confidence in you, and be gladly obedient. Study antiquity as a preparation for entering on

[1] Out of these six ministers and their departments have grown the Six Boards of the Chinese Government of the present day:—the Board of Civil Office; the Board of Revenue; the Board of Rites; the Board of War; the Board of Punishment; and the Board of Works.

your offices. In deliberating on affairs, form your determinations by help (of such study), and your measures will be free from error. Make the regular statutes of (our own) dynasty your rule, and do not with artful speeches introduce disorder into your offices. To accumulate doubts is the way to ruin your plans; to be idle and indifferent is the way to ruin your government. Without study, you stand facing a wall, and your management of affairs will be full of trouble.

'I warn you, my high ministers and officers, that exalted merit depends on the high aim, and a patrimony is enlarged only by diligence; it is by means of bold decision that future difficulties are avoided. Pride comes, along with rank, unperceived, and extravagance in the same way with emolument. Let reverence and economy be (real) virtues with you, unaccompanied with hypocritical display. Practise them as virtues, and your minds will be at ease, and you will daily become more admirable. Practise them in hypocrisy, and your minds will be toiled, and you will daily become more stupid. In the enjoyment of favour think of peril, and never be without a cautious apprehension;—he who is without such apprehension finds himself amidst what is really to be feared. Push forward the worthy, and show deference to the able; and harmony will prevail among all your officers. When they are not harmonious, the government becomes a mass of confusion. If those whom you advance be able for their offices, the ability is yours; if you advance improper men, you are not equal to your position.'

5. The king said, 'Oh! ye (charged) with the

threefold business (of government)[1], and ye great officers, reverently attend to your departments, and conduct well the affairs under your government, so as to assist your sovereign, and secure the lasting happiness of the millions of the people;—so shall there be no dissatisfaction throughout the myriad states.'

Book XXI. The *Kün-khăn*.

Kün-khăn was the successor in 'the eastern capital' of the duke of *K*âu, who has now passed off the stage of the Shû, which he occupied so long. Between 'the Officers of *K*âu' and this Book, there were, when the Shû was complete, two others, which are both lost. We must greatly deplore the loss of the second of them, for it contained an account of the death of the duke of *K*âu, and an announcement made by king *Kh*ăng by his bier.

Who *K*ün-*kh*ăn, the charge to whom on entering on his important government is here preserved, really was, we are not informed. Some have supposed that he was a son of the duke of *K*âu; but we may be sure, from the analogy of other charges, that if he had been so, the fact would have been alluded to in the text. *K*ün-*kh*ăn might be translated 'the prince *Kh*ăn,' like *K*ün Shih in the title of Book xvi, but we know nothing of any territory with which he was invested.

The following summary of the contents is given by a Chinese critic:—'The whole Book may be divided into three chapters. The first relates *K*ün-*kh*ăn's appointment to the government of the eastern capital. The concluding words, "Be reverent,"

---

[1] 'The threefold business of government' is the appointment of the men of office, the officers of law, and the pastors, 'the three concerns of those in the three highest positions,' as described in the last Book, ch. 4. The king, probably, intends the Kung, the Kû, and the six ministers, whose duties he has spoken of. The 'great officers' will be all the officers inferior to these in their several departments.

are emphatic, and give the key-note to all that follows. The second chapter enjoins on him to exert himself to illustrate the lessons of the duke of *K*âu, and thereby transform the people of Yin. The third requires him to give full development to those lessons, and instances various particulars in which his doing so would appear;—all illustrative of the command at the commencement, that he should be reverent.'

1. The king spake to the following effect:—'*K*ün-*kh*ăn, it is you who are possessed of excellent virtue, filial and respectful. Being filial, and friendly with your brethren, you can display these qualities in the exercise of government. I appoint you to rule this eastern border. Be reverent.'

2. 'Formerly, the duke of *K*âu acted as teacher and guardian of the myriads of the people, who cherish (the remembrance of) his virtue. Go and with sedulous care enter upon his charge; act in accordance with his regular ways, and exert yourself to illustrate his lessons;—so shall the people be regulated. I have heard that he said, "Perfect government has a piercing fragrance, and influences the spiritual intelligences.* It is not the millet which has the piercing fragrance; it is bright virtue." Do you make this lesson of the duke of *K*âu your rule, being diligent from day to day, and not presuming to indulge in luxurious ease. Ordinary men, while they have not yet seen a sage, (are full of desire) as if they should never get a sight of him; and after they have seen him, they are still unable to follow him. Be cautioned by this! You are the wind; the inferior people are the grass. In revolving the plans of your government, never hesitate to acknowledge the difficulty of the subject. Some things have to be abolished, and some new things to be enacted;—

going out and coming in, seek the judgment of your people about them, and, when there is a general agreement, exert your own powers of reflection. When you have any good plans or counsels, enter and lay them before your sovereign in the palace. Thereafter, when you are acting abroad in accordance with them, say, "This plan or this view is all due to our sovereign." Oh! if all ministers were to act thus, how excellent would they be, and how distinguished!'

3. The king said, '*K*ün-*kh*ăn, do you give their full development to the great lessons of the duke of *K*âu. Do not make use of your power to exercise oppression; do not make use of the laws to practise extortion. Be gentle, but with strictness of rule. Promote harmony by the display of an easy forbearance.

'When any of the people of Yin are amenable to punishment, if I say "Punish," do not you therefore punish; and if I say "Spare," do not you therefore spare. Seek the due middle course. Those who are disobedient to your government, and uninfluenced by your instructions, you will punish, remembering that the end of punishment is to make an end of punishing. Those who are inured to villainy and treachery, those who violate the regular duties of society, and those who introduce disorder into the public manners:—those three classes you will not spare, though their particular offences be but small.

'Do not cherish anger against the obstinate, and dislike them. Seek not every quality in one individual. You must have patience, and you will be successful; have forbearance, and your virtue will be great. Mark those who discharge their duties well, and also mark those who do not do so, (and distinguish them from one another.) Advance the good, to induce those who may not be so to follow (their example).

'The people are born good, and are changed by (external) things,* so that they resist what their superiors command, and follow what they (themselves) love. Do you but reverently observe the statutes, and they will be found in (the way of) virtue; they will thus all be changed, and truly advance to a great degree of excellence. Then shall I, the One man, receive much happiness, and your excellent services will be famous through long ages!'

Book XXII. The Testamentary Charge.

This Book brings us to the closing act of the life of king *Kh*ăng, whose reign, according to the current chronology, lasted thirty-seven years, ending in B.C. 1079. From the appointment of *K*ün-*kh*ăn to his death, the king's history is almost a blank. The only events chronicled by Sze-mâ *Kh*ien are a coinage of round money with a square hole in the centre,—the prototype of the present cash; and an enactment about the width and length in which pieces of silk and cloth were to be manufactured.

King *Kh*ăng, feeling that his end is near, calls his principal ministers and other officers around his bed, and commits his son *K*âo to their care and guidance. The record of all these things and the dying charge form a chapter that ends with the statement of the king's death. The rest of the Book forms a second chapter, in which we have a detailed account of the ceremonies connected with the publication of the charge, and the accession of *K*âo to the throne. It is an interesting account of the ways of that distant time on such occasions.

1. In the fourth month, when the moon began to wane, the king was indisposed. On the day *K*iâ-

ȝze, he washed his hands and face; his attendants put on him his cap and robes[1]; (and he sat up), leaning on a gem-adorned bench[2]. He then called together the Grand-Guardian Shih, the earls of *Z*ui and Thung, the duke of Pî, the marquis of Wei, the duke of Mâo, the master of the warders, the master of the guards, the heads of the various departments, and the superintendents of affairs[3].

The king said, 'Oh! my illness has greatly increased, and it will soon be over with me. The malady comes on daily with more violence, and maintains its hold. I am afraid I may not find (another opportunity) to declare my wishes about my successor, and therefore I (now) lay my charge upon you with special instructions. The former rulers, our kings Wăn and Wû, displayed in succession their equal glory, making sure provision for the support of the people, and setting forth their

[1] The king's caps or crowns and robes were many, and for each there was the appropriate occasion. His attendants, no doubt, now dressed king *Kh*ăng as the rules of court fashions required.

[2] In those days they sat on the ground upon mats; and for the old or infirm benches or stools were placed, in front of them, to lean forward on. The king had five kinds of stools variously adorned. That with gems was the most honourable.

[3] The Grand-Guardian Shih, or the duke of Shâo, and the other five dignitaries were, no doubt, the six ministers of the 20th Book. *Z*ui is referred to the present district of *K*âo-yî, department Hsî-an; and Thung to Hwâ *K*âu, department Thung-*k*âu;—both in Shen-hsî. The earl of *Z*ui, it is supposed, was Minister of Instruction, and he of Thung Minister of Religion. Pî corresponded to the present district of *Kh*ang-an, department Hsî-an. The duke of Pî was Minister of War, called Duke or Kung, as Grand-Master. It is not known where Mâo was. The lord of it was Minister of Works, and Grand-Assistant. The marquis of Wei,—see on Book ix. He was now, it is supposed, Minister of Crime.

instructions. (The people) accorded a practical submission, without any opposition, and the influence (of their example and instructions) extended to Yin, and the great appointment (of Heaven) was secured *. After them, I, the stupid one, received with reverence the dread (decree) of Heaven, and continued to keep the great instructions of Wăn and Wû, not daring blindly to transgress them.*

'Now Heaven has laid affliction on me, and it seems as if I should not again rise or be myself. Do you take clear note of these my words, and in accordance with them watch reverently over my eldest son *K*âo, and greatly assist him in the difficulties of his position. Be kind to those who are far off, and help those who are near. Promote the tranquillity of the states, small and great, and encourage them (to well-doing). I think how a man has to govern himself in dignity and with decorum;—do not you allow *K*âo to proceed heedlessly on the impulse of improper motives.' Immediately on receiving this charge, (the ministers and others) withdrew. The tent[1] was then carried out into

[1] The tent had been prepared when the king sent for his ministers and officers to give them his last charge, and set up outside his chamber in the hall where he was accustomed to hold 'the audience of government.' He had walked or been carried to it, and then returned to his apartment when he had expressed his last wishes, while the tent—the curtains and canopy—was carried out into the courtyard.

The palace was much more long or deep than wide, consisting of five series of buildings continued one after another, so that, if all the gates were thrown open, one could walk in a direct line from the first gate to the last. The different parts of it were separated by courts that embraced a large space of ground, and were partly open overhead. The gates leading to the different parts had their particular names, and were all fronting

the court; and on the next day, (being) Yî-*kh*âu, the king died.

2. The Grand-Guardian then ordered *K*ung Hwan[1] and Nan-Kung Mâo[1] to instruct Lü *K*î, the marquis of *Kh*î[2], with two shield-and-spearmen, and a hundred guards, to meet the prince *K*âo outside the south gate[3], and conduct him to (one of) the side-apartments (near to that where the king lay), there to be as chief mourner[4].

On the day Ting-mâo, (two days after the king's death), he ordered (the charge) to be recorded on

---

the south. Outside the second was held 'the outer levee,' where the king received the princes and officers generally. Outside the fifth was held 'the audience of government,' when he met his ministers to consult with them on the business of the state. Inside this gate were the buildings which formed the private apartments, in the hall leading to which was held 'the inner audience,' and where the sovereign feasted those whom he designed specially to honour. Such is the general idea of the ancient palace given by *K*û Hsî. The gateways included a large space, covered by a roof, supported on pillars.

[1] We know nothing more of these officers but what is here related.

[2] The marquis of *Kh*î was the son of Thâi-kung, a friend and minister of king Wăn, who had been enfeoffed by king Wû with the state of *Kh*î, embracing the present department of *Kh*ing-*k*âu, in Shan-tung, and other territory. His place at court was that of master of the guards.

[3] All the gates might be called 'south gates.' It is not certain whether that intended here was the outer gate of all, or the last, immediately in front of the hall, where the king had given his charge. Whichever it was, the meeting *K*âo in the way described was a public declaration that he had been appointed successor to the throne.

[4] 'The mourning shed,' spoken of in Part IV, viii, ch. 1, had not yet been set up, and the apartment here indicated—on the east of the hall of audience—was the proper one for the prince to occupy in the mean time.

tablets, and the forms (to be observed in publishing it). Seven days after, on Kwei-yû, as chief (of the west) and premier, he ordered the (proper) officers to prepare the wood (for all the requirements of the funeral)[1].

The salvage men[2] set out the screens[3], ornamented with figures of axes, and the tents. Between the window (and the door), facing the south, they placed the (three)fold mat of fine bamboo splints, with its striped border of white and black silk, and the usual bench adorned with different-coloured gems. In the side-space on the west, which faced the east, they placed the threefold rush mat, with its variegated border, and the usual bench adorned with beautiful shells. In the side-space on the east, which faced the west, they placed the threefold mat of fine grass, with its border of painted silk, and the usual bench carved, and adorned with gems. Before the western side-chamber, and facing the south, they placed the threefold mat of fine bamboo, with its dark mixed border, and the usual lacquered bench[4].

---

[1] On the seventh day after his death the king had been shrouded and put into his coffin. But there were still the shell or outer coffin, &c., to be provided.

[2] These 'salvage men' were, I suppose, natives of the wild Tî tribes, employed to perform the more servile offices about the court. Some of them, we know, were enrolled among the guards.

[3] The screens were ornamented with figures of axe-heads, and placed behind the king, under the canopy that overshadowed him.

[4] All these arrangements seem to have been made in the hall where king *Kh*ăng had delivered his charge. He had been accustomed to receive his guests at all the places where the tents, screens, and mats were now set. It was presumed he would be present in spirit at the ceremony of proclaiming his son, and

(They set forth) also the five pairs of gems (or jade), and the precious things of display. There were the red knife, the great lessons, the large round-and-convex symbol of jade, and the rounded and pointed maces,—all in the side-space on the west; the large piece of jade, the pieces contributed by the wild tribes of the east, the heavenly sounding-stone, and the river-Plan,—all in the side-space on the east; the dancing habits of Yin, the large tortoise-shell, and the large drum,—all in the western apartment; the spear of Tûi, the bow of Ho, and the bamboo arrows of *Kh*ui,—all in the eastern apartment[1].

The grand carriage was by the guests' steps, facing (the south); the next was by the eastern (or host's) steps, facing (the south). The front carriage was placed before the left lobby, and the one that followed it before the right lobby[2].

---

making known to him his dying charge; and as they could not tell at what particular spot the spirit would be, they made all the places ready for it.

[1] The western and eastern apartments were two rooms, east and west of the hall, forming part of the private apartments, behind the side rooms, and of large dimensions. The various articles enumerated were precious relics, and had been favourites with king *Kh*ăng. They were now displayed to keep up the illusion of the king's still being present in spirit. 'They were set forth,' it is said, 'at the ancestral sacrifices to show that the king could preserve them, and at the ceremony of announcing a testamentary charge to show that he could transmit them.' About the articles themselves it is not necessary to append particular notes. They perished thousands of years ago, and the accounts of them by the best scholars are little more than conjectural.

[2] The royal carriages were of five kinds, and four of them at least were now set forth inside the last gate, that everything might again be done, as when the king was alive. On the west side of the hall were the guests' steps (or staircase), by which visitors

Two men in brownish leather caps, and holding three-cornered halberts, stood inside the gate leading to the private apartments. Four men in caps of spotted deer-skin, holding spears with blades upturned from the base of the point, stood, one on each side of the steps east and west, and near to the platform of the hall. One man in a great officer's cap, and holding an axe, stood in the hall, (near the steps) at the east (end). One man in a great officer's cap, and holding an axe of a different pattern, stood in the hall, (near the steps) at the west end. One man in a great officer's cap, and holding a lance, stood at the front and east of the hall, close by the steps. One man in a great officer's cap, and holding a lance of a different pattern, stood in the corresponding place on the west. One man in a great officer's cap, and holding a pointed weapon, stood by the steps on the north side of the hall.

The king, in a linen cap and the variously figured skirt, ascended by the guests' steps, followed by the high ministers, (great) officers, and princes of states, in linen caps and dark-coloured skirts[1]. Arrived in the hall, they all took their (proper) places. The Grand-Guardian, the Grand-Historiographer, and the Minister of Religion were all in

ascended, and on the east were those used by the host himself. If one of the royal carriages was absent on this occasion, it must have been that used in war, as not being appropriate at such a time.

[1] All was now ready for the grand ceremony, and the performers, in their appropriate mourning and sacrificial array, take their places in the hall. *K*âo is here for the first time styled 'king;' but still he goes up by the guests' steps, not presuming to ascend by the others, while his father's corpse was in the hall.

linen caps and red skirts. The Grand-Guardian bore the great mace. The Minister of Religion bore the cup and the mace-cover. These two ascended by the steps on the east[1]. The Grand-Historiographer bore the testamentary charge. He ascended by the guests' steps (on the west), and advanced to the king with the tablets containing the charge, and said, 'Our royal sovereign, leaning on the gem-adorned bench, declared his last charge, and commanded you to continue (the observance of) the lessons, and to take the rule of the kingdom of *K*âu, complying with the great laws, and securing the harmony of all under the sky, so as to respond to and display the bright instructions of Wăn and Wû.'

The king twice bowed (low), and then arose, and replied, 'I am utterly insignificant and but a child, how should I be able to govern the four quarters (of the kingdom) with a corresponding reverent awe of the dread majesty of Heaven!'* He then received the cup and the mace-cover. Thrice he slowly and reverently advanced with a cup of spirits (to the east of the coffin); thrice he sacrificed (to the spirit of his father);* and thrice he put the cup down. The Minister of Religion said, 'It is accepted[2].'*

[1] The Grand-Guardian and the Minister of Religion ascended by the eastern steps, because the authority of king *Kh*ăng was in their persons, to be conveyed by the present ceremony to his son. 'The great mace' was one of the emblems of the royal sovereignty, and 'the cup' also must have been one that only the king could use. 'The mace-cover' was an instrument by which the genuineness of the symbols of their rank conferred on the different princes was tested.

[2] According to Khung Ying-tâ, when the king received the record of the charge, he was standing at the top of the eastern steps, a little eastwards, with his face to the north. The Historiographer stood by king *Kh*ăng's coffin, on the south-west of it, with his face

The Grand-Guardian received the cup, descended the steps, and washed his hands[1]. He then took another cup, (placed it on) a half-mace which he carried, and repeated the sacrifice[2].* He then gave the cup to one of the attendants of the Minister of Religion, and did obeisance. The king returned the obeisance. The Grand-Guardian took a cup again, and poured out the spirits in sacrifice.* He then just tasted the spirits, returned to his place, gave the cup to the attendant, and did obeisance. The king returned the obeisance. The Grand-Guardian descended from the hall, after which the various (sacrificial) articles were removed, and the princes all went out at the temple gate[3] and waited.

---

to the east. There he read the charge, after which the king bowed twice, and the Minister of Religion, on the south-west of the king, presented the cup and mace-cover. The king took them, and, having given the cover in charge to an attendant, advanced with the cup to the place between the pillars where the sacrificial spirits were placed. Having filled a cup, he advanced to the east of the coffin, and stood with his face to the west; then going to the spot where his father's spirit was supposed to be, he sacrificed, pouring out the spirits on the ground, and then he put the cup on the bench appropriated for it. This he repeated three times. At the conclusion the Minister of Religion conveyed to him a message from the spirit of his father, that his offering was accepted.

[1] Preparatory, that is, to his offering a sacrifice.

[2] That is, probably, repeated the sacrifice to the spirit of king *Kh*ăng, as if to inform him that his charge had been communicated to his son. The half-mace was used as a handle for the sacrificial cup. This ceremony appears to have been gone through twice. The Grand-Guardian's bowing was to the spirit of king *Kh*ăng, and the new king returned the obeisance for his father.

[3] Meaning the fifth or last gate of the palace. The private apartments had for the time, through the presence of the coffin and by the sacrifices, been converted into a sort of ancestral temple.

BOOK XXIII.

THE ANNOUNCEMENT OF KING KHANG.

KHANG was the honorary sacrificial title conferred on *K*âo, the son and successor of king *Kh*ăng. His reign lasted from B.C. 1078 to 1053. Khang, as an honorary title, has various meanings. In the text it probably denotes—'Who caused the people to be tranquil and happy.'

Immediately on his accession to the throne, as described in the last Book, king Khang made the Announcement which is here recorded. Indeed the two Books would almost seem to form only one, and as such they appeared in the Shû of Fû, as related in the Introduction.

The princes, with whose departure from the inner hall of the palace the last Book concludes, are introduced again to the king in the court between the fourth and fifth gates, and do homage to him after their fashion, cautioning also and advising him about the discharge of his high duties. He responds with the declaration which has given name to the Book, referring to his predecessors, and asking the assistance of all his hearers, that his reign may be a not unworthy sequel of theirs. With this the proceedings terminate, and the king resumes his mourning dress which he had put off for the occasion. The whole thus falls into three chapters.

1. The king came forth and stood (in the space) within the fourth gate of the palace, when the Grand-Guardian led in the princes of the western regions by the left (half) of the gate, and the duke of Pî those of the eastern regions by the right (half)[1]. They then all caused their teams of light bay horses, with their manes and tails dyed red, to be exhibited;—and, (as the king's) guests, lifted up their rank-symbols, and (the other) presents (they had brought)[2],

---

[1] See note on these ministers, p. 235.

[2] These presents were in addition to the teams of horses exhibited in the courtyard;—silks and lighter productions of their various territories.

saying, 'We your servants, defenders (of the throne), venture to bring the productions of our territories, and lay them here.' (With these words) they all did obeisance twice, laying their heads on the ground. The king, as the righteous successor to the virtue of those who had gone before him, returned their obeisance.

The Grand-Guardian and the earl of *Z*ui, with all the rest, then advanced and bowed to each other, after which they did obeisance twice, with their heads to the ground, and said, 'O Son of Heaven, we venture respectfully to declare our sentiments. Great Heaven altered its decree which the great House of Yin had received, and Wăn and Wû of our *K*âu grandly received the same, and carried it out, manifesting their kindly government in the western regions. His recently ascended majesty,* rewarding and punishing exactly in accordance with what was right, fully established their achievements, and transmitted this happy state to his successors. Do you, O king, now be reverent. Maintain your armies in great order, and do not allow the rarely equalled appointment of our high ancestors to come to harm.'*

2. The king spoke to the following effect:—'Ye princes of the various states, chiefs of the Hâu, Tien, Nan, and Wei domains, I, *K*âo, the One man, make an announcement in return (for your advice). The former rulers, Wăn and Wû, were greatly just and enriched (the people). They did not occupy themselves to find out people's crimes. Pushing to the utmost and maintaining an entire impartiality and sincerity, they became gloriously illustrious all under heaven. Then they had officers brave as bears and

grisly bears, and ministers of no double heart, who (helped them) to maintain and regulate the royal House. Thus (did they receive) the true favouring decree from God, and thus did great Heaven approve of their ways, and give them the four quarters (of the land).* Then they appointed and set up principalities, and established bulwarks (to the throne), for the sake of us, their successors. Now do ye, my uncles[1], I pray you, consider with one another, and carry out the service which the dukes, your predecessors, rendered to my predecessors. Though your persons be distant, let your hearts be in the royal House. Enter thus into my anxieties, and act in accordance with them, so that I, the little child, may not be put to shame.'

3. The dukes and all the others, having heard this charge, bowed to one another, and hastily withdrew. The king put off his cap, and assumed again his mourning dress.

BOOK XXIV. THE CHARGE TO THE DUKE OF PÎ.

THE king who delivers the charge in this Book was Khang, and the only events of his reign of twenty-six years of which we have any account in the Shû and in Sze-mâ *Kh*ien are it and the preceding announcement.

Book xxi relates the appointment of *K*ün-*kh*ăn, by king *Kh*ăng, to the charge which was now, on his death, entrusted to the duke of Pî, who is mentioned at the commencement of 'the Testamentary Charge.' By the labours of the duke of *K*âu and *K*ün-*kh*ăn a considerable change had been effected in the character of the people of Yin, who had been transferred to the new capital and its neighbourhood; and king Khang now

---

[1] Meaning the various princes, and especially those bearing the same surname as himself.

appoints the duke of Pî to enter into and complete their work.

After an introductory paragraph, the charge, in three chapters, occupies all the rest of the Book. The first of them speaks of what had been accomplished, and the admirable qualities of the duke which fitted him to accomplish what remained to be done. The second speaks of the special measures which were called for by the original character and the altered character of the people. The third dwells on the importance of the charge, and stimulates the duke, by various considerations, to address himself to fulfil it effectually.

1. In the sixth month of his twelfth year, the day of the new moon's appearance was Kăng-wû, and on *Z*ăn-shăn, the third day after, the king walked in the morning from the honoured capital of *K*âu to Făng[1], and there, with reference to the multitudes of *Kh*ăng-*k*âu[2], gave charge to the duke of Pî[3] to protect and regulate the eastern border.

2. The king spoke to the following effect:—'Oh! Grand-Master, it was when Wăn and Wû had diffused their great virtue all under heaven, that they therefore received the appointment which Yin had enjoyed.* The duke of *K*âu acted as assistant to my royal predecessors, and tranquillized and established their kingdom. Cautiously did he deal with the refractory people of Yin, and removed them to the city of Lo, that they might be quietly near the royal House, and be transformed by its

[1] That is, he went from Hâo, founded by king Wû, to Făng the capital of Wăn. The king wished to give his charge in the temple of king Wăn, because the duke of Pî had been one of his ministers.

[2] *Kh*ăng-*k*âu was a name of the new or 'lower' capital of Lo, perhaps as giving 'completion,' or full establishment to the dynasty.

[3] The duke of Pî had succeeded the duke of *K*âu, in the office of Grand-Master, under king *Kh*ăng.

lessons. Six and thirty years have elapsed[1]; the generation has been changed; and manners have altered. Through the four quarters of the land there is no occasion for anxiety, and I, the One man, enjoy repose.

'The prevailing ways now tend to advancement and now to degeneracy, and measures of government must be varied according to the manners (of the time). If you (now) do not manifest your approval of what is good, the people will not be led to stimulate themselves in it. But your virtue, O duke, is strenuous, and you are cautiously attentive to the smallest things. You have been helpful to and brightened four reigns[2]; with deportment all correct leading on the inferior officers, so that there is not one who does not reverently take your words as a law. Your admirable merits were many (and great) in the times of my predecessors; I, the little child, have but to let my robes hang down, and fold my hands, while I look up for the complete effect (of your measures).'

3. The king said, Oh! Grand-Master, I now reverently charge you with the duties of the duke of *K*âu. Go! Signalize the good, separating the bad from them; give tokens of your approbation in their neighbourhoods[3], making it ill for the evil by such distinction of the good, and thus establishing the influence and reputation (of their virtue). When the people will not obey your lessons and statutes,

---

[1] Probably, from the death of the duke of *K*âu.

[2] Those of Wăn, Wû, *Kh*ăng, and the existing reign of Khang.

[3] Setting up, that is, some conspicuous monument, with an inscription testifying his approbation. All over China, at the present day, such testimonials are met with.

mark off the boundaries of their hamlets, making them fear (to do evil), and desire (to do good). Define anew the borders and frontiers, and be careful to strengthen the guard-posts through the territory, in order to secure tranquillity (within) the four seas. In measures of government to be consistent and constant, and in proclamations a combination of completeness and brevity, are valuable. There should not be the love of what is extraordinary. Among the customs of Shang was the flattery of superiors; sharp-tonguedness was the sign of worth. The remains of these manners are not yet obliterated. Do you, O duke, bear this in mind. I have heard the saying, "Families which have for generations enjoyed places of emolument seldom observe the rules of propriety. They become dissolute, and do violence to virtue, setting themselves in positive opposition to the way of Heaven. They ruin the formative principles of good; encourage extravagance and display; and tend to carry all (future ages) on the same stream with them." Now the officers of Yin had long relied on the favour which they enjoyed. In the confidence of their prideful extravagance they extinguished their (sense of) righteousness. They displayed before men the beauty of their robes, proud, licentious, arrogant, and boastful;—the natural issue was that they should end in being thoroughly bad. Although their lost minds have (in a measure) been recovered, it is difficult to keep them under proper restraint. If with their property and wealth they can be brought under the influence of instruction, they may enjoy lengthened years, virtue, and righteousness!—these are the great lessons. If you do not follow in dealing with them these lessons of antiquity, wherein will you instruct them?'

4. The king said, 'Oh! Grand-Master, the security or the danger of the kingdom depends on those officers of Yin. If you are not (too) stern with them nor (too) mild, their virtue will be truly cultivated. The duke of *K*âu exercised the necessary caution at the beginning (of the undertaking); *K*ün-*kh*ăn displayed the harmony proper to the middle of it; and you, O duke, can bring it at last to a successful issue. You three princes will have been one in aim, and will have equally pursued the proper way. The penetrating power of your principles, and the good character of your measures of government, will exert an enriching influence on the character of the people, so that the wild tribes, with their coats buttoning on the left[1], will all find their proper support in them, and I, the little child, will long enjoy much happiness. Thus, O duke, there in *Kh*ăng-*k*âu will you establish for ever the power (of *K*âu), and you will have an inexhaustible fame. Your descendants will follow your perfect pattern, governing accordingly.

'Oh! do not say, "I am unequal to this;" but exert your mind to the utmost. Do not say, "The people are few;" but attend carefully to your business. Reverently follow the accomplished achievements of the former kings, and complete the excellence of the government of your predecessors.'

---

[1] Confucius once praised Kwan *K*ung, a great minister of *Kh*î, in the seventh century B.C., for his services against the wild tribes of his time, saying, that but for him they in China would be wearing their hair dishevelled, and buttoning the lappets of their coats on the left side. See Analects, XIV, xviii. The long robes and jackets of the Chinese generally stretch over on the right side of the chest, and are there buttoned.

Book XXV. The *K*ün-yâ.

According to the note in the Preface to the Shû, the charge delivered in this Book to *K*ün-yâ, or possibly 'the prince Yâ,' was by king Mû; and its dictum is not challenged by any Chinese critic. The reign of king *Kh*âo, who succeeded to Khang, is thus passed over in the documents of the Shû. Mû was the son and successor of *Kh*âo, and reigned from B.C. 1001 to 947.

*K*ün-yâ's surname is not known. He is here appointed to be Minister of Instruction, and as it is intimated that his father and grandfather had been in the same office, it is conjectured that he was the grandson of the earl of *Z*ui, who was Minister of Instruction at the beginning of the reign of king Khang.

The Book is short, speaking of the duties of the office, and stimulating Yâ to the discharge of them by considerations drawn from the merits of his forefathers, and the services which he would render to the dynasty and his sovereign.

1. The king spoke to the following effect:—'Oh! *K*ün-yâ, your grandfather and your father, one after the other, with a true loyalty and honesty, laboured in the service of the royal House, accomplishing a merit that was recorded on the grand banner[1]. I, the little child, have become charged by inheritance with the line of government transmitted from Wăn and Wû, from *Kh*ăng and Khang; I also keep thinking of their ministers who aided them in the good government of the kingdom; the trembling anxiety of my mind makes me feel as if I were treading on a tiger's tail, or walking upon spring ice. I now give you charge to assist me;

[1] The grand banner was borne aloft when the king went to sacrifice. There were figures of the sun and moon on it, and dragons lying along its breadth, one over the other, head above tail. The names of meritorious ministers were inscribed on it during their lifetime, preparatory to their sharing in the sacrifices of the ancestral temple after their death.

be as my limbs to me, as my heart and backbone. Continue their old service, and do not disgrace your grandfather and father.

'Diffuse widely (the knowledge of) the five invariable relations (of society), and reverently seek to produce a harmonious observance of the duties belonging to them among the people. If you are correct in your own person, none will dare to be but correct. The minds of the people cannot attain to the right mean (of duty);—they must be guided by your attaining to it. In the heat and rains of summer, the inferior people may be described as murmuring and sighing. And so it is with them in the great cold of winter. How great are their hardships! Think of their hardships in order to seek to promote their ease; and the people will be tranquil. Oh! how great and splendid were the plans of king Wăn! How greatly were they carried out by the energy of king Wû! All in principle correct, and deficient in nothing, they are for the help and guidance of us their descendants. Do you with reverence and wisdom carry out your instructions, enabling me to honour and follow the example of my (immediate) predecessors, and to respond to and display the bright decree conferred on Wăn and Wû;—so shall you be the mate of your by-gone fathers.'

2. The king spoke to the following effect:—'*K*ün-yâ, do you take for your rule the lessons afforded by the courses of your excellent fathers. The good or the bad order of the people depends on this. You will thus follow the practice of your grandfather and father, and make the good government of your sovereign illustrious.'

BOOK XXVI. THE CHARGE TO *KH*IUNG.

THE charge recorded here, like that in the last Book, is assigned to king Mû. It was delivered on the appointment of a *Kh*iung or Po-*kh*iung (that is, the eldest *Kh*iung, the eldest brother in his family) to be High Chamberlain. Of this *Kh*iung we know nothing more than we learn from the Shû. He was no high dignitary of state. That the charge to him found a place in the Shû, we are told, shows how important it was thought that men in the lowest positions, yet coming into contact with the sovereign, should possess correct principles and an earnest desire for his progress in intelligence and virtue.

King Mû represents himself as conscious of his own incompetencies, and impressed with a sense of the high duties devolving on him. His predecessors, much superior to himself, were yet greatly indebted to the aid of the officers about them;—how much more must this be the case with him!

He proceeds to appoint *Kh*iung to be the High Chamberlain, telling him how he should guide correctly all the other servants about the royal person, so that none but good influences should be near to act upon the king;—telling him also the manner of men whom he should employ, and the care he should exercise in the selection of them.

The king spoke to the following effect:—'Po-*kh*iung, I come short in virtue, and have succeeded to the former kings, to occupy the great throne. I am fearful, and conscious of the peril (of my position). I rise at midnight, and think how I can avoid falling into errors. Formerly Wăn and Wû were endowed with all intelligence, august and sage, while their ministers, small and great, all cherished loyalty and goodness. Their servants, charioteers, chamberlains, and followers were all men of correctness; morning and evening waiting on their sovereign's wishes, or supplying his deficiencies. (Those kings), going out and coming in, rising up and sitting down, were thus made reverent. Their every warning or command was good. The people yielded a reverent obedience, and the myriad regions were all happy. But I, the One man, am destitute of goodness, and really depend on the officers who have places about me to help my deficiencies, applying the line to my faults, and exhibiting my errors, thus correcting my bad heart, and enabling me to be the successor of my meritorious predecessors.

'Now I appoint you to be High Chamberlain, to see that all the officers in your department and my personal attendants are upright and correct, that they strive to promote the virtue of their sovereign, and together supply my deficiencies. Be careful in selecting your officers. Do not employ men of artful speech and insinuating looks, men whose likes and dislikes are ruled by mine, one-sided men and flatterers; but employ good men. When these household officers are correct, the sovereign will be correct; when they are flatterers, the sovereign will consider himself a sage. His virtue or his want of it equally depends on them. Cultivate no intimacy with flatterers, nor get them to do duty for me as my ears and eyes;—they will lead their sovereign to disregard the statutes of the former kings. If you choose the men not for their personal goodness, but for the sake of their bribes, their offices will be made of no effect, your great want of reverence for your sovereign will be apparent, and I will hold you guilty.'

The king said, 'Oh! be reverent! Ever help your sovereign to follow the regular laws of duty (which he should exemplify).'

Book XXVII.

The Marquis of Lü on Punishments.

The charge or charges recorded in this Book were given in the hundredth year of the king's age. The king, it is again understood, was Mû; and the hundredth year of his age would be B.C. 952. The title of the Book in Chinese is simply 'Lü's Punishments,' and I conclude that Lü, or the marquis of Lü, was a high minister who prepared, by the king's orders, a code of punishments for the regulation of the kingdom, in connexion with the undertaking, or the completion, of which the king delivered to his princes and judges the sentiments that are here preserved.

The common view is that Lü is the name of a principality, the marquis of which was Mû's Minister of Crime. Where it was is not well known, and as the Book is quoted in the Lî *K*î several times under the title of 'Fû on Punishments,' it is supposed that Lü and Fû (a small marquisate in the present Ho-nan) were the same.

The whole Book is divided into seven chapters. The first is merely a brief introduction, the historiographer's account of the circumstances in which king Mû delivered his lessons. Each of the other chapters begins with the words, 'The king said.' The first two of them are an historical resumé of the lessons of antiquity on the subject of punishments, and an inculcation on the princes and officers of justice to give heed to them, and learn from them. The next two tell the princes of the diligence and carefulness to be employed in the use of punishments, and how they can make punishments a blessing. The fourth chapter treats principally of the commutation or redemption of punishments, and has been very strongly condemned by critics and moralists. They express their surprise that such a document should be in the Shû, and, holding that the collection was made by Confucius, venture to ask what the sage meant by admitting it. There is, in fact, no evidence that the redemption of punishments on the scale here laid down, existed in China before Mû's time. It has entered, however, into the penal code of every subsequent dynasty. Great official corruption and depravation of the general morality would seem to be inseparable from such a system. The fifth chapter returns again to the reverence with which punishments should be employed; and the sixth and last is addressed to future generations, and directs them to the ancient models, in order that punishments may never be but a blessing to the kingdom.

A Chinese critic says that throughout the Book 'virtue' and 'exact adaptation' are the terms that carry the weight of the meaning. Virtue must underlie the use of punishments, of which their exact adaptation will be the manifestation.

1. In reference to the charge to (the marquis of) Lü:—When the king had occupied the throne till he reached the age of a hundred years, he gave great consideration to the appointment of punishments, in order to deal with (the people of) the four quarters.

2. The king said, 'According to the teachings of ancient times, *Kh*ih Yû was the first to produce disorder, which spread among the quiet, orderly people, till all became robbers and murderers, owl-like and yet self-complacent in their conduct, traitors and villains, snatching and filching, dissemblers and oppressors[1].

'Among the people of Miâo, they did not use the power of goodness, but the restraint of punishments. They made the five punishments engines of oppression[2], calling them the laws. They

---

[1] *Kh*ih Yû, as has been observed in the Introduction, p. 27, is the most ancient name mentioned in the Shû, and carries us back, according to the Chinese chronologists, nearly to the beginning of the twenty-seventh century B.C. P. Gaubil translates the characters which appear in the English text here as 'According to the teachings of ancient times' by 'Selon les anciens documents,' which is more than the Chinese text says.—It is remarkable that at the commencement of Chinese history, Chinese tradition placed a period of innocence, a season when order and virtue ruled in men's affairs.

[2] I do not think it is intended to say here that 'the five punishments' were invented by the chiefs of the Miâo; but only that

slaughtered the innocent, and were the first also to go to excess in cutting off the nose, cutting off the ears, castration, and branding. All who became liable to those punishments were dealt with without distinction, no difference being made in favour of those who could offer some excuse. The people were gradually affected by this state of things, and became dark and disorderly. Their hearts were no more set on good faith, but they violated their oaths and covenants. The multitudes who suffered from the oppressive terrors, and were (in danger of) being murdered, declared their innocence to Heaven. God surveyed the people, and there was no fragrance of virtue arising from them, but the rank odour of their (cruel) punishments.*

'The great Tî[1] compassionated the innocent multitudes that were (in danger of) being murdered, and made the oppressors feel the terrors of his majesty. He restrained and (finally) extinguished the people of Miâo, so that they should not con-

these used them excessively and barbarously. From two passages in the Canon of Shun, we conclude that that monarch was acquainted with 'the five great inflictions or punishments,' and gave instructions to his minister Kâo-yâo as to their use.

[1] Here is the name—Hwang Tî—by which the sovereigns of China have been styled from B.C. 221, since the emperor of *Kh*in, on his extinction of the feudal states, enacted that it should be borne by himself and his descendants. I have spoken of the meaning of Tî and of the title Hwang Tî in the note on the translation of the Shû appended to the Preface. There can be no doubt that it was Shun whom king Mû intended by the name. A few sentences further on, the mention of Po-î and Yü leads us to the time subsequent to Yâo, and there does not appear to be any change of subject in the paragraph. We get from this Book a higher idea of the power of the Miâo than from the Books of Part II.

tinue to future generations. Then he commissioned *Kh*ung and Lî[1] to make an end of the communications between earth and heaven; and the descents (of spirits) ceased[1]. From the princes down to the

[1] *Kh*ung and Lî are nowhere met with in the previous parts of the Shû, nor in any other reliable documents of history, as officers of Shun. Ȝhâi *Kh*ăn and others would identify them with the Hsî and Ho of the Canon of Yâo, and hold those to have been descended from a *Kh*ung and a Lî, supposed to belong to the time of Shâo Hâo in the twenty-sixth century B.C.

Whoever they were, the duty with which they were charged was remarkable. In the Narratives of the States (a book of the *K*âu dynasty), we find a conversation on it, during the lifetime of Confucius, between king *Kh*âo of *Kh*û (B.C. 515–489) and one of his ministers, called Kwan Yî-fû. 'What is meant,' asked the king, 'by what is said in one of the Books of *K*âu about *Kh*ung and Lî, that they really brought it about that there was no intercourse between heaven and earth? If they had not done so, would people have been able to ascend to heaven?' The minister replied that that was not the meaning at all, and gave his own view of it at great length, to the following effect.—Anciently, the people attended to the discharge of their duties to one another, and left the worship of spiritual beings—the seeking intercourse with them, and invoking and effecting their descent on earth—to the officers who were appointed for that purpose. In this way things proceeded with great regularity. The people minded their own affairs, and the spirits minded theirs. Tranquillity and prosperity were the consequence. But in the time of Shâo Hâo, through the lawlessness of *K*iû-lî, a change took place. The people intruded into the functions of the regulators of the spirits and their worship. They abandoned their duties to their fellow men, and tried to bring down spirits from above. The spirits themselves, no longer kept in check and subjected to rule, made their appearance irregularly and disastrously. All was confusion and calamity, when *K*wan Hsü (B.C. 2510–2433) took the case in hand. He appointed *Kh*ung, the Minister of the South, to the superintendency of heavenly things, to prescribe the laws for the spirits, and Lî, the Minister of Fire, to the superintendency of earthly things, to prescribe the rules for the people. In this way both spirits and people were

inferior officers, all helped with clear intelligence (the spread of) the regular principles of duty, and the solitary and widows were no longer overlooked. The great Tî with an unprejudiced mind carried his enquiries low down among the people, and the solitary and widows laid before him their complaints against the Miâo. He awed the people by the majesty of his virtue, and enlightened them by its brightness. He thereupon charged the three princely (ministers)[1] to labour with compassionate anxiety in the people's behalf. Po-î delivered his statutes to prevent the people from rendering themselves obnoxious to punishment; Yü reduced to order the water and the land, and presided over the naming of the hills and rivers; *K*î spread abroad a knowledge of agriculture, and (the people) extensively cultivated the admirable grains. When the three princes had accomplished their work, it was abundantly well with the people. The Minister of Crime[2] exercised among them the restraint of

brought back to their former regular courses, and there was no unhallowed interference of the one with the other. This was the work described in the text. But subsequently the chief of San-miâo showed himself a *K*iû-lî redivivus, till Yâo called forth the descendants of *Kh*ung and Lî, who had not forgotten the virtue and functions of their fathers, and made them take the case in hand again.

According to Yî-fû's statements *Kh*ung's functions were those of the Minister of Religion, and Lî's those of the Minister of Instruction; but Hsî and Ho were simply Ministers of Astronomy and the Calendar, and their descendants continue to appear as such in the Shû to the reign of *K*ung Khang, long after we know that men of other families were appointed to the important ministries of *Kh*ung and Lî.

[1] Those immediately mentioned,—Po-î, Yü, and *K*î. See the Canon of Shun and other Books of Part II.

[2] Kâo-yâo.

punishment in exact adaptation to each offence, and taught them to reverence virtue. The greatest gravity and harmony in the sovereign, and the greatest intelligence in those below him, thus shining forth to all quarters (of the land), all were rendered diligent in cultivating their virtue. Hence, (if anything more were wanted), the clear adjudication of punishments effected the regulation of the people, and helped them to observe the regular duties of life. The officers who presided over criminal cases executed the law (fearlessly) against the powerful, and (faithfully) against the wealthy. They were reverent and cautious. They had no occasion to make choice of words to vindicate their conduct. The virtue of Heaven was attained to by them; from them was the determination of so great a matter as the lives (of men). In their low sphere they yet corresponded (to Heaven) and enjoyed (its favour).' *

3. The king said, 'Ah! you who direct the government and preside over criminal cases through all the land, are you not constituted the shepherds of Heaven? * To whom ought you now to look as your pattern? Is it not to Po-î, spreading among the people his lessons to avert punishments? And from whom ought you now to take warning? Is it not from the people of Miâo, who would not examine into the circumstances of criminal cases, and did not make choice of good officers that should see to the right apportioning of the five punishments, but chose the violent and bribe-snatchers, who determined and administered them, so as to oppress the innocent, until God would no longer hold them guiltless, and sent down calamity on

Miâo, when the people had no plea to allege in mitigation of their punishment, and their name was cut off from the world?' *

4. The king said, 'Oh! lay it to heart. My uncles, and all ye, my brethren and cousins, my sons and my grandsons[1], listen all of you to my words, in which, it may be, you will receive a most important charge. You will only tread the path of satisfaction by being daily diligent;—do not have occasion to beware of the want of diligence. Heaven, in its wish to regulate the people, allows us for a day to make use of punishments.* Whether crimes have been premeditated, or are unpremeditated, depends on the parties concerned;—do you (deal with them so as to) accord with the mind of Heaven, and thus serve me, the One man. Though I would put them to death, do not you therefore put them to death; though I would spare them, do not you therefore spare them. Reverently apportion the five punishments, so as fully to exhibit the three virtues[2]. Then shall I, the One man, enjoy felicity; the people will look to you as their sure dependance; the repose of such a state will be perpetual.'

5. The king said, 'Ho! come, ye rulers of states and territories[3], I will tell you how to make punishments a blessing. It is yours now to give repose to the people;—what should you be most concerned

[1] Meaning all the princes of the same surname as himself. As he was a hundred years old, there might well be among them those who were really his sons and grandsons.

[2] 'The three virtues' are those of the Great Plan; those of 'correctness and straightforwardness,' of 'strong government,' and of 'mild government.'

[3] Meaning all the princes;—of the king's own and other surnames.

about the choosing of? Should it not be the proper men? What should you deal with the most reverently? Should it not be punishments? What should you calculate the most carefully? Should it not be to whom these will reach?

'When both parties are present, (with their documents and witnesses) all complete, let the judges listen to the fivefold statements that may be made[1]. When they have examined and fully made up their minds on those, let them adjust the case to one of the five punishments. If the five punishments do not meet it, let them adjust it to one of the five redemption-fines; and if these, again, are not sufficient for it, let them reckon it among the five cases of error[2].

'In (settling) the five cases of error there are evils (to be guarded against);—being warped by the influence of power, or by private grudge, or by female solicitation, or by bribes, or by applications. Any one of these things should be held equal to the crime (before the judges). Do you carefully examine, and prove yourselves equal to (every difficulty).

'When there are doubts as to the infliction of any of the five punishments, that infliction should be forborne. When there are doubts as to the

[1] That is, the statements, with the evidence on both sides, whether incriminating or exculpating. They are called fivefold, as the case might have to be dealt with by one or other of 'the five punishments.'

[2] That is, the offences of inadvertence. What should ensue on the adjudication of any case to be so ranked does not appear. It would be very leniently dealt with, and perhaps pardoned. In 'the Counsels of Yü,' Kâo-yâo says to Shun, 'You pardon inadvertent offences however great.'

infliction of any of the five fines, it should be forborne. Do you carefully examine, and prove yourselves equal to overcome (every difficulty). When you have examined and many things are clear, yet form a judgment from studying the appearance of the parties. If you find nothing out on examination, do not listen (to the case any more). In everything stand in awe of the dread majesty of Heaven.*

'When, in a doubtful case, the punishment of branding is forborne, the fine to be laid on instead is 600 ounces (of copper); but you must first have satisfied yourselves as to the crime. When the case would require the cutting off the nose, the fine must be double this;—with the same careful determination of the crime. When the punishment would be the cutting off the feet, the fine must be 3000 ounces;—with the same careful determination of the crime. When the punishment would be castration[1], the fine must be 3600 ounces;—with the same determination. When the punishment would be death, the fine must be 6000 ounces;—with the same determination. Of crimes that may be redeemed by the fine in lieu of branding there are 1000; and the same number of those that would otherwise incur cutting off the nose. The fine in lieu of cutting off the feet extends to 500 cases; that in lieu of castration, to 300; and that in lieu of death, to 200. Altogether, set against the five punishments, there are 3000 crimes. (In the case of others not exactly defined), you must class them with the (next) higher or (next) lower offences, not

[1] Or solitary confinement in the case of a female.

admitting assumptive and disorderly pleadings, and not using obsolete laws. Examine and act lawfully, judging carefully, and proving yourselves equal (to every difficulty).

'Where the crime should incur one of the higher punishments, but there are mitigating circumstances, apply to it the next lower. Where it should incur one of the lower punishments, but there are aggravating circumstances, apply to it the next higher. The light and heavy fines are to be apportioned (in the same way) by the balance of circumstances. Punishments and fines should (also) be light in one age, and heavy in another. To secure uniformity in this (seeming) irregularity, there are certain relations of things (to be considered), and the essential principle (to be observed).

'The chastisement of fines is short of death, yet it will produce extreme distress. They are not (therefore) persons of artful tongues who should determine criminal cases, but really good persons, whose awards will hit the right mean. Examine carefully where there are any discrepancies in the statements; the view which you were resolved not to follow, you may see occasion to follow; with compassion and reverence settle the cases; examine carefully the penal code, and deliberate with all about it, that your decisions may be likely to hit the proper mean and be correct;—whether it be the infliction of a punishment or a fine, examining carefully and mastering every difficulty. When the case is thus concluded, all parties will acknowledge the justice of the sentence; and when it is reported, the sovereign will do the same. In sending up reports of cases, they must be full and complete.

If a man have been tried on two counts, his two punishments (must be recorded).'

6. The king said, 'Oh! let there be a feeling of reverence. Ye judges and princes, of the same surname with me, and of other surnames, (know all) that I speak in much fear. I think with reverence of the subject of punishment, for the end of it is to promote virtue. Now Heaven, wishing to help the people, has made us its representatives here below.* Be intelligent and pure in hearing (each) side of a case. The right ordering of the people depends on the impartial hearing of the pleas on both sides;—do not seek for private advantage to yourselves by means of those pleas. Gain (so) got by the decision of cases is no precious acquisition; it is an accumulation of guilt, and will be recompensed with many judgments:—you should ever stand in awe of the punishment of Heaven.* It is not Heaven that does not deal impartially with men, but men ruin themselves. If the punishment of Heaven were not so extreme, nowhere under the sky would the people have good government.'

7. The king said, 'Oh! ye who shall hereafter inherit (the dignities and offices of) the present time, to whom are ye to look for your models? Must it not be to those who promoted the virtue belonging to the unbiassed nature of the people? I pray you give attention to my words. The wise men (of antiquity) by their use of punishments obtained boundless fame. Everything relating to the five punishments exactly hit with them the due mean, and hence came their excellence. Receiving from your sovereigns the good multitudes, behold in the case of those men punishments made felicitous!'

Book XXVIII.

The Charge to the Marquis Wăn.

The king to whom this charge is ascribed was Phing (B.C. 770–719). Between him and Mû there was thus a period of fully two centuries, of which no documents are, or ever were, in the collection of the Shû. The time was occupied by seven reigns, the last of which was that of Nieh, known as king Yû, a worthless ruler, and besotted in his attachment to a female favourite, called Pâo-sze. For her sake he degraded his queen, and sent their son, Î-*kh*iû, to the court of the lord of Shăn, her father, 'to learn good manners.' The lord of Shăn called in the assistance of some barbarian tribes, by which the capital was sacked, and the king slain; and with him ended the sway of 'the Western *K*âu.' Several of the feudal princes went to the assistance of the royal House, drove away the barbarians, brought back Î-*kh*iû from Shăn, and hailed him as king. He is known as king Phing, 'the Tranquillizer.' His first measure was to transfer the capital from the ruins of Hâo to Lo, thus fulfilling at length, but under disastrous circumstances, the wishes of the duke of *K*âu; and from this time (B.C. 770) dates the history of 'the Eastern *K*âu.'

Among king Phing's early measures was the rewarding the feudal lords to whom he owed his throne. The marquis of *K*in was one of them. His name was *Kh*iû, and that of Î-ho, by which he is called in the text, is taken as his 'style,' or designation assumed by him on his marriage. Wăn, 'the Accomplished,' was his sacrificial title. The lords of *K*in were descended from king Wû's son, Yü, who was appointed marquis of Thang, corresponding to the present department of Thâi-yüan, in Shan-hsî. The name of Thang was afterwards changed into *K*in. The state became in course of time one of the largest and most powerful in the kingdom.

The charge in this Book is understood to be in connexion with Wăn's appointment to be president or chief of several of the other princes. The king begins by celebrating the virtues and happy times of kings Wăn and Wû, and the services rendered by the worthy ministers of subsequent reigns. He contrasts with this the misery and distraction of his own times, deploring his want of wise counsellors and helpers, and praising the marquis for the services which he had rendered. He then concludes with the special charge by which he would reward the prince's merit in the past, and stimulate him to greater exertions in the future.

1. The king spoke to the following effect:—'Uncle Î-ho, how illustrious were Wăn and Wû! Carefully did they make their virtue brilliant, till it rose brightly on high, and the fame of it was widely diffused here below. Therefore God caused his favouring decree to light upon king Wăn.* There were ministers also (thereafter), who aided and illustriously served their sovereigns, following and carrying out their plans, great and small, so that my fathers sat tranquilly on the throne.

'Oh! an object of pity am I, who am (but as) a little child. Just as I have succeeded to the throne, Heaven has severely chastised me.* Through the interruption of the (royal) bounties that ceased to descend to the inferior people, the invading barbarous tribes of the west have greatly (injured) our kingdom. Moreover, among the managers of my affairs there are none of age and experience and distinguished ability in their offices. I am (thus) unequal (to the difficulties of my position), and say to myself, "My grand-uncles and uncles, you ought to compassionate my case." Oh! if there were those who could establish their merit in behalf of me, the One man, I might long enjoy repose upon the throne.

'Uncle Î-ho, you render still more glorious your illustrious ancestor. You were the first to imitate the example of Wăn and Wû, collecting (the scattered powers), and continuing (the all but broken line of) your sovereign. Your filial piety goes back to your accomplished ancestor, (and is equal to his.) You have done much to repair my (losses), and defend me in my difficulties, and of you, being such, I am full of admiration.'

2. The king said, 'Uncle Î-ho, return home, survey your multitudes, and tranquillize your state. I reward you with a jar of spirits, distilled from the black millet, and flavoured with odoriferous herbs [1], with a red bow, and a hundred red arrows [2]; with a black bow, and a hundred black arrows; and with four horses. Go, my uncle. Show kindness to those that are far off, and help those who are near at hand; cherish and secure the repose of the inferior people; do not idly seek your ease; exercise an inspection and (benign) compassion in your capital (and all your borders);—thus completing your illustrious virtue.'

BOOK XXIX. THE SPEECH AT PÎ.

THE Speech at Pî carries us back from the time of Phing to that of king *Kh*ăng. In the Preface to the Shû it is attributed to Po-*kh*in, the son of the duke of *K*âu; and there is a general acquiescence of tradition and critics in this view. We may account for its position out of the chronological order from

---

[1] Compare king *Kh*ăng's gift to the duke of *K*âu, in the Announcement concerning Lo, ch. 6.

[2] The conferring on a prince of a bow and arrows, invested him with the power of punishing throughout the states within his jurisdiction all who were disobedient to the royal commands, but not of taking life without first reporting to the court. The gift was also a tribute to the merit of the receiver. See the Book of Poetry, II, iii, ode 1.

the Book's being the record not of any royal doings, but of the words of the ruler of a state.

The speech has reference to some military operations against the wild tribes on the Hwâi river and in other parts of the province of Hsü; and we have seen that they were in insurrection many times during the reign of *Kh*ăng. We thus cannot tell exactly the year in which the speech was delivered. Po-*kh*in presided over his state of Lû for the long period of fifty-three years, and died B.C. 1063.

The name of Pî is retained in the district still so called of the department of Î-*k*âu. At first it was an independent territory, but attached to Lû, and under the jurisdiction of its marquises, by one of whom it had been incorporated with Lû before the time of Confucius.

Po-*kh*in appears at the head of his host, approaching the scene of active operations. Having commanded silence, he issues his orders, first, that the soldiers shall have their weapons in good order; next, that the people of the country shall take care of the oxen and horses of the army; further, that the troops on no account leave their ranks or go astray; and finally, he names the day when he will commence operations against the enemy, and commands all the requisite preparations to be made.

The duke said, 'Ah! ye men, make no noise, but listen to my commands. We are going (to punish) those wild tribes of the Hwâi and of Hsü, which have risen up together.

'Have in good repair your buff coats and helmets; have the laces of your shields well secured;—presume not to have any of them but in perfect order. Prepare your bows and arrows; temper your lances and spears; sharpen your pointed and edged weapons;—presume not to have any of them but in good condition.

'We must now largely let the oxen and horses loose, and not keep them in enclosures;—(ye people), do you close your traps and fill up your pitfalls, and do not presume to injure any of the animals (so let loose). If any of them be injured, you shall be dealt with according to the regular punishments.

'When the horses or cattle are seeking one another, or when your followers, male or female, abscond, presume not to leave the ranks to pursue them. But let them be carefully returned. I will reward you (among the people) who return them according to their value. But if you leave your places to pursue them, or if you who find them do not restore them, you shall be dealt with according to the regular punishments.

'And let none of you presume to commit any robbery or detain any creature that comes in your way, to jump over enclosures and walls to steal (people's) horses or oxen, or to decoy away their servants or female attendants. If you do so, you shall be dealt with according to the regular punishments.

'On the day *K*iâ-hsü I will take action against the hordes of Hsü;—prepare the roasted grain and other provisions, and presume not to have any deficiency. If you have, you shall suffer the severest punishment. Ye men of Lû, from the three environing territories and the three tracts beyond[1],

---

[1] Outside the capital city was an environing territory called the *K*iâo, and beyond the *K*iâo was the Sui. The *K*iâo of the royal domain was divided again into six Hsiang, which furnished the six royal hosts, while the Sui beyond furnished subsidiary hosts. The *K*iâo and Sui of a large state furnished three hosts, and if need were, subsidiary battalions. The language of the text is equivalent, I conceive, simply to 'ye men of the army of Lû;' but, as P. Gaubil observes, it is difficult at the present day to get correct ideas of what is meant by the designations, and to account for the mention of three *K*iâo and three Sui.

be ready with your posts and planks. On *K*iâ-hsü I will commence my intrenchments;—dare not but be provided with a supply of these. (If you be not so provided), you shall be subjected to various punishments, short only of death. Ye men of Lû, from the three environing territories and the three tracts beyond, be ready with the forage, and do not dare to let it be other than abundant. (If you do), you shall suffer the severest punishment.'

Book XXX.

The Speech of (the Marquis of) *Kh*in.

The state of *Kh*in, at the time to which this speech belongs, was one of the most powerful in the kingdom, and already giving promise of what it would grow to. Ultimately, one of its princes overthrew the dynasty of *K*âu, and brought feudal China to an end. Its earliest capital was in the present district of *Kh*ăng-shui, *Kh*in *K*âu, Kan-sû.

*Kh*in and *K*in were engaged together in B.C. 631 in besieging the capital of *K*ăng, and threatened to extinguish that state. The marquis of *Kh*in, however, was suddenly induced to withdraw his troops, leaving three of his officers in friendly relations with the court of *K*ăng, and under engagement to defend the state from aggression. These men played the part of spies in the interest of *Kh*in, and in B.C. 629, one of them, called *Kh*î-ȝze, sent word that he was in charge of one of the gates, and if an army were sent to surprise the capital, *K*ăng might be added to the territories of *Kh*in. The marquis—known in history as duke Mû—laid the matter before his counsellors. The most experienced of them—Pâi-lî Hsî and *Kh*ien-shû—were against taking advantage of the proposed treachery; but the marquis listened rather to the promptings of ambition; and the next year he sent a large force, under his three ablest commanders, hoping to find *K*ăng unprepared for any resistance. The attempt, however, failed; and the army, on its way back to

*Kh*in, was attacked by the forces of *K*in, and sustained a terrible defeat. It was nearly annihilated, and the three commanders were taken prisoners.

The marquis of *K*in was intending to put these captives to death, but finally sent them to *Kh*in, that duke Mû might himself sacrifice them to his anger for their want of success. Mû, however, did no such thing. He went from his capital to meet the disgraced generals, and comforted them, saying that the blame of their defeat was due to himself, who had refused to listen to the advice of his wise counsellors. Then also, it is said, he made the speech here preserved for the benefit of all his ministers, describing the good and bad minister, and the different issues of listening to them and deploring how he had himself foolishly rejected the advice of his aged counsellors, and followed that of new men;—a thing which he would never do again.

The duke[1] said, 'Ah! my officers, listen to me without noise. I solemnly announce to you the most important of all sayings. (It is this which) the ancients have said, "Thus it is with all people,—they mostly love their ease. In reproving others there is no difficulty, but to receive reproof, and allow it to have free course,—this is difficult." The sorrow of my heart is, that the days and months have passed away, and it is not likely they will come again, (so that I might pursue a different course.)

'There were my old counsellors[2].—I said, "They will not accommodate themselves to me," and I hated them. There were my new counsellors, and I would for the time give my confidence to them[3]. So indeed it was with me; but hereafter I will

[1] The prince of *Kh*in was only a marquis; but the historiographers or recorders of a state always gave their ruler the higher title. This shows that this speech is taken from the chronicles of *Kh*in.

[2] Pâi-lî Hsî and *Kh*ien-shû.

[3] *Kh*î-ȝze and others.

take advice from the men of yellow hair, and then I shall be free from error. That good old officer! —his strength is exhausted, but I would rather have him (as my counsellor). That dashing brave officer!—his shooting and charioteering are faultless, but I would rather not wish to have him. As to men of quibbles, skilful at cunning words, and able to make the good man change his purposes, what have I to do to make much use of them?

'I have deeply thought and concluded.—Let me have but one resolute minister, plain and sincere, without other ability, but having a straightforward mind, and possessed of generosity, regarding the talents of others as if he himself possessed them; and when he finds accomplished and sage men, loving them in his heart more than his mouth expresses, really showing himself able to bear them: —such a minister would be able to preserve my descendants and people, and would indeed be a giver of benefits.

'But if (the minister), when he finds men of ability, be jealous and hates them; if, when he finds accomplished and sage men, he oppose them and does not allow their advancement, showing himself really not able to bear them:—such a man will not be able to protect my descendants and people; and will he not be a dangerous man?

'The decline and fall of a state may arise from one man. The glory and tranquillity of a state may also arise from the goodness of one man.'

THE SHIH KING

OR

BOOK OF POETRY:

ALL THE PIECES AND STANZAS IN IT ILLUSTRATING
THE RELIGIOUS VIEWS AND PRACTICES OF
THE WRITERS AND THEIR TIMES.

THE SHIH KING

OR

BOOK OF POETRY.

INTRODUCTION.

CHAPTER I.

THE NAME AND CONTENTS OF THE CLASSIC.

1. Among the Chinese classical books next after the Shû in point of antiquity comes the Shih or Book of Poetry.

The meaning of the character Shih.

The character Shû[1], as formed by the combination of two others, one of which signified 'a pencil,' and the other 'to speak,' supplied, we saw, in its structure, an indication of its primary significance, and furnished a clue to its different applications. The character Shih[2] was made on a different principle,—that of phonetical formation, in the peculiar sense of these words when applied to a large class of Chinese terms. The significative portion of it is the character for 'speech,' but the other half is merely phonetical, enabling us to approximate to its pronunciation or name. The meaning of the compound has to be learned from its usage. Its most common significations are 'poetry,' 'a poem, or poems,' and 'a collection of poems.' This last is its meaning when we speak of the Shih or the Shih King.

The earliest Chinese utterance that we have on the subject of poetry is that in the Shû by the ancient Shun, when he said to his Minister of Music, 'Poetry is the expression of earnest thought, and singing is the prolonged

---

[1] 書 [2] 詩

utterance of that expression.' To the same effect is the language of a Preface to the Shih, sometimes ascribed to Confucius, and certainly older than our Christian era:—'Poetry is the product of earnest thought. Thought cherished in the mind becomes earnest; then expressed in words, it becomes poetry. The feelings move inwardly, and are embodied in words. When words are insufficient for them, recourse is had to sighs and exclamations. When sighs and exclamations are insufficient for them, recourse is had to the prolonged utterance of song. When this again is insufficient, unconsciously the hands begin to move and the feet to dance. . . . . To set forth correctly the successes and failures (of government), to affect Heaven and Earth, and to move spiritual beings, there is no readier instrument than poetry.'

Rhyme, it may be added here, is a necessary accompaniment of poetry in the estimation of the Chinese. Only in a very few pieces of the Shih is it neglected.

The contents of the Shih.

2. The Shih King contains 305 pieces and the titles of six others. The most recent of them are assigned to the reign of king Ting of the *K*âu dynasty, B.C. 606 to 586, and the oldest, forming a group of only five, to the period of the Shang dynasty which preceded that of *K*âu, B.C. 1766 to 1123. Of those five, the latest piece should be referred to the twelfth century B.C., and the most ancient may have been composed five centuries earlier. All the other pieces in the Shih have to be distributed over the time between Ting and king Wăn, the founder of the line of *K*âu. The distribution, however, is not equal nor continuous. There were some reigns of which we do not have a single poetical fragment.

The whole collection is divided into four parts, called the Kwo Făng, the Hsiâo Yâ, the Tâ Yâ, and the Sung.

The Kwo Făng, in fifteen Books, contains 160 pieces, nearly all of them short, and descriptive of manners and events in several of the feudal states of *K*âu. The title has been translated by The Manners of the Different States, 'Les Mœurs des Royaumes,' and, which I prefer, by Lessons from the States.

The Hsiâo Yâ, or Lesser Yâ, in eight Books, contains seventy-four pieces and the titles of six others, sung at gatherings of the feudal princes, and their appearances at the royal court. They were produced in the royal territory, and are descriptive of the manners and ways of the government in successive reigns. It is difficult to find an English word that shall fitly represent the Chinese Yâ as here used. In his Latin translation of the Shih, P. Lacharme translated Hsiâo Yâ by 'Quod rectum est, sed inferiore ordine,' adding in a note :—'Siâo Yâ, latine Parvum Rectum, quia in hac Parte mores describuntur, recti illi quidem, qui tamen nonnihil a recto deflectunt.' But the manners described are not less correct or incorrect, as the case may be, than those of the states in the former Part or of the kingdom in the next. I prefer to call this Part 'Minor Odes of the Kingdom,' without attempting to translate the term Yâ.

The Tâ Yâ or Greater Yâ, in three Books, contains thirty-one pieces, sung on great occasions at the royal court and in the presence of the king. P. Lacharme called it 'Magnum Rectum (Quod rectum est superiore ordine).' But there is the same objection here to the use of the word 'correct' as in the case of the pieces of the previous Part. I use the name 'Major Odes of the Kingdom.' The greater length and dignity of most of the pieces justify the distinction of the two Parts into Minor and Major.

The Sung, also in three Books, contains forty pieces, thirty-one of which belong to the sacrificial services at the royal court of *K*âu ; four, to those of the marquises of Lû ; and five to the corresponding sacrifices of the kings of Shang. P. Lacharme denominated them correctly 'Parentales Cantus.' In the Preface to the Shih, to which I have made reference above, it is said, 'The Sung are pieces in admiration of the embodied manifestation of complete virtue, announcing to the spiritual Intelligences their achievement thereof.' *K*û Hsî's account of the Sung was—'Songs for the Music of the Ancestral Temple ;' and that of *K*iang Yung of the present dynasty—'Songs for the Music at Sacrifices.' I have united these two definitions, and call the Part—'Odes of the Temple and the Altar.' There is a difference between the pieces of Lû and the other two collections in this Part, to which I will call attention in giving the translation of them.

Only the pieces of the fourth Part have professedly a religious character.

From the above account of the contents of the Shih, it will be seen that only the pieces in the last of its four Parts are professedly of a religious character. Many of those, however, in the other Parts, especially the second and third, describe religious services, and give expression to religious ideas in the minds of their authors.

Classification of the pieces from their form and style.

3. Some of the pieces in the Shih are ballads, some are songs, some are hymns, and of others the nature can hardly be indicated by any English denomination. They have often been spoken of by the general name of odes, understanding by that term lyric poems that were set to music.

My reason for touching here on this point is the earliest account of the Shih, as a collection either already formed or in the process of formation, that we find in Chinese literature. In the Official Book of *K*âu, generally supposed to be a work of the twelfth or eleventh century B.C., among the duties of the Grand Music-Master there is 'the teaching,' (that is, to the musical performers,) 'the six classes of poems:—the Făng; the Fû; the Pî; the Hsing; the Yâ; and the Sung.' That the collection of the Shih, as it now is, existed so early as the date assigned to the Official Book could not be; but we find the same account of it given in the so-called Confucian Preface. The Făng, the Yâ, and the Sung are the four Parts of the classic described in the preceding paragraph, the Yâ embracing both the Minor and Major Odes of the Kingdom. But what were the Fû, the Pî, and the Hsing? We might suppose that they were the names of three other distinct Parts or Books. But they were not so. Pieces so discriminated are found in all the four Parts, though there are more of them in the first two than in the others.

The Fû may be described as Narrative pieces, in which the writers tell what they have to say in a simple, straightforward manner, without any hidden meaning reserved in the mind. The metaphor and other figures of speech enter into their composition as freely as in descriptive poems in any other language.

The Pî are Metaphorical pieces, in which the poet has under his language a different meaning from what it expresses,—a meaning which there should be nothing in that language to indicate. Such a piece may be compared to the Æsopic fable; but, while it is the object of the fable to inculcate the virtues of morality and prudence, an historical interpretation has to be sought for the metaphorical pieces of the Shih. Generally, moreover, the moral of the fable is subjoined to it, which is never done in the case of these pieces.

The Hsing have been called Allusive pieces. They are very remarkable, and more numerous than the metaphorical. They often commence with a couple of lines which are repeated without change, or with slight rhythmical changes, in all the stanzas. In other pieces different stanzas have allusive lines peculiar to themselves. Those lines are descriptive, for the most part, of some object or circumstance in the animal or vegetable world, and after them the poet proceeds to his proper subject. Generally, the allusive lines convey a meaning harmonizing with those which follow, where an English poet would begin the verses with Like or As. They are really metaphorical, but the difference between an allusive and a metaphorical piece is this,—that in the former the writer proceeds to state the theme which his mind is occupied with, while no such intimation is given in the latter. Occasionally, it is difficult, not to say impossible, to discover the metaphorical idea in the allusive lines, and then we can only deal with them as a sort of refrain.

In leaving this subject, it is only necessary to say further that the allusive, the metaphorical, and the narrative elements sometimes all occur in the same piece.

CHAPTER II.

THE SHIH BEFORE CONFUCIUS, AND WHAT, IF ANY, WERE HIS LABOURS UPON IT.

1. Sze-mâ *Kh*ien, in his memoir of Confucius, says:—'The old poems amounted to more than 3000. Confucius removed those which were only repetitions of others, and selected those which would be serviceable for the inculcation of propriety and righteousness. Ascending as high as Hsieh and Hâu-*k*î, and descending through the prosperous eras of Yin and *K*âu to the times of decadence under kings Yû and Lî, he selected in all 305 pieces, which he sang over to his lute, to bring them into accordance with the musical style of the Shâo, the Wû, the Yâ, and the Făng.'

Statement of Sze-mâ *Kh*ien.

In the History of the Classical Books in the Records of the Sui Dynasty (A.D. 589 to 618), it is said:—'When royal benign rule ceased, and poems were no more collected, *K*ih, the Grand Music-Master of Lû, arranged in order those that were existing, and made a copy of them. Then Confucius expurgated them; and going up to the Shang dynasty, and coming down to the state of Lû, he compiled altogether 300 pieces.'

The writer of the Records of the Sui Dynasty.

*K*û Hsî, whose own standard work on the Shih appeared in A.D. 1178, declined to express himself positively on the expurgation of the odes, but summed up his view of what Confucius did for them in the following words:—'Royal methods had ceased, and poems were no more collected. Those which were extant were full of errors, and wanting in arrangement. When Confucius returned from Wei to Lû, he brought with him the odes that he had gotten in other states, and digested them, along with those that were to be found in Lû, into a collection of 300 pieces.'

Opinion of *K*û Hsî.

I have not been able to find evidence sustaining these

representations, and must adopt the view that, before the birth of Confucius, the Book of Poetry existed, substantially the same as it was at his death, and that while he may have somewhat altered the arrangement of its Books and pieces, the service which he rendered to it was not that of compilation, but the impulse to study it which he communicated to his disciples.

View of the author.

2. If we place *Kh*ien's composition of the memoir of Confucius in B.C. 100, nearly four hundred years will have elapsed between the death of the sage and any statement to the effect that he expurgated previously existing poems, or compiled the collection that we now have; and no writer in the interval affirmed or implied any such things. The further statement in the Sui Records about the Music-Master of Lû is also without any earlier confirmation. But independently of these considerations, there is ample evidence to prove, first, that the poems current before Confucius were not by any means so numerous as *Kh*ien says, and, secondly, that the collection of 300 pieces or thereabouts, digested under the same divisions as in the present classic, existed before the sage's time.

Groundlessness of *Kh*ien's statement.

3. i. It would not be surprising, if, floating about and current among the people of China in the sixth century before our era, there had been more than 3000 pieces of poetry. The marvel is that such was not the case. But in the Narratives of the States, a work of the *K*âu dynasty, and ascribed by many to 3o *Kh*iû-ming, there occur quotations from thirty-one poems, made by statesmen and others, all anterior to Confucius; and of those poems there are not more than two which are not in the present classic. Even of those two, one is an ode of it quoted under another name. Further, in the 3o *K*wan, certainly the work of *Kh*iû-ming, we have quotations from not fewer than 219 poems, of which only thirteen are not found in the classic. Thus of 250 poems current in China before the supposed compilation of the Shih, 236 are found in it, and only fourteen are absent. To use the words of *K*âo Yî, a scholar of the present dynasty, 'If the poems existing in

Confucius' time had been more than 3000, the quotations of poems now lost in these two works should have been ten times as numerous as the quotations from the 305 pieces said to have been preserved by him, whereas they are only between a twenty-first and twenty-second part of the existing pieces. This is sufficient to show that *Kh*ien's statement is not worthy of credit.'

ii. Of the existence of the Book of Poetry before Confucius, digested in four Parts, and much in the same order as at present, there may be advanced the following proofs:—

First. There is the passage in the Official Book of *K*âu, quoted and discussed in the last paragraph of the preceding chapter. We have in it a distinct reference to poems, many centuries before the sage, arranged and classified in the same way as those of the existing Shih. Our Shih, no doubt, was then in the process of formation.

Second. In the ninth piece of the sixth decade of the Shih, Part II, an ode assigned to the time of king Yû, B.C. 781 to 771, we have the words,

'They sing the Yâ and the Nan,
Dancing to their flutes without error.

So early, therefore, as the eighth century B.C. there was a collection of poems, of which some bore the name of the Nan, which there is much reason to suppose were the *K*âu Nan and the Shâo Nan, forming the first two Books of the first Part of the present Shih; and of which others bore the name of the Yâ, being, probably, the earlier pieces that now compose a large portion of the second and third Parts.

Third. In the narratives of 3o *Kh*iû-ming, under the twenty-ninth year of duke Hsiang, B.C. 544, when Confucius was only seven or eight years old, we have an account of a visit to the court of Lû by an envoy from Wû, an eminent statesman of the time, and a man of great learning. We are told that as he wished to hear the music of *K*âu, which he could do better in Lû than in any other state, they sang to him the odes of the *K*âu Nan and the Shâo Nan; those of Phei, Yung, and Wei; of the Royal Domain; of Kăng; of *Kh*î; of Pin; of *Kh*in; of Wei; of

Thang; of *Kh*ăn; of Kwei; and of *3h*âo. They sang to him also the odes of the Minor Yâ and the Greater Yâ; and they sang finally the pieces of the Sung. We have thus, existing in the boyhood of Confucius, what we may call the present Book of Poetry, with its Făng, its Yâ, and its Sung. The only difference discernible is slight,—in the order in which the Books of the Făng followed one another.

Fourth. We may appeal in this matter to the words of Confucius himself. Twice in the Analects he speaks of the Shih as a collection consisting of 300 pieces[1]. That work not being made on any principle of chronological order, we cannot positively assign those sayings to any particular years of Confucius' life; but it is, I may say, the unanimous opinion of Chinese critics that they were spoken before the time to which *Kh*ien and *K*û Hsî refer his special labour on the Book of Poetry.

To my own mind the evidence that has been adduced is decisive on the points which I specified. The Shih, arranged very much as we now have it, was current in China before the time of Confucius, and its pieces were in the mouths of statesmen and scholars, constantly quoted by them on festive and other occasions. Poems not included in it there doubtless were, but they were comparatively few. Confucius may have made a copy for the use of himself and his disciples; but it does not appear that he rejected any pieces which had been previously received into the collection, or admitted any which had not previously found a place in it.

What Confucius did for the Shih.

4. The question now arises of what Confucius did for the Shih, if, indeed, he did anything at all. The only thing from which we can hazard an opinion on the point we have from himself. In the Analects, IX, xiv, he tells us:—'I returned from Wei to Lû, and then the music was reformed, and the pieces in

[1] In stating that the odes were 300, Confucius probably preferred to use the round number. There are, as I said in the former chapter, altogether 305 pieces, which is the number given by Sze-mâ *Kh*ien. There are also the titles of six others. It is contended by *K*û Hsî and many other scholars that these titles were only the names of tunes. More likely is the view that the text of the pieces so styled was lost after Confucius' death.

the Yâ and the Sung received their proper places.' The return from Wei to Lû took place only five years before the sage's death. He ceased from that time to take an active part in political affairs, and solaced himself with music, the study of the ancient literature of his nation, the writing of 'the Spring and Autumn,' and familiar intercourse with those of his disciples who still kept around him. He reformed the music,—that to which the pieces of the Shih were sung; but wherein the reformation consisted we cannot tell. And he gave to the pieces of the Yâ and the Sung their proper places. The present order of the Books in the Făng, slightly differing from what was common in his boyhood, may have now been determined by him. More than this we cannot say.

While we cannot discover, therefore, any peculiar and important labours of Confucius on the Shih, and we have it now, as will be shown in the next chapter, substantially as he found it already compiled to his hand, the subsequent preservation of it may reasonably be attributed to the admiration which he expressed for it, and the enthusiasm for it with which he sought to inspire his disciples. It was one of the themes on which he delighted to converse with them [1]. He taught that it is from the poems that the mind receives its best stimulus [2]. A man ignorant of them was, in his opinion, like one who stands with his face towards a wall, limited in his view, and unable to advance [3]. Of the two things that his son could specify as enjoined on him by the sage, the first was that he should learn the odes [4]. In this way Confucius, probably, contributed largely to the subsequent preservation of the Shih,—the preservation of the tablets on which the odes were inscribed, and the preservation of it in the memory of all who venerated his authority, and looked up to him as their master.

[1] Analects, VII, xvii.
[2] Analects, VIII, viii, XVII, ix.
[3] Analects, XVII, x.
[4] Analects, XVI, xiii.

CHAPTER III.

THE SHIH FROM THE TIME OF CONFUCIUS TILL THE GENERAL ACKNOWLEDGMENT OF THE PRESENT TEXT.

From Confucius to the rise of the *Kh*in dynasty.

1. Of the attention paid to the study of the Shih from the death of Confucius to the rise of the *Kh*in dynasty, we have abundant evidence in the writings of his grandson Ȝze-sze, of Mencius, and of Hsün *Kh*ing. One of the acknowledged distinctions of Mencius is his acquaintance with the odes, his quotations from which are very numerous; and Hsün *Kh*ing survived the extinction of the *K*âu dynasty, and lived on into the times of *Kh*in.

The Shih was all recovered after the fires of *Kh*in.

2. The Shih shared in the calamity which all the other classical works, excepting the Yî, suffered, when the tyrant of *Kh*in issued his edict for their destruction. But I have shown, in the Introduction to the Shû, p. 7, that that edict was in force for less than a quarter of a century. The odes were all, or very nearly all[1], recovered; and the reason assigned for this is, that their preservation depended on the memory of scholars more than on their inscription on tablets of bamboo and on silk.

Three different texts.

3. Three different texts of the Shih made their appearance early in the Han dynasty, known as the Shih of Lû, of *Kh*î, and of Han; that is, the Book of Poetry was recovered from three different quarters. Liû Hin's Catalogue of the Books in the Imperial Library of Han (B.C. 6 to 1) commences, on the Shih King, with a collection of the three texts, in twenty-eight chapters.

---

[1] All, in fact, unless we except the six pieces of Part II, of which we have only the titles. It is contended by *K*û Hsî and others that the text of these had been lost before the time of Confucius. It may have been lost, however, after the sage's death; see note on p. 283.

i. Immediately after the mention of the general collection in the Catalogue come the titles of two works of commentary on the text of Lû. The former of them was by a Shăn Phei of whom we have some account in the Literary Biographies of Han. He was a native of Lû, and had received his own knowledge of the odes from a scholar of *Kh*î, called Fâu *Kh*iû-po. He was resorted to by many disciples, whom he taught to repeat the odes. When the first emperor of the Han dynasty was passing through Lû, Shăn followed him to the capital of that state, and had an interview with him. Subsequently the emperor Wû (B.C. 140 to 87), in the beginning of his reign, sent for him to court when he was more than eighty years old; and he appears to have survived a considerable number of years beyond that advanced age. The names of ten of his disciples are given, all of them men of eminence, and among them Khung An-kwo. Rather later, the most noted adherent of the school of Lû was Wei Hsien, who arrived at the dignity of prime minister (from B.C. 71 to 67), and published the Shih of Lû in Stanzas and Lines. Up and down in the Books of Han and Wei are to be found quotations of the odes, that must have been taken from the professors of the Lû recension; but neither the text nor the writings on it long survived. They are said to have perished during the *K*in dynasty (A.D. 265 to 419). When the Catalogue of the Sui Library was made, none of them were existing.

The text of Lû.

ii. The Han Catalogue mentions five different works on the Shih of *Kh*î. This text was from a Yüan Kû, a native of *Kh*î, about whom we learn, from the same collection of Literary Biographies, that he was one of the great scholars of the court in the time of the emperor *K*ing (B.C. 156 to 141),—a favourite with him, and specially distinguished for his knowledge of the odes and his advocacy of orthodox Confucian doctrine. He died in the succeeding reign of Wû, more than ninety years old; and we are told that all the scholars of *Kh*î who got a name in those days for their acquaintance with the Shih sprang from his school. Among his disciples was the well-

The text of *Kh*î.

known name of Hsiâ-hâu Shih-*kh*ang, who communicated his acquisitions to Hâu ʒ*h*ang, a native of the present Shan-tung province, and author of two of the works in the Han Catalogue. Hâu had three disciples of note, and by them the Shih of *Kh*î was transmitted to others, whose names, with quotations from their writings, are scattered through the Books of Han. Neither text nor commentaries, however, had a better fate than the Shih of Lû. There is no mention of them in the Catalogue of Sui. They are said to have perished even before the rise of the *K*in dynasty.

iii. The text of Han was somewhat more fortunate. Hin's Catalogue contains the names of four works, all by Han Ying, whose surname is thus perpetuated in the text of the Shih that emanated from him. He was a native, we are told, of Yen, and a great scholar in the time of the emperor Wăn (B.C. 179 to 155), and on into the reigns of *K*ing and Wû. 'He laboured,' it is said, 'to unfold the meaning of the odes, and published an Explanation of the Text, and Illustrations of the Poems, containing several myriads of characters. His text was somewhat different from the texts of Lû and *Kh*î, but substantially of the same meaning.' Of course, Han founded a school; but while almost all the writings of his followers soon perished, both the works just mentioned continued on through the various dynasties to the time of Sung. The Sui Catalogue contains the titles of his Text and two works on it; the Thang, those of his Text and his Illustrations; but when we come to the Catalogue of Sung, published under the Yüan dynasty, we find only the Illustrations, in ten books or chapters; and Âu-yang Hsiû (A.D. 1017 to 1072) tells us that in his time this was all of Han that remained. It continues entire, or nearly so, to the present day.

The text of Han Ying.

4. But while those three different recensions of the Shih all disappeared, with the exception of a single treatise of Han Ying, their unhappy fate was owing not more to the convulsions by which the empire was often rent, and the consequent destruction of literary monuments such as we

have witnessed in China in our own day, than to the appearance of a fourth text, which displaced them by its superior correctness, and the ability with which it was advocated and commented on. This was what is called the Text of Mâo. It came into the field rather later than the others; but the Han Catalogue contains the Shih of Mâo, in twenty-nine chapters, and a Commentary on it in thirty-nine. According to *K*ăng Hsüan, the author of this was a native of Lû, known as Mâo Hăng or 'the Greater Mâo,' who had been a disciple, we are told by Lü Teh-ming, of Hsün *Kh*ing. The work is lost. He had communicated his knowledge of the Shih, however, to another Mâo,—Mâo *K*ang, 'the Lesser Mâo,' who was a great scholar, at the court of king Hsien of Ho-*k*ien, a son of the emperor *K*ing. King Hsien was one of the most diligent labourers in the recovery of the ancient books, and presented the text and work of Hăng at the court of his father,—probably in B.C. 129. Mâo *K*ang published Explanations of the Shih, in twenty-nine chapters, —a work which we still possess; but it was not till the reign of Phing (A.D. 1 to 5) that Mâo's recension was received into the Imperial College, and took its place along with those of Lû, *Kh*î, and Han Ying.

A fourth text; that of Mâo.

The Chinese critics have carefully traced the line of scholars who had charge of Mâo's Text and Explanations down to the reign of Phing. The names of the men and their works are all given. By the end of the first quarter of our first century we find the most famous scholars addicting themselves to Mâo's text. The well-known *K*iâ Khwei (A.D. 30 to 101) published a work on the Meaning and Difficulties of Mâo's Shih, having previously compiled a digest of the differences between its text and those of the other three recensions, at the command of the emperor Ming (A.D. 58 to 75). The equally celebrated Mâ Yung (A.D. 79 to 166) followed with another commentary;—and we arrive at *K*ăng Hsüan or *K*ăng Khang-*kh*ăng (A.D. 127 to 200), who wrote a Supplementary Commentary to the Shih of Mâo, and a Chronological Introduction to the Shih. The former of these two works complete, and portions of the latter, are still extant. After the time of *K*ăng the other three texts were little heard of, while the name of the commentators on Mâo's text speedily becomes legion. It was inscribed, moreover, on the stone tablets of the emperor Ling (A. D. 168 to 189). The grave of Mâo *K*ăng is still shown near the village of Ȝun-fû, in the departmental district of Ho-*k*ien, *K*ih-lî.

The different texts guarantee the genuineness of the recovered Shih.

5. Returning now to what I said in the second paragraph, it will be granted that the appearance of three different and independent texts, soon after the rise of the Han dynasty, affords the most satisfactory evidence of the recovery of the Book of Poetry as it had continued from the time of Confucius. Unfortunately, only fragments of those texts remain now; but they were, while they were current, diligently compared with one another, and with the fourth text of Mâo, which subsequently got the field to itself. When a collection is made of their peculiar readings, so far as it can now be done, it is clear that their variations from one another and from Mâo's text arose from the alleged fact that the preservation of the odes was owing to their being transmitted by recitation. The rhyme helped the memory to retain them, and while wood, bamboo, and silk had all been consumed by the flames of *Kh*in, when the time of repression ceased, scholars would be eager to rehearse their stores. It was inevitable, and more so in China than in a country possessing an alphabet, that the same sounds when taken down by different writers should be represented by different characters.

On the whole, the evidence given above is as full as could be desired in such a case, and leaves no reason for us to hesitate in accepting the present received text of the Shih as a very close approximation to that which was current in the time of Confucius.

CHAPTER IV.

THE FORMATION OF THE COLLECTION OF THE SHIH; HOW IT CAME TO BE SO SMALL AND INCOMPLETE; THE INTERPRETATION AND AUTHORS OF THE PIECES; ONE POINT OF TIME CERTAINLY INDICATED IN IT; AND THE CONFUCIAN PREFACE.

1. It has been shown above, in the second chapter, that the Shih existed as a collection of poetical pieces before the time of Confucius[1]. In order to complete this Introduction to it, it is desirable to give some account of the various subjects indicated in the heading of the present chapter.

How were the odes collected in the first place? In his Account of a Conversation concerning 'a Right Regulation of Governments for the Common Good of Mankind' (Edinburgh, 1704), p. 10, Sir Andrew Fletcher, of Saltoun, tells us the opinion of 'a very wise man,' that 'if a man were permitted to make all the ballads of a nation, he need not care who should make its laws.' A writer in the Spectator, no. 502, refers to a similar opinion as having been entertained in England earlier than the time of Fletcher. 'I have heard,' he says, 'that a minister of state in the reign of Elizabeth had all manner of books and ballads brought to him, of what kind soever, and took great notice how they took with the people; upon which he would, and certainly might, very well judge of their present dispositions, and of the most proper way of applying them according to his own purposes[2].'

---

[1] As in the case of the Shû, Confucius generally speaks of 'the Shih,' never using the name of 'the Shih King.' In the Analects, IX, xiv, however, he mentions also the Yâ and the Sung; and in XVII, x, he specifies the *K*âu Nan and the Shâo Nan, the first two books of the Kwo Făng. Mencius similarly speaks of 'the Shih;' and in III, i, ch. 4, he specifies 'the Sung of Lû,' Book ii of Part IV. In VI, ii, ch. 3, he gives his views of the Hsiâo Phan, the third ode of decade 5, Part II, and of the Khâi Fung, the seventh ode of Book iii of Part I.

[2] This passage from the Spectator is adduced by Sir John Davis in his treatise on the Poetry of the Chinese, p. 35.

The theory of the Chinese scholars about a collection of poems for governmental purposes.

In harmony with the views thus expressed is the theory of the Chinese scholars, that it was the duty of the ancient kings to make themselves acquainted with all the poems current in the different states, and to judge from them of the rule exercised by the several princes, so that they might minister praise or blame, reward or punishment accordingly.

The rudiments of this theory may be found in the Shû, in the Canon of Shun; but the one classical passage which is appealed to in support of it is in the Record of Rites, III, ii, parr. 13, 14:—'Every fifth year, the Son of Heaven made a progress through the kingdom, when the Grand Music-Master was commanded to lay before him the poems of the different states, as an exhibition of the manners and government of the people.' Unfortunately, this Book of the Lî *K*î, the Royal Ordinances, was compiled only in the reign of the emperor Wăn of the Han dynasty (B.C. 179 to 155). The scholars entrusted with the work did their best, we may suppose, with the materials at their command. They made much use, it is evident, of Mencius, and of the Î Lî. The *K*âu Lî, or the Official Book of *K*âu, had not then been recovered. But neither in Mencius nor in the Î Lî do we meet with any authority for the statement before us. The Shû mentions that Shun every fifth year made a tour of inspection; but there were then no odes for him to examine, for to him and his minister Kâo-yâo is attributed the first rudimentary attempt at the poetic art. Of the progresses of the Hsiâ and Yin sovereigns we have no information; and those of the kings of *K*âu were made, we know, only once in twelve years. The statement in the Royal Ordinances, therefore, was probably based only on tradition.

Notwithstanding the difficulties that beset this passage of the Lî *K*î, I am not disposed to reject it altogether. It derives a certain amount of confirmation from the passage quoted from the Official Book of *K*âu on p. 278, showing that in the *K*âu dynasty there was a collection of poems, under the divisions of the Făng, the Yâ, and the Sung, which it was the business of the Grand Music-Master to teach the musicians of the court. It may be accepted then, that the duke of *K*âu, in legislating for his dynasty, enacted that the poems produced in the different feudal states should be collected on occasion of the royal progresses, and lodged thereafter among the archives of the bureau of music at the royal court. The same thing, we may presume à fortiori, would be done, at certain other stated times, with those produced within the royal domain itself.

The music-master of the king would get the odes of each state from its music-master.

But the feudal states were modelled after the pattern of the royal state. They also had their music-masters, their musicians, and their historiographers. The kings in their progresses did not visit each particular state, so that the Grand Music-Master could have the opportunity to collect the odes in it for himself. They met, at well-known points, the marquises, earls, barons, &c., of the different quarters of the kingdom; there gave audience to them; adjudicated on their merits, and issued to them their orders. We are obliged to suppose that the princes were attended to the places of rendezvous by their music-masters, carrying with them the poetical compositions gathered in their several regions, to present them to their superior of the royal court. We can understand how, by means of the above arrangement, the poems of the whole kingdom were accumulated and arranged among the archives of the capital. Was there any provision for disseminating thence the poems of one state among all the others? There is sufficient evidence that such dissemination was effected in some way. Throughout the Narratives of the States, and the details of 3o *Kh*iû-ming on the history of the Spring and Autumn, the officers of the states generally are presented to us as familiar not only with the odes of their particular states, but with those of other states as well. They appear equally well acquainted with all the Parts and Books of our present Shih; and we saw how the whole of it was sung over to *K*î *K*â of Wû, when he visited the court of Lû in the boyhood of Confucius. There was,

How the collected poems were disseminated throughout the states.

probably, a regular communication from the royal court to the courts of the various states of the poetical pieces that for one reason or another were thought worthy of preservation. This is nowhere expressly stated, but it may be contended for by analogy from the accounts which I have given, in the Introduction to the Shû, pp. 4, 5, of the duties of the royal historiographers or recorders.

2. But if the poems produced in the different states were thus collected in the capital, and thence again disseminated throughout the kingdom, we might conclude that the collection would have been far more extensive and complete than we have it now. The smallness of it is to be accounted for by the disorder into which the kingdom fell after the lapse of a few reigns from king Wû. Royal progresses ceased when royal government fell into decay, and then the odes were no more collected [1]. We have no account of any progress of the kings during the *Kh*un *Kh*iû period. But before that period there is a long gap of nearly 150 years between kings *Kh*ăng and Î, covering the reigns of Khang, *K*âo, Mû, and Kung, if we except two doubtful pieces among the Sacrificial Odes of *K*âu. The reign of Hsiâo, who succeeded to Î, is similarly uncommemorated; and the latest odes are of the time of Ting, when 100 years of the *Kh*un *Kh*iû period had still to run their course. Many odes must have been made and collected during the 140 and more years after king *Kh*ăng. The probability is that they perished during the feeble reigns of Î and the three monarchs who followed him. Then came the long and vigorous reign of Hsüan (B.C. 827 to 782), when we may suppose that the ancient custom of collecting the poems was revived. After him all was in the main decadence and confusion. It was probably in the latter part of his reign that *K*ăng-khâo, an ancestor of Confucius, obtained from the Grand Music-Master at the court of *K*âu twelve of the sacrificial odes of the previous dynasty, as will be related under the Sacrificial Odes of Shang, with which he returned to Sung,

How the Shih is so small and incomplete.

[1] See Mencius, IV, ii, ch. 21.

which was held by representatives of the line of Shang. They were used there in sacrificing to the old Shang kings; yet seven of the twelve were lost before the time of the sage.

The general conclusion to which we come is, that the existing Shih is the fragment of various collections made during the early reigns of the kings of *K*âu, and added to at intervals, especially on the occurrence of a prosperous rule, in accordance with the regulation that has been preserved in the Lî *K*î. How it is that we have in Part I odes of comparatively few of the states into which the kingdom was divided, and that the odes of those states extend only over a short period of their history:—for these things we cannot account further than by saying that such were the ravages of time and the results of disorder. We can only accept the collection as it is, and be thankful for it. How long before Confucius the collection was closed we cannot tell.

Bearing of these views on the interpretation of particular pieces.

3. The conclusions which I have thus sought to establish concerning the formation of the Shih as a collection have an important bearing on the interpretation of many of the pieces. The remark of Sze-mâ *Kh*ien that 'Confucius selected those pieces which would be serviceable for the inculcation of propriety and righteousness' is as erroneous as the other, that he selected 305 pieces out of more than 3000. The sage merely studied and taught the pieces which he found existing, and the collection necessarily contained odes illustrative of bad government as well as of good, of licentiousness as well as of a pure morality. Nothing has been such a stumbling-block in the way of the reception of *K*û Hsî's interpretation of the pieces as the readiness with which he attributes a licentious meaning to many of those in the seventh Book of Part I. But the reason why the kings had the odes of the different states collected and presented to them was, 'that they might judge from them of the manners of the people,' and so come to a decision regarding the government and morals of their rulers. A student and translator of the odes has simply to allow them

to speak for themselves, and has no more reason to be surprised by references to vice in some of them than by the language of virtue in many others. Confucius said, indeed, in his own enigmatical way, that the single sentence, 'Thought without depravity,' covered the whole 300 pieces[1]; and it may very well be allowed that they were collected and preserved for the promotion of good government and virtuous manners. The merit attaching to them is that they give us faithful pictures of what was good and what was bad in the political state of the country, and in the social, moral, and religious habits of the people.

The writers of the odes.

The pieces were of course made by individuals who possessed the gift, or thought that they possessed the gift, of poetical composition. Who they were we could tell only on the authority of the pieces themselves, or of credible historical accounts, contemporaneous with them or nearly so. It is not worth our while to question the opinion of the Chinese critics who attribute very many of them to the duke of *K*âu, to whom we owe so much of the fifth Part of the Shû. There is, however, independent testimony only to his composition of a single ode,—the second of the fifteenth Book in Part I[2]. Some of the other pieces in that Part, of which the historical interpretation may be considered as sufficiently fixed, are written in the first person; but the author may be personating his subject.

In Part II, the seventh ode of decade 2 was made by a *K*iâ-fû, a noble of the royal court, but we know nothing more about him; the sixth of decade 6, by a eunuch styled Măng-ȝze; and the sixth of decade 7, from a concurrence of external testimonies, should be ascribed to duke Wû of Wei, B.C. 812 to 758.

In the third decade of Part III, the second piece was composed by the same duke Wû; the third by an earl of *Z*ui in the royal domain; the fourth must have been made by one of king Hsüan's ministers, to express the king's

[1] Analects, II, ii. [2] See the Shû, V, vi, par. 2.

feelings under the drought that was exhausting the kingdom; and the fifth and sixth claim to be the work of Yin *K*î-fû, one of Hsüan's principal officers.

4. The ninth ode of the fourth Book, Part II, gives us a note of time that enables us to fix the year of its composition in a manner entirely satisfactory, and proves also the correctness, back to that date, of the ordinary Chinese chronology. The piece is one of a group which their contents lead us to refer to the reign of king Yû, the son of Hsüan, B.C. 781 to 771. When we examine the chronology of his period, it is said that in his sixth year, B.C. 776, there was an eclipse of the sun. Now the ode commences:—

'At the conjunction (of the sun and moon) in the tenth month, on the first day of the moon, which was Hsin-mâo, the sun was eclipsed.'

This eclipse is verified by calculation as having taken place in B.C. 776, on August 29th, the very day and month assigned to it in the poem.

The Preface to the Shih.

5. In the Preface which appeared along with Mâo's text of the Shih, the occasion and authorship of many of the odes are given; but I do not allow much weight to its testimony. It is now divided into the Great Preface and the Little Preface; but Mâo himself made no such distinction between its parts. It will be sufficient for me to give a condensed account of the views of *K*û Hsî on the subject:—

'Opinions of scholars are much divided as to the authorship of the Preface. Some ascribe it to Confucius; some to (his disciple) 3ze-hsiâ; and some to the historiographers of the states. In the absence of clear testimony it is impossible to decide the point, but the notice about Wei Hung (first century) in the Literary Biographies of Han[1] would seem to make it clear that the Preface was

[1] The account is this: 'Hung became the disciple of Hsieh Man-*kh*ing, who was famous for his knowledge of Mâo's Shih; and he afterwards made the Preface to it, remarkable for the accuracy with which it gives the meaning of the pieces in the Făng and the Yâ, and which is now current in the world.'

his work. We must take into account, however, on the other hand the statement of *K*ăng Khang-*kh*ăng, that the Preface existed as a separate document when Mâo appeared with his text, and that he broke it up, prefixing to each ode the portion belonging to it. The natural conclusion is, that the Preface had come down from a remote period, and that Hung merely added to it, and rounded it off. In accordance with this, scholars generally hold that the first sentences in the introductory notices formed the original Preface, which Mâo distributed, and that the following portions were subsequently added.

'This view may appear reasonable; but when we examine those first sentences themselves, we find that some of them do not agree with the obvious meaning of the odes to which they are prefixed, and give only rash and baseless expositions. Evidently, from the first, the Preface was made up of private speculations and conjectures on the subject-matter of the odes, and constituted a document by itself, separately appended to the text. Then on its first appearance there were current the explanations of the odes that were given in connexion with the texts of Lû, *Kh*î, and Han Ying, so that readers could know that it was the work of later hands, and not give entire credit to it. But when Mâo no longer published the Preface as a separate document, but each ode appeared with the introductory notice as a portion of the text, this seemed to give it the authority of the text itself. Then after the other texts disappeared and Mâo's had the field to itself, this means of testing the accuracy of its prefatory notices no longer existed. They appeared as if they were the production of the poets themselves, and the odes seemed to be made from them as so many themes. Scholars handed down a faith in them from one to another, and no one ventured to express a doubt of their authority. The text was twisted and chiseled to bring it into accordance with them, and no one would undertake to say plainly that they were the work of the scholars of the Han dynasty.'

There is no western sinologist, I apprehend, who will

not cordially concur with me in the principle of *K*û Hsî that we must find the meaning of the poems in the poems themselves, instead of accepting the interpretation of them given by we know not whom, and to follow which would reduce many of them to absurd enigmas.

THE SHIH KING.

ODES OF THE TEMPLE AND THE ALTAR.

It was stated in the Introduction, p. 278, that the poems in the fourth Part of the Shih are the only ones that are professedly religious; and there are some even of them, it will be seen, which have little claim on internal grounds to be so considered. I commence with them my selections from the Shih for the Sacred Books of the Religions of the East. I will give them all, excepting the first two of the Praise Odes of Lû, the reason for omitting which will be found, when I come to that division of the Part.

The Odes of the Temple and the Altar are, most of them, connected with the ancestral worship of the sovereigns of the Shang and *K*âu dynasties, and of the marquises of Lû. Of the ancestral worship of the common people we have almost no information in the Shih. It was binding, however, on all, and two utterances of Confucius may be given in illustration of this. In the eighteenth chapter of the Doctrine of the Mean, telling how the duke of *K*âu, the legislator of the dynasty so called, had 'completed the virtuous course of Wăn and Wû, carrying up the title of king to Wăn's father and grandfather, and sacrificing to the dukes before them with the royal ceremonies,' he adds, 'And this rule he extended to the feudal princes, the great officers, the other officers, and the common people. In the mourning and other duties rendered to a deceased father or mother, he allowed no difference between the noble and the mean.' Again, his summary in the tenth chapter of the Hsiâo King, of the duties

The ancestral worship of the common people.

of filial piety, is the following:—'A filial son, in serving his parents, in his ordinary intercourse with them, should show the utmost respect; in supplying them with food, the greatest delight; when they are ill, the utmost solicitude; when mourning for their death, the deepest grief; and when sacrificing to them, the profoundest solemnity. When these things are all complete, he is able to serve his parents.'

Of the ceremonies in the royal worship of ancestors, and perhaps on some other occasions, we have much information in the pieces of this Part, and in many others in the second and third Parts. They were preceded by fasting and various purifications on the part of the king and the parties who were to assist in the performance of them. There was a great concourse of the feudal princes, and much importance was attached to the presence among them of the representatives of former dynasties; but the duties of the occasion devolved mainly on the princes of the same surname as the royal House. Libations of fragrant spirits were made, especially in the *K*âu period, to attract the Spirits, and their presence was invoked by a functionary who took his place inside the principal gate. The principal victim, a red bull in the temple of *K*âu, was killed by the king himself, using for the purpose a knife to the handle of which small bells were attached. With this he laid bare the hair, to show that the animal was of the required colour, inflicted the wound of death, and cut away the fat, which was burned along with southernwood to increase the incense and fragrance. Other victims were numerous, and the fifth ode of the second decade, Part II, describes all engaged in the service as greatly exhausted with what they had to do, flaying the carcases, boiling the flesh, roasting it, broiling it, arranging it on trays and stands, and setting it forth. Ladies from the palace are present to give their assistance; music peals; the cup goes round. The description is that of a feast as much as of a sacrifice; and in fact, those great seasonal occasions were what we might call grand family reunions, where the dead and the living met, eating and drinking together, where the living worshipped the dead, and the dead blessed the living.

The royal worship of ancestors.

This characteristic of these ceremonies appeared most strikingly in the custom which required that the departed ancestors should be represented by living relatives of the same surname, chosen according to certain rules that are not mentioned in the Shih. These took for the time the place of the dead, received the honours which were due to them, and were supposed to be possessed by their spirits. They ate and drank as those whom they personated would have done ; accepted for them the homage rendered by their descendants ; communicated their will to the principal in the service, and pronounced on him and on his line their benediction, being assisted in this point by a mediating priest, as we may call him for want of a more exact term. On the next day, after a summary repetition of the ceremonies of the sacrifice, those personators of the dead were specially feasted, and, as it is expressed in the second decade of Part III, ode 4, 'their happiness and dignity were made complete.' We have an allusion to this strange custom in Mencius (VI, i, ch. 5), showing how a junior member of a family, when chosen to represent one of his ancestors, was for the time exalted above his elders, and received the demonstrations of reverence due to the ancestor.

When the sacrifice to ancestors was finished, the king feasted his uncles and younger brothers or cousins, that is, all the princes and nobles of the same surname with himself, in another apartment. The musicians who had discoursed with instrument and voice during the worship and entertainment of the ancestors, followed the convivial party 'to give their soothing aid at the second blessing.' The viands that had been provided, we have seen, in great abundance, were brought in from the temple, and set forth anew. The guests ate to the full and drank to the full, and at the conclusion they all did obeisance, while one of them declared the satisfaction of the Spirits, and assured the king of their favour to him and his posterity, so long as they did not neglect those observances. During the feast the king showed particular respect to those among his relatives who were aged, filled their cups again and again, and desired 'that their old age might be blessed, and their bright happiness ever increased.'

The above sketch of the seasonal sacrifices to ancestors shows that they were intimately related to the duty of filial piety, and were designed mainly to maintain the unity of the family connexion. There was implied in them a belief in the continued existence of the spirits of the departed ; and by means of them the ancestors of the kings were raised to the position of the Tutelary spirits of the dynasty ; and the ancestors of each family became its Tutelary spirits. Several of the pieces in Part IV are appropriate, it will be observed, to sacrifices offered to some one monarch. They would be used on particular occasions connected with his achievements in the past, or when it was supposed that his help would be valuable in contemplated enterprises. With regard to all the ceremonies of the ancestral temple, Confucius gives the following account of the purposes which they were intended to serve, hardly adverting to their religious significance, in the nineteenth chapter of the Doctrine of the Mean:—'By means of them they distinguished the royal kindred according to their order of descent. By arranging those present according to their rank, they distinguished the more noble and the less. By the apportioning of duties at them, they made a distinction of talents and worth. In the ceremony of general pledging, the inferiors presented the cup to their superiors, and thus something was given to the lowest to do. At the (concluding) feast places were given according to the hair, and thus was marked the distinction of years.'

The worship paid to God.

The Shih does not speak of the worship which was paid to God, unless it be incidentally. There were two grand occasions on which it was rendered by the sovereign,—the summer and winter solstices. These two sacrifices were offered on different altars, that in winter being often described as offered to Heaven, and that in summer to Earth; but we have the testimony of Confucius, in the nineteenth chapter of the Doctrine of the Mean, that the object of them both was to serve Shang-Tî. Of the ceremonies on these two occasions, however, I do not speak here, as there is nothing said about them in the Shih. But there were other sacrifices to God, at stated periods in the course of the year, of at least two of which we have some intimation in the pieces of this fourth Part. The last in the first decade of the Sacrificial Odes of *K*âu is addressed to Hâu *K*î as having proved himself the correlate of Heaven, in teaching men to cultivate the grain which God had appointed for the nourishment of all. This was appropriate to a sacrifice in spring, offered to God to seek His blessing on the agricultural labours of the year, Hâu *K*î, as the ancestor of the House of *K*âu, being associated with Him in it. The seventh piece of the same decade again was appropriate to a sacrifice to God in autumn, in the Hall of Light, at a great audience to the feudal princes, when king Wăn was associated with Him as being the founder of the dynasty of *K*âu.

With these preliminary observations to assist the reader in understanding the pieces in this Part, I proceed to give—

I. The Sacrificial Odes of Shang.

These odes of Shang constitute the last Book in the ordinary editions of the Shih. I put them here in the first place, because they are the oldest pieces in the collection. There are only five of them.

The sovereigns of the dynasty of Shang occupied the throne from B.C. 1766 to 1123. They traced their lineage to Hsieh, who appears in the Shû as Minister of Instruction to Shun. By Yâo or by Shun, Hsieh was invested with the principality of Shang, corresponding to the small department which is so named in Shen-hsî. Fourteenth in descent from him came Thien-yî, better known as *Kh*ăng Thang, or Thang the Successful, who dethroned the last descendant of the line of Hsiâ, and became the founder of a new dynasty. We meet with him first at a considerable distance from the ancestral fief (which, however, gave name to the dynasty), having as his capital the southern Po, which seems correctly referred to the present district of Shang-*kh*iû, in the department of Kwei-teh, Ho-nan. Among the twenty-seven sovereigns who followed Thang, there were three especially distinguished:—Thâi *K*iâ, his grandson and successor (B.C. 1753 to 1721), who received the title of Thâi Ȝung; Thâi Mâu (B.C. 1637 to 1563), canonized as *K*ung Ȝung; and Wû-ting (B.C. 1324 to 1266), known as Kâo Ȝung. The shrines of these three sovereigns and that of Thang retained their places in the ancestral temple ever after they were first set up, and if all the sacrificial odes of the dynasty had been preserved, most of them would have been in praise of one or other of the four. But it so happened that at least all the odes of which Thâi Ȝung was the subject were lost; and of the others we have only the small portion that has been mentioned above.

Of how it is that we have even these, we have the following account in the Narratives of the States, compiled, probably, by a contemporary of Confucius. The count of Wei was made duke of Sung by king Wû of *K*âu, as related in the Shû, V, viii, there to continue the sacrifices of the House of Shang; but the government of Sung fell subsequently into disorder, and the memorials of the dynasty were lost. In the time of duke Tâi (B.C. 799 to 766), one of his ministers, *K*ăng-khâo, an ancestor of Confucius, received from the Grand Music-Master at the court of *K*âu twelve of the sacrificial odes of Shang with which he returned to Sung, where they were used in sacrificing to the old Shang kings. It is supposed that seven of these were lost subsequently, before the collection of the Shih was formed.

Ode 1. The Nâ[1].

APPROPRIATE TO A SACRIFICE TO THANG, THE FOUNDER OF THE SHANG DYNASTY, DWELLING ESPECIALLY ON THE MUSIC AND THE REVERENCE WITH WHICH THE SACRIFICE WAS PERFORMED.

We cannot tell by which of the kings of Shang the sacrifice here referred to was first performed. He is simply spoken of as 'a descendant of Thang.' The ode seems to have been composed by some one, probably a member of the royal House, who had taken part in the service.

How admirable! how complete! Here are set our hand-drums and drums. The drums resound harmonious and loud, To delight our meritorious ancestor[2].

The descendant of Thang invites him with this music, That he may soothe us with the realization of our thoughts[3]. Deep is the sound of our hand-

---

[1] The piece is called the Nâ, because a character so named is an important part of the first line. So generally the pieces in the Shih receive their names from a character or phrase occurring in them. This point will not be again touched on.

[2] The 'meritorious ancestor' is Thang. The sacrifices of the Shang dynasty commenced with music; those of the *K*âu with libations of fragrant spirits;—in both cases with the same object, to attract the spirit, or spirits, sacrificed to, and secure their presence at the service. *Kh*ăn Hâo (Ming dynasty) says, 'The departed spirits hover between heaven and earth, and sound goes forth, filling the region of the air. Hence in sacrificing, the people of Yin began with a performance of music.'

[3] The Lî *K*î, XXIV, i, parr. 2, 3, tells us, that the sacrificer, as preliminary to the service, had to fast for some days, and to think of the person of his ancestor,—where he had stood and sat, how he had smiled and spoken, what had been his cherished aims,

drums and drums; Shrilly sound the flutes; All harmonious and blending together, According to the notes of the sonorous gem. Oh! majestic is the descendant of Thang; Very admirable is his music.

The large bells and drums fill the ear; The various dances are grandly performed[1]. We have the admirable visitors[2], Who are pleased and delighted.

From of old, before our time, The former men set us the example;—How to be mild and humble from morning to night, And to be reverent in discharging the service.

May he regard our sacrifices of winter and autumn[3], (Thus) offered by the descendant of Thang!

ODE 2. THE LIEH ȜÛ.

PROBABLY LIKE THE LAST ODE, APPROPRIATE TO A SACRIFICE TO THANG, DWELLING ON THE SPIRITS, THE SOUP, AND THE GRAVITY OF THE SERVICE, AND ON THE ASSISTING PRINCES.

Neither can we tell by which of the kings of Shang this ode was first used. *K*û Hsî says that the object of the sacrifice was Thang. The Preface assigns it to Thâi Mâu, the *K*ung Ȝung, or second of the three 'honoured ones.' But there is not a

pleasures, and delights; and on the third day he would have a complete image of him in his mind's eye. Then on the day of sacrifice, when he entered the temple, he would seem to see him in his shrine, and to hear him, as he went about in the discharge of the service. This line seems to indicate the realization of all this.

[1] Dancing thus entered into the service as an accompaniment of the music. Two terms are employed; one denoting the movements appropriate to a dance of war, the other those appropriate to a dance of peace.

[2] The visitors would be the representatives of the lines of Hsiâ, Shun, and Yâo.

[3] Two of the seasonal sacrifices are thus specified, by synecdoche, for all the four.

word in praise of *K*ung Ʒung, and the 'meritorious ancestor' of the first line is not to be got over. Still more clearly than in the case of the former ode does this appear to have been made by some one who had taken part in the service, for in line 4 he addresses the sacrificing king as 'you.'

Ah! ah! our meritorious ancestor! Permanent are the blessings coming from him, Repeatedly conferred without end;—They have come to you in this place.

The clear spirits are in our vessels, And there is granted to us the realization of our thoughts. There are also the well-tempered soups, Prepared beforehand, with the ingredients rightly proportioned. By these offerings we invite his presence, without a word, Without (unseemly) contention (among the worshippers). He will bless us with the eyebrows of longevity, With the grey hair and wrinkled face in unlimited degree.

With the naves of their wheels bound with leather, and their ornamented yokes, With the eight bells at their horses' bits all tinkling, (The princes) come to assist at the offerings[1]. We have received the appointment in all its greatness, And from Heaven is our prosperity sent down, Fruitful years of great abundance. (Our ancestor) will come and enjoy (our offerings), And confer on us happiness without limit.

May he regard our sacrifices of winter and autumn, (Thus) offered by the descendant of Thang!

[1] These lines are descriptive of the feudal princes, who were present and assisted at the sacrificial service. The chariot of each was drawn by four horses yoked abreast, two insides and two outsides, on each side of the bits of which small bells were attached.

ODE 3. THE HSÜAN NIÂO.

APPROPRIATE TO A SACRIFICE IN THE ANCESTRAL TEMPLE OF SHANG;—INTENDED SPECIALLY TO DO HONOUR TO THE KING WÛ-TING.

If this ode were not intended to do honour to Wû-ting, the Kâo Ȝung of Shang, we cannot account for the repeated mention of him in it. *K*û Hsî, however, in his note on it, says nothing about Wû-ting, but simply that the piece belonged to the sacrifices in the ancestral temple, tracing back the line of the kings of Shang to its origin, and to its attaining the sovereignty of the kingdom. Not at all unlikely is the view of *K*ăng Hsüan, that the sacrifice was in the third year after the death of Wû-ting, and offered to him in the temple of Hsieh, the ancestor of the Shang dynasty.

Heaven commissioned the swallow, To descend and give birth to (the father of our) Shang[1]. (His descendants) dwelt in the land of Yin, and became great. (Then) long ago God appointed the martial Thang, To regulate the boundaries throughout the four quarters (of the kingdom).

(In those) quarters he appointed the princes, And grandly possessed the nine regions[2]. The

[1] The father of Shang is Hsieh, who has already been mentioned. The mother of Hsieh was a daughter of the House of the ancient state of Sung, and a concubine of the ancient ruler Khû (B. C. 2435). According to Mâo, she accompanied Khû, at the time of the vernal equinox, when the swallow made its appearance, to sacrifice and pray to the first match-maker, and the result was the birth of Hsieh. Sze-mâ *Kh*ien and *K*ăng make Hsieh's birth more marvellous:—The lady was bathing in some open place, when a swallow made its appearance, and dropt an egg, which she took and swallowed; and from this came Hsieh. The editors of the imperial edition of the Shih, of the present dynasty, say we need not believe the legends;—the important point is to believe that the birth of Hsieh was specially ordered by Heaven.

[2] 'The nine regions' are the nine provinces into which Yü divided the kingdom.

first sovereign of Shang[1] Received the appointment without any element of instability in it, And it is (now) held by the descendant of Wû-ting[2].

The descendant of Wû-ting Is a martial sovereign, equal to every emergency. Ten princes, (who came) with their dragon-emblazoned banners, Bear the large dishes of millet.

The royal domain of a thousand lî Is where the people rest; But the boundaries that reach to the four seas commence there.

From the four seas[3] they come (to our sacrifices); They come in multitudes. *K*ing has the Ho for its outer border[4]. That Yin[5] should have received the appointment (of Heaven) was entirely right;—(Its sovereign) sustains all its dignities.

ODE 4. THE *KH*ANG FÂ.

CELEBRATING HSIEH, THE ANCESTOR OF THE HOUSE OF SHANG; HSIANG-THÛ, HIS GRANDSON; THANG, THE FOUNDER OF THE DYNASTY; AND Î-YIN, THANG'S CHIEF MINISTER AND ADVISER.

It does not appear on occasion of what sacrifice this piece was made. The most probable view is that of Mâo, that it was the

---

[1] That is, Thang.

[2] If this ode were used, as *K*ăng supposes, in the third year after Wû-ting's death, this 'descendant' would be his son 3û-kăng, B.C. 1265 to 1259.

[3] This expression, which occurs also in the Shû, indicates that the early Chinese believed that their country extended to the sea, east, west, north, and south.

[4] *K*û Hsî says he did not understand this line; but there is ground in the 3o *K*wan for our believing that *K*ing was the name of a hill in the region where the capital of Shang was.

[5] We saw in the Shû that the name Shang gave place to Yin after the time of Pan-kăng, B.C. 1401 to 1374. Wû-ting's reign was subsequent to that of Pan-kăng.

'great Tî sacrifice,' when the principal object of honour would be the ancient Khû, the father of Hsieh, with Hsieh as his correlate, and all the kings of the dynasty, with the earlier lords of Shang, and their famous ministers and advisers, would have their places at the service. I think this is the oldest of the odes of Shang.

Profoundly wise were (the lords of) Shang, And long had there appeared the omens (of their dignity).

When the waters of the deluge spread vast abroad, Yü arranged and divided the regions of the land, And assigned to the exterior great states their boundaries, With their borders extending all over (the kingdom). (Even) then the chief of Sung was beginning to be great, And God raised up the son (of his daughter), and founded (the line of) Shang[1].

The dark king exercised an effective sway[2]. Charged with a small state, he commanded success; Charged with a large state, he commanded success[3]. He followed his rules of conduct without error; Wherever he inspected (the people), they responded (to his instructions)[4]. (Then came) Hsiang-thû all ardent[5], And all within the four seas, beyond (the middle regions), acknowledged his restraints.

---

[1] This line refers to the birth of Hsieh, as described in the previous ode, and his being made lord of Shang.

[2] It would be hard to say why Hsieh is here called 'the dark king.' There may be an allusion to the legend about the connexion of the swallow,—'the dark bird,'—with his birth. He never was 'a king;' but his descendants here represented him as such.

[3] All that is meant here is, that the territory of Shang was enlarged under Hsieh.

[4] There is a reference here to Hsieh's appointment by Shun to be Minister of Instruction.

[5] Hsiang-thû appears in the genealogical lists as grandson of Hsieh. We know nothing of him but what is related here.

The favour of God did not leave (Shang), And in Thang was found the fit object for its display. Thang was not born too late, And his wisdom and reverence daily advanced:—Brilliant was the influence of his character (on Heaven) for long. God he revered, And God appointed him to be the model for the nine regions.

He received the rank-tokens of the states, small and large, Which depended on him like the pendants of a banner:—So did he receive the blessing of Heaven. He was neither violent nor remiss, Neither hard nor soft. Gently he spread his instructions abroad, And all dignities and riches were concentrated in him.

He received the tribute of the states, small and large, And he supported them as a strong steed (does its burden):—So did he receive the favour of Heaven. He displayed everywhere his valour, Unshaken, unmoved, Unterrified, unscared:—All dignities were united in him.

The martial king displayed his banner, And with reverence grasped his axe. It was like (the case of) a blazing fire which no one can repress. The root, with its three shoots, Could make no progress, no growth[1]. The nine regions were effectually secured by Thang. Having smitten (the princes of) Wei and Kû, He dealt with (him of) *K*ün-wû and with *K*ieh of Hsiâ.

Formerly, in the middle of the period (before

[1] By 'the root' we are to understand Thang's chief opponent, *K*ieh, the last king of Hsiâ. *K*ieh's three great helpers were 'the three shoots,'—the princes of Wei, Kû, and *K*ün-wû; but the exact sites of their principalities cannot be made out.

Thang), There was a time of shaking and peril[1]. But truly did Heaven (then) deal with him as a son, And sent him down a high minister, Namely, Â-hăng[2], Who gave his assistance to the king of Shang.

ODE 5. THE YIN WÛ.

CELEBRATING THE WAR OF WÛ-TING AGAINST *KING-KHÛ*, ITS SUCCESS, AND THE GENERAL HAPPINESS AND VIRTUE OF HIS REIGN;—MADE, PROBABLY, WHEN A SPECIAL AND PERMANENT TEMPLE WAS BUILT FOR HIM AS THE 'HIGH AND HONOURED' KING OF SHANG.

The concluding lines indicate that the temple was made on the occasion which I thus assign to it. After Wû-ting's death, his spirit-tablet would be shrined in the ancestral temple, and he would have his share in the seasonal sacrifices; but several reigns would elapse before there was any necessity to make any other arrangement, so that his tablet should not be removed, and his share in the sacrifices not be discontinued. Hence the composition of the piece has been referred to the time of Tî-yî, the last but one of the kings of Shang.

Rapid was the warlike energy of (our king of) Yin, And vigorously did he attack *K*ing-*Kh*û[3].

---

[1] We do not know anything of this time of decadence in the fortunes of Shang between Hsieh and Thang.

[2] Â-hăng is Î Yin, who plays so remarkable a part in the Shû, IV, Books iv, v, and vi.

[3] *K*ing, or *Kh*û, or *K*ing-*Kh*û, as the two names are combined here, was a large and powerful half-savage state, having its capital in the present Wû-pei. So far as evidence goes, we should say, but for this ode, that the name of *Kh*û was not in use till long after the Shang dynasty. The name *K*ing appears several times in 'the Spring and Autumn' in the annals of duke *K*wang (B. C. 693 to 662), and then it gives place to the name *Kh*û in the first year of duke Hsî (B. C. 659), and subsequently disappears itself altogether. In consequence of this some critics make this piece out to have been composed under the *K*âu dynasty. The point cannot be fully cleared up; but on the whole I accept the words of the ode as sufficient proof against the silence of other documents.

Boldly he entered its dangerous passes, And brought the multitudes of *K*ing together, Till the country was reduced under complete restraint:—Such was the fitting achievement of the descendant of Thang!

'Ye people,' (he said), 'of *K*ing-*Kh*û, Dwell in the southern part of my kingdom. Formerly, in the time of Thang the Successful, Even from the *K*iang of Tî[1], They dared not but come with their offerings; (Their chiefs) dared not but come to seek acknowledgment[2]:—Such is the regular rule of Shang.'

Heaven had given their appointments (to the princes), But where their capitals had been assigned within the sphere of the labours of Yü, For the business of every year they appeared before our king[3], (Saying), 'Do not punish nor reprove us; We have not been remiss in our husbandry.'

When Heaven by its will is inspecting (the kingdom), The lower people are to be feared. (Our king) showed no partiality (in rewarding), no excess (in punishing); He dared not to allow himself in indolence:—So was his appointment (established)

[1] The Tî *K*iang, or *K*iang of Tî, still existed in the time of the Han dynasty, occupying portions of the present Kan-sû.

[2] The chiefs of the wild tribes, lying beyond the nine provinces of the kingdom, were required to present themselves once in their lifetime at the royal court. The rule, in normal periods, was for each chief to appear immediately after he had succeeded to the headship of his tribe.

[3] The feudal lords had to appear at court every year. They did so, we may suppose, at the court of Wû-ting, the more so because of his subjugation of *K*ing-*Kh*û.

over the states, And he made his happiness grandly secure.

The capital of Shang was full of order, The model for all parts of the kingdom. Glorious was (the king's) fame; Brilliant his energy. Long lived he and enjoyed tranquillity, And so he preserves us, his descendants.

We ascended the hill of *K*ing[1], Where the pines and cypresses grew symmetrical. We cut them down and conveyed them here; We reverently hewed them square. Long are the projecting beams of pine; Large are the many pillars. The temple was completed,—the tranquil abode (of the martial king of Yin).

II. The Sacrificial Odes of *K*âu.

In this division we have thirty-one sacrificial odes of *K*âu, arranged in three decades, the third of which, however, contains eleven pieces. They belong mostly to the time of king Wăn, the founder of the *K*âu dynasty, and to the reigns of his son and grandson, kings Wû and *Kh*ăng. The decades are named from the name of the first piece in each.

The First Decade, or that of *Kh*ing Miâo.

Ode 1. The *Kh*ing Miâo.

CELEBRATING THE REVERENTIAL MANNER IN WHICH A SACRIFICE TO KING WĂN WAS PERFORMED, AND FURTHER PRAISING HIM.

Chinese critics agree in assigning this piece to the sacrifice mentioned in the Shû, in the end of the thirteenth Book of Part V, when, the building of Lo being finished, king *Kh*ăng came to

---

[1] See on the last line but two of ode 3.

the new city, and offered a red bull to Wăn, and the same to Wû. It seems to me to have been sung in honour of Wăn, after the service was completed. This determination of the occasion of the piece being accepted, we should refer it to B.C. 1108.

Oh! solemn is the ancestral temple in its pure stillness. Reverent and harmonious were the distinguished assistants[1]; Great was the number of the officers[2]:—(All) assiduous followers of the virtue of (king Wăn). In response to him in heaven, Grandly they hurried about in the temple. Distinguished is he and honoured, And will never be wearied of among men.

ODE 2. THE WEI THIEN *K*IH MING.

CELEBRATING THE VIRTUE OF KING WĂN AS COMPARABLE TO THAT OF HEAVEN, AND LOOKING TO HIM FOR BLESSING IN THE FUTURE.

According to the Preface, there is an announcement here of the realization of complete peace throughout the kingdom, and some of the old critics refer the ode to a sacrifice to king Wăn by the duke of *K*âu, when he had completed the statutes for the new dynasty. But there is nothing to authorize a more definite argument of the contents than I have given.

The ordinances of Heaven,—How deep are they and unintermitting! And oh! how illustrious Was the singleness of the virtue of king Wăn[3]!

How does he (now) show his kindness? We will receive it, Striving to be in accord with him, our

[1] These would be the princes who were assembled on the occasion, and assisted the king in the service.

[2] That is, the officers who took part in the libations, prayers, and other parts of the sacrifice.

[3] See what 3ze-sze says on these four lines in the Doctrine of the Mean, XXVI, par. 10.

king Wăn; And may his remotest descendant be abundantly the same!

Ode 3. The Wei *Kh*ing.

APPROPRIATE AT SOME SACRIFICE TO KING WĂN, AND CELEBRATING HIS STATUTES.

Nothing more can, with any likelihood of truth, be said of this short piece, which moreover has the appearance of being a fragment.

Clear and to be preserved bright, Are the statutes of king Wăn. From the first sacrifice (to him), Till now when they have issued in our complete state, They have been the happy omen of (the fortunes of) *K*âu.

Ode 4. The Lieh Wăn.

A SONG IN PRAISE OF THE PRINCES WHO HAVE ASSISTED AT A SACRIFICE, AND ADMONISHING THEM.

The Preface says that this piece was made on the occasion of king *Kh*ăng's accession to the government, when he thus addressed the princes who had assisted him in the ancestral temple. *K*û Hsî considers that it was a piece for general use in the ancestral temple, to be sung when the king presented a cup to his assisting guests, after they had thrice presented the cup to the representatives of the dead. There is really nothing in it to enable us to decide in favour of either view.

Ye, brilliant and accomplished princes, Have conferred on me this happiness. Your favours to me are without limit, And my descendants will preserve (the fruits of) them.

Be not mercenary nor extravagant in your states, And the king will honour you. Thinking of this great service, He will enlarge the dignity of your successors.

What is most powerful is the being the man:—Its influence will be felt throughout your states. What is most distinguished is the being virtuous:—It will secure the imitation of all the princes. Ah! the former kings cannot be forgotten!

Ode 5. The Thien 3o.

APPROPRIATE TO A SACRIFICE TO KING THÂI.

We cannot tell what the sacrifice was; and the Preface, indeed, says that the piece was used in the seasonal sacrifices to all the former kings and dukes of the House of *K*âu. King Thâi was the grandfather of king Wăn, and, before he received that title, was known as 'the ancient duke Than-fû.' In B.C. 1327, he moved with his followers from Pin, an earlier seat of his House, and settled in the plain of *Kh*î, about fifty lî to the north-east of the present district city of *Kh*î-shan, in Shen-hsî.

Heaven made the lofty hill[1], And king Thâi brought (the country about) it under cultivation. He made the commencement with it, And king Wăn tranquilly (carried on the work), (Till) that rugged (mount) *Kh*î Had level roads leading to it. May their descendants ever preserve it!

Ode 6. The Hâo Thien yû *Kh*ăng Ming.

APPROPRIATE TO A SACRIFICE TO KING *KH*ĂNG.

*Kh*ăng was the honorary title of Sung, the son and successor of king Wû, B.C. 1115 to 1079.

Heaven made its determinate appointment, Which our two sovereigns received[2]. King *Kh*ăng did not dare to rest idly in it, But night and day enlarged

[1] Meaning mount *Kh*î.

[2] Wăn and Wû.

its foundations by his deep and silent virtue. How did he continue and glorify (his heritage), Exerting all his heart, And so securing its tranquillity!

ODE 7. THE WO *K*IANG.

APPROPRIATE TO A SACRIFICE TO KING WĂN, ASSOCIATED WITH HEAVEN, IN THE HALL OF AUDIENCE.

There is, happily, an agreement among the critics as to the occasion to which this piece is referred. It took place in the last month of autumn, in the Hall of Audience, called also 'the Brilliant Hall,' and 'the Hall of Light.' We must suppose that the princes are all assembled at court, and that the king receives them in this hall. A sacrifice is then presented to God, and with him is associated king Wăn, the two being the fountain from which, and the channel through which, the sovereignty had come to *K*âu.

I have brought my offerings, A ram and a bull. May Heaven accept them[1]!

I imitate and follow and observe the statutes of king Wăn, Seeking daily to secure the tranquillity of the kingdom. King Wăn, the Blesser, has descended on the right, and accepted (the offerings).

Do I not, night and day, Revere the majesty of Heaven, Thus to preserve (its favour)?

ODE 8. THE SHIH MÂI.

APPROPRIATE TO KING WÛ'S SACRIFICING TO HEAVEN, AND TO THE SPIRITS OF THE HILLS AND RIVERS, ON A PROGRESS THROUGH THE KINGDOM, AFTER THE OVERTHROW OF THE SHANG DYNASTY.

Here again there is an agreement among the critics. We find from the Ȝo *K*wan and 'the Narratives of the States,' that the

[1] This is a prayer. The worshipper, it is said, in view of the majesty of Heaven, shrank from assuming that God would certainly accept his sacrifice. He assumes, below, that king Wăn does so.

piece was, when those compilations were made, considered to be the work of the duke of *K*âu; and, no doubt, it was made by him soon after the accession of Wû to the kingdom, and when he was making a royal progress in assertion of his being appointed by Heaven to succeed to the rulers of Shang. The 'I' in the fourteenth line is, most probably, to be taken of the duke of *K*âu, who may have recited the piece on occasion of the sacrifices, in the hearing of the assembled princes and lords.

Now is he making a progress through his states; May Heaven deal with him as its son!

Truly are the honour and succession come from it to the House of *K*âu. To his movements All respond with tremulous awe. He has attracted and given rest to all spiritual beings[1], Even to (the spirits of) the Ho and the highest hills. Truly is the king our sovereign lord.

Brilliant and illustrious is the House of *K*âu. He has regulated the positions of the princes; He has called in shields and spears; He has returned to their cases bows and arrows[2]. I will cultivate admirable virtue, And display it throughout these great regions. Truly will the king preserve the appointment.

---

[1] 'All spiritual beings' is, literally, 'the hundred spirits,' meaning the spirits presiding, under Heaven, over all nature, and especially the spirits of the rivers and hills throughout the kingdom. Those of the Ho and the lofty mountains are mentioned, because if their spirits were satisfied with Wû, those of all other mountains and hills, no doubt, were so.

[2] Compare with these lines the last chapter of 'the Completion of the War' in the Shû.

ODE 9. THE *K*IH *K*ING.

AN ODE APPROPRIATE IN SACRIFICING TO THE KINGS WŬ, *KH*ĂNG, AND KHANG.

The Chinese critics differ in the interpretation of this ode, the Preface and older scholars restricting it to a sacrifice to king Wû, while *K*û Hsî and others find reference in it, as to me also seems most natural, to *Kh*ăng and Khang, who succeeded him.

The arm of king Wû was full of strength; Irresistible was his ardour. Greatly illustrious were *Kh*ăng and Khang[1], Kinged by God.

When we consider how *Kh*ăng and Khang Grandly held all within the four quarters (of the kingdom), How penetrating was their intelligence!

The bells and drums sound in harmony; The sounding-stones and flutes blend their notes; Abundant blessing is sent down.

Blessing is sent down in large measure. Careful and exact is all our deportment; We have drunk, and we have eaten, to the full; Our happiness and dignity will be prolonged.

ODE 10. THE SZE WĂN.

APPROPRIATE TO ONE OF THE BORDER SACRIFICES, WHEN HÂU-*K*Î WAS WORSHIPPED AS THE CORRELATE OF GOD, AND CELEBRATING HIM.

Hâu-*k*î was the same as *Kh*î, who appears in Part II of the Shû, as Minister of Agriculture to Yâo and Shun, and co-operating with

[1] If the whole piece be understood only of a sacrifice to Wû, this line will have to be translated—'How illustrious was he, who completed (his great work), and secured its tranquillity.' We must deal similarly with the next line. This construction is very forced; nor is the text clear on the view of *K*û Hsî.

Yü in his labours on the flooded land. The name Hâu belongs to him as lord of Thâi; that of *K*î, as Minister of Agriculture. However the combination arose, Hâu-*k*î became historically the name of *Kh*î of the time of Yâo and Shun, the ancestor to whom the kings of *K*âu traced their lineage. He was to the people the Father of Husbandry, who first taught men to plough and sow and reap. Hence, when the kings offered sacrifice and prayer to God at the commencement of spring for his blessing on the labours of the year, they associated Hâu-*k*î with him at the service.

O accomplished Hâu-*k*î, Thou didst prove thyself the correlate of Heaven. Thou didst give grain-food to our multitudes:—The immense gift of thy goodness. Thou didst confer on us the wheat and the barley, Which God appointed for the nourishment of all. And without distinction of territory or boundary, The rules of social duty were diffused throughout these great regions.

The Second Decade, or that of *Kh*ăn Kung.

Ode 1. The *Kh*ăn Kung.

INSTRUCTIONS GIVEN TO THE OFFICERS OF HUSBANDRY.

The place of this piece among the sacrificial odes makes us assign it to the conclusion of some sacrifice; but what the sacrifice was we cannot tell. The Preface says that it was addressed, at the conclusion of the spring sacrifice to ancestors, to the princes who had been present and taken part in the service. *K*û Hsî says nothing but what I have stated in the above argument of the piece.

Ah! ah! ministers and officers, Reverently attend to your public duties. The king has given you perfect rules;—Consult about them, and consider them.

Ah! ah! ye assistants, It is now the end of

spring[1]; And what have ye to seek for? (Only) how to manage the new fields and those of the third year. How beautiful are the wheat and the barley! The bright and glorious God Will in them give us a good year. Order all our men To be provided with their spuds and hoes:—Anon we shall see the sickles at work.

ODE 2. THE Î HSÎ.

FURTHER INSTRUCTIONS TO THE OFFICERS OF HUSBANDRY.

Again there is a difficulty in determining to what sacrifice this piece should be referred. The Preface says it was sung on the occasions of sacrifice by the king to God, in spring and summer, for a good year. But the note on the first two lines will show that this view cannot be accepted without modification.

Oh! yes, king *Kh*ăng[2] Brightly brought himself near[2]. Lead your husbandmen To sow their various kinds of grain, Going vigorously to work

[1] It is this line which makes it difficult to determine after what sacrifice we are to suppose these instructions to have been delivered. The year, during the Hsiâ dynasty, began with the first month of spring, as it now does in China, in consequence of Confucius having said that that was the proper time. Under the Shang dynasty, it commenced a month earlier; and during the *K*âu period, it ought always to have begun with the new moon preceding the winter solstice,—between our November 22 and December 22. But in the writings of the *K*âu period we find statements of time continually referred to the calendar of Hsiâ,—as here.

[2] These first two lines are all but unmanageable. The old critics held that there was no mention of king *Kh*ăng in them; but the text is definite on this point. We must suppose that a special service had been performed at his shrine, asking him to intimate the day when the sacrifice after which the instructions were given should be performed; and that a directing oracle had been received.

on your private fields[1], All over the thirty lî[2]. Attend to your ploughing, With your ten thousand men all in pairs.

Ode 3. The *K*âu Lû.

CELEBRATING THE REPRESENTATIVES OF FORMER DYNASTIES, WHO HAD COME TO COURT TO ASSIST AT A SACRIFICE IN THE ANCESTRAL TEMPLE.

This piece may have been used when the king was dismissing his distinguished guests in the ancestral temple. See the introductory note to this Part, pp. 300, 301.

A flock of egrets is flying, About the marsh there in the west[3]. My visitors came, With an (elegant) carriage like those birds.

There, (in their states), not disliked, Here, (in *K*âu), never tired of;—They are sure, day and night, To perpetuate their fame.

---

[1] The mention of 'the private fields' implies that there were also 'the public fields,' cultivated by the husbandmen in common, in behalf of the government. As the people are elsewhere introduced, wishing that the rain might first fall on 'the public fields,' to show their loyalty, so the king here mentions only 'the private fields,' to show his sympathy and consideration for the people.

[2] For the cultivation of the ground, the allotments of single families were separated by a small ditch; ten allotments, by a larger; a hundred, by what we may call a brook; a thousand, by a small stream; and ten thousand, by a river. The space occupied by 10,000 families formed a square of a little more than thirty-two lî. We may suppose that this space was intended by the round number of thirty lî in the text. So at least *K*ăng Khang-*kh*ăng explained it.

[3] These two lines make the piece allusive. See the Introduction, p. 279.

ODE 4. THE FĂNG NIEN.

AN ODE OF THANKSGIVING FOR A PLENTIFUL YEAR.

The Preface says the piece was used at sacrifices in autumn and winter. *K*û Hsî calls it an ode of thanksgiving for a good year,—without any specification of time. He supposes, however, that the thanks were given to the ancient Shăn-năng, 'the father of Agriculture,' Hâu-*k*î, 'the first Husbandman,' and the spirits presiding over the four quarters of the heavens. To this the imperial editors rightly demur, saying that the blessings which the piece speaks of could come only from God.

Abundant is the year with much millet and much rice; And we have our high granaries, With myriads, and hundreds of thousands, and millions (of measures in them); For spirits and sweet spirits, To present to our forefathers, male and female, And to supply all our ceremonies. The blessings sent down on us are of every kind.

ODE 5. THE YÛ KÛ.

THE BLIND MUSICIANS OF THE COURT OF *K*ÂU; THE INSTRUMENTS OF MUSIC; AND THEIR HARMONY.

The critics agree in holding that this piece was made on occasion of the duke of *K*âu's completing his instruments of music for the ancestral temple, and announcing the fact at a grand performance in the temple of king Wăn. It can hardly be regarded as a sacrificial ode.

There are the blind musicians; there are the blind musicians; In the court of (the temple of) *K*âu[1].

[1] The blind musicians at the court of *K*âu were numerous. The blindness of the eyes was supposed to make the ears more acute in hearing, and to be favourable to the powers of the voice. In the Official Book of *K*âu, III, i, par. 22, the enumeration of

There are (the music-frames with their) face-boards and posts, The high toothed-edge (of the former), and the feathers stuck (in the latter); With the drums, large and small, suspended from them; And the hand-drums and sounding-stones, the instrument to give the signal for commencing, and the stopper. These being all complete, the music is struck up. The pan-pipe and the double flute begin at the same time [1].

Harmoniously blend their sounds; In solemn unison they give forth their notes. Our ancestors will give ear. Our visitors will be there;—Long to witness the complete performance.

ODE 6. THE *KH*IEN.

SUNG IN THE LAST MONTH OF WINTER, AND IN SPRING, WHEN THE KING PRESENTED A FISH IN THE ANCESTRAL TEMPLE.

Such is the argument of this piece given in the Preface, and in which the critics generally concur. In the Lî *K*î, IV, vi, 49, it is recorded that the king, in the third month of winter, gave orders to his chief fisher to commence his duties, and went himself to see his operations. He partook of the fish first captured, but previously presented some as an offering in the back apartment of the ancestral temple. In the third month of spring, again, when the sturgeons began to make their appearance (Lî *K*î, IV, i, 25), the king presented one in the same place. On

these blind musicians gives 2 directors of the first rank, and 4 of the second; 40 performers of the first grade, 100 of the second, and 160 of the third; with 300 assistants who were possessed of vision. But it is difficult not to be somewhat incredulous as to this great collection of blind musicians about the court of *K*âu.

[1] All the instruments here enumerated were performed on in the open court below the hall. Nothing is said of the stringed instruments which were used in the hall itself; nor is the enumeration of the instruments in the courtyard complete.

these passages, the prefatory notice was, no doubt, constructed. Choice specimens of the earliest-caught fish were presented by the sovereign to his ancestors, as an act of duty, and an acknowledgment that it was to their favour that he and the people were indebted for the supplies of food, which they received from the waters.

Oh! in the *Kh*î and the *Kh*ü, There are many fish in the warrens;—Sturgeons, large and snouted, Thryssas, yellow-jaws, mud-fish, and carp;—For offerings, for sacrifice, That our bright happiness may be increased.

ODE 7. THE YUNG.

APPROPRIATE, PROBABLY, AT A SACRIFICE BY KING WÛ TO HIS FATHER WĂN.

From a reference in the Analects, III, ii, to an abuse of this ode in the time of Confucius, we learn that it was sung when the sacrificial vessels and their contents were being removed.

They come full of harmony; They are here in all gravity;—The princes assisting, While the Son of Heaven looks profound.

(He says), 'While I present (this) noble bull, And they assist me in setting forth the sacrifice, O great and august Father, Comfort me, your filial son.

'With penetrating wisdom thou didst play the man, A sovereign with the gifts both of peace and war, Giving rest even to great Heaven[1], And ensuring prosperity to thy descendants.

---

[1] To explain this line one commentator refers to the seventh stanza of the first piece in the Major Odes of the Kingdom, where it is said, 'God surveyed the four quarters of the kingdom, seeking for some one to give settlement and rest to the people;' and adds, 'Thus what Heaven has at heart is the settlement of the people. When they have rest given to them, then Heaven is at rest.'

'Thou comfortest me with the eyebrows of longevity; Thou makest me great with manifold blessings, I offer this sacrifice to my meritorious father, And to my accomplished mother[1].'

Ode 8. The 3âi Hsien.

APPROPRIATE TO AN OCCASION WHEN THE FEUDAL PRINCES HAD BEEN ASSISTING KING *KH*ĂNG AT A SACRIFICE TO HIS FATHER.

They appeared before their sovereign king, To seek from him the rules (they were to observe). With their dragon-emblazoned banners, flying bright, The bells on them and their front-boards tinkling, And with the rings on the ends of the reins glittering, Admirable was their majesty and splendour.

He led them to appear before his father shrined on the left[2], Where he discharged his filial duty, and presented his offerings;—That he might have granted to him long life, And ever preserve (his dignity). Great and many are his blessings. They are the brilliant and accomplished princes, Who cheer him with his many sources of happiness,

---

[1] At sacrifices to ancestors, the spirit tablets of wives were placed along with those of their husbands in their shrines, so that both shared in the honours of the service. So it is now in the imperial ancestral temple in Peking. The 'accomplished mother' here would be Thâi Sze, celebrated often in the pieces of the first Book of Part I, and elsewhere.

[2] Among the uses of the services of the ancestral temple, specified by Confucius and quoted on p. 302, was the distinguishing the order of descent in the royal House. According to the rules for that purpose, the characters here used enable us to determine the subject of this line as king Wû, in opposition to his father Wăn.

Enabling him to perpetuate them in their brightness as pure blessing.

ODE 9. THE YÛ KHO.

CELEBRATING THE DUKE OF SUNG ON ONE OF HIS APPEARANCES AT THE CAPITAL TO ASSIST AT THE SACRIFICE IN THE ANCESTRAL TEMPLE OF *K*ÂU;—SHOWING HOW HE WAS ESTEEMED AND CHERISHED BY THE KING.

The mention of the white horses here in the chariot of the visitor sufficiently substantiates the account in the Preface that he was the famous count of Wei, mentioned in the Shû, IV, xi, and whose subsequent investiture with the duchy of Sung, as the representative of the line of the Shang kings, is also related in the Shû, V, viii. With the dynasty of Shang white had been the esteemed and sacred colour, as red was with *K*âu, and hence the duke had his carriage drawn by white horses. 'The language,' says one critic, 'is all in praise of the visitor, but it was sung in the temple, and is rightly placed therefore among the Sung.' There is, in the last line, an indication of the temple in it.

The noble visitor! The noble visitor! Drawn, like his ancestors, by white horses! The reverent and dignified, Polished members of his suite!

The noble guest will stay (but) a night or two! The noble guest will stay (but) two nights or four! Give him ropes, To bind his horses[1].

I will convoy him (with a parting feast); I will comfort him in every possible way. Adorned with such great dignity, It is very natural that he should be blessed.

[1] These four lines simply express the wish of the king to detain his visitor, from the delight that his presence gave him. Compare the similar language in the second ode of the fourth decade of Part II.

Ode 10. The Wû.

SUNG IN THE ANCESTRAL TEMPLE TO THE MUSIC REGULATING THE DANCE IN HONOUR OF THE ACHIEVEMENTS OF KING WÛ.

This account of the piece, given in the Preface, is variously corroborated, and has not been called in question by any critic. Perhaps this brief ode was sung as a prelude to the dance, or it may be that the seven lines are only a fragment. This, indeed, is most likely, as we have several odes in the next decade, all said to have been used at the same occasion.

Oh! great wast thou, O king Wû, Displaying the utmost strength in thy work. Truly accomplished was king Wăn, Opening the path for his successors. Thou didst receive the inheritance from him. Thou didst vanquish Yin, and put a stop to its cruelties;—Effecting the firm establishment of thy merit.

The Third Decade, or that of Min Yü Hsiâo Ʒze.

Ode 1. The Min Yü.

APPROPRIATE TO THE YOUNG KING *KH*ĂNG, DECLARING HIS SENTIMENTS IN THE TEMPLE OF HIS FATHER.

The speaker in this piece is, by common consent, king *Kh*ăng. The only question is as to the date of its composition, whether it was made for him, in his minority, on his repairing to the temple when the mourning for his father was completed, or after the expiration of the regency of the duke of *K*âu. The words 'little child,' according to their usage, are expressive of humility and not of age. They do not enable us to determine the above point.

Alas for me, who am a little child, On whom has devolved the unsettled state! Solitary am I and full of distress. Oh! my great Father, All thy life long, thou wast filial.

Thou didst think of my great grandfather, (Seeing

him, as it were) ascending and descending in the court, I, the little child, Day and night will be as reverent.

Oh! ye great kings, As your successor, I will strive not to forget you.

ODE 2. THE FANG LO.

THE YOUNG KING TELLS OF HIS DIFFICULTIES AND INCOMPETENCIES; ASKS FOR COUNSEL TO KEEP HIM TO COPY THE EXAMPLE OF HIS FATHER; STATES HOW HE MEANT TO DO SO; AND CONCLUDES WITH AN APPEAL OR PRAYER TO HIS FATHER.

This seems to be a sequel to the former ode. We can hardly say anything about it so definite as the statement in the Preface, that it relates to a council held by *Kh*ăng and his ministers in the ancestral temple.

I take counsel at the beginning of my (rule), How I can follow (the example of) my shrined father. Ah! far-reaching (were his plans), And I am not yet able to carry them out. However I endeavour to reach to them, My continuation of them will still be all-deflected. I am a little child, Unequal to the many difficulties of the state. Having taken his place, (I will look for him) to go up and come down in the court, To ascend and descend in the house. Admirable art thou, O great Father, (Condescend) to preserve and enlighten me.

ODE 3. THE *K*ING *K*IH.

KING *KH*ĂNG SHOWS HIS SENSE OF WHAT WAS REQUIRED OF HIM TO PRESERVE THE FAVOUR OF HEAVEN, A CONSTANT JUDGE; INTIMATES HIS GOOD PURPOSES; AND ASKS THE HELP OF HIS MINISTERS TO BE ENABLED TO PERFORM THEM.

Let me be reverent! Let me be reverent! (The way of) Heaven is evident, And its appointment is not easily preserved[1]. Let me not say that it is high aloft above me. It ascends and descends about our doings; It daily inspects us wherever we are.

I am a little child, Without intelligence to be reverently (attentive to my duties); But by daily progress and monthly advance, I will learn to hold fast the gleams (of knowledge), till I arrive at bright intelligence. Assist me to bear the burden (of my position), And show me how to display a virtuous conduct.

Ode 4. The Hsiâo Pî.

KING *KH*ĂNG ACKNOWLEDGES THAT HE HAD ERRED, AND STATES HIS PURPOSE TO BE CAREFUL IN THE FUTURE; HE WILL GUARD AGAINST THE SLIGHT BEGINNINGS OF EVIL; AND IS PENETRATED WITH A SENSE OF HIS OWN INCOMPETENCIES.

This piece has been considered by some critics as the conclusion of the council in the ancestral temple, with which the previous two also are thought to be connected. The Preface says that the king asks in it for the assistance of his ministers, but no such request is expressed. I seem myself to see in it, with Sû *Kh*eh and others, a reference to the suspicions which *Kh*ăng at one time, we know, entertained of the fidelity of the duke of *K*âu, when he was inclined to believe the rumours spread against him by his other uncles, who joined in rebellion with the son of the last king of Shang.

I condemn myself (for the past), And will be on my guard against future calamity. I will have nothing to do with a wasp, To seek for myself its painful sting. At first indeed it seemed to be

[1] The meaning is this: 'The way of Heaven is very clear, to bless the good, namely, and punish the bad. But its favour is thus dependent on men themselves, and hard to preserve.'

(but) a wren[1], But it took wing, and became a large bird. I am unequal to the many difficulties of the kingdom, And am placed in the midst of bitter experiences.

ODE 5. THE 3ÂI SHÛ.

THE CULTIVATION OF THE GROUND FROM THE FIRST BREAKING OF IT UP, TILL IT YIELDS ABUNDANT HARVESTS;—AVAILABLE SPECIALLY FOR SACRIFICES AND FESTIVE OCCASIONS. WHETHER INTENDED TO BE USED ON OCCASIONS OF THANKSGIVING, OR IN SPRING WHEN PRAYING FOR A GOOD YEAR, CANNOT BE DETERMINED.

The Preface says that this ode was used in spring, when the king in person turned up some furrows in the field set apart for that purpose, and prayed at the altars of the spirits of the land and the grain, for an abundant year. *K*û Hsî says he does not know on what occasion it was intended to be used; but comparing it with the fourth ode of the second decade, he is inclined to rank it with that as an ode of thanksgiving. There is nothing in the piece itself to determine us in favour of either view. It brings before us a series of pleasing pictures of the husbandry of those early times. The editors of the imperial edition say that its place in the Sung makes it clear that it was an accompaniment of some royal sacrifice. We need not controvert this; but the poet evidently singled out some large estate, and describes the labour on it, from the first bringing it under cultivation to the state in which it was before his eyes, and concludes by saying that the picture which he gives of it had long been applicable to the whole country.

They clear away the grass and the bushes; And the ground is laid open by their ploughs.

In thousands of pairs they remove the roots, Some in the low wet land, some along the dykes.

---

[1] The Chinese characters here mean, literally, 'peach-tree insect,' or, as Dr. Williams has it, 'peach-bug.' Another name for the bird is 'the clever wife,' from the artistic character of its nest, which would point it out as the small 'tailor bird.' But the name is applied to various small birds.

There are the master and his eldest son; His younger sons, and all their children; Their strong helpers, and their hired servants. How the noise of their eating the viands brought to them resounds! (The husbands) think lovingly of their wives; (The wives) keep close to their husbands. (Then) with their sharp ploughshares They set to work on the south-lying acres.

They sow their various kinds of grain, Each seed containing in it a germ of life.

In unbroken lines rises the blade, And, well nourished, the stalks grow long.

Luxuriant looks the young grain, And the weeders go among it in multitudes.

Then come the reapers in crowds, And the grain is piled up in the fields, Myriads, and hundreds of thousands, and millions (of stacks); For spirits and for sweet spirits, To offer to our ancestors, male and female, And to provide for all ceremonies.

Fragrant is their aroma, Enhancing the glory of the state. Like pepper is their smell, To give comfort to the aged.

It is not here only that there is this (abundance); It is not now only that there is such a time:— From of old it has been thus.

Ode 6. The Liang Sze.

PRESUMABLY, AN ODE OF THANKSGIVING IN THE AUTUMN TO THE SPIRITS OF THE LAND AND GRAIN.

Very sharp are the excellent shares, With which they set to work on the south-lying acres.

They sow their various kinds of grain, Each seed containing in it a germ of life.

There are those who come to see them, With their baskets round and square, Containing the provisions of millet.

With their light splint hats on their heads, They ply their hoes on the ground, Clearing away the smartweed on the dry land and wet.

The weeds being decayed, The millets grow luxuriantly.

They fall rustling before the reapers. The gathered crop is piled up solidly, High as a wall, United together like the teeth of a comb; And the hundred houses are opened (to receive the grain)[1].

Those hundred houses being full, The wives and children have a feeling of repose.

(Now) we kill this black-muzzled tawny bull[2], with his crooked horns, To imitate and hand down, To hand down (the observances of) our ancestors.

ODE 7. THE SZE Î.

AN ODE APPROPRIATE TO THE PREPARATIONS AND PROGRESS OF A FEAST AFTER A SACRIFICE.

The Preface and the editors of the Yung-*kh*ăng Shih say that the piece has reference to the entertainment given, the day after a

[1] 'The hundred houses,' or chambers in a hundred family residences, are those of the hundred families, cultivating the space which was bounded by a brook;—see note on the second ode of the preceding decade. They formed a society, whose members helped one another in their field work, so that their harvest might be said to be carried home at the same time. Then would come the threshing or treading, and winnowing, after which the grain would be brought into the houses.

[2] It has been observed that under the *K*âu dynasty, red was the

sacrifice, in the ancestral temple, to the personators of the dead, described on p. 301. *K*û Hsî denies this, and holds simply that it belongs to the feast after a sacrifice, without further specifying what sacrifice. The old view is probably the more correct.

In his silken robes, clean and bright, With his cap on his head, looking so respectful, From the hall he goes to the foot of the stairs, And (then) from the sheep to the oxen[1]. (He inspects) the tripods, large and small, And the curved goblet of rhinoceros horn[2]. The good spirits are mild, (But) there is no noise, no insolence:—An auspice (this) of great longevity.

ODE 8. THE *K*O.

AN ODE IN PRAISE OF KING WÛ, AND RECOGNISING THE DUTY TO FOLLOW HIS COURSE.

This was sung, according to the Preface, at the conclusion of the dance in honour of king Wû;—see on the last piece of the second decade.

Oh! powerful was the king's army, But he nursed it, in obedience to circumstances, while the

colour of the sacrificial victims. So it was for the ancestral temple; but in sacrificing to the spirits of the land and grain, the victim was a 'yellow' bull with black lips.

[1] The subject of these lines must be an ordinary officer, for to such the silk robes and a purple cap were proper, when he was assisting at the sacrifices of the king or of a feudal prince. There were two buildings outside the principal gate leading to the ancestral temple, and two corresponding inside, in which the personators of the departed ancestors were feasted. We must suppose the officer in question descending from the upper hall to the vestibule of the gate, to inspect the dishes, arranged for the feast, and then proceeding to see the animals, and the tripods for boiling the flesh, &c.

[2] The goblet of rhinoceros horn was to be drained, as a penalty, by any one offending at the feast against the rules of propriety; but here there was no occasion for it.

time was yet dark. When the time was clearly bright, He thereupon donned his grand armour. We have been favoured to receive What the martial king accomplished. To deal aright with what we have inherited, We have to be sincere imitators of thy course, (O king).

Ode 9. The Hwan.

CELEBRATING THE MERIT AND SUCCESS OF KING WÛ.

According to a statement in the Ȝo *K*wan, this piece also was sung in connexion with the dance of Wû. The Preface says it was used in declarations of war, and in sacrificing to God and the Father of War. Perhaps it came to be used on such occasions; but we must refer it in the first place to the reign of king *Kh*ăng.

There is peace throughout our myriad regions. There has been a succession of plentiful years:— Heaven does not weary in its favour. The martial king Wû Maintained (the confidence of) his officers, And employed them all over the kingdom, So securing the establishment of his family. Oh! glorious was he in the sight of Heaven, Which kinged him in the room (of Shang).

Ode 10. The Lâi.

CELEBRATING THE PRAISE OF KING WĂN.

This is the only account of the piece that can be given from itself. The Ȝo *K*wan, however, refers it to the dance of king Wû; and the Preface says it contains the words with which Wû accompanied his grant of fiefs and appanages in the ancestral temple to his principal followers.

King Wăn laboured earnestly:—Right is it we should have received (the kingdom). We will diffuse (his virtue), ever cherishing the thought of him; Henceforth we will seek only the settlement (of the kingdom). It was he through whom came the appointment of *K*âu. Oh! let us ever cherish the thought of him.

Ode 11. The Pan.

CELEBRATING THE GREATNESS OF *K*ÂU, AND ITS FIRM POSSESSION OF THE KINGDOM, AS SEEN IN THE PROGRESSES OF ITS REIGNING SOVEREIGN.

In the eighth piece of the first decade we have an ode akin to this, relating a tentative progress of king Wû, to test the acceptance of his sovereignty. This is of a later date, and should be referred, probably, to the reign of king *Kh*ăng, when the dynasty was fully acknowledged. Some critics, however, make it, like the three preceding, a portion of what was sung at the Wû dance.

Oh! great now is *K*âu. We ascend the high hills, Both those that are long and narrow, and the lofty mountains. Yes, and (we travel) along the regulated Ho, All under the sky, Assembling those who now respond to me. Thus it is that the appointment belongs to *K*âu.

III. The Praise Odes of Lû.

It is not according to the truth of things to class the Sung of Lû among the sacrificial odes, and I do not call them such. *K*û Hsî says:—'King *Kh*ăng, because of the great services rendered by the duke of *K*âu, granted to Po-*kh*in, (the duke's eldest son, and first marquis of Lû), the privilege of using the royal ceremonies and music, in consequence of which Lû had its Sung, which were sung to the music in its ancestral temple. Afterwards, they made in Lû other odes in praise of their rulers, which they also called Sung.' In this way it is endeavoured to account for there being such pieces in this part of the Shih as the four in this division of it. Confucius, it is thought, found them in Lû, bearing the name of Sung, and so he classed them with the true sacrificial odes, bearing that designation. If we were to admit, contrary to the evidence in the case, that the Shih was compiled by Confucius, this explanation of the place of the Sung of Lû in this Part would not be complimentary to his discrimination.

Whether such a privilege as *K*û states was really granted to the first marquis of Lû, is a point very much controverted. Many contend that the royal ceremonies were usurped in the state, in the time of duke Hsî (B.C. 659 to 627). But if this should be conceded, it would not affect the application to the odes in this division of the name of Sung. They are totally unlike the Sung of Shang and of *K*âu. It has often been asked why there are no Făng of Lû in the first Part of the Shih. The pieces here are really the Făng of Lû, and may be compared especially with the Făng of Pin.

Lû was one of the states in the east, having its capital in *Kh*ü-fâu, which is still the name of a district in the department of Yen-*k*âu, Shan-tung. According to *K*û, king *Kh*ăng invested the duke of *K*âu's eldest son with the territory. According to Sze-mâ *Kh*ien, the duke of *K*âu was himself appointed marquis of Lû; but being unable to go there in consequence of his duties at the royal court, he sent his son instead. After the expiration of his regency, the territory was largely augmented, but he still remained in *K*âu.

I pass over the first two odes, which have no claim to a place among 'sacred texts.' And only in one stanza of the third is there the expression of a religious sentiment. I give it entire, however.

ODE 3. THE PHAN SHUI.

IN PRAISE OF SOME MARQUIS OF LÛ, CELEBRATING HIS INTEREST IN THE STATE COLLEGE, WHICH HE HAD, PROBABLY, REPAIRED, TESTIFYING HIS VIRTUES, AND AUSPICING FOR HIM A COMPLETE TRIUMPH OVER THE TRIBES OF THE HWÂI, WHICH WOULD BE CELEBRATED IN THE COLLEGE.

The marquis here celebrated was, probably, Shăn, or 'duke Hsî,' mentioned above. The immediate occasion of its composition must have been some opening or inauguration service in connexion with the repair of the college.

1. Pleasant is the semicircular water[1], And we gather the cress about it. The marquis of Lû is coming to it, And we see his dragon-figured banner. His banner waves in the wind, And the bells of his horses tinkle harmoniously. Small and great, All follow the prince in his progress to it.

2. Pleasant is the semicircular water, And we gather the pondweed in it. The marquis of Lû has come to it, With his horses so stately. His horses are grand; His fame is brilliant. Blandly he looks and smiles; Without any impatience he delivers his instructions.

3. Pleasant is the semicircular water, And we gather the mallows about it. The marquis of Lû has come to it, And in the college he is drinking. He is drinking the good spirits. May there be

---

[1] It is said in the tenth ode of the first decade of the Major Odes of the Kingdom, that king Wû in his capital of Hâo built 'his hall with its circlet of water.' That was the royal college built in the middle of a circle of water; each state had its grand college with a semicircular pool in front of it, such as may now be seen in front of the temples of Confucius in the metropolitan cities of the provinces. It is not easy to describe all the purposes which the building served. In this piece the marquis of Lû appears feasting in it, delivering instructions, taking counsel with his ministers, and receiving the spoils and prisoners of war. The Lî *K*î, VIII, ii, 7, refers to sacrifices to Hâu-*k*î in connexion with the college of Lû. There the officers of the state in autumn learned ceremonies; in winter, literary studies; in spring and summer, the use of arms; and in autumn and winter, dancing. There were celebrated trials of archery; there the aged were feasted: there the princes held council with their ministers. The college was in the western suburb of each capital.

given to him such old age as is seldom enjoyed! May he accord with the grand ways, So subduing to himself all the people!

4. Very admirable is the marquis of Lû, Reverently displaying his virtue, And reverently watching over his deportment, The pattern of the people. With great qualities, both civil and martial, Brilliantly he affects his meritorious ancestors[1]. In everything entirely filial, He seeks the blessing that is sure to follow.

5. Very intelligent is the marquis of Lû, Making his virtue illustrious. He has made this college with its semicircle of water, And the tribes of the Hwâi will submit to him[2]. His martial-looking tiger-leaders Will here present the left ears (of their foes)[3]. His examiners, wise as Kâo-yâo[4], Will here present the prisoners.

6. His numerous officers, Men who have enlarged their virtuous minds, With martial energy conducting their expedition, Will drive far away those tribes of the east and south. Vigorous and

---

[1] The meaning is that the fine qualities of the marquis 'reached to' and affected his ancestors in their spirit-state, and would draw down their protecting favour. Their blessing, seen in his prosperity, was the natural result of his filial piety.

[2] The Hwâi rises in the department of Nan-yang, Ho-nan, and flows eastward to the sea. South of it, down to the time of this ode, were many rude and wild tribes that gave frequent occupation to the kings of *K*âu.

[3] When prisoners refused to submit, their left ears were cut off, and shown as trophies.

[4] The ancient Shun's Minister of Crime. The 'examiners' were officers who questioned the prisoners, especially the more important of them, to elicit information, and decide as to the amount of their guilt and punishment.

grand, Without noise or display, Without appeal to the judges [1], They will here present (the proofs of) their merit.

7. How they draw their bows adorned with bone! How their arrows whiz forth! Their war chariots are very large! Their footmen and charioteers never weary! They have subdued the tribes of Hwâi, And brought them to an unrebellious submission. Only lay your plans securely, And all the tribes of the Hwâi will be won [2].

8. They come flying on the wing, those owls, And settle on the trees about the college; They eat the fruit of our mulberry trees, And salute us with fine notes [3]. So awakened shall be those tribes of the Hwâi. They will come presenting their precious things, Their large tortoises, and their elephants' teeth, And great contributions of the southern metals [4].

---

[1] The 'judges' decided all questions of dispute in the army, and on the merits of different men who had distinguished themselves.

[2] In this stanza the poet describes a battle with the wild tribes, as if it were going on before his eyes.

[3] An owl is a bird with a disagreeable scream, instead of a beautiful note; but the mulberries grown about the college would make them sing delightfully. And so would the influence of Lû, going forth from the college, transform the nature of the tribes about the Hwâi.

[4] That is, according to 'the Tribute of Yü,' in the Shû, from *K*ing-*k*âu and Yang-*k*âu.

ODE 4. THE PÎ KUNG.

IN PRAISE OF DUKE HSÎ, AND AUSPICING FOR HIM A MAGNIFICENT CAREER OF SUCCESS, WHICH WOULD MAKE LÛ ALL THAT IT HAD EVER BEEN:—WRITTEN, PROBABLY, ON AN OCCASION WHEN HSÎ HAD REPAIRED THE TEMPLES OF THE STATE, OF WHICH PIOUS ACT HIS SUCCESS WOULD BE THE REWARD.

There is no doubt that duke Hsî is the hero of this piece. He is mentioned in the third stanza as 'the son of duke *K*wang,' and the Hsî-sze referred to in the last stanza as the architect under whose superintendence the temples had been repaired was his brother, whom we meet with elsewhere as 'duke's son, Yü.' The descriptions of various sacrifices prove that the lords of Lû, whether permitted to use royal ceremonies or not, did really do so. The writer was evidently in a poetic rapture as to what his ruler was, and would do. The piece is a genuine bardic effusion.

The poet traces the lords of Lû to *K*iang Yüan and her son Hâu-*k*î. He then comes to the establishment of the *K*âu dynasty, and under it of the marquisate of Lû; and finally to duke Hsî, dilating on his sacrificial services, the military power of Lû, and the achievements which he might be expected to accomplish in subjugating all the territory lying to the east, and a long way south, of Lû.

1. How pure and still are the solemn temples, In their strong solidity and minute completeness! Highly distinguished was *K*iang Yüan[1], Of virtue undeflected. God regarded her with favour, And without injury or hurt, Immediately, when her months were completed, She gave birth to Hâu-*k*î! On him were conferred all blessings,—(To know) how the (ordinary) millet ripened early, and the sacrificial millet late; How first to sow pulse

[1] About *K*iang Yüan and her conception and birth of Hâu-*k*î, see the first piece in the third decade of the Major Odes of the Kingdom. There also Hâu-*k*î's teaching of husbandry is more fully described.

and then wheat. Anon he was invested with an inferior state, And taught the people how to sow and to reap, The (ordinary) millet and the sacrificial, Rice and the black millet; Ere long over the whole country:—(Thus) continuing the work of Yü.

2. Among the descendants of Hâu-*k*î, There was king Thâi[1], Dwelling on the south of (mount) *Kh*î, Where the clipping of Shang began. In process of time Wăn and Wû Continued the work of king Thâi, And (the purpose of) Heaven was carried out in its time, In the plain of Mû[2]. 'Have no doubts, no anxieties,' (it was said), 'God is with you[3].' Wû disposed of the troops of Shang; He and his men equally shared in the achievement. (Then) king (*Kh*ăng) said, 'My uncle[4], I will set up your eldest son, And make him marquis of Lû. I will greatly enlarge your territory there, To be a help and support to the House of *K*âu.'

3. Accordingly he appointed (our first) duke of Lû, And made him marquis in the east, Giving him the hills and rivers, The lands and fields, and the attached states[5]. The (present) descendant of the duke of *K*âu, The son of duke *K*wang, With dragon-emblazoned banner, attends the sacrifices, (Grasping) his six reins soft and pliant. In spring

[1] See on the Sacrificial Odes of *K*âu, decade i, ode 5.

[2] See the Shû, V, iii.

[3] Shang-fû, one of Wû's principal leaders, encouraged him at the battle of Mû with these words.

[4] That is, the duke of *K*âu.

[5] That is, small territories, held by chiefs of other surnames, but acknowledging the jurisdiction of the lords of Lû, and dependent on them for introduction to the royal court.

and autumn he is not remiss; His offerings are all without error[1]. To the great and sovereign God, And to his great ancestor Hâu-*k*î, He offers the victims, red and pure[2]. They enjoy, they approve, And bestow blessings in large number. The duke of *K*âu, and (your other) great ancestors, Also bless you.

4. In autumn comes the sacrifice of the season[3], But the bulls for it have had their horns capped in summer[4]; They are the white bull and the red one[5]. (There are) the bull-figured goblet in its dignity[6]; Roast pig, minced meat, and soups; The dishes of bamboo and wood, and the large stands[7], And the dancers all complete. The filial descendant

[1] These lines refer to the seasonal sacrifices in the temple of ancestors, two seasons being mentioned for all the four, as in some of the odes of Shang.

[2] From the seasonal sacrifices the poet passes to the sacrifice to God at the border altar in the spring,—no doubt the same which is referred to in the last ode of the first decade of the Sacrificial Odes of *K*âu.

[3] The subject of the seasonal sacrifices is resumed.

[4] A piece of wood was fixed across the horns of the victim-bulls, to prevent their injuring them by pushing or rubbing against any hard substance. An animal injured in any way was not fit to be used in sacrifice.

[5] In sacrificing to the duke of *K*âu, a white bull was used by way of distinction. His great services to the dynasty had obtained for him the privilege of being sacrificed to with royal ceremonies. A white bull, such as had been offered to the kings of Shang, was therefore devoted to him; while for Po-*kh*in, and the other marquises (or dukes as spoken of by their own subjects), a victim of the orthodox *K*âu colour was employed.

[6] This goblet, fashioned in the shape of a bull, or with a bull pictured on it, must have been well known in connexion with these services.

[7] 'The large stand' was of a size to support half the roasted body of a victim.

will be blessed. (Your ancestors) will make you gloriously prosperous, They will make you long-lived and good, To preserve this eastern region, Long possessing the state of Lû, Unwaning, unfallen, Unshaken, undisturbed! They will make your friendship with your three aged (ministers)[1] Like the hills, like the mountains.

5. Our prince's chariots are a thousand, And (in each) are (the two spears with their) vermilion tassels, and (the two bows with their) green bands. His footmen are thirty thousand, With shells on vermilion strings adorning their helmets[2]. So numerous are his ardent followers, To deal with the tribes of the west and north, And to punish those of *K*ing and Shû[3], So that none of them will dare to withstand us. (The spirits of your ancestors) shall make you grandly prosperous; They

[1] Referring, probably, to the three principal ministers of the state.

[2] These lines describe Hsî's resources for war. A thousand chariots was the regular force which a great state could at the utmost bring into the field. Each chariot contained three mailed men;—the charioteer in the middle, a spearman on the right, and an archer on the left. Two spears rose aloft with vermilion tassels, and there were two bows, bound with green bands to frames in their cases. Attached to every chariot were seventy-two foot-soldiers and twenty-five followers, making with the three men in it, 100 in all; so that the whole force would amount to 100,000 men. But in actual service the force of a great state was restricted to three 'armies' or 375 chariots, attended by 37,500 men, of whom 27,500 were foot-soldiers, put down here in round numbers as 30,000.

[3] *K*ing is the *K*ing-*kh*û of the last of the Sacrificial Odes of Shang, and the name Shû was applied to several half-civilized states to the east of it, which it brought, during the *Kh*un *Kh*iû period, one after another under its jurisdiction.

shall make you long-lived and wealthy. The hoary hair and wrinkled back, Marking the aged men, shall always be in your service. They shall grant you old age, ever vigorous, For myriads and thousands of years, With the eyebrows of longevity, and ever unharmed.

6. The mountain of Thâi is lofty, Looked up to by the state of Lû [1]. We grandly possess also Kwei and Măng [2]; And we shall extend to the limits of the east, Even the states along the sea. The tribes of the Hwâi will seek our alliance; All will proffer their allegiance:—Such shall be the achievements of the marquis of Lû.

7. He shall maintain the possession of Hû and Yî [3], And extend his sway to the regions of Hsü [4], Even to the states along the sea. The tribes of the Hwâi, the Man, and the Mo [5], And those tribes (still more) to the south, All will proffer their allegiance;—Not one will dare not to answer to his call, Thus showing their obedience to the marquis of Lû.

8. Heaven will give great blessing to our prince, So that with the eyebrows of longevity he shall

[1] Mount Thâi is well known, the eastern of the four great mountains of China in the time of Shun. It is in the department of Thâi-an, Shan-tung.

[2] These were two smaller hills in Lû.

[3] These were two hills of Lû, in the present district of Ȝâu.

[4] Hsü was the name of one of Yü's nine provinces, embracing portions of the present Shan-tung, *K*iang-sû, and An-hui.

[5] Mo was properly the name of certain wild tribes in the north, as Man was that of the tribes of the south. But we cannot suppose any tribes to be meant here but such as lay south of Lû.

maintain Lû. He shall possess *K*ang and Hsü[1], And recover all the territory of the duke of *K*âu. Then shall the marquis of Lû feast and be glad, With his admirable wife and aged mother; With his excellent ministers and all his (other) officers[2]. Our region and state shall he hold, Thus receiving many blessings, To hoary hair, and with teeth ever renewed like a child's.

9. The pines of 3û-lâi[3], And the cypresses of Hsin-fû[3], Were cut down and measured, With the cubit line and the eight cubits' line. The projecting beams of pine were made very large; The grand inner apartments rose vast. Splendid look the new temples, The work of Hsî-sze, Very wide and large, Answering to the expectations of all the people.

---

[1] *K*ang was a city with some adjacent territory, in the present district of Thăng, that had been taken from Lû by *Kh*î. Hsü, called in the Spring and Autumn 'the fields of Hsü,' was west from Lû, and had been granted to it as a convenient place for its princes to stop at on their way to the royal court; but it had been sold or parted with to *K*ăng in the first year of duke Hwan (B.C. 711). The poet desires that Hsî should recover these and all other territory which had at any time belonged to Lû.

[2] He would feast with the ladies in the inner apartment of the palace, suitable for such a purpose; with his ministers in the outer banqueting-room.

[3] These were two hills, in the present department of Thâi-an.

THE MINOR ODES OF THE KINGDOM.

PIECES AND STANZAS ILLUSTRATING THE RELIGIOUS VIEWS AND PRACTICES OF THE WRITERS AND THEIR TIMES.

The First Decade, or that of Lû-ming.

ODE 5, STANZA 1. THE FÂ MÛ.

THE FÂ MÛ IS A FESTAL ODE, WHICH WAS SUNG AT THE ENTERTAINMENT OF FRIENDS;—INTENDED TO CELEBRATE THE DUTY AND VALUE OF FRIENDSHIP, EVEN TO THE HIGHEST.

On the trees go the blows *k*ăng-*k*ăng; And the birds cry out ying-ying. One issues from the dark valley, And removes to the lofty tree. Ying goes its cry, Seeking with its voice its companion. Look at the bird, Bird as it is, seeking with its voice its companion; And shall a man Not seek to have his friends? Spiritual beings will then hearken to him[1]; He shall have harmony and peace.

ODE 6. THE THIEN PÂO.

A FESTAL ODE, RESPONSIVE TO ANY OF THE FIVE THAT PRECEDE IT. THE KING'S OFFICERS AND GUESTS, HAVING BEEN FEASTED BY HIM, CELEBRATE HIS PRAISES, AND DESIRE FOR HIM THE BLESSING OF HEAVEN AND HIS ANCESTORS.

Ascribed, like the former, to the duke of *K*âu.

Heaven protects and establishes thee, With the greatest security; Makes thee entirely virtuous.

[1] This line and the following show the power and value of the cultivation of friendship in affecting spiritual beings. That designation is understood in the widest sense.

That thou mayest enjoy every happiness; Grants thee much increase, So that thou hast all in abundance.

Heaven protects and establishes thee. It grants thee all excellence, So that thine every matter is right, And thou receivest every Heavenly favour. It sends down to thee long-during happiness, Which the days are not sufficient to enjoy.

Heaven protects and establishes thee, So that in everything thou dost prosper. Like the high hills and the mountain masses, Like the topmost ridges and the greatest bulks, Like the stream ever coming on, Such is thine increase.

With happy auspices and purifications thou bringest the offerings, And dost filially present them, In spring, summer, autumn, and winter, To the dukes and former kings[1]; And they say, 'We give to thee myriads of years, duration unlimited[2].'

The spirits come[3], And confer on thee many blessings. The people are simple and honest, Daily enjoying their meat and drink. All the black-haired race, in all their surnames, Universally practise thy virtue.

Like the moon advancing to the full, Like the sun ascending the heavens, Like the everlasting southern hills, Never waning, never falling, Like

[1] These dukes and former kings are all the ancestors of the royal House of *K*âu, sacrificed to at the four seasons of the year.

[2] Here we have the response of the dukes and kings communicated to the sacrificing king by the individuals chosen to represent them at the service.

[3] The spirits here are, of course, those of the former dukes and kings.

the luxuriance of the fir and the cypress;—May such be thy succeeding line!

ODE 9, STANZA 4. THE TÎ TÛ.

THE TÎ TÛ IS AN ODE OF CONGRATULATION, INTENDED FOR THE MEN WHO HAVE RETURNED FROM MILITARY DUTY AND SERVICE ON THE FRONTIERS.

The congratulation is given in a description of the anxiety and longing of the soldiers' wives for their return. We must suppose one of the wives to be the speaker throughout. The fourth stanza shows how she had resorted to divination to allay her fears about her husband.

They have not packed up, they do not come. My sorrowing heart is greatly distressed. The time is past, and he is not here, To the multiplication of my sorrows. Both by the tortoise-shell and the reeds have I divined, And they unite in saying he is near. My warrior is at hand.

The Fourth Decade, or that of *Kh*î fû.

ODE 5, STANZAS 5 TO 9. THE SZE KAN.

THE SZE KAN WAS PROBABLY MADE FOR A FESTIVAL ON THE COMPLETION OF A PALACE; CONTAINING A DESCRIPTION OF IT, AND PROCEEDING TO GOOD WISHES FOR THE BUILDER AND HIS POSTERITY. THE STANZAS HERE GIVEN SHOW HOW DIVINATION WAS RESORTED TO FOR THE INTERPRETATION OF DREAMS.

The piece is referred to the time of king Hsüan (B.C. 827 to 782).

Level and smooth is the courtyard, And lofty are the pillars around it. Pleasant is the exposure of the chamber to the light, And deep and wide are its recesses. Here will our noble lord repose.

On the rush-mat below and that of fine bamboos above it, May he repose in slumber! May he sleep and awake, (Saying), 'Divine for me my dreams[1]. What dreams are lucky? They have been of bears and grisly bears; They have been of cobras and (other) snakes.'

The chief diviner will divine them. 'The bears and grisly bears Are the auspicious intimations of sons; The cobras and (other) snakes Are the auspicious intimations of daughters[2].'

Sons shall be born to him:—They will be put to sleep on couches; They will be clothed in robes; They will have sceptres to play with; Their cry will be loud. They will be (hereafter) resplendent with red knee-covers, The (future) king, the princes of the land.

Daughters shall be born to him:—They will be put to sleep on the ground; They will be clothed with wrappers; They will have tiles to play with[3]. It will be theirs neither to do wrong nor to do good[4]. Only about the spirits and the food will

---

[1] In the Official Book of *K*âu, ch. 24, mention is made of the Diviner of Dreams and his duties:—He had to consider the season of the year when a dream occurred, the day of the cycle, and the then predominant influence of the two powers of nature. By the positions of the sun, moon, and planets in the zodiacal spaces he could determine whether any one of the six classes of dreams was lucky or unlucky. Those six classes were ordinary and regular dreams, terrible dreams, dreams of thought, dreams in waking, dreams of joy, and dreams of fear.

[2] The boy would have a sceptre, a symbol of dignity, to play with; the girl, a tile, the symbol of woman's work, as, sitting with a tile on her knee, she twists the threads of hemp.

[3] That is, the red apron of a king and of the prince of a state.

[4] The woman has only to be obedient. That is her whole duty. The line does not mean, as it has been said, that 'she is incapable of good or evil;' but it is not her part to take the initiative even in what is good.

they have to think, And to cause no sorrow to their parents.

Ode 6, Stanza 4. The Wû Yang.

THE WÛ YANG IS SUPPOSED TO CELEBRATE THE LARGENESS AND EXCELLENT CONDITION OF KING HSÜAN'S FLOCKS AND HERDS. THE CONCLUDING STANZA HAS REFERENCE TO THE DIVINATION OF THE DREAMS OF HIS HERDSMEN.

Your herdsmen shall dream, Of multitudes and then of fishes, Of the tortoise-and-serpent, and then of the falcon, banners[1]. The chief diviner will divine the dreams;—How the multitudes, dissolving into fishes, Betoken plentiful years; How the tortoise-and-serpent, dissolving into the falcon, banners, Betoken the increasing population of the kingdom.

Ode 7. The *K*ieh Nan Shan.

A LAMENTATION OVER THE UNSETTLED STATE OF THE KINGDOM; DENOUNCING THE INJUSTICE AND NEGLECT OF THE CHIEF MINISTER, BLAMING ALSO THE CONDUCT OF THE KING, WITH APPEALS TO HEAVEN, AND SEEMINGLY CHARGING IT WITH CRUELTY AND INJUSTICE.

This piece is referred to the time of king Yû (B.C. 781 to 771), the unworthy son of king Hsüan. The 'Grand-Master' Yin must have been one of the 'three Kung,' the highest ministers at the court of *K*âu, and was, probably, the chief of the three, and administrator of the government under Yû.

Lofty is that southern hill[2], With its masses of rocks! Awe-inspiring are you, O (Grand-)Master

[1] The tortoise-and-serpent banner marked the presence in a host of its leader on a military expedition. On its field were the figures of tortoises, with snakes coiled round them. The falcon banners belonged to the commanders of the divisions of the host. They bore the figures of falcons on them.

[2] 'The southern hill' was also called the *K*ung-nan, and rose right to the south of the western capital of *K*âu.

Yin, And the people all look to you! A fire burns in their grieving hearts; They do not dare to speak of you even in jest. The kingdom is verging to extinction;—How is it that you do not consider the state of things?

Lofty is that southern hill, And vigorously grows the vegetation on it! Awe-inspiring are you, O (Grand-)Master Yin, But how is it that you are so unjust? Heaven is continually redoubling its inflictions; Deaths and disorder increase and multiply; No words of satisfaction come from the people; And yet you do not correct nor bemoan yourself.

The Grand-Master Yin Is the foundation of our *K*âu, And the balance of the kingdom is in his hands. He should be keeping its four quarters together; He should be aiding the Son of Heaven, So as to preserve the people from going astray. O unpitying great Heaven, It is not right he should reduce us all to such misery!

He does nothing himself personally, And the people have no confidence in him. Making no enquiry about them, and no trial of their services, He should not deal deceitfully with superior men. If he dismissed them on the requirement of justice, Mean men would not be endangering (the commonweal); And his mean relatives Would not be in offices of importance.

Great Heaven, unjust, Is sending down these exhausting disorders. Great Heaven, unkind, Is sending down these great miseries. Let superior men come (into office), And that would bring rest to the people's hearts. Let superior men execute their justice, And the animosities and angers would disappear[1].

O unpitying great Heaven, There is no end to the disorder! With every month it continues to grow, So that the people have no repose. I am as if intoxicated with the grief of my heart. Who holds the ordering of the kingdom? He attends not himself to the government, And the result is toil and pain to the people.

I yoke my four steeds, My four steeds, long-necked. I look to the four quarters (of the kingdom); Distress is everywhere; there is no place I can drive to.

Now your evil is rampant[2], And I can see your spears. Anon you are pacified and friendly as if you were pledging one another.

From great Heaven is the injustice, And our king has no repose. (Yet) he will not correct his heart, And goes on to resent endeavours to rectify him.

I, *K*iâ-fû, have made this poem, To lay bare the king's disorders. If you would but change your heart, Then would the myriad regions be nourished.

---

[1] In this stanza, as in the next and the last but one, the writer complains of Heaven, and charges it foolishly. He does so by way of appeal, however, and indicates the true causes of the misery of the kingdom,—the reckless conduct, namely, of the king and his minister.

[2] The parties spoken of here are the followers of the minister, 'mean men,' however high in place and great in power, now friendly, now hostile to one another.

ODE 8, STANZAS 4, 5, AND 7. THE *K*ĂNG YÜEH.

THE *K*ĂNG YÜEH IS, LIKE THE PRECEDING ODE, A LAMENTATION OVER THE MISERIES OF THE KINGDOM, AND THE RUIN COMING ON IT; WITH A SIMILAR, BUT MORE HOPEFULLY EXPRESSED, APPEAL TO HEAVEN, 'THE GREAT GOD.'

Look into the middle of the forest; There are (only) large faggots and small branches in it[1]. The people now amidst their perils Look to Heaven, all dark; But let its determination be fixed, And there is no one whom it will not overcome. There is the great God,—Does he hate any one?

If one say of a hill that it is low, There are its ridges and its large masses. The false calumnies of the people,—How is it that you do not repress them[2]? You call those experienced ancients, You consult the diviner of dreams. They all say, 'We are very wise, But who can distinguish the male and female crow[3]?'

Look at the rugged and stony field;—Luxuriantly rises in it the springing grain. (But) Heaven moves and shakes me, As if it could not overcome me[4]

[1] By introducing the word 'only,' I have followed the view of the older interpreters, who consider the forest, with merely some faggots and twigs left in it, to be emblematic of the ravages of oppressive government in the court and kingdom. *K*û Hsî takes a different view of them:—'In a forest you can easily distinguish the large faggots from the small branches, while Heaven appears unable to distinguish between the good and bad.'

[2] The calumnies that were abroad were as absurd as the assertion in line 1, and yet the king could not, or would not, see through them and repress them.

[3] This reference to the diviners of dreams is in derision of their pretensions.

[4] That is, the productive energy of nature manifests itself in the most unlikely places; how was it that 'the great God, who hates no one,' was contending so with the writer?

They sought me (at first) to be a pattern (to them), (Eagerly) as if they could not get me; (Now) they regard me with great animosity, And will not use my strength.

ODE 9. THE SHIH YÜEH *K*IH *K*IÂO.

THE LAMENTATION OF AN OFFICER OVER THE PRODIGIES CELESTIAL AND TERRESTRIAL, ESPECIALLY AN ECLIPSE OF THE SUN, THAT WERE BETOKENING THE RUIN OF *K*ÂU. HE SETS FORTH WHAT HE CONSIDERED TO BE THE TRUE CAUSES OF THE PREVAILING MISERY, WHICH WAS BY NO MEANS TO BE CHARGED ON HEAVEN.

Attention is called in the Introduction, p. 296, to the date of the solar eclipse mentioned in this piece.

At the conjunction (of the sun and moon) in the tenth month, On the first day of the moon, which was hsin-mâo, The sun was eclipsed, A thing of very evil omen. Before, the moon became small, And now the sun became small. Henceforth the lower people Will be in a very deplorable case.

The sun and moon announce evil, Not keeping to their proper paths. Throughout the kingdom there is no (proper) government, Because the good are not employed. For the moon to be eclipsed Is but an ordinary matter. Now that the sun has been eclipsed,—How bad it is!

Grandly flashes the lightning of the thunder. There is a want of rest, a want of good. The streams all bubble up and overflow. The crags on the hill-tops fall down. High banks become valleys; Deep valleys become hills. Alas for the men of this time! How does (the king) not stop these things?

Hwang-fû is the President; Fan is the Minister

of Instruction; *K*iâ-po is the (chief) Administrator; *K*ung-yün is the chief Cook; 3âu is the Recorder of the Interior; Khwei is Master of the Horse; Yü is Captain of the Guards; And the beautiful wife blazes, now in possession of her place[1].

This Hwang-fû Will not acknowledge that he is acting out of season. But why does he call us to move, Without coming and consulting with us? He has removed our walls and roofs; And our fields are all either a marsh or a moor. He says, 'I am not injuring you; The laws require that thus it should be.'

Hwang-fû is very wise; He has built a great city for himself in Hsiang. He chose three men as his ministers, All of them possessed of great wealth. He could not bring himself to leave a single minister, Who might guard our king. He (also) selected those who had chariots and horses, To go and reside in Hsiang[2].

---

[1] We do not know anything from history of the ministers of Yû mentioned in this stanza. Hwang-fû appears to have been the leading minister of the government at the time when the ode was written, and, as appears from the next two stanzas, was very crafty, oppressive, and selfishly ambitious. The mention of 'the chief Cook' among the high ministers appears strange; but we shall find that functionary mentioned in another ode; and from history it appears that 'the Cook,' at the royal and feudal courts, sometimes played an important part during the times of *K*âu. 'The beautiful wife,' no doubt, was the well-known Sze of Pâo, raised by king Yû from her position as one of his concubines to be his queen, and whose insane folly and ambition led to her husband's death, and great and disastrous changes in the kingdom.

[2] Hsiang was a district of the royal domain, in the present district of Măng, department of Hwâi-*kh*ing, Ho-nan. It had been assigned to Hwang-fû, and he was establishing himself there, without any loyal regard to the king. As a noble in the royal domain,

I have exerted myself to discharge my service, And do not dare to make a report of my toils. Without crime or offence of any kind, Slanderous mouths are loud against me. (But) the calamities of the lower people Do not come down from Heaven. A multitude of (fair) words, and hatred behind the back;—The earnest, strong pursuit of this is from men.

Distant far is my village, And my dissatisfaction is great. In other quarters there is ease, And I dwell here, alone and sorrowful. Everybody is going into retirement, And I alone dare not seek rest. The ordinances of Heaven are inexplicable, But I will not dare to follow my friends, and leave my post.

ODE 10, STANZAS 1 AND 3. THE YÜ WÛ *K*ĂNG.

THE WRITER OF THIS PIECE MOURNS OVER THE MISERABLE STATE OF THE KINGDOM, THE INCORRIGIBLE COURSE OF THE KING, AND OTHER EVILS, APPEALING ALSO TO HEAVEN, AND SURPRISED THAT IT ALLOWED SUCH THINGS TO BE.

Great and wide Heaven, How is it you have contracted your kindness, Sending down death and famine, Destroying all through the kingdom? Compassionate Heaven, arrayed in terrors, How is it you exercise no forethought, no care? Let alone the criminals:—They have suffered for their guilt. But those who have no crime Are indiscriminately involved in ruin.

---

he was entitled only to two ministers, but he had appointed three as in one of the feudal states, encouraging, moreover, the resort to himself of the wealthy and powerful, while the court was left weak and unprotected.

How is it, O great Heaven, That the king will not hearken to the justest words? He is like a man going (astray), Who knows not where he will proceed to. All ye officers, Let each of you attend to his duties. How do ye not stand in awe of one another? Ye do not stand in awe of Heaven.

The Fifth Decade, or that of Hsiâo Min.

Ode 1, Stanzas 1, 2, and 3. The Hsiâo Min.

A LAMENTATION OVER THE RECKLESSNESS AND INCAPACITY OF THE KING AND HIS COUNSELLORS. DIVINATION HAS BECOME OF NO AVAIL, AND HEAVEN IS DESPAIRINGLY APPEALED TO.

This is referred, like several of the pieces in the fourth decade, to the time of king Yû.

The angry terrors of compassionate Heaven Extend through this lower world. (The king's) counsels and plans are crooked and bad; When will he stop (in his course)? Counsels that are good he will not follow, And those that are not good he employs. When I look at his counsels and plans, I am greatly pained.

Now they agree, and now they defame one another;—The case is greatly to be deplored. If a counsel be good, They are all found opposing it. If a counsel be bad, They are all found according with it. When I look at such counsels and plans, What will they come to?

Our tortoise-shells are wearied out, And will not tell us anything about the plans. The counsellors are very many, But on that account nothing is accomplished. The speakers fill the court, But who dares to take any responsibility on himself? We are as if we consulted (about a journey) without taking a step in advance, And therefore did not get on on the road.

ODE 2, STANZAS 1 AND 2. THE HSIÂO YÜAN.

SOME OFFICER IN A TIME OF DISORDER AND MISGOVERNMENT URGES ON HIS BROTHERS THE DUTY OF MAINTAINING THEIR OWN VIRTUE, AND OF OBSERVING THE GREATEST CAUTION.

Small is the cooing dove, But it flies aloft to heaven. My heart is wounded with sorrow, And I think of our forefathers. When the dawn is breaking, and I cannot sleep, The thoughts in my breast are of our parents.

Men who are grave and wise, Though they drink, are mild and masters of themselves; But those who are benighted and ignorant Become devoted to drink, and more so daily. Be careful, each of you, of your deportment; What Heaven confers, (when once lost), is not regained [1].

The greenbeaks come and go, Picking up grain about the stackyard. Alas for the distressed and the solitary, Deemed fit inmates for the prisons! With a handful of grain I go out and divine [2], How I may be able to become good.

---

[1] 'What Heaven confers' is, probably, the good human nature, which by vice, and especially by drunkenness, may be irretrievably ruined.

[2] A religious act is here referred to, on which we have not sufficient information to be able to throw much light. It was the practice to spread some finely ground rice on the ground, in connexion with divination, as an offering to the spirits. The poet represents himself here as using a handful of grain for the purpose,—probably on account of his poverty.

ODE 3, STANZAS 1 AND 3. THE HSIÂO PAN.

THE ELDEST SON AND HEIR-APPARENT OF KING YÛ BEWAILS HIS DEGRADATION, APPEALING TO HEAVEN AS TO HIS INNOCENCE, AND COMPLAINING OF ITS CASTING HIS LOT IN SUCH A TIME.

It is allowed that this piece is clearly the composition of a banished son, and there is no necessity to call in question the tradition preserved in the Preface which prefers it to Î-*kh*iû, the eldest son of king Yû. His mother was a princess of the House of Shăn; but when Yû became enamoured of Sze of Pâo, the queen was degraded, and the son banished to Shăn.

With flapping wings the crows Come back, flying all in a flock[1]. Other people are happy, And I only am full of misery. What is my offence against Heaven? What is my crime? My heart is sad;— What is to be done?

Even the mulberry trees and the rottleras Must be regarded with reverence[2]; But no one is to be looked up to like a father, No one is to be depended on as a mother. Have I not a connexion with the hairs (of my father)? Did I not dwell in the womb (of my mother)? O Heaven, who gave me birth! How was it at so inauspicious a time?

---

[1] The sight of the crows, all together, suggests to the prince his own condition, solitary and driven from court.

[2] The mulberry tree and the rottlera were both planted about the farmsteadings, and are therefore mentioned here. They carried the thoughts back to the father or grandfather, or the more remote ancestor, who first planted them, and so a feeling of reverence attached to themselves.

ODE 4, STANZA 1. THE *KHIÂO* YEN.

SOME ONE, SUFFERING FROM THE KING THROUGH SLANDER, APPEALS TO HEAVEN, AND GOES ON TO DWELL ON THE NATURE AND EVIL OF SLANDER.

This piece has been referred to the time of king Lî, B.C. 878 to 828.

O vast and distant Heaven, Who art called our parent, That, without crime or offence, I should suffer from disorders thus great! The terrors of great Heaven are excessive, But indeed I have committed no crime. (The terrors of) great Heaven are very excessive, But indeed I have committed no offence.

ODE 6, STANZAS 5 AND 6. THE HSIANG PO.

A EUNUCH, HIMSELF THE VICTIM OF SLANDER, COMPLAINS OF HIS FATE, AND WARNS AND DENOUNCES HIS ENEMIES; APPEALING AGAINST THEM, AS HIS LAST RESORT, TO HEAVEN.

The proud are delighted, And the troubled are in sorrow. O azure Heaven! O azure Heaven! Look on those proud men, Pity those who are troubled.

Those slanderers! Who devised their schemes for them? I would take those slanderers, And throw them to wolves and tigers. If these refused to devour them, I would cast them into the north[1]. If the north refused to receive them, I would throw them into the hands of great (Heaven)[2].

---

[1] 'The north,' i.e. the region where there are the rigours of winter and the barrenness of the desert.

[2] 'Great Heaven;' 'Heaven' has to be supplied here, but there

Ode 9. The Tâ Tung.

AN OFFICER OF ONE OF THE STATES OF THE EAST DEPLORES THE EXACTIONS MADE FROM THEM BY THE GOVERNMENT, COMPLAINS OF THE FAVOUR SHOWN TO THE WEST, CONTRASTS THE MISERY OF THE PRESENT WITH THE HAPPINESS OF THE PAST, AND APPEALS TO THE STARS OF HEAVEN IDLY BEHOLDING THEIR CONDITION.

I give the whole of this piece, because it is an interesting instance of Sabian views. The writer, despairing of help from men, appeals to Heaven; but he distributes the Power that could help him among many heavenly bodies, supposing that there are spiritual beings in them, taking account of human affairs.

Well loaded with millet were the dishes, And long and curved were the spoons of thorn-wood. The way to *K*âu was like a whetstone, And straight as an arrow. (So) the officers trod it, And the common people looked on it. When I look back and think of it, My tears run down in streams.

In the states of the east, large and small, The looms are empty. Then shoes of dolichos fibre Are made to serve to walk on the hoar-frost. Slight and elegant gentlemen[1] Walk along that road to *K*âu. Their going and coming makes my heart sad.

Ye cold waters, issuing variously from the spring, Do not soak the firewood I have cut. Sorrowful I awake and sigh;—Alas for us toiled people! The firewood has been cut;—Would that it were

---

is no doubt as to the propriety of doing so; and, moreover, the peculiar phraseology of the line shows that the poet did not rest in the thought of the material heavens.

[1] That is, 'slight-looking,' unfit for toil; and yet they are obliged to make their journey on foot.

conveyed home! Alas for us the toiled people! Would that we could have rest[1]!

The sons of the east Are summoned only (to service), without encouragement; While the sons of the west Shine in splendid dresses. The sons of boatmen Have furs of the bear and grisly bear. The sons of the poorest families Form the officers in public employment.

If we present them with spirits, They regard them as not fit to be called liquor. If we give them long girdle pendants with their stones, They do not think them long enough.

There is the Milky Way in heaven[2], Which looks down on us in light; And the three stars together are the Weaving Sisters[3], Passing in a day through seven stages (of the sky).

Although they go through their seven stages, They complete no bright work for us. Brilliant shine the Draught Oxen[4], But they do not serve to draw our carts. In the east there is Lucifer[5]; In the west there is Hesperus[5]; Long and curved

[1] This stanza describes, directly or by symbol, the exactions from which the people of the east were suffering.

[2] 'The Milky Way' is here called simply the Han, = in the sky what the Han river is in China.

[3] 'The Weaving Sisters, or Ladies,' are three stars in Lyra, that form a triangle. To explain what is said of their passing through seven spaces, it is said: 'The stars seem to go round the circumference of the heavens, divided into twelve spaces, in a day and night. They would accomplish six of them in a day; but as their motion is rather in advance of that of the sun, they have entered into the seventh space by the time it is up with them again.'

[4] 'The Draught Oxen' is the name of some stars in the neck of Aquila.

[5] Liû Î (Sung dynasty) says: 'The metal star (Venus) is in the

is the Rabbit Net of the sky[1];—But they only occupy their places.

In the south is the Sieve[2], But it is of no use to sift. In the north is the Ladle[3], But it lades out no liquor. In the south is the Sieve, Idly showing its mouth. In the north is the Ladle, Raising its handle in the west.

The Sixth Decade, or that of Pei Shan.

Ode 3, Stanzas 1, 4, and 5. The Hsiâo Ming.

AN OFFICER, KEPT LONG ABROAD ON DISTANT SERVICE, APPEALS TO HEAVEN, DEPLORING THE HARDSHIPS OF HIS LOT, AND TENDERS GOOD ADVICE TO HIS MORE FORTUNATE FRIENDS AT COURT.

O bright and high Heaven, Who enlightenest and rulest this lower world! I marched on this expedition to the west, As far as this wilderness of *Kh*iû. From the first day of the second month, I have passed through the cold and the heat. My heart is sad; The poison (of my lot) is too bitter. I think of those (at court) in their offices, And my tears flow down like rain. Do I not wish to return? But I fear the net for crime.

Ah! ye gentlemen, Do not reckon on your rest

east in the morning, thus "opening the brightness of the day;" and it is in the west in the evening, thus "prolonging the day."' The author of the piece, however, evidently took Lucifer and Hesperus to be two stars.

[1] 'The Rabbit Net' is the Hyades.

[2] 'The Sieve' is the name of one of the twenty-eight constellations of the zodiac,—part of Sagittarius.

[3] 'The Ladle' is the constellation next to 'the Sieve,'—also part of Sagittarius.

being permanent. Quietly fulfil the duties of your offices, Associating with the correct and upright; So shall the spirits hearken to you, And give you good.

Ah! ye gentlemen, Do not reckon on your repose being permanent. Quietly fulfil the duties of your offices, Loving the correct and upright; So shall the spirits hearken to you, And give you large measures of bright happiness.

Ode 5. The *Khû Ʒhze*.

SACRIFICIAL AND FESTAL SERVICES IN THE ANCESTRAL TEMPLE; AND THEIR CONNEXION WITH ATTENTION TO HUSBANDRY.

See the remarks on the Services of the Ancestral Temple, pp. 300, 301.

Thick grew the tribulus (on the ground), But they cleared away its thorny bushes. Why did they this of old? That we might plant our millet and sacrificial millet; That our millet might be abundant, And our sacrificial millet luxuriant. When our barns are full, And our stacks can be counted by tens of myriads, We proceed to make spirits and prepared grain, For offerings and sacrifice. We seat the representatives of the dead, and urge them to eat[1]:—Thus seeking to increase our bright happiness.

[1] The poet hurries on to describe the sacrifices in progress. The persons selected to personate the departed were necessarily inferior in rank to the principal sacrificer, yet for the time they were superior to him. This circumstance, it was supposed, would make them feel uncomfortable; and therefore, as soon as they appeared in the temple, the director of the ceremonies instructed the sacrificer to ask them to be seated, and to place them at ease; after which they were urged to take some refreshment.

With correct and reverent deportment, The bulls and rams all pure, We proceed to the winter and autumnal sacrifices. Some flay (the victims); some cook (their flesh); Some arrange (the meat); some adjust (the pieces of it). The officer of prayer sacrifices inside the temple gate[1], And all the sacrificial service is complete and brilliant. Grandly come our progenitors; Their spirits happily enjoy the offerings; Their filial descendant receives blessing:—They will reward him with great happiness, With myriads of years, life without end.

They attend to the furnaces with reverence; They prepare the trays, which are very large;—Some for the roast meat, some for the broiled. Wives presiding are still and reverent[2], Preparing the numerous (smaller) dishes. The guests and visitors[3] Present the cup all round[4]. Every form is according to rule; Every smile and word are as they should be. The spirits quietly come, And respond

---

[1] The *K*û, who is mentioned here, was evidently an officer, 'one who makes or recites prayers.' The sacrifice he is said to offer was, probably, a libation, the pouring out fragrant spirits, as a part of the general service, and likely to attract the hovering spirits of the departed, on their approach to the temple. Hence his act was performed just inside the gate.

[2] 'Wives presiding,' i.e. the wife of the sacrificer, the principal in the service, and other ladies of the harem. The dishes under their care, the smaller dishes, would be those containing sauces, cakes, condiments, &c.

[3] 'The guests and visitors' would be nobles and officers of different surnames from the sacrificer, chosen by divination to take part in the sacrificial service.

[4] 'Present the cup all round' describes the ceremonies of drinking, which took place between the guests and visitors, the representatives of the dead, and the sacrificer.

with great blessings,—Myriads of years as the (fitting) reward.

We are very much exhausted, And have performed every ceremony without error. The able officer of prayer announces (the will of the spirits)[1], And goes to the filial descendant to convey it[1]:—'Fragrant has been your filial sacrifice, And the spirits have enjoyed your spirits and viands. They confer on you a hundred blessings; Each as it is desired, Each as sure as law. You have been exact and expeditious; You have been correct and careful; They will ever confer on you the choicest favours, In myriads and tens of myriads.'

The ceremonies having thus been completed, And the bells and drums having given their warning[2], The filial descendant goes to his place[3], And the able officer of prayer makes his announcement, 'The spirits have drunk to the full.' The great representatives of the dead then rise, And the bells and drums escort their withdrawal, (On which) the spirits tranquilly return (to whence they came)[4]. All the servants, and the presiding wives, Remove (the trays and dishes) without delay. The

---

[1] The officer of prayer had in the first place obtained, or professed to have obtained, this answer of the progenitors from their personators.

[2] The music now announced that the sacrificial service in the temple was ended.

[3] The sacrificer, or principal in the service, now left the place which he had occupied, descended from the hall, and took his position at the foot of the steps on the east,—the place appropriate to him in dismissing his guests.

[4] Where did they return to? According to *K*ang Hsüan, 'To heaven.'

(sacrificer's) uncles and cousins All repair to the private feast[1].

The musicians all go in to perform, And give their soothing aid at the second blessing[2]. Your[3] viands are set forth; There is no dissatisfaction, but all feel happy. They drink to the full, and eat to the full; Great and small, they bow their heads, (saying), 'The spirits enjoyed your spirits and viands, And will cause you to live long. Your sacrifices, all in their seasons, Are completely discharged by you. May your sons and your grandsons Never fail to perpetuate these services!'

Ode 6. The Hsin Nan Shan.

HUSBANDRY TRACED TO ITS FIRST AUTHOR; DETAILS ABOUT IT, GOING ON TO THE SUBJECT OF SACRIFICES TO ANCESTORS.

The Preface refers this piece to the reign of king Yû; but there is nothing in it to suggest the idea of its having been made in a time of disorder and misgovernment. 'The distant descendant' in the first stanza is evidently the principal in the sacrifice of the last two stanzas:—according to *K*û, a noble or great landholder in the royal domain; according to others, some one of the kings of *K*âu. I incline myself to this latter view. The three pieces,

[1] These uncles and cousins were all present at the sacrifice, and of the same surname as the principal. The feast to them was to show his peculiar affection for his relatives.

[2] The feast was given in the apartment of the temple behind the hall where the sacrifice had been performed, so that the musicians are represented as going in to continue at the feast the music they had discoursed at the sacrifice.

[3] The transition to the second person here is a difficulty. We can hardly make the speech, made by some one of the guests on behalf of all the others, commence here. We must come to the conclusion that the ode was written, in compliment to the sacrificer, by one of the relatives who shared in the feast; and so here he addresses him directly.

of which this is the middle one, seem all to be royal odes. The mention of 'the southern hill' strongly confirms this view.

Yes, (all about) that southern hill Was made manageable by Yü[1]. Its plains and marshes being opened up, It was made into fields by the distant descendant. We define their boundaries, We form their smaller divisions, And make the acres lie, here to the south, there to the east.

The heavens overhead are one arch of clouds, Snowing in multitudinous flakes; There is superadded the drizzling rain. When (the land) has received the moistening, Soaking influence abundantly, It produces all our kinds of grain.

The boundaries and smaller divisions are nicely adjusted, And the millets yield abundant crops, The harvest of the distant descendant. We proceed to make therewith spirits and food, To supply our representatives of the departed, and our guests;—To obtain long life, extending over myriads of years.

In the midst of the fields are the huts[2], And

[1] There is here a recognition of the work of the great Yü, as the real founder of the kingdom of China, extending the territory of former elective chiefs, and opening up the country. 'The southern hill' bounded the prospect to the south from the capital of *K*âu, and hence the writer makes mention of it. He does not mean to confine the work of Yü to that part of the country; but, on the other hand, there is nothing in his language to afford a confirmation to the account given in the third Part of the Shû of that hero's achievements.

[2] In every *K*ing, or space of 900 Chinese acres or mâu, assigned to eight families, there were in the centre 100 mâu of 'public fields,' belonging to the government, and cultivated by the husbandmen in common. In this space of 100 mâu, two mâu and a half were again assigned to each family, and on them were

along the bounding divisions are gourds. The fruit is sliced and pickled, To be presented to our great ancestors, That their distant descendant may have long life, And receive the blessing of Heaven[1].

We sacrifice (first) with clear spirits, And then follow with a red bull; Offering them to our ancestors, (Our lord) holds the knife with tinkling bells, To lay open the hair of the victim, And takes the blood and fat[2].

Then we present, then we offer; All round the fragrance is diffused. Complete and brilliant is the sacrificial service; Grandly come our ancestors. They will reward (their descendant) with great blessing, Long life, years without end.

ODE 7. THE PHÛ THIEN.

PICTURES OF HUSBANDRY, AND SACRIFICES CONNECTED WITH IT. HAPPY UNDERSTANDING BETWEEN THE PEOPLE AND THEIR SUPERIORS.

It is difficult to say who the 'I' in the piece is, but evidently he and the 'distant descendant' are different persons. I suppose he may have been an officer, who had charge of the farms, as we may call them, in the royal domain.

Bright are those extensive fields, A tenth of whose produce is annually levied[3]. I take the old

---

erected the huts in which they lived, while they were actively engaged in their agricultural labours.

[1] Here, as in so many other places, the sovereign Power, ruling in the lots of men, is referred to as Heaven.

[2] The fat was taken from the victim, and then burnt along with fragrant herbs, so as to form a cloud of incense. On the taking of the 'blood,' it is only said, that it was done to enable the sacrificer to announce that a proper victim had been slain.

[3] This line, literally, is, 'Yearly are taken ten (and a) thousand;' meaning the produce of ten acres in every hundred, and of a thousand in every ten thousand.

stores, And with them feed the husbandmen. From of old we have had good years; And now I go to the south-lying acres, Where some are weeding, and some gather the earth about the roots. The millets look luxuriant; And in a spacious resting-place, I collect and encourage the men of greater promise [1].

With my vessels full of bright millet, And my pure victim-rams, We sacrificed at the altar of the spirits of the land, and at (the altars of those of the four) quarters [2]. That my fields are in such good condition Is matter of joy to the husbandmen. With lutes, and with drums beating, We will invoke the Father of Husbandry [3], And pray for sweet rain, To increase the produce of our millets, And to bless my men and their wives.

The distant descendant comes, When their wives and children Are bringing food to those (at work) in the south-lying acres. The surveyor of the fields (also) comes and is glad. He takes (of the food) on the left and the right, And tastes whether

[1] The general rule was that the sons of husbandmen should continue husbandmen; but their superior might select those among them in whom he saw promising abilities, and facilitate their advancement to the higher grade of officers.

[2] The sacrifices here mentioned were of thanksgiving at the end of the harvest of the preceding year. The one was to 'sovereign Earth,' supposed to be the supreme Power in correlation with Heaven, or, possibly, to the spirits supposed to preside over the productive energies of the land; the other to the spirits presiding over the four quarters of the sky, and ruling all atmospherical influences.

[3] This was the sacrifice that had been, or was about to be, offered in spring to 'the Father of Husbandry,'—probably the ancient mythical Tî, Shăn Năng.

it be good or not. The grain is well cultivated, all the acres over; Good will it be and abundant. The distant descendant has no displacency; The husbandmen are encouraged to diligence.

The crops of the distant descendant Look (thick) as thatch, and (swelling) like a carriage-cover. His stacks will stand like islands and mounds. He will seek for thousands of granaries; He will seek for tens of thousands of carts. The millets, the paddy, and the maize Will awake the joy of the husbandmen; (And they will say), 'May he be rewarded with great happiness, With myriads of years, life without end!'

Ode 8. The Tâ Thien.

FURTHER PICTURES OF HUSBANDRY, AND SACRIFICES CONNECTED WITH IT.

Large are the fields, and various is the work to be done. Having selected the seed, and looked after the implements, So that all preparations have been made for our labour, We take our sharp ploughshares, And commence on the south-lying acres. We sow all the kinds of grain, Which grow up straight and large. So that the wish of the distant descendant is satisfied.

It ears and the fruit lies soft in its sheath; It hardens and is of good quality; There is no wolf's-tail grass nor darnel. We remove the insects that eat the heart and the leaf, And those that eat the roots and the joints, So that they shall not hurt the young plants of our fields. May the spirit, the Father of Husbandry [1], Lay hold of them, and put them in the blazing fire!

[1] The ancient Shăn Năng, as in the preceding ode.

The clouds form in dense masses, And the rain comes down slowly. May it first rain on our public fields[1], And then come to our private[1]! Yonder shall be young grain unreaped, And here some bundles ungathered; Yonder shall be handfuls left on the ground, And here ears untouched:—For the benefit of the widow[2].

The distant descendant will come, When their wives and children Are bringing food to those (at work) on the south-lying acres. The surveyor of the fields (also) will come and be glad. They will come and offer pure sacrifices to (the spirits of the four) quarters, With their victims red and black[3], With their preparations of millet:—Thus offering, thus sacrificing, Thus increasing our bright happiness.

The Seventh Decade, or that of Sang Hû.

Ode 1, Stanza 1. The Sang Hû.

THE KING, ENTERTAINING THE CHIEF AMONG THE FEUDAL PRINCES, EXPRESSES HIS ADMIRATION OF THEM, AND GOOD WISHES FOR THEM.

They flit about, the greenbeaks[4], With their

---

[1] These are two famous lines, continually quoted as showing the loyal attachment of the people to their superiors in those ancient times.

[2] Compare the legislation of Moses, in connexion with the harvest, for the benefit of the poor, in Deuteronomy xxiv. 19–22.

[3] They would not sacrifice to these spirits all at once, or all in one place, but in the several quarters as they went along on their progress through the domain. For each quarter the colour of the victim was different. A red victim was offered to the spirit of the south, and a black to that of the north.

[4] The greenbeaks appeared in the second ode of the fifth decade. The bird had many names, and a beautiful plumage,

variegated wings. To be rejoiced in are these princes! May they receive the blessing of Heaven[1]!

ODE 6, STANZAS 1 AND 2. THE PIN *KIH KHÛ* YEN.

AGAINST DRUNKENNESS. DRINKING ACCORDING TO RULE AT ARCHERY CONTESTS AND THE SEASONAL SACRIFICES, AND DRINKING TO EXCESS.

There are good grounds for referring the authorship of this piece to duke Wû of Wei (B.C. 812 to 758), who played an important part in the kingdom, during the affairs which terminated in the death of king Yû, and the removal of the capital from Hâo to Lo. The piece, we may suppose, is descriptive of things as they were at the court of king Yû.

When the guests first approach the mats[2], They take their places on the left and the right in an orderly manner. The dishes of bamboo and wood are arranged in rows, With the sauces and kernels displayed in them. The spirits are mild and good, And they drink, all equally reverent. The bells and drums are properly arranged[3], And they raise their pledge-cups with order and ease[4]. (Then) the great

---

made use of here to compliment the princes on the elegance of their manners, and perhaps also the splendour of their equipages. The bird is here called the 'mulberry Hû,' because it appeared when the mulberry tree was coming into leaf.

[1] This line is to be understood, with *K*û Hsî, as a prayer of the king to Heaven for his lords.

[2] The mats were spread on the floor, and also the viands of the feast. Chairs and tables were not used in that early time.

[3] The archery took place in the open court, beneath the hall or raised apartment, where the entertainment was given. Near the steps leading up to the hall was the regular place for the bells and drums, but it was necessary now to remove them more on one side, to leave the ground clear for the archers.

[4] The host first presented a cup to the guest, which the latter drank, and then he returned a cup to the host. After this pre-

target is set up; The bows and arrows are made ready for the shooting. The archers are arranged in classes; 'Show your skill in shooting,' (it is said by one). 'I shall hit that mark' (is the response), 'And pray you to drink the cup [1].'

The dancers move with their flutes to the notes of the organ and drum, While all the instruments perform in harmony. All this is done to please the meritorious ancestors, Along with the observance of all ceremonies. When all the ceremonies have been fully performed, Grandly and fully, (The personators of the dead say), 'We confer on you great blessings, And may your descendants also be happy!' These are happy and delighted, And each of them exerts his ability. A guest [2] draws the spirits; An attendant enters again with a cup, And fills it,—the cup of rest [2]. Thus are performed your seasonal ceremonies [3].

---

liminary ceremony, the company all drank to one another,—'took up their cups,' as it is here expressed.

[1] Each defeated archer was obliged to drink a large cup of spirits as a penalty.

[2] This guest was, it is supposed, the eldest of all the scions of the royal House present on the occasion. At this point, he presented a cup to the chief among the personators of the ancestors, and received one in return. He then proceeded to draw more spirits from one of the vases of supply, and an attendant came in and filled other cups,—we may suppose for all the other personators. This was called 'the cup of repose or comfort;' and the sacrifice was thus concluded,—in all sobriety and decency.

[3] The three stanzas that follow this, graphically descriptive of the drunken revel, are said to belong to the feast of the royal relatives that followed the conclusion of the sacrificial service, and is called 'the second blessing' in the sixth ode of the preceding decade. This opinion probably is correct; but as the piece does not itself say so, and because of the absence from the text of religious sentiments, I have not given the stanzas here.

The Eighth Decade, or that of Po Hwâ.

Ode 5, Stanzas 1 and 2. The Po Hwâ.

THE QUEEN OF KING YÛ COMPLAINS OF BEING DEGRADED AND FORSAKEN.

The fibres from the white-flowered rush Are bound with the white grass [1]. This man's sending me away makes me dwell solitary.

The light and brilliant clouds Bedew the rush and the grass [2]. The way of Heaven is hard and difficult [3];—This man does not conform (to good principle).

---

[1] The stalks of the rush were tied with the grass in bundles, in order to be steeped;—an operation which ladies in those days might be supposed to be familiar with. The two lines suggest the idea of the close connexion between the two plants, and the necessariness of the one to the other;—as it should be between husband and wife.

[2] The clouds bestowed their dewy influence on the plants, while her husband neglected the speaker.

[3] 'The way of Heaven' is equivalent to our 'The course of Providence.' The lady's words are, literally, 'The steps of Heaven.' She makes but a feeble wail; but in Chinese opinion discharges thereby, all the better, the duty of a wife.

THE MAJOR ODES OF THE KINGDOM.

PIECES AND STANZAS ILLUSTRATING THE RELIGIOUS VIEWS AND PRACTICES OF THE WRITERS AND THEIR TIMES.

The First Decade, or that of Wăn Wang.

ODE 1. THE WĂN WANG.

CELEBRATING KING WĂN, DEAD AND ALIVE, AS THE FOUNDER OF THE DYNASTY OF *K*ÂU, SHOWING HOW HIS VIRTUES DREW TO HIM THE FAVOURING REGARD OF HEAVEN OR GOD, AND MADE HIM A BRIGHT PATTERN TO HIS DESCENDANTS AND THEIR MINISTERS.

The composition of this and the other pieces of this decade is attributed to the duke of *K*âu, king Wăn's son, and was intended by him for the benefit of his nephew, the young king *Kh*ăng. Wăn, it must be borne in mind, was never actually king of China. He laid the foundations of the kingly power, which was established by his son king Wû, and consolidated by the duke of *K*âu. The title of king was given to him and to others by the duke, according to the view of filial piety, that has been referred to on p. 299.

King Wăn is on high. Oh! bright is he in heaven. Although *K*âu was an old country, The (favouring) appointment lighted on it recently[1]. Illustrious was the House of *K*âu, And the

---

[1] The family of *K*âu, according to its traditions, was very ancient, but it did not occupy the territory of *K*âu, from which it subsequently took its name, till B.C. 1326; and it was not till the time of Wăn (B.C. 1231 to 1135) that the divine purpose concerning its supremacy in the kingdom was fully manifested.

appointment of God came at the proper season. King Wăn ascends and descends On the left and the right of God[1].

Full of earnest activity was king Wăn, And his fame is without end. The gifts (of God) to *K*âu Extend to the descendants of king Wăn, In the direct line and the collateral branches for a hundred generations[2]. All the officers of *K*âu Shall (also) be illustrious from age to age.

They shall be illustrious from age to age, Zealously and reverently pursuing their plans. Admirable are the many officers, Born in this royal kingdom. The royal kingdom is able to produce them, The supporters of (the House of) *K*âu. Numerous is the array of officers, And by them king Wăn enjoys his repose.

Profound was king Wăn; Oh! continuous and bright was his feeling of reverence. Great is the appointment of Heaven! There were the descendants of (the sovereigns of) Shang[3]—The descendants of the sovereigns of Shang Were in number more

---

[1] According to *K*û Hsî, the first and last two lines of this stanza are to be taken of the spirit of Wăn in heaven. Attempts have been made to explain them otherwise, or rather to explain them away. But language could not more expressly intimate the existence of a supreme personal God, and the continued existence of the human spirit.

[2] The text, literally, is, 'The root and the branches:' the root (and stem) denoting the eldest sons, by the recognised queen, succeeding to the throne; and the branches, the other sons by the queen and concubines. The former would grow up directly from the root; and the latter, the chief nobles of the kingdom, would constitute the branches of the great *K*âu tree.

[3] The Shang or Yin dynasty of kings superseded by *K*âu.

than hundreds of thousands. But when God gave the command, They became subject to *K*âu.

They became subject to *K*âu, (For) the appointment of Heaven is not unchangeable. The officers of Yin, admirable and alert, Assist at the libations in our capital[1]. They assist at those libations, Always wearing the hatchet-figures on their lower garments and their peculiar cap[2]. O ye loyal ministers of the king, Ever think of your ancestor!

Ever think of your ancestor, Cultivating your virtue, Always seeking to accord with the will (of Heaven):—So shall you be seeking for much happiness, Before Yin lost the multitudes, (Its kings) were the correlates of God[3]. Look to Yin as a beacon; The great appointment is not easily preserved.

The appointment is not easily (preserved):—Do not cause your own extinction. Display and make bright your righteousness and fame, And look at (the fate of) Yin in the light of Heaven. The doings of high Heaven Have neither sound nor

---

[1] These officers of Yin would be the descendants of the Yin kings and of their principal nobles, scions likewise of the Yin stock. They would assist, at the court of *K*âu, at the services in the ancestral temple, which began with a libation of fragrant spirits to bring down the spirits of the departed.

[2] These, differing from the dress worn by the representatives of the ruling House, were still worn by the officers of Yin or Shang, by way of honour, and also by way of warning.

[3] There was God in heaven hating none, desiring the good of all the people; there were the sovereigns on earth, God's vicegerents, maintained by him so long as they carried out in their government his purpose of good.

smell[1]. Take your pattern from king Wăn, And the myriad regions will repose confidence in you.

Ode 2. The Tâ Ming.

HOW THE APPOINTMENT OF HEAVEN OR GOD CAME FROM HIS FATHER TO KING WĂN, AND DESCENDED TO HIS SON, KING WÛ, WHO OVERTHREW THE DYNASTY OF SHANG BY HIS VICTORY AT MÛ; CELEBRATING ALSO THE MOTHER AND WIFE OF KING WĂN.

The illustration of illustrious (virtue) is required below, And the dread majesty is on high[2]. Heaven is not readily to be relied on; It is not easy to be king. Yin's rightful heir to the heavenly seat Was not permitted to possess the kingdom.

*Z*ăn, the second of the princesses of *K*ih[3], From (the domain of) Yin-shang, Came to be married to (the prince of) *K*âu, And became his wife in his

---

[1] These two lines are quoted in the last paragraph of the Doctrine of the Mean, as representing the ideal of perfect virtue. They are indicative of Power, operating silently, and not to be perceived by the senses, but resistless in its operations.

[2] 'The first two lines,' says the commentator Yen Ȝ*h*an, 'contain a general sentiment, expressing the principle that governs the relation between Heaven and men. According to line 1, the good or evil of a ruler cannot be concealed; according to 2, Heaven, in giving its favour or taking it away, acts with strict decision. When below there is the illustrious illustration (of virtue), that reaches up on high. When above there is the awful majesty, that exercises a survey below. The relation between Heaven and men ought to excite our awe.'

[3] The state of *K*ih must have been somewhere in the royal domain of Yin. Its lords had the surname of *Z*ăn, and the second daughter of the House became the wife of *K*î of *K*âu. She is called in the eighth line Thâi-*z*ăn, by which name she is still famous in China. 'She commenced,' it is said, 'the instruction of her child when he was still in her womb, looking on no improper sight, listening to no licentious sound, uttering no word of pride.'

capital. Both she and king *K*î Were entirely virtuous. (Then) Thâi-*z*ăn became pregnant, And gave birth to our king Wăn.

This king Wăn, Watchfully and reverently, With entire intelligence served God, And so secured the great blessing. His virtue was without deflection; And in consequence he received (the allegiance of) the states from all quarters.

Heaven surveyed this lower world; And its appointment lighted (on king Wăn). In his early years, It made for him a mate[1];—On the north of the Hsiâ, On the banks of the Wei. When king Wăn would marry, There was the lady in a large state[2].

In a large state was the lady, Like a fair denizen of heaven. The ceremonies determined the auspiciousness (of the union)[3], And in person he met her on the Wei. Over it he made a bridge of boats; The glory (of the occasion) was illustrious.

The favouring appointment was from Heaven, Giving the throne to our king Wăn, In the capital of *K*âu. The lady-successor was from Hsin, Its eldest daughter, who came to marry him. She was blessed to give birth to king Wû, Who was preserved, and helped, and received (also) the appoint-

---

[1] Heaven is here represented as arranging for the fulfilment of its purposes beforehand.

[2] The name of the state was Hsin, and it must have been near the Hsiâ and the Wei, somewhere in the south-east of the present Shen-hsî.

[3] 'The ceremonies' would be various; first of all, divination by means of the tortoise-shell.

ment, And in accordance with it smote the great Shang.

The troops of Yin-shang Were collected like a forest, And marshalled in the wilderness of Mû. We rose (to the crisis); 'God is with you,' (said Shang-fû to the king), 'Have no doubts in your heart[1].'

The wilderness of Mû spread out extensive; Bright shone the chariots of sandal; The teams of bays, black-maned and white-bellied, galloped along; The Grand-Master Shang-fû Was like an eagle on the wing, Assisting king Wû, Who at one onset smote the great Shang. That morning's encounter was followed by a clear, bright (day).

Ode 3. The Mien.

SMALL BEGINNINGS AND SUBSEQUENT GROWTH OF THE HOUSE OF *K*ÂU IN *K*ÂU. ITS REMOVAL FROM PIN UNDER THAN-FÛ, WITH ITS FIRST SETTLEMENT IN *K*ÂU, WITH THE PLACE THEN GIVEN TO THE BUILDING OF THE ANCESTRAL TEMPLE, AND THE ALTAR TO THE SPIRITS OF THE LAND. CONSOLIDATION OF ITS FORTUNES BY KING WĂN.

'The ancient duke Than-fû' was the grandfather of king Wăn, and was canonized by the duke of *K*âu as 'king Thâi.' As mentioned in a note on p. 316, he was the first of his family to settle in *K*âu, removing there from Pin, the site of their earlier settlement, 'the country about the *Kh*ü and the *Kh*î.'

In long trains ever increasing grow the gourds[2]. When (our) people first sprang, From the country about the *Kh*ü and the *Kh*î[3], The ancient duke

[1] See the account of the battle of Mû in the third Book of the fifth Part of the Shû. Shang-fû was one of Wû's principal leaders and counsellors, his 'Grand-Master Shang-fû' in the next stanza.

[2] As a gourd grows and extends, with a vast development of its tendrils and leaves, so had the House of *K*âu increased.

[3] These were two rivers in the territory of Pin, which name still

Than-fû Made for them kiln-like huts and caves, Ere they had yet any houses[1].

The ancient duke Than-fû Came in the morning, galloping his horses, Along the banks of the western rivers, To the foot of mount *Kh*î[2]; And there he and the lady *K*iang[3] Came and together looked out for a site.

The plain of *K*âu looked beautiful and rich, With its violets, and sowthistles (sweet) as dumplings. There he began by consulting (with his followers); There he singed the tortoise-shell, (and divined). The responses were there to stay and then; And they proceeded there to build[4].

He encouraged the people, and settled them; Here on the left, there on the right. He divided the ground, and subdivided it; He dug the ditches; he defined the acres. From the east to the west, There was nothing which he did not take in hand[5].

---

remains in the small department of Pin *K*âu, in Shen-hsî. The *Kh*ü flows into the Lo, and the *Kh*î into the Wei.

[1] According to this ode then, up to the time of Than-fû, the *K*âu people had only had the dwellings here described; but this is not easily reconciled with other accounts, or even with other stanzas of this piece.

[2] See a graphic account of the circumstances in which this migration took place, in the fifteenth chapter of the second Part of the first Book of Mencius, very much to the honour of the ancient duke.

[3] This lady is known as Thâi-*k*iang, the worthy predecessor of Thâi-*z*ăn.

[4] This stanza has reference to the choice—by council and divination—of a site for what should be the chief town of the new settlement.

[5] This stanza describes the general arrangements for the occupancy and cultivation of the plain of *K*âu, and the distribution of the people over it.

He called his Superintendent of Works; He called his Minister of Instruction; And charged them with the rearing of the houses. With the line they made everything straight; They bound the frame-boards tight, so that they should rise regularly: Uprose the ancestral temple in its solemn grandeur[1].

Crowds brought the earth in baskets; They threw it with shouts into the frames; They beat it with responsive blows. They pared the walls repeatedly, till they sounded strong. Five thousand cubits of them arose together, So that the roll of the great drums did not overpower (the noise of the builders)[2].

They reared the outer gate (of the palace), Which rose in lofty state. They set up the gate of audience, Which rose severe and exact. They reared the great altar to the spirits of the land, From which all great movements should proceed[3].

---

[1] This stanza describes the preparations and processes for erecting the buildings of the new city. The whole took place under the direction of two officers, in whom we have the germ probably of the Six Heads of the Boards or Departments, whose functions are described in the Shû and the Official Book of *K*âu. The materials of the buildings were earth and lime pounded together in frames, as is still to be seen in many parts of the country. The first great building taken in hand was the ancestral temple. Than-fû would make a home for the spirits of his fathers, before he made one for himself. However imperfectly directed, the religious feeling asserted the supremacy which it ought to possess.

[2] The bustle and order of the building all over the city is here graphically set forth.

[3] Than-fû was now at leisure to build the palace for himself, which appears to have been not a very large building, though the Chinese names of its gates are those belonging to the two which

Thus though he could not prevent the rage of his foes[1], He did not let fall his own fame. The oaks and the buckthorns were (gradually) thinned, And roads for travellers were opened. The hordes of the Khwăn disappeared, Startled and panting.

(The chiefs of) Yü and *Z*ui[2] were brought to an agreement By king Wăn's stimulating their natural virtue. Then, I may say, some came to him, previously not knowing him; Some, drawn the last by the first; Some, drawn by his rapid successes; And some by his defence (of the weak) from insult.

---

were peculiar to the palaces of the kings of *K*âu in the subsequent times of the dynasty. Outside the palace were the altars appropriate to the spirits of the four quarters of the land, the 'great' or royal altar being peculiar to the kings, though the one built by Than-fû is here so named. All great undertakings, and such as required the co-operation of all the people, were preceded by a solemn sacrifice at this altar.

[1] Referring to Than-fû's relations with the wild hordes, described by Mencius, and which obliged him to leave Pin. As the new settlement in *K*âu grew, they did not dare to trouble it.

[2] The poet passes on here to the time of king Wăn. The story of the chiefs of Yü and *Z*ui (two states on the east of the Ho) is this:—They had a quarrel about a strip of territory, to which each of them laid claim. Going to lay their dispute before the lord of *K*âu, as soon as they entered his territory, they saw the ploughers readily yielding the furrow, and travellers yielding the path, while men and women avoided one another on the road, and old people had no burdens to carry. At his court, they beheld the officers of each inferior grade giving place to those above them. They became ashamed of their own quarrel, agreed to let the disputed ground be an open territory, and withdrew without presuming to appear before Wăn. When this affair was noised abroad, more than forty states, it is said, tendered their submission to *K*âu.

Ode 4, Stanzas 1 and 2. The Yî Pho.

IN PRAISE OF KING WĂN, CELEBRATING HIS INFLUENCE, DIGNITY IN THE TEMPLE SERVICES, ACTIVITY, AND CAPACITY TO RULE.

Abundant is the growth of the buckthorn and shrubby trees, Supplying firewood; yea, stores of it[1]. Elegant and dignified was our prince and king; On the left and the right they hastened to him.

Elegant and dignified was our prince and king; On his left and his right they bore their half-mace (libation-cups)[2]:—They bore them with solemn gravity, As beseemed such eminent officers.

Ode 5. The Han Lû.

IN PRAISE OF THE VIRTUE OF KING WĂN, BLESSED BY HIS ANCESTORS, AND RAISED TO THE HIGHEST DIGNITY WITHOUT SEEKING OF HIS OWN.

Look at the foot of the Han[3], How abundantly grow the hazel and arrow-thorn[4]. Easy and self-possessed was our prince, In his pursuit of dignity (still) easy and self-possessed.

Massive is that libation-cup of jade, With the

---

[1] It is difficult to trace the connexion between these allusive lines and the rest of the piece.

[2] Here we have the lord of *K*âu in his ancestral temple, assisted by his ministers or great officers in pouring out the libations to the spirits of the departed. The libation-cup was fitted with a handle of jade, that used by the king having a complete kwei, the obelisk-like symbol of rank, while the cups used by a minister had for a handle only half a kwei.

[3] Where mount Han was cannot now be determined.

[4] As the foot of the hill was favourable to vegetable growth, so were king Wăn's natural qualities to his distinction and advancement.

yellow liquid sparkling in it[1]. Easy and self-possessed was our prince, The fit recipient of blessing and dignity.

The hawk flies up to heaven, The fishes leap in the deep[2]. Easy and self-possessed was our prince:—Did he not exert an influence on men?

His clear spirits were in the vessels; His red bull was ready[3];—To offer, to sacrifice, To increase his bright happiness.

Thick grow the oaks and the buckthorn, Which the people use for fuel[4]. Easy and self-possessed was our prince, Cheered and encouraged by the spirits[4].

Luxuriant are the dolichos and other creepers, Clinging to the branches and stems. Easy and self-possessed was our prince, Seeking for happiness by no crooked ways.

ODE 6. THE SZE *K*ÂI.

THE VIRTUE OF WĂN, WITH HIS FILIAL PIETY AND CONSTANT REVERENCE, AND THEIR WONDERFUL EFFECTS. THE EXCELLENT CHARACTER OF HIS MOTHER AND WIFE.

Pure and reverent was Thâi *Z*ăn[5], The mother of king Wăn. Loving was she to *K*âu *K*iang[6];—

[1] As a cup of such quality was the proper receptacle for the yellow, herb-flavoured spirits, so was the character of Wăn such that all blessing must accrue to him.

[2] It is the nature of the hawk to fly and of fishes to swim, and so there went out an influence from Wăn unconsciously to himself.

[3] Red, we have seen, was the proper colour for victims in the ancestral temple of *K*âu.

[4] As it was natural for the people to take the wood and use it, so it was natural for the spirits of his ancestors, and spiritual beings generally, to bless king Wăn.

[5] Thâi *Z*ăn is celebrated, above, in the second ode.

[6] *K*âu *K*iang is 'the lady *K*iang' of ode 3, the wife of Than-fû or

A wife becoming the House of *K*âu. Thâi Sze[1] inherited her excellent fame, And from her came a hundred sons[2].

He conformed to the example of his ancestors, And their spirits had no occasion for complaint. Their spirits had no occasion for dissatisfaction; And his example acted on his wife, Extended to his brethren, And was felt by all the clans and states.

Full of harmony was he in his palace; Full of reverence in the ancestral temple. Unseen (by men), he still felt that he was under inspection[3]: Unweariedly he maintained his virtue.

Though he could not prevent (some) great calamities, His brightness and magnanimity were without stain. Without previous instruction he did what was right; Without admonition he went on (in the path of goodness).

So, grown up men became virtuous (through him), And young men made (constant) attainments. (Our) ancient prince never felt weariness, And from him were the fame and eminence of his officers.

---

king Thâi, who came with him from Pin. She is here called *K*âu, as having married the lord of *K*âu.

[1] Thâi Sze, the wife of Wăn, we are told in ode 2, was from the state of Hsin. The surname Sze shows that its lords must have been descended from the Great Yü.

[2] We are not to suppose that Thâi Sze had herself a hundred sons. She had ten, and her freedom from jealousy so encouraged the fruitfulness of the harem, that all the sons born in it are ascribed to her.

[3] Where there was no human eye to observe him, Wăn still felt that he was open to the observation of spiritual beings.

ODE 7. THE HWANG Î.

SHOWING THE RISE OF THE HOUSE OF *K*ÂU TO THE SOVEREIGNTY OF THE KINGDOM THROUGH THE FAVOUR OF GOD. THE ACHIEVEMENTS OF KINGS THÂI AND *K*Î, AND ESPECIALLY OF KING WĂN.

Great is God, Beholding this lower world in majesty. He surveyed the four quarters (of the kingdom), Seeking for some one to give establishment to the people. Those two earlier dynasties [1] Had failed to satisfy him with their government; So, throughout the various states, He sought and considered For one on whom he might confer the rule. Hating all the great states, He turned his kind regards on the west, And there gave a settlement (to king Thâi).

(King Thâi) raised up and removed The dead trunks and the fallen trees. He dressed and regulated The bushy clumps and the (tangled) rows. He opened up and cleared The tamarisk trees and the stave trees. He hewed and thinned The mountain mulberry trees. God having brought about the removal thither of this intelligent ruler, The Kwan hordes fled away [2]. Heaven had raised up a helpmeet for him, And the appointment he had received was made sure.

God surveyed the hills, Where the oaks and the buckthorn were thinned, And paths made through the firs and cypresses. God, who had raised the

[1] Those of Hsiâ and Shang.

[2] The same as 'the hordes of the Khwăn' in ode 3. Mr. T. W. Kingsmill says that 'Kwan' here should be 'Chun,' and charges the transliteration Kwan with error (Journal of the Royal Asiatic Society for April, 1878). He had not consulted his dictionary for the proper pronunciation of the Chinese character.

state, raised up a proper ruler[1] for it,—From the time of Thâi-po and king *K*î (this was done)[1]. Now this king *K*î In his heart was full of brotherly duty. Full of duty to his elder brother, He gave himself the more to promote the prosperity (of the country), And secured to him the glory (of his act)[2]. He accepted his dignity and did not lose it, And (ere long his family) possessed the whole kingdom.

This king *K*î Was gifted by God with the power of judgment, So that the fame of his virtue silently grew. His virtue was highly intelligent,—Highly intelligent, and of rare discrimination; Able to lead, able to rule, To rule over this great country; Rendering a cordial submission, effecting a cordial union[3]. When (the sway) came to king Wăn, His

[1] King Wăn is 'the proper ruler' intended here, and the next line intimates that this was determined before there was any likelihood of his becoming the ruler even of the territory of *K*âu;—another instance of the foreseeing providence ascribed to God. Thâi-po was the eldest son of king Thâi, and king *K*î was, perhaps, only the third. The succession ought to have come to Thâi-po; but he, seeing the sage virtues of *Kh*ang (afterwards king Wăn), the son of *K*î, and seeing also that king Thâi was anxious that this boy should ultimately become ruler of *K*âu, voluntarily withdrew from *K*âu altogether, and left the state to *K*î and his son. See the remark of Confucius on Thâi-po's conduct, in the Analects, VIII, i.

[2] The lines from six to ten speak of king *K*î in his relation to his elder brother. He accepted Thâi-po's act without any failure of his own duty to him, and by his own improvement of it, made his brother more glorious through it. His feeling of brotherly duty was simply the natural instinct of his heart. Having accepted the act, it only made him the more anxious to promote the good of the state, and thus he made his brother more glorious by showing what advantages accrued from his resignation and withdrawal from *K*âu.

[3] This line refers to *K*î's maintenance of his own loyal duty

virtue left nothing to be dissatisfied with, He received the blessing of God, And it was extended to his descendants.

God said to king Wăn[1], 'Be not like those who reject this and cling to that; Be not like those who are ruled by their likings and desires;' So he grandly ascended before others to the height (of virtue). The people of Mî[2] were disobedient, Daring to oppose our great country, And invaded Yüan, marching to Kung[3]. The king rose, majestic in his wrath; He marshalled his troops, To stop the invading foes; To consolidate the prosperity of *K*âu; To meet the expectations of all under heaven.

He remained quietly in the capital, But (his troops) went on from the borders of Yüan. They ascended our lofty ridges, And (the enemy) arrayed no forces on our hills, On our hills, small or large, Nor drank at our springs, Our springs or our pools. He then determined the finest of the plains, And settled on the south of *Kh*î[4], On the banks of

---

to the dynasty of Shang, and his making all the states under his presidency loyal also.

[1] The statement that 'God spake to king Wăn,' repeated in stanza 7, vexes the Chinese critics, and they find in it simply an intimation that Wăn's conduct was 'in accordance with the will of Heaven.' I am not prepared to object to that view of the meaning; but it is plain that the writer, in giving such a form to his meaning, must have conceived of God as a personal Being, knowing men's hearts, and able to influence them.

[2] Mî or Mî-hsü was a state in the present *K*ing-ning *K*âu, of Phing-liang department, Kan-sû.

[3] Yüan was a state adjacent to Mî,—the present *K*ing *K*âu, and Kung must have been a place or district in it.

[4] Wăn, it appears, made now a small change in the site of his capital, but did not move to Făng, where he finally settled.

the Wei, The centre of all the states, The resort of the lower people.

God said to king Wăn, 'I am pleased with your intelligent virtue, Not loudly proclaimed nor pourtrayed, Without extravagance or changeableness, Without consciousness of effort on your part, In accordance with the pattern of God.' God said to king Wăn, 'Take measures against the country of your foes. Along with your brethren, Get ready your scaling ladders, And your engines of onfall and assault, To attack the walls of *Kh*ung[1].'

The engines of onfall and assault were (at first) gently plied, Against the walls of *Kh*ung high and great; Captives for the question were brought in, one after another; The left ears (of the slain) were taken leisurely[2]. He had sacrificed to God and to the Father of War[3], Thus seeking to induce

[1] *Kh*ung was a state, in the present district of Hû, department Hsî-an, Shen-hsî. His conquest of *Kh*ung was an important event in the history of king Wăn. He moved his capital to it, advancing so much farther towards the east, nearer to the domain of Shang. According to Sze-mâ *Kh*ien the marquis of *Kh*ung had slandered the lord of *K*âu, who was president of the states of the west, to *K*âu-hsin, the king of Shang, and our hero was put in prison. His friends succeeded in effecting his deliverance by means of various gifts to the tyrant, and he was reinstated in the west with more than his former power. Three years afterwards he attacked the marquis of *Kh*ung.

[2] So far the siege was prosecuted slowly and, so to say, tenderly, Wăn hoping that the enemy would be induced to surrender without great sacrifice of life.

[3] The sacrifice to God had been offered in *K*âu, at the commencement of the expedition; that to the Father of War, on the army's arriving at the borders of *Kh*ung. We can hardly tell who is intended by the Father of War. *K*û Hsî and others would require the plural 'Fathers,' saying the sacrifice was to Hwang Tî and *Kh*ih Yû, who are found engaged in hostilities far back in the

submission, And throughout the region none had dared to insult him. The engines of onfall and assault were (then) vigorously plied, Against the walls of *Kh*ung very strong. He attacked it, and let loose all his forces; He extinguished (its sacrifices)[1], and made an end of its existence; And throughout the kingdom none dared to oppose him.

Ode 9. The Hsiâ Wû.

IN PRAISE OF KING WÛ, WALKING IN THE WAYS OF HIS FOREFATHERS, AND BY HIS FILIAL PIETY SECURING THE THRONE TO HIMSELF AND HIS POSTERITY.

Successors tread in the steps (of their predecessors) in our *K*âu. For generations there had been wise kings; The three sovereigns were in heaven[2]; And king (Wû) was their worthy successor in his capital[3].

King (Wû) was their worthy successor in his capital, Rousing himself to seek for the hereditary virtue, Always striving to be in accordance with the

---

mythical period of Chinese history. But *Kh*ih Yû appears as a rebel, or opposed to the One man in all the country who was then fit to rule. It is difficult to imagine how they could be associated, and sacrificed together.

[1] The extinction of its sacrifices was the final act in the extinction of a state. Any members of its ruling House who might survive could no longer sacrifice to their ancestors as having been men of princely dignity. The family was reduced to the ranks of the people.

[2] 'The three sovereigns,' or 'wise kings,' are to be understood of the three celebrated in ode 7,—Thâi, *K*î, and Wăn. We are thus obliged, with all Chinese scholars, to understand this ode of king Wû. The statement that 'the three kings were in heaven' is very express.

[3] The capital here is Hâo, to which Wû removed in B.C. 1134, the year after his father's death. It was on the east of the river Făng, and only about eight miles from Wăn's capital of Făng.

will (of Heaven); And thus he secured the confidence due to a king.

He secured the confidence due to a king, And became the pattern of all below him. Ever thinking how to be filial, His filial mind was the model (which he supplied).

Men loved him, the One man, And responded (to his example) with a docile virtue. Ever thinking how to be filial, He brilliantly continued the doings (of his fathers).

Brilliantly! and his posterity, Continuing to walk in the steps of their forefathers, For myriads of years, Will receive the blessing of Heaven.

They will receive the blessing of Heaven, And from the four quarters (of the kingdom) will felicitations come to them. For myriads of years Will there not be their helpers?

Ode 10. The Wăn Wang yû Shăng.

THE PRAISE OF KINGS WĂN AND WÛ:—HOW THE FORMER DISPLAYED HIS MILITARY PROWESS ONLY TO SECURE THE TRANQUILLITY OF THE PEOPLE; AND HOW THE LATTER, IN ACCORDANCE WITH THE RESULTS OF DIVINATION, ENTERED IN HIS NEW CAPITAL OF HÂO, INTO THE SOVEREIGNTY OF THE KINGDOM WITH THE SINCERE GOOD WILL OF ALL THE PEOPLE.

King Wăn is famous; Yea, he is very famous. What he sought was the repose (of the people); What he saw was the completion (of his work). A sovereign true was king Wăn!

King Wăn received the appointment (from Heaven), And achieved his martial success. Having overthrown *Kh*ung[1] He fixed his (capital) city in Făng[2]. A sovereign true was king Wăn!

[1] As related in ode 7.

[2] Făng had, probably, been the capital of *Kh*ung, and Wăn

He repaired the walls along the (old) moat. His establishing himself in Făng was according to (the pattern of his forefathers), It was not that he was in haste to gratify his wishes;—It was to show the filial duty that had come down to him. A sovereign true was the royal prince!

His royal merit was brightly displayed By those walls of Făng. There were collected (the sympathies of the people of) the four quarters, Who regarded the royal prince as their protector. A sovereign true was the royal prince!

The Făng-water flowed on to the east (of the city), Through the meritorious labour of Yü. There were collected (the sympathies of the people of) the four quarters, Who would have the great king as their ruler. A sovereign true was the great king[1]!

In the capital of Hâo he built his hall with its circlet of water[2]. From the west to the east, From the south to the north, There was not a thought but did him homage. A sovereign true was the great king!

He examined and divined, did the king, About settling in the capital of Hâo. The tortoise-shell decided the site[3], And king Wû completed the city. A sovereign true was king Wû!

---

removed to it, simply making the necessary repairs and alterations. This explains how we find nothing about the divinations which should have preceded so important a step as the founding of a new capital.

[1] The writer has passed on to Wû, who did actually become king.

[2] See on the third of the Praise Odes of Lû in Part IV.

[3] Hâo was built by Wû, and hence we have the account of his divining about the site and the undertaking.

By the Făng-water grows the white millet[1];— Did not king Wû show wisdom in his employment of officers? He would leave his plans to his descendants, And secure comfort and support to his son. A sovereign true was king Wû!

The Second Decade, or that of Shăng Min.

Ode 1. The Shăng Min.

THE LEGEND OF HÂU-*K*Î:—HIS CONCEPTION; HIS BIRTH; THE PERILS OF HIS INFANCY; HIS BOYISH HABITS OF AGRICULTURE; HIS SUBSEQUENT METHODS AND TEACHING OF AGRICULTURE; HIS FOUNDING OF CERTAIN SACRIFICES; AND THE HONOURS OF SACRIFICE PAID TO HIM BY THE HOUSE OF *K*ÂU.

Of Hâu-*k*î there is some notice on the tenth ode of the first decade of the Sacrificial Odes of *K*âu. To him the kings of *K*âu traced their lineage. Of *K*iang Yüan, his mother, our knowledge is very scanty. It is said that she was a daughter of the House of Thâi, which traced its lineage up to Shăn-nung in præhistoric times. From the first stanza of this piece it appears that she was married, and had been so for some time without having any child. But who her husband was it is impossible to say with certainty. As the *K*âu surname was *K*î, he must have been one of the descendants of Hwang Tî.

The first birth of (our) people[2] Was from *K*iang Yüan. How did she give birth to (our) people? She had presented a pure offering and sacrificed[3],

---

[1] 'The white millet,' a valuable species, grown near the Făng, suggests to the writer the idea of all the men of ability whom Wû collected around him.

[2] Our 'people' is of course the people of *K*âu. The whole piece is about the individual from whom the House of *K*âu sprang, of which were the kings of the dynasty so called.

[3] To whom *K*iang Yüan sacrificed and prayed we are not told, but I receive the impression that it was to God,—see the next stanza,—and that she did so all alone with the special object which is mentioned.

That her childlessness might be taken away. She then trod on a toe-print made by God, and was moved[1], In the large place where she rested. She became pregnant; she dwelt retired; She gave birth to, and nourished (a son), Who was Hâu-*k*î.

When she had fulfilled her months, Her first-born son (came forth) like a lamb. There was no bursting, nor rending, No injury, no hurt; Showing how wonderful he would be. Did not God give her the comfort? Had he not accepted her pure offering and sacrifice, So that thus easily she brought forth her son?

He was placed in a narrow lane, But the sheep and oxen protected him with loving care[2]. He was placed in a wide forest, Where he was met with by the wood-cutters. He was placed on the cold ice, And a bird screened and supported him with its wings. When the bird went away, Hâu-*k*î began to wail. His cry was long and loud, So that his voice filled the whole way[2].

---

[1] The 'toe-print made by God' has occasioned much speculation of the critics. We may simply draw the conclusion that the poet meant to have his readers believe with him that the conception of his hero was supernatural. We saw in the third of the Sacrificial Odes of Shang that there was also a legend assigning a præternatural birth to the father of the House of Shang.

[2] It does not appear from the ode who exposed the infant to these various perils; nor did Chinese tradition ever fashion any story on the subject. Mâo makes the exposure to have been made by *K*iang Yüan's husband, dissatisfied with what had taken place; *K*ăng, by the mother herself, to show the more the wonderful character of her child. Readers will compare the accounts with the Roman legends about Romulus and Remus, their mother and her father; but the two legends differ according to the different characters of the Chinese and Roman peoples.

When he was able to crawl, He looked majestic and intelligent. When he was able to feed himself, He fell to planting beans. The beans grew luxuriantly; His rows of paddy shot up beautifully; His hemp and wheat grew strong and close; His gourds yielded abundantly.

The husbandry of Hâu-*k*î Proceeded on the plan of helping (the growth). Having cleared away the thick grass, He sowed the ground with the yellow cereals. He managed the living grain, till it was ready to burst; Then he used it as seed, and it sprang up; It grew and came into ear; It became strong and good; It hung down, every grain complete; And thus he was appointed lord of Thâi [1].

He gave (his people) the beautiful grains;—The black millet and the double-kernelled, The tall red and the white. They planted extensively the black and the double-kernelled, Which were reaped and stacked on the ground. They planted extensively the tall red and the white, Which were carried on their shoulders and backs, Home for the sacrifices which he founded [2].

And how as to our sacrifices (continued from him)?

---

[1] Hâu-*k*î's mother, we have seen, was a princess of Thâi, in the present district of Wû-kung, *Kh*ien *K*âu, Shen-hsî. This may have led to his appointment to that principality, and the transference of the lordship from *K*iangs to *K*îs. Evidently he was appointed to that dignity for his services in the promotion of agriculture. Still he has not displaced the older Shăn-nung, with whom on his father's side he had a connexion, as 'the Father of Husbandry.'

[2] This is not to be understood of sacrifice in general, as if there had been no such thing before Hâu-*k*î; but of the sacrifices of the House of *K*âu,—those in the ancestral temple and others,—which began with him as its great ancestor.

Some hull (the grain); some take it from the mortar; Some sift it; some tread it. It is rattling in the dishes; It is distilled, and the steam floats about. We consult[1]; we observe the rites of purification; We take southernwood and offer it with the fat; We sacrifice a ram to the spirit of the path[2]; We offer roast flesh and broiled:—And thus introduce the coming year[3].

We load the stands with the offerings, The stands both of wood and of earthenware. As soon as the fragrance ascends, God, well pleased, smells the sweet savour. Fragrant it is, and in its due season[4]. Hâu-*k*î founded our sacrifices, And no one, we presume, has given occasion for blame or regret in regard to them, Down to the present day.

Ode 2. The Hsin Wei.

A FESTAL ODE, CELEBRATING SOME ENTERTAINMENT GIVEN BY THE KING TO HIS RELATIVES, WITH THE TRIAL OF ARCHERY AFTER THE FEAST; CELEBRATING ESPECIALLY THE HONOUR DONE ON SUCH OCCASIONS TO THE AGED.

This ode is given here, because it is commonly taken as a prelude to the next. *K*û Hsî interprets it of the feast, given by the

[1] That is, we divine about the day, and choose the officers to take part in the service.

[2] A sacrifice was offered to the spirit of the road on commencing a journey, and we see here that it was offered also in connexion with the king's going to the ancestral temple or the border altar.

[3] It does not appear clearly what sacrifices the poet had in view here. I think they must be all those in which the kings of *K*âu appeared as the principals or sacrificers. The concluding line is understood to intimate that the kings were not to forget that a prosperous agriculture was the foundation of their prosperity.

[4] In this stanza we have the peculiar honour paid to Hâu-*k*î by his descendants at one of the great border sacrifices to God,—the same to which the last ode in the first decade of the Sacrificial Odes of *K*âu belongs.

king, at the close of the sacrifice in the ancestral temple, to the princes of his own surname. There are difficulties in the interpretation of the piece on this view, which, however, is to be preferred to any other.

In thick patches are those rushes, Springing by the way-side:—Let not the cattle and sheep trample them. Anon they will grow up; anon they will be completely formed, With their leaves soft and glossy[1]. Closely related are brethren; Let none be absent, let all be near. For some there are mats spread; For some there are given stools[2].

The mats are spread, and a second one above; The stools are given, and there are plenty of servants. (The guests) are pledged, and they pledge (the host) in return; He rinses the cups (and refills them, but the guests) put them down, Sauces and pickles are brought in, With roasted meat and broiled. Excellent provisions there are of tripe and palates; With singing to lutes, and with drums.

The ornamented bows are strong, And the four arrows are all balanced. They discharge the arrows, and all hit, And the guests are arranged according to their skill. The ornamented bows are drawn to the full, And the arrows are grasped in the hand. They go straight to the mark as if planted

[1] In the rushes growing up densely from a common root we have an emblem of brothers all sprung from the same ancestor; and in the plants developing so finely, when preserved from injury, an emblem of the happy fellowships of consanguinity, when nothing is allowed to interfere with mutual confidence and good feeling.

[2] In a previous note I have said that chairs and tables had not come into use in those early times. Guests sat and feasts were spread on mats on the floor; for the aged, however, stools were placed on which they could lean forward.

in it, And the guests are arranged according to the humble propriety of their behaviour.

The distant descendant presides over the feast; His sweet spirits are strong. He fills their cups from a large vase, And prays for the hoary old (among his guests):—That with hoary age and wrinkled back, They may lead on one another (to virtue), and support one another (in it); That so their old age may be blessed, And their bright happiness ever increased.

Ode 3. The *Kî* 3ui.

RESPONSIVE TO THE LAST:—THE UNCLES AND BRETHREN OF THE KING EXPRESS THEIR SENSE OF HIS KINDNESS, AND THEIR WISHES FOR HIS HAPPINESS, MOSTLY IN THE WORDS IN WHICH THE PERSONATORS OF THE DEPARTED ANCESTORS HAD CONVEYED THEIR SATISFACTION WITH THE SACRIFICE OFFERED TO THEM, AND PROMISED TO HIM THEIR BLESSING.

You have made us drink to the full of your spirits; You have satiated us with your kindness. May you enjoy, O our lord, myriads of years! May your bright happiness (ever) be increased!

You have made us drink to the full of your spirits; Your viands were set out before us. May you enjoy, O our lord, myriads of years! May your bright intelligence ever be increased!

May your bright intelligence become perfect, High and brilliant, leading to a good end! That good end has (now) its beginning:—The personators of your ancestors announced it in their blessing.

What was their announcement? '(The offerings) in your dishes of bamboo and wood are clean and fine. Your friends[1], assisting in the service, Have done their part with reverent demeanour.

'Your reverent demeanour was altogether what the occasion required; And also that of your filial son[2]. For such filial piety, continued without ceasing, There will ever be conferred blessings upon you.'

What will the blessings be? 'That along the passages of your palace, You shall move for ten thousand years, And there will be granted to you for ever dignity and posterity.'

How as to your posterity? 'Heaven invests you with your dignity; Yea, for ten thousand years, The bright appointment is attached (to your line).'

How is it attached? 'There is given you a heroic wife. There is given you a heroic wife, And from her shall come the (line of) descendants.'

Ode 4. The Hû Î.

AN ODE APPROPRIATE TO THE FEAST GIVEN TO THE PERSONATORS OF THE DEPARTED, ON THE DAY AFTER THE SACRIFICE IN THE ANCESTRAL TEMPLE.

This supplementary sacrifice on the day after the principal service in the temple appeared in the ninth Book of the fourth Part of the Shû; and of the feast after it to the personators of the dead I have spoken on p. 301.

The wild-ducks and widgeons are on the *K*ing[3];

---

[1] That is, the guests, visitors, and officers of the court.

[2] Towards the end of the sacrificial service, the eldest son of the king joined in pledging the representatives of their ancestors.

[3] The *K*ing is an affluent of the Wei, not far from Wû's capital of Hâo. The birds, feeling at home in its waters, on its sands, &c., serve to introduce the parties feasted, in a situation where they might relax from the gravity of the preceding day, and be happy.

The personators of your ancestors feast and are happy. Your spirits are clear; Your viands are fragrant. The personators of your ancestors feast and drink;—Their happiness and dignity are made complete.

The wild-ducks and widgeons are on the sand; The personators of the dead enjoy the feast, their appropriate tribute. Your spirits are abundant; Your viands are good. The personators of your ancestors feast and drink;—Happiness and dignity lend them their aids.

The wild-ducks and widgeons are on the islets; The personators of your ancestors feast and enjoy themselves. Your spirits are strained; Your viands are in slices. The personators of your ancestors feast and drink;—Happiness and dignity descend on them.

The wild-ducks and widgeons are where the waters meet; The personators of your ancestors feast and are honoured. The feast is spread in the ancestral temple, The place where happiness and dignity descend. The personators of your ancestors feast and drink;—Their happiness and dignity are at the highest point.

The wild-ducks and widgeons are in the gorge; The personators of your ancestors rest, full of complacency. The fine spirits are delicious; Your meat, roast and broiled, is fragrant. The personators of your ancestors feast and drink;—No troubles will be theirs after this.

Ode 5, Stanza 1. The *K*iâ Lo.

IN PRAISE OF SOME KING, WHOSE VIRTUE SECURED TO HIM THE FAVOUR OF HEAVEN.

Perhaps the response of the feasted personators of the ancestors.

Of our admirable, amiable sovereign Most illustrious is the excellent virtue. He orders rightly the people, orders rightly the officers, And receives his dignity from Heaven, Which protects and helps him, and (confirms) his appointment, By repeated acts of renewal from heaven.

Ode 8. The *Kh*üan Â.

ADDRESSED, PROBABLY, BY THE DUKE OF SHÂO TO KING *KH*ĂNG, DESIRING FOR HIM LONG PROSPERITY, AND CONGRATULATING HIM, IN ORDER TO ADMONISH HIM, ON THE HAPPINESS OF HIS PEOPLE, THE NUMBER OF HIS ADMIRABLE OFFICERS, AND THE AUSPICIOUS OMEN ARISING FROM THE APPEARANCE OF THE PHŒNIX.

The duke of Shâo was the famous Shih, who appears in the fifth and other Books of the fifth Part of the Shû, the colleague of the duke of *K*âu in the early days of the *K*âu dynasty. This piece may have been composed by him, but there is no evidence in it that it was so. The assigning it to him rests entirely on the authority of the preface. The language, however, is that in which an old statesman of that time might express his complacency in his young sovereign.

Into the recesses of the large mound Came the wind, whirling from the south. There was (our) happy, courteous sovereign, Rambling and singing; And I took occasion to give forth my notes.

'Full of spirits you ramble; Full of satisfaction you rest. O happy and courteous sovereign, May you fulfil your years, And end them like your ancestors!

'Your territory is great and glorious, And perfectly secure. O happy and courteous sovereign, May you fulfil your years, As the host of all the spirits[1]!

'You have received the appointment long acknowledged, With peace around your happiness and dignity. O happy and courteous sovereign, May you fulfil your years, With pure happiness your constant possession!

'You have helpers and supporters, Men of filial piety and of virtue, To lead you on, and act as wings to you, (So that), O happy and courteous sovereign, You are a pattern to the four quarters (of the kingdom).

'Full of dignity and majesty (are they), Like a

---

[1] 'Host of the hundred—i.e., of all—the spirits' is one of the titles of the sovereign of China. It was and is his prerogative to offer the great 'border sacrifices' to Heaven and Earth, or, as Confucius explains them, to God, and to the spirits of his ancestors in his ancestral temple; and in his progresses (now neglected), among the states, to the spirits of the hills and rivers throughout the kingdom. Every feudal prince could only sacrifice to the hills and streams within his own territory. Under the changed conditions of the government of China, the sacrificial ritual of the emperor still retains the substance of whatever belonged to the sovereigns in this respect from the earliest dynasties. On the text here, Khung Ying-tâ of the Thang dynasty said, 'He who possesses all under the sky, sacrifices to all the spirits, and thus he is the host of them all.' *K*û Hsî said on it, 'And always be the host of (the spirits of) Heaven and Earth, of the hills and rivers, and of the departed.' The term 'host' does not imply any superiority of rank on the part of the entertainer. In the greatest sacrifices the emperor acknowledges himself as 'the servant or subject of Heaven.' See the prayer of the first of the present Manchâu line of emperors, in announcing that he had ascended the throne, at the altar of Heaven and Earth, in 1644, as translated by the Rev. Dr. Edkins in the chapter on Imperial Worship, in the recent edition of his 'Religion in China.'

jade-mace (in its purity), The subject of praise, the contemplation of hope. O happy and courteous sovereign, (Through them) the four quarters (of the kingdom) are guided by you.

'The male and female phœnix fly about[1], Their wings rustling, While they settle in their proper resting-place. Many are your admirable officers, O king, Ready to be employed by you, Loving you, the Son of Heaven.

'The male and female phœnix fly about, Their wings rustling, As they soar up to heaven. Many are your admirable officers, O king, Waiting for your commands, And loving the multitudes of the people.

'The male and female phœnix give out their notes, On that lofty ridge. The dryandras grow, On those eastern slopes. They grow luxuriantly; And harmoniously the notes resound.

---

[1] The phœnix (so the creature has been named) is a fabulous bird, 'the chief of the 360 classes of the winged tribes.' It is mentioned in the fourth Book of the second Part of the Shû, as appearing in the courtyard of Shun; and the appearance of a pair of them has always been understood to denote a sage on the throne and prosperity in the country. Even Confucius (Analects, IX, viii) could not express his hopelessness about his own times more strongly than by saying that 'the phœnix did not make its appearance.' He was himself also called 'a phœnix,' in derision, by one of the recluses of his time (Analects, XVIII, v). The type of the bird was, perhaps, the Argus pheasant, but the descriptions of it are of a monstrous creature, having 'a fowl's head, a swallow's chin, a serpent's neck, a fish's tail,' &c. It only lights on the dryandra cordifolia, of which tree also many marvellous stories are related. The poet is not to be understood as saying that the phœnix actually appeared; but that the king was sage and his government prosperous, as if it had appeared.

'Your chariots, O sovereign, Are numerous, many. Your horses, O sovereign, Are well trained and fleet. I have made my few verses, In prolongation of your song.'

ODE 9, STANZA 1. THE MIN LÂO.

IN A TIME OF DISORDER AND SUFFERING, SOME OFFICER OF DISTINCTION CALLS ON HIS FELLOWS TO JOIN WITH HIM TO EFFECT A REFORMATION IN THE CAPITAL, AND PUT AWAY THE PARTIES WHO WERE THE CAUSE OF THE PREVAILING MISERY.

With the *Kh*üan Â, what are called the 'correct' odes of Part III, or those belonging to a period of good government, and the composition of which is ascribed mainly to the duke of *K*âu, come to an end; and those that follow are the 'changed' Major Odes of the Kingdom, or those belonging to a degenerate period, commencing with this. Some among them, however, are equal to any of the former class. The Min Lâo has been assigned to duke Mû of Shâo, a descendant of duke Khang, the Shih of the Shû, the reputed author of the *Kh*üan Â, and was directed against king Lî, B.C. 878 to 828.

The people indeed are heavily burdened, But perhaps a little relief may be got for them. Let us cherish this centre of the kingdom, To secure the repose of the four quarters of it. Let us give no indulgence to the wily and obsequious, In order to make the unconscientious careful, And to repress robbers and oppressors, Who have no fear of the clear will (of Heaven)[1]. Then let us show kindness to those who are distant, And help those who are near,—Thus establishing (the throne of) our king.

---

[1] 'The clear will,' according to *K*û Hsî, is 'the clear appointment of Heaven;' according to *K*û Kung-*kh*ien, 'correct principle.' They both mean the law of human duty, as gathered from the nature of man's moral constitution conferred by Heaven.

Ode 10. The Pan.

AN OFFICER OF EXPERIENCE MOURNS OVER THE PREVAILING MISERY; COMPLAINS OF THE WANT OF SYMPATHY WITH HIM SHOWN BY OTHER OFFICERS; ADMONISHES THEM, AND SETS FORTH THE DUTY REQUIRED OF THEM, ESPECIALLY IN THE ANGRY MOOD IN WHICH IT MIGHT SEEM THAT HEAVEN WAS.

This piece, like the last, is assigned to the time of king Lî.

God has reversed (his usual course of procedure)[1], And the lower people are full of distress. The words which you utter are not right; The plans which you form are not far-reaching. As there are not sages, you think you have no guidance;—You have no real sincerity. (Thus) your plans do not reach far, And I therefore strongly admonish you.

Heaven is now sending down calamities;—Do not be so complacent. Heaven is now producing such movements;—Do not be so indifferent. If your words were harmonious, The people would become united. If your words were gentle and kind, The people would be settled.

Though my duties are different from yours, I am your fellow-servant. I come to advise with you, And you hear me with contemptuous indifference. My words are about the (present urgent) affairs;—Do not think them matter for laughter. The ancients had a saying:—'Consult the gatherers of grass and firewood[2].'

---

[1] The proof of God's having reversed his usual course of procedure was to be found in the universal misery of the people, whose good He was understood to desire, and for the securing of which government by righteous kings was maintained by him.

[2] If ancient worthies thought that persons in such mean employments were to be consulted, surely the advice of the writer deserved to be taken into account by his comrades.

Heaven is now exercising oppression;—Do not in such a way make a mock of things. An old man, (I speak) with entire sincerity; But you, my juniors, are full of pride. It is not that my words are those of age, But you make a joke of what is sad. But the troubles will multiply like flames, Till they are beyond help or remedy.

Heaven is now displaying its anger;—Do not be either boastful or flattering, Utterly departing from all propriety of demeanour, Till good men are reduced to personators of the dead[1]. The people now sigh and groan, And we dare not examine (into the causes of their trouble). The ruin and disorder are exhausting all their means of living, And we show no kindness to our multitudes.

Heaven enlightens the people[2], As the bamboo flute responds to the earthen whistle; As two half-maces form a whole one; As you take a thing, and bring it away in your hand, Bringing it away, without any more ado. The enlightenment of the people is very easy. They have (now) many perversities;—Do not you set up your perversity before them.

Good men are a fence; The multitudes of the people are a wall; Great states are screens; Great families are buttresses; The cherishing of virtue

[1] During all the time of the sacrifice, the personators of the dead said not a word, but only ate and drank. To the semblance of them good men were now reduced.

[2] The meaning is, that Heaven has so attuned the mind to virtue, that, if good example were set before the people, they would certainly and readily follow it. This is illustrated by various instances of things, in which the one succeeded the other freely and as if necessarily; so that government by virtue was really very easy.

secures repose; The circle of (the king's) relatives is a fortified wall. We must not let the fortified wall get destroyed; We must not let (the king) be solitary and consumed with terrors.

Revere the anger of Heaven, And presume not to make sport or be idle. Revere the changing moods of Heaven, And presume not to drive about (at your pleasure). Great Heaven is intelligent, And is with you in all your goings. Great Heaven is clear-seeing, And is with you in your wanderings and indulgences.

The Third Decade, or that of Tang.

Ode 1. The Tang.

WARNINGS, SUPPOSED TO BE ADDRESSED TO KING LÎ, ON THE ISSUES OF THE COURSE WHICH HE WAS PURSUING, SHOWING THAT THE MISERIES OF THE TIME AND THE IMMINENT DANGER OF RUIN WERE TO BE ATTRIBUTED, NOT TO HEAVEN, BUT TO HIMSELF AND HIS MINISTERS.

This ode, like the ninth of the second decade, is attributed to duke Mû of Shâo. The structure of the piece is peculiar, for, after the first stanza, we have king Wăn introduced delivering a series of warnings to *K*âu-hsin, the last king of the Shang dynasty. They are put into Wăn's mouth, in the hope that Lî, if, indeed, he was the monarch whom the writer had in view, would transfer the figure of *K*âu-hsin to himself, and alter his course so as to avoid a similar ruin.

How vast is God, The ruler of men below! How arrayed in terrors is God, With many things irregular in his ordinations. Heaven gave birth to the multitudes of the people, But the nature it confers is not to be depended on. All are (good) at first, But few prove themselves to be so at the last[1].

King Wăn said, 'Alas! Alas! you sovereign of Shang, That you should have such violently oppressive ministers, That you should have such extortionate exactors, That you should have them in offices, That you should have them in the conduct of affairs! "Heaven made them with their insolent dispositions;" But it is you who employ them, and give them strength.'

King Wăn said, 'Alas! Alas! you (sovereign of) Yin-shang, You ought to employ such as are good, But (you employ instead) violent oppressors, who cause many dissatisfactions. They respond to you with baseless stories, And (thus) robbers and thieves are in your court. Hence come oaths and curses, Without limit, without end.'

King Wăn said, 'Alas! Alas! you (sovereign of) Yin-shang, You show a strong fierce will in the centre of the kingdom, And consider the contracting of enmities a proof of virtue. All-unintelligent are you of your (proper) virtue, And so you have no (good) men behind you, nor by your side. Without any intelligence of your (proper) virtue, You have no (good) intimate adviser or minister.'

King Wăn said, 'Alas! Alas! you (sovereign of) Yin-shang, It is not Heaven that flushes your face with spirits, So that you follow what is evil and imitate it. You go wrong in all your conduct; You make no distinction between the light and the

---

[1] The meaning seems to be that, whatever miseries might prevail, and be ignorantly ascribed to God, they were in reality owing to men's neglect of the law of Heaven inscribed on their hearts.

darkness; But amid clamour and shouting, You turn the day into night[1].'

King Wăn said, 'Alas! Alas! you (sovereign of) Yin-shang, (All round you) is like the noise of cicadas, Or like the bubbling of boiling soup. Affairs, great and small, are approaching to ruin, And still you (and your creatures) go on in this course. Indignation is rife against you here in the Middle Kingdom, And extends to the demon regions[2].'

King Wăn said, 'Alas! Alas! you (sovereign of) Yin-shang, It is not God that has caused this evil time, But it arises from Yin's not using the old (ways). Although you have not old experienced men, There are still the ancient statutes and laws. But you will not listen to them, And so your great appointment is being overthrown.'

King Wăn said, 'Alas! Alas! you (sovereign of) Shang, People have a saying, "When a tree falls utterly, While its branches and leaves are yet uninjured, It must first have been uprooted." The beacon of Yin is not far distant;—It is in the age of the (last) sovereign of Hsiâ.'

---

[1] We speak of 'turning night into day.' The tyrant of Shang turned day into night. Excesses, generally committed in darkness, were by him done openly.

[2] These 'demon regions' are understood to mean the seat of the Turkic tribes to the north of China, known from the earliest times by various names—'The hill *Z*ung,' 'the northern Lî,' 'the Hsien-yun,' &c. Towards the beginning of our era, they were called Hsiung-nû, from which, perhaps, came the name Huns; and some centuries later, Thû-*k*üeh (Thuh-*k*üeh), from which came Turk. We are told in the Yî, under the diagram *K*î-*k*î, that Kâo Ʒung (B.C. 1324–1266) conducted an expedition against the demon regions, and in three years subdued them.

ODE 2. THE YÎ.

CONTAINING VARIOUS COUNSELS WHICH DUKE WÛ OF WEI MADE TO ADMONISH HIMSELF, WHEN HE WAS OVER HIS NINETIETH YEAR; ESPECIALLY ON THE DUTY OF A RULER TO BE CAREFUL OF HIS OUTWARD DEMEANOUR, FEELING THAT HE IS EVER UNDER THE INSPECTION OF SPIRITUAL BEINGS, AND TO RECEIVE WITH DOCILITY INSTRUCTIONS DELIVERED TO HIM.

The sixth ode in the seventh decade of the Minor Odes of the Kingdom is attributed to the same duke of Wei as this; and the two bear traces of having proceeded from the same writer. The external authorities for assigning this piece to duke Wû are the statement of the preface and an article in the 'Narratives of the States,' a work already referred to as belonging to the period of the *K*âu dynasty. That article relates how Wû, at the age of ninety-five, insisted on all his ministers and officers being instant, in season and out of season, to admonish him on his conduct, and that 'he made the warnings in the Î to admonish himself.' The Î is understood to be only another name for this Yî. Thus the speaker throughout the piece is Wû, and 'the young son,' whom he sometimes addresses, is himself also. The conception of the writer in taking such a method to admonish himself, and give forth the lessons of his long life, is very remarkable; and the execution of it is successful.

Outward demeanour, cautious and grave, Is an indication of the (inward) virtue. People have the saying, 'There is no wise man who is not (also) stupid.' The stupidity of the ordinary man Is determined by his (natural) defects. The stupidity of the wise man Is from his doing violence (to his proper character).

What is most powerful is the being the man[1];—

[1] Wû writes as the marquis of Wei, the ruler of a state; but what he says is susceptible of universal application. In every smaller sphere, and in the largest, 'being the man,' displaying, that is, the proper qualities of humanity, will be appreciated and felt.

In all quarters (of the state) men are influenced by it. To an upright virtuous conduct All in the four quarters of the state render obedient homage. With great counsels and determinate orders, With far-reaching plans and timely announcements, And with reverent care of his outward demeanour, One will become the pattern of the people.

As for the circumstances of the present time, You are bent on error and confusion in your government. Your virtue is subverted; You are besotted by drink [1]. Although you thus pursue nothing but pleasure, How is it you do not think of your relation to the past, And do not widely study the former kings, That you might hold fast their wise laws?

Shall not those whom great Heaven does not approve of, Surely as the waters flow from a spring, Sink down together in ruin? Rise early and go to bed late, Sprinkle and sweep your courtyard;—So as to be a pattern to the people [2]. Have in good order your chariots and horses, Your bows and arrows, and (other) weapons of war;—To be prepared for warlike action, To keep at a distance (the hordes of) the south.

Perfect what concerns your officers and people;

---

[1] Han Ying (who has been mentioned in the Introduction) says that Wû made the sixth ode of the seventh decade of the former Part against drunkenness, when he was repenting of his own giving way to that vice. His mention of the habit here, at the age of ninety-five, must be understood as a warning to other rulers.

[2] Line 3 describes things important to the cultivation of one's self; and line 4, things important to the regulation of one's family. They may seem unimportant, it is said, as compared with the defence of the state, spoken of in the last four lines of the stanza; but the ruler ought not to neglect them.

Be careful of your duties as a prince (of the kingdom). To be prepared for unforeseen dangers, Be cautious of what you say; Be reverentially careful of your outward behaviour; In all things be mild and correct. A flaw in a mace of white jade May be ground away; But for a flaw in speech Nothing can be done.

Do not speak lightly; your words are your own [1]. Do not say, 'This is of little importance; No one can hold my tongue for me.' Words are not to be cast away. Every word finds its answer; Every good deed has its recompense. If you are gracious among your friends, And to the people, as if they were your children, Your descendants will continue in unbroken line, And all the people will surely be obedient to you.

Looked at in friendly intercourse with superior men, You make your countenance harmonious and mild; Anxious not to do anything wrong. Looked at in your chamber, You ought to be equally free from shame before the light which shines in. Do not say, 'This place is not public; No one can see me here.' The approaches of spiritual beings Cannot be calculated beforehand; But the more should they not be slighted [2].

---

[1] And therefore every one is himself responsible for his words.

[2] *K*û Hsî says that from the fourth line this stanza only speaks of the constant care there should be in watching over one's thoughts; but in saying so, he overlooks the consideration by which such watchful care is enforced. Compare what is said of king Wăn in the third stanza of the sixth ode of the first decade. King Wăn and duke Wû were both influenced by the consideration that their inmost thoughts, even when 'unseen by men,' were open to the inspection of spiritual beings.

O prince, let your practice of virtue Be entirely good and admirable. Watch well over your behaviour, And allow nothing wrong in your demeanour. Committing no excess, doing nothing injurious, There are few who will not in such a case take you for their pattern. When one throws to me a peach, I return to him a plum[1]. To look for horns on a young ram Will only weary you, my son[2].

The tough and elastic wood Can be fitted with the silken string[3]. The mild and respectful man Possesses the foundation of virtue. There is a wise man;—I tell him good words, And he yields to them the practice of docile virtue. There is a stupid man;—He says on the contrary that my words are not true:—So different are people's minds.

Oh! my son, When you did not know what was good, and what was not good, Not only did I lead you by the hand, But I showed the difference between them by appealing to instances. Not (only) did I charge you face to face, But I held you by the ear[4]. And still perhaps you do not know, Although you have held a son in your arms. If people be not self-sufficient, Who comes to a late maturity after early instruction?

Great Heaven is very intelligent, And I pass

---

[1] That is, every deed, in fact, meets with its recompense.

[2] See the conclusion of duke Wû's ode against drunkenness. Horns grow as the young ram grows. Effects must not be expected where there have not been the conditions from which they naturally spring.

[3] Such wood is the proper material for a bow.

[4] That is, to secure your attention.

my life without pleasure. When I see you so dark and stupid, My heart is full of pain. I taught you with assiduous repetition, And you listened to me with contempt. You would not consider me as your teacher, But regarded me as troublesome. Still perhaps you do not know;—But you are very old.

Oh! my son, I have told you the old ways. Hear and follow my counsels:—Then shall you have no cause for great regret. Heaven is now inflicting calamities, And is destroying the state. My illustrations are not taken from things remote:—Great Heaven makes no mistakes. If you go on to deteriorate in your virtue, You will bring the people to great distress.

Ode 3, Stanzas 1, 2, 3, 4, and 7. The Sang *Z*âu.

THE WRITER MOURNS OVER THE MISERY AND DISORDER OF THE TIMES, WITH A VIEW TO REPREHEND THE MISGOVERNMENT OF KING LÎ, APPEALING ALSO TO HEAVEN TO HAVE COMPASSION.

King Lî is not mentioned by name in the piece, but the second line of stanza 7 can only be explained of him. He was driven from the throne, in consequence of his misgovernment, in B.C. 842, and only saved his life by flying to *K*ih, a place in the present Ho *K*âu, department Phing-yang, Shan-hsî, where he remained till his death in B.C. 828. The government in the meantime was carried on by the dukes of Shâo and *K*âu, whose administration, called the period of 'Mutual Harmony,' forms an important chronological era in Chinese history. On the authority of a reference in the Ȝo Kwan, the piece is ascribed to an earl of *Z*ui.

Luxuriant is that young mulberry tree, And beneath it wide is the shade; But they will pluck its leaves till it is quite destroyed[1]. The distress

[1] These three lines are metaphorical of the once flourishing kingdom, which was now brought to the verge of ruin.

inflicted on these (multitudes of the) people, Is an unceasing sorrow to my heart; My commiseration fills (my breast). O thou bright and great Heaven, Shouldest thou not have compassion on us?

The four steeds (gallop about), eager and strong[1]; The tortoise-and-serpent and the falcon banners fly about. Disorder grows, and no peace can be secured. Every state is being ruined; There are no black heads among the people[2]. Everything is reduced to ashes by calamity. Oh! alas! The doom of the kingdom hurries on.

There is nothing to arrest the doom of the kingdom; Heaven does not nourish us. There is no place in which to stop securely; There is no place to which to go. Superior men are the bonds (of the social state)[3], Allowing no love of strife in their hearts. Who reared the steps of the dissatisfaction[4], Which has reached the present distress?

The grief of my heart is extreme, And I dwell on (the condition of) our land. I was born at an unhappy time, To meet with the severe anger of Heaven. From the west to the east, There is no quiet place of abiding. Many are the distresses I meet with; Very urgent is the trouble on our borders.

Heaven is sending down death and disorder, And

---

[1] That is, the war-chariots, each drawn by its team of four horses.

[2] The young and able-bodied of the people were slain or absent on distant expeditions, and only old and gray-headed men were to be seen.

[3] Intimating that no such men were now to be found in office.

[4] Meaning the king by his misgovernment and employment of bad men.

has put an end to our king. It is (now) sending down those devourers of the grain, So that the husbandry is all in evil case. Alas for our middle states[1]! All is in peril and going to ruin. I have no strength (to do anything), And think of (the Power in) the azure vault.

ODE 4. THE YUN HAN.

KING HSÜAN, ON OCCASION OF A GREAT DROUGHT, EXPOSTULATES WITH GOD AND ALL THE SPIRITS, WHO MIGHT BE EXPECTED TO HELP HIM AND HIS PEOPLE; ASKS THEM WHEREFORE THEY WERE CONTENDING WITH HIM; AND DETAILS THE MEASURES HE HAD TAKEN, AND WAS STILL TAKING, FOR THE REMOVAL OF THE CALAMITY.

King Hsüan does not occur by name in the ode, though the remarkable prayer which it relates is ascribed to a king in stanza 1. All critics have admitted the statement of the Preface that the piece was made, in admiration of king Hsüan, by *Z*ăng Shû, a great officer, we may presume, of the court. The standard chronology places the commencement of the drought in B. C. 822, the sixth year of Hsüan's reign. How long it continued we cannot tell.

Bright was the milky way, Shining and revolving in the sky. The king said, 'Oh! What crime is chargeable on us now, That Heaven (thus) sends down death and disorder? Famine comes again and again. There is no spirit I have not sacrificed to[2]; There is no victim I have grudged; Our

---

[1] We must translate here in the plural, 'the middle states' meaning all the states subject to the sovereign of *K*âu.

[2] In the Official Book of *K*âu, among the duties of the Minister of Instruction, or, as Biot translates the title, 'the Director of the Multitudes,' it is stated that one of the things he has to do, on occurrences of famine, is 'to seek out the spirits,' that is, as explained by the commentators, to see that sacrifices are offered to all the spirits, even such as may have been discontinued. This rule had, no doubt, been acted on during the drought which this ode describes.

jade symbols, oblong and round, are exhausted[1];—How is it that I am not heard?

'The drought is excessive; Its fervours become more and more tormenting. I have not ceased offering pure sacrifices; From the border altars I have gone to the ancestral temple[2]. To the (Powers) above and below I have presented my offerings and then buried them[3];—There is no spirit whom I have not honoured. Hâu-*k*î is not equal to the occasion; God does not come to us. This wasting and ruin of our country,—Would that it fell (only) on me!

'The drought is excessive, And I may not try to excuse myself. I am full of terror, and feel the peril, Like the clap of thunder or the roll. Of the remnant of *K*âu, among the black-haired people, There will not be half a man left; Nor will God from his great heaven exempt (even) me. Shall

---

[1] We have, in the sixth Book of the fifth Part of the Shû, an instance of the use of the symbols here mentioned in sacrificing to the spirits of departed kings. The Official Book, among the duties of the Minister of Religion, mentions the use of these and other symbols—in all six, of different shapes and colours—at the different sacrifices.

[2] By 'the border altars' we are to understand the altars in the suburbs of the capital, where Heaven and Earth were sacrificed to;—the great services at the solstices, and any other seasons. The mention of Hâu-*k*î in the seventh line makes us think especially of the service in the spring, to pray for a good year, when Hâu-*k*î was associated with God.

[3] 'The (Powers) above and below' are Heaven and Earth. The offerings, during the progress of the service, were placed on the ground, or on the altars, and buried in the earth at the close of it. This explains what the king says in the first stanza about the offerings of jade being exhausted.

we not mingle our fears together? (The sacrifices to) my ancestors will be extinguished[1].

'The drought is excessive, And it cannot be stopped. More fierce and fiery, It is leaving me no place. My end is near;—I have none to look up, none to look round, to. The many dukes and their ministers of the past[2] Give me no help. O ye parents and (nearer) ancestors[3], How can ye bear to see me thus?

'The drought is excessive;—Parched are the hills, and the streams are dried. The demon of drought exercises his oppression, As if scattering flames and fire[4] My heart is terrified with the heat;—My sorrowing heart is as if on fire. The

---

[1] Equivalent to the extinction of the dynasty.

[2] The king had sacrificed to all the early lords of *K*âu. 'The many dukes' may comprehend kings Thâi and *K*î. He had also sacrificed to their ministers. Compare what Pan-kăng says in the Shû, p. 109, about his predecessors and their ministers. Some take 'the many dukes, and the ministers,' of all princes of states who had signalised themselves by services to the people and kingdom.

[3] The king could hardly hope that his father, the oppressive Lî, would in his spirit-state give him any aid; but we need only find in his words the expression of natural feeling. Probably it was the consideration of the character of Lî which has made some critics understand by 'parents' and 'ancestors' the same individuals, namely, kings Wăn and Wû, 'the ancestors' of Hsüan, and who had truly been 'the parents' of the people.

[4] Khung Ying-tâ, from 'the Book of Spirits and Marvels,' gives the following account of 'the demon of drought:'—'In the southern regions there is a man, two or three cubits in height, with the upper part of his body bare, and his eyes in the top of his head. He runs with the speed of the wind, and is named Po. In whatever state he appears, there ensues a great drought.' The Book of Spirits and Marvels, however, as it now exists, cannot be older than our fourth or fifth century.

many dukes and their ministers of the past Do not hear me. O God, from thy great heaven, Grant me the liberty to withdraw (into retirement[1]).

'The drought is excessive;—I struggle and fear to go away. How is it that I am afflicted with this drought? I cannot ascertain the cause of it. In praying for a good year I was abundantly early[2]. I was not late (in sacrificing) to (the spirits of) the four quarters and of the land[3]. God in great heaven Does not consider me. Reverent to the intelligent spirits, I ought not to be thus the object of their anger.

'The drought is excessive;—All is dispersion, and the bonds of government are relaxed. Reduced to extremities are the heads of departments; Full of distress are my chief ministers, The Master of the Horse, the Commander of the Guards, The chief Cook[4], and my attendants. There is no one who has not (tried to) help (the people); They have not refrained on the ground of being unable. I look up to the great heaven;—Why am I plunged in this sorrow?

'I look up to the great heaven, But its stars sparkle bright. My great officers and excellent men, Ye have reverently drawn near (to Heaven) with all

---

[1] That is, to withdraw and give place to a more worthy sovereign.

[2] This was the border sacrifice to God, when Hâu-*k*î was associated with him. Some critics add a sacrifice in the first month of winter, for a blessing on the ensuing year, offered to 'the honoured ones of heaven,'—the sun, moon, and zodiacal constellations.

[3] See note 2 on p. 371.

[4] See note 1 on p. 356.

your powers. Death is approaching. But do not cast away what you have done. You are seeking not for me only, But to give rest to all our departments. I look up to the great heaven;—When shall I be favoured with repose?'

Ode 5, Stanzas 1, 2, and 4. The Sung Kâo.

CELEBRATING THE APPOINTMENT BY KING HSÜAN OF A RELATIVE TO BE THE MARQUIS OF SHĂN, AND DEFENDER OF THE SOUTHERN BORDER OF THE KINGDOM, WITH THE ARRANGEMENTS MADE FOR HIS ENTERING ON HIS CHARGE.

That the king who appears in this piece was king Hsüan is sufficiently established. He appears in it commissioning 'his great uncle,' an elder brother, that is, of his mother, to go and rule, as marquis of Shăn, and chief or president of the states in the south of the kingdom, to defend the borders against the encroaching hordes of the south, headed by the princes of *Kh*û, whose lords had been rebellious against the middle states even in the time of the Shang dynasty;—see the last of the Sacrificial Odes of Shang.

Grandly lofty are the mountains, With their large masses reaching to the heavens. From those mountains was sent down a spirit, Who produced the birth of (the princes of) Fû and Shăn[1]. Fû and

[1] Shăn was a small marquisate, a part of what is the present department of Nan-yang, Ho-nan. Fû, which was also called Lü, was another small territory, not far from Shăn. The princes of both were *K*iangs, descended from the chief minister of Yâo, called in the first Book of the Shû, 'the Four Mountains.' Other states were ruled by his descendants, particularly the great state of *Kh*î. When it is said here that a spirit was sent down from the great mountains, and produced the birth of (the princes of) Fû and Shăn, we have, probably, a legendary tradition concerning the birth of Yâo's minister, which was current among all his descendants; and with which we may compare the legends that have come under our notice about the supernatural births of the ancestors of the founders of the Houses of Shang and *K*âu. The character for

Shăn Are the support of *K*âu, Screens to all the states, Diffusing (their influence) over the four quarters of the kingdom.

Full of activity is the chief of Shăn, And the king would employ him to continue the services (of his fathers), With his capital in Hsieh [1], Where he should be a pattern to the states of the south. The king gave charge to the earl of Shâo, To arrange all about the residence of the chief of Shăn, Where he should do what was necessary for the regions of the south, And where his posterity might maintain his merit.

Of the services of the chief of Shăn The foundation was laid by the earl of Shâo, Who first built the walls (of his city), And then completed his ancestral temple [2]. When the temple was completed, wide and grand, The king conferred on the chief of Shâo Four noble steeds, With the hooks for the trappings of the breast-bands, glittering bright [3].

'mountains' in lines 1 and 3 is the same that occurs in the title of Yâo's minister. On the statement about the mountains sending down a spirit, Hwang Hsün, a critic of the Sung dynasty, says that 'it is merely a personification of the poet, to show how high Heaven had a mind to revive the fortunes of *K*âu, and that we need not trouble ourselves about whether there was such a spirit or not.'

[1] Hsieh was in the present Făng *K*âu of the department of Nan-yang.

[2] Compare with this the account given, in ode 3 of the first decade, of the settling of 'the ancient duke Than-fû' in the plain of *K*âu. Here, as there, the great religious edifice, the ancestral temple, takes precedence of all other buildings in the new city.

[3] The steeds with their equipments were tokens of the royal favour, usually granted on occasions of investiture. The conferring of them was followed immediately by the departure of the newly-invested prince to his charge.

ODE 6, STANZAS 1 AND 7. THE *K*ĂNG MIN.

CELEBRATING THE VIRTUES OF *K*UNG SHAN-FÛ, WHO APPEARS TO HAVE BEEN ONE OF THE PRINCIPAL MINISTERS OF KING HSÜAN, AND HIS DESPATCH TO THE EAST, TO FORTIFY THE CAPITAL OF THE STATE OF *KH*Î.

Heaven, in giving birth to the multitudes of the people, To every faculty and relationship annexed its law. The people possess this normal nature, And they (consequently) love its normal virtue[1]. Heaven beheld the ruler of *K*âu, Brilliantly affecting it by his conduct below, And to maintain him, its Son, Gave birth to *K*ung Shan-fû[2].

*K*ung Shan-fû went forth, having sacrificed to the spirit of the road[3]. His four steeds were strong;

---

[1] We get an idea of the meaning which has been attached to these four lines from a very early time by Mencius' quotation of them (VI, i, ch. 6) in support of his doctrine of the goodness of human nature, and the remark on the piece which he attributes to Confucius, that 'the maker of it knew indeed the constitution (of our nature).' Every faculty, bodily or mental, has its function to fulfil, and every relationship its duty to be discharged. The function and the duty are the things which the human being has to observe:—the seeing clearly, for instance, with the eyes, and hearing distinctly with the ears; the maintenance of righteousness between ruler and minister, and of affection between parent and child. This is the 'normal nature,' and the 'normal virtue' is the nature fulfilling the various laws of its constitution.

[2] The connexion between these four lines and those that precede is this:—that while Heaven produces all men with the good nature there described, on occasions it produces others with virtue and powers in a super-eminent degree. Such an occasion was presented by the case of king Hsüan, and therefore, to mark its appreciation of him, and for his help, it now produced *K*ung Shan-fû.

[3] This was a special sacrifice at the commencement of a journey, or of an expedition. See note 2 on p. 399.

His men were alert, He was always anxious lest he should not be equal to his commission; His steeds went on without stopping, To the tinkling of their eight bells. The king had given charge to *K*ung Shan-fû, To fortify the city there in the east.

ODE 7, STANZAS 1 AND PART OF 3. THE HAN YÎ.

CELEBRATING THE MARQUIS OF HAN:—HIS INVESTITURE, AND THE KING'S CHARGE TO HIM; THE GIFTS HE RECEIVED, AND THE PARTING FEAST AT THE COURT; HIS MARRIAGE; THE EXCELLENCE OF HIS TERRITORY; AND HIS SWAY OVER THE REGIONS OF THE NORTH.

Only one line—the first of stanza 3—in this interesting piece serves to illustrate the religious practices of the time, and needs no further note than what has been given on the first line of stanza 7 in the preceding ode. The name of the marquisate of Han remains in the district of Han-*kh*ăng, department of Hsî-an, Shen-hsî, in which also is mount Liang.

Very grand is the mountain of Liang, Which was made cultivable by Yü. Bright is the way from it, (Along which came) the marquis of Han to receive investiture. The king in person gave the charge:—'Continue the services of your ancestors; Let not my charge to you come to nought. Be diligent early and late, And reverently discharge your duties:—So shall my appointment of you not change. Be a support against those princes who do not come to court, Thus assisting your sovereign.'

When the marquis of Han left the court, he sacrificed to the spirit of the road. He went forth, and lodged for the night in Tû.

ODE 8, STANZAS 4 AND 5. THE *K*IANG HAN.

CELEBRATING AN EXPEDITION AGAINST THE SOUTHERN TRIBES OF THE HWÂI, AND THE WORK DONE FOR THE KING IN THEIR COUNTRY, BY HÛ, THE EARL OF SHÂO, WITH THE MANNER IN WHICH THE KING REWARDED HIM, AND HE RESPONDED TO THE ROYAL FAVOUR.

Hû was probably the same earl of Shâo, who is mentioned in ode 5, as building his capital of Hsieh for the new marquis of Shăn. The lords of Shâo had been distinguished in the service of *K*âu ever since the rise of the dynasty.

The king gave charge to Hû of Shâo:—'You have everywhere made known (and carried out my orders). When (the kings) Wăn and Wû received their appointment, The duke of Shâo was their strong support. You not (only) have a regard to me the little child, But you try to resemble that duke of Shâo. You have commenced and earnestly displayed your merit; And I will make you happy.

'I give you a large libation-cup of jade [1], And a jar of herb-flavoured spirits from the black millet [2]. I have made announcement to the Accomplished one [3], And confer on you hills, lands, and fields. In (*Kh*î-)*k*âu shall you receive investiture, According as your ancestor received his.' Hû bowed with

---

[1] See note 2 on p. 386.

[2] The cup and the spirits would be used by the earl when sacrificing in his ancestral temple. Compare the similar gift from king *Kh*ăng to the duke of *K*âu, in the Shû, p. 194. More substantial gifts are immediately specified.

[3] 'The Accomplished one' is understood to be king Wăn (='the Accomplished king'). He was the founder of the *K*âu dynasty. To him the kingdom had first come by the appointment and gift of Heaven. It was the duty therefore of his successors, in making grants of territory to meritorious officers, to announce them to him in *Kh*î-kâu, the old territory of the family, and obtain, as it were, his leave for what they were doing.

his head to the ground (and said), 'May the Son of Heaven live for ever!'

ODE 10, STANZAS 1, 5, 6, AND 7. THE *K*AN *Z*ANG.

THE WRITER DEPLORES, WITH AN APPEALING WAIL TO HEAVEN, THE MISERY AND OPPRESSION THAT PREVAILED, AND INTIMATES THAT THEY WERE CAUSED BY THE INTERFERENCE OF WOMEN AND EUNUCHS IN THE GOVERNMENT.

The king addressed in this piece was most probably Yû. It suits his character and reign.

I look up to great Heaven, But it shows us no kindness. Very long have we been disquieted, And these great calamities are sent down (upon us). There is nothing settled in the country; Officers and people are in distress. Through the insects from without and from within, There is no peace or limit (to our misery). The net of crime is not taken up[1], And there is no peace nor cure (for our state).

Why is it that Heaven is (thus) reproving (you)? Why is it that Heaven is not blessing (you)? You neglect your great barbarian (foes), And regard me with hatred. You are regardless of the evil omens (that abound[2]), And your demeanour is all unseemly. (Good) men are going away, And the country is sure to go to ruin.

Heaven is letting down its net, And many (are the calamities in it). (Good) men are going away, And my heart is sorrowful. Heaven is letting down

---

[1] By 'the net of crime' we are to understand the multitude of penal laws, to whose doom people were exposed. In stanza 6, Heaven is represented as letting it down.

[2] Compare ode 9 of the fourth decade in the former Part.

its net, And soon (all will be caught in it). (Good) men are going away, And my heart is sad.

Right from the spring comes the water bubbling, Revealing its depth. The sorrow of my heart,—Is it (only) of to-day? Why were these things not before me? Or why were they not after me? But mysteriously great Heaven Is able to strengthen anything. Do not disgrace your great ancestors:—This will save your posterity[1].

Ode 11, Stanzas 1 and 2. The Shâo Min.

THE WRITER APPEALS TO HEAVEN, BEMOANING THE MISERY AND RUIN WHICH WERE GOING ON, AND SHOWING HOW THEY WERE DUE TO THE KING'S EMPLOYMENT OF MEAN AND WORTHLESS CREATURES.

Compassionate Heaven is arrayed in angry terrors. Heaven is indeed sending down ruin, Afflicting us with famine, So that the people are all wandering fugitives. In the settled regions, and on the borders, all is desolation.

Heaven sends down its net of crime;—Devouring insects, who weary and confuse men's minds, Ignorant, oppressive, negligent, Breeders of confusion, utterly perverse:—These are the men employed.

---

[1] The writer in these concluding lines ventures to summon the king to repentance, and to hold out a hope that there might come a change in their state. He does this, believing that all things are possible with Heaven.

LESSONS FROM THE STATES.

ODES AND STANZAS ILLUSTRATING THE RELIGIOUS VIEWS AND PRACTICES OF THE WRITERS AND THEIR TIMES.

IT has been stated in the Introduction, p. 276, that the first Part of the Shih, called the Kwo Făng, or 'Lessons from the States,' consists of 160 pieces, descriptive of manners and events in several of the feudal states into which the kingdom of *K*âu was divided. Nearly all of them are short; and the passages illustrating the religious views and practices of their times are comparatively few. What passages there are, however, of this nature will all be found below. The pieces are not arranged in decades, as in the Odes of the Kingdom, but in Books, under the names of the states in which they were produced.

Although the Kwo Făng form, as usually published, the first Part of the Shih, nearly all of them are more recent in their origin than the pieces of the other Parts. They bring us face to face with the states of the kingdom, and the ways of their officers and people for several centuries of the dynasty of *K*âu.

BOOK II. THE ODES OF SHÂO AND THE SOUTH.

THE Shû and previous portions of the Shih have made us familiar with Shâo, the name of the appanage of Shih, one of the principal ministers at the court of *K*âu in the first two reigns of the dynasty. The site of the city of Shâo was in the present department of Făng-*kh*iang, Shen-hsî. The first possessor of it, along with the still more famous duke of *K*âu, remained at court, to watch over the fortunes of the new dynasty. They were known as 'the highest dukes' and 'the two great chiefs,' the duke of *K*âu having charge of the eastern portions of the kingdom, and the other of the western. The pieces in this Book are supposed to have been produced in Shâo, and the principalities south of it within his jurisdiction, by the duke.

ODE 2. THE *ZH*ÂI FAN.

CELEBRATING THE INDUSTRY AND REVERENCE OF A PRINCE'S WIFE, ASSISTING HIM IN SACRIFICING.

We must suppose the ladies of a harem, in one of the states of the south, admiring and praising in these simple stanzas the way in which their mistress discharged her duties. A view of the ode maintained by many is that the lady gathered the southernwood, not to use it in sacrificing, but in the nurture of the silkworms under her care; but the evidence of the characters in the text is, on the whole, in favour of the more common view. Constant reference is made to the piece by Chinese moralists, to show that the most trivial things are accepted in sacrifice, when there are reverence and sincerity in the presenting of them.

One critic asked *K*û Hsî whether it was conceivable that the wife of a prince did herself what is here related, and he replied that the poet said so. Another has observed that if the lady ordered and employed others, it was still her own doing. But that the lady did it herself is not incredible, when we consider the simplicity of those early times, in the twelfth century B. C.

She gathers the white southernwood, By the ponds, on the islets. She employs it, In the business of our prince.

She gathers the white southernwood, Along the streams in the valleys. She employs it, In the temple[1] of our prince.

[1] If the character here translated 'temple' had no other signification but that, there would be an end of the dispute about the meaning of the piece. But while we find it often used of the ancestral temple, it may also mean any building, especially one of a large and public character, such as a palace or mansion; and hence some contend that it should be interpreted here of 'the silkworm house.' We are to conceive of the lady, after having gathered the materials for sacrificial use, then preparing them according to rule, and while it is yet dark on the morning of the sacrificial day, going with them into the temple, and setting them forth in their proper vessels and places.

With head-dress reverently rising aloft, Early, while yet it is night, she is in the prince's (temple). In her head-dress, slowly retiring, She returns (to her own apartments).

ODE 4. THE *ZHÂI* PIN.

CELEBRATING THE DILIGENCE AND REVERENCE OF THE YOUNG WIFE OF AN OFFICER, DOING HER PART IN SACRIFICIAL OFFERINGS.

She gathers the large duckweed, By the banks of the stream in the southern valley. She gathers the pondweed, In those pools left by the floods.

She deposits what she gathers, In her square baskets and round ones. She boils it, In her tripods and pans.

She sets forth her preparations, Under the window in the ancestral chamber[1]. Who superintends the business? It is (this) reverent young lady.

---

[1] 'The ancestral chamber' was a room behind the temple of the family, dedicated specially to the ancestor of the officer whose wife is the subject of the piece. The princes of states were succeeded, as a rule, by the eldest son of the wife proper. Their sons by other wives were called 'other sons.' The eldest son by the wife proper of one of them became the 'great ancestor' of the clan descended from him, and 'the ancestral chamber' was an apartment dedicated to him. Mâo and other interpreters, going on certain statements as to the training of daughters in the business of sacrificing in this apartment for three months previous to their marriage, contend that the lady spoken of here was not yet married, but was only undergoing this preparatory education. It is not necessary, however, to adopt this interpretation. The lady appears doing the same duties as the wife in the former piece.

BOOK III. THE ODES OF PHEI.

WHEN king Wû overthrew the dynasty of Shang, the domain of its kings was divided into three portions, the northern portion being called Phei, the southern Yung, and the eastern Wei, the rulers of which last in course of time absorbed the other two. It is impossible to say why the old names were retained in the arrangement of the odes in this Part of the Shih, for it is acknowledged on all hands that the pieces in Books iii and iv, as well as those of Book v, are all odes of Wei.

ODE 4. THE *Z*ĂH YÜEH.

SUPPOSED TO BE THE COMPLAINT AND APPEAL OF *K*WANG *K*IANG, A MARCHIONESS OF WEI, AGAINST THE BAD TREATMENT SHE RECEIVED FROM HER HUSBAND.

All the Chinese critics give this interpretation of the piece. *K*wang *K*iang was a daughter of the house of *Kh*î, about the middle of the eighth century B.C., and was married to the marquis Yang, known in history as 'duke *K*wang,' of Wei. She was a lady of admirable character, and beautiful; but her husband proved faithless and unkind. In this ode she makes her subdued moan, appealing to the sun and moon, as if they could take cognizance of the way in which she was treated. Possibly, however, the addressing those bodies may simply be an instance of prosopopoeia.

O sun, O moon, Which enlighten this lower earth! Here is this man, Who treats me not according to the ancient rule. How can he get his mind settled? Would he then not regard me?

O sun, O moon, Which overshadow this lower earth! Here is this man, Who will not be friendly with me. How can he get his mind settled? Would he then not respond to me?

O sun, O moon, Which come forth from the east! Here is this man, With virtuous words, but really not good. How can he get his mind settled? Would he then allow me to be forgotten?

O sun, O moon, From the east that come forth! O father, O mother, There is no sequel to your nourishing of me. How can he get his mind settled? Would he then respond to me contrary to all reason?

ODE 15, STANZA 1. THE PEI MĂN.

AN OFFICER OF WEI SETS FORTH HIS HARD LOT, THROUGH DISTRESSES AND THE BURDENS LAID UPON HIM, AND HIS SILENCE UNDER IT IN SUBMISSION TO HEAVEN.

I go out at the north gate, With my heart full of sorrow. Straitened am I and poor, And no one takes knowledge of my distress. So it is! Heaven has done it[1];—What then shall I say?

BOOK IV. THE ODES OF YUNG.

See the preliminary note on p. 433.

ODE 1. THE PAI *K*ÂU.

PROTEST OF A WIDOW AGAINST BEING URGED TO MARRY AGAIN, AND HER APPEAL TO HER MOTHER AND TO HEAVEN.

THIS piece, it is said, was made by Kung *K*iang, the widow of Kung-po, son of the marquis Hsî of Wei (B.C. 855–814). Kung-po having died an early death, her parents (who must have been the marquis of *Kh*î and his wife or one of the ladies of his harem) wanted to force her to a second marriage, against which she protests. The ode was preserved, no doubt, as an example of

---

[1] The 'Complete Digest of Comments on the Shih' warns its readers not to take 'Heaven' here as synonymous with Ming, 'what is decreed or commanded.' The writer does not go on to define the precise idea which he understood the character to convey. This appears to be what we often mean by 'Providence,' when we speak of anything permitted, rather than appointed, by the supreme ruling Power.

what the Chinese have always considered a great virtue,—the refusal of a widow to marry again.

It floats about, that boat of cypress wood, There in the middle of the Ho[1]. With his two tufts of hair falling over his forehead[2], He was my mate; And I swear that till death I will have no other. O mother, O Heaven[3], Why will you not understand me?

It floats about, that boat of cypress wood, There by the side of the Ho. With his two tufts of hair falling over his forehead, He was my only one; And I swear that till death I will not do the evil thing. O mother, O Heaven, Why will you not understand me?

ODE 3, STANZA 2. THE *K*ÜN-ȜZE *K*IEH LÂO.

CONTRAST BETWEEN THE BEAUTY AND SPLENDOUR OF HSÜAN *K*IANG AND HER VICIOUSNESS.

Hsüan *K*iang was a princess of *Kh*î, who, towards the close of the seventh century B.C., became wife to the marquis of Wei, known as duke Hsüan. She was beautiful and unfortunate, but various things are related of her indicative of the grossest immoralities prevailing in the court of Wei.

How rich and splendid Is her pheasant-figured

[1] These allusive lines, probably, indicate the speaker's widowhood, which left her like 'a boat floating about on the water.'

[2] Such was the mode in which the hair was kept, while a boy or young man's parents were alive, parted into two tufts from the pia mater, and brought down as low as the eyebrows on either side of the forehead.

[3] Mâo thought that the lady intended her father by 'Heaven;' while *K*û held that her father may have been dead, and that the mother is called Heaven, with reference to the kindness and protection that she ought to show. There seems rather to be in the term a wild, and not very intelligent, appeal to the supreme Power in heaven.

robe[1]! Her black hair in masses like clouds, No false locks does she descend to. There are her ear-plugs of jade, Her comb-pin of ivory, And her high forehead, so white. She appears like a visitant from heaven! She appears like a goddess[2].

ODE 6, STANZAS 1 AND 2. THE TING *K*IH FANG *K*UNG.

CELEBRATING THE PRAISE OF DUKE WĂN;—HIS DILIGENCE, FORESIGHT, USE OF DIVINATION, AND OTHER QUALITIES.

The state of Wei was reduced to extremity by an irruption of some northern hordes in B.C. 660, and had nearly disappeared from among the states of *K*âu. Under the marquis Wei, known in history as duke Wăn, its fortunes revived, and he became a sort of second founder of the state.

When Ting culminated (at night-fall)[3], He began to build the palace at *Kh*û[4], Determining

[1] The lady is introduced arrayed in the gorgeous robes worn by the princess of a state in the ancestral temple.

[2] P. Lacharme translated these two concluding lines by 'Tu primo aspectu coelos (pulchritudine), et imperatorem (majestate) adaequas,' without any sanction of the Chinese critics; and moreover there was no Tî (帝) in the sense of imperator then in China. The sovereigns of *K*âu were wang or kings. *K*û Hsî expands the lines thus:—'Such is the beauty of her robes and appearance, that beholders are struck with awe, as if she were a spiritual being.' Hsü *Kh*ien (Yüan dynasty) deals with them thus:—'With such splendour of beauty and dress, how is it that she is here? She has come down from heaven! She is a spiritual being!'

[3] Ting is the name of a small space in the heavens, embracing *α* Markab and another star of Pegasus. Its culminating at night-fall was the signal that the labours of husbandry were over for the year, and that building operations should be taken in hand. Great as was the urgency for the building of his new capital, duke Wăn would not take it in hand till the proper time for such a labour was arrived.

[4] *Kh*û, or *Kh*û-*kh*iû, was the new capital of Wei, in the present district of *Kh*ăng-wû, department Ȝ*h*âo-*k*âu, Shan-tung.

its aspects by means of the sun. He built the palace at *Kh*û. He planted about it hazel and chesnut trees, The Î, the Thung, the 3ze, and the varnish tree. Which, when cut down, might afford materials for lutes.

He ascended those old walls, And thence surveyed (the site of) *Kh*û. He surveyed *Kh*û and Thang[1], With the lofty hills and high elevations about. He descended and examined the mulberry trees. He then divined by the tortoise-shell, and got a favourable response[2]; And thus the issue has been truly good.

Book V. The Odes of Wei.

It has been said on the title of Book iii, that Wei at first was the eastern portion of the old domain of the kings of Shang. With this a brother of king Wû, called Khang-shû, was invested. The principality was afterwards increased by the absorption of Phei and Yung. It came to embrace portions of the present provinces of *K*ih-lî, Shan-tung, and Ho-nan. It outlasted the dynasty of *K*âu itself, the last prince of Wei being reduced to the ranks of the people only during the dynasty of *Kh*in.

Ode 4, Stanzas 1 and 2. The Măng.

AN UNFORTUNATE WOMAN, WHO HAD BEEN SEDUCED INTO AN IMPROPER CONNEXION, NOW CAST OFF, RELATES AND BEMOANS HER SAD CASE.

An extract is given from the pathetic history here related, because it shows how divination was used among the common people, and entered generally into the ordinary affairs of life.

A simple-looking lad you were, Carrying cloth

---

[1] Thang was the name of a town, evidently not far from *Kh*û.

[2] We have seen before how divination was resorted to on occasion of new undertakings, especially in proceeding to rear a city.

to exchange it for silk. (But) you came not so to purchase silk;—You came to make proposals to me. I convoyed you through the *Kh*î[1], As far as Tun-*kh*iû[2], 'It is not I,' (I said), 'who would protract the time; But you have had no good go-between. I pray you be not angry, And let autumn be the time.'

I ascended that ruinous wall, To look towards Fû-kwan[3]; And when I saw (you) not (coming from) it, My tears flowed in streams. When I did see (you coming from) Fû-kwan, I laughed and I spoke. You had consulted, (you said), the tortoise-shell and the divining stalks, And there was nothing unfavourable in their response[4]. 'Then come,' (I said), 'with your carriage, And I will remove with my goods.'

Book VI. The Odes of the Royal Domain.

King Wăn, it has been seen, had for his capital the city of Făng, from which his son, king Wû, moved the seat of government to Hâo. In the time of king *Kh*ăng, a city was built by the duke

---

[1] The *Kh*î was a famous river of Wei.

[2] Tun-*kh*iû was a well-known place—'the mound or height of Tun'—south of the Wei.

[3] Fû-kwan must have been the place where the man lived, according to *K*û. Rather, it must have been a pass (Fû-kwan may mean 'the gate or pass of Fû'), through which he would come, and was visible from near the residence of the woman.

[4] Ying-tâ observes that the man had never divined about the matter, and said that he had done so only to complete the process of seduction. The critics dwell on the inconsistency of divination being resorted to in such a case:—'Divination is proper only if used in reference to what is right and moral.'

of *K*âu, near the present Lo-yang, and called 'the eastern capital.' Meetings of the princes of the states assembled there; but the court continued to be held at Hâo till the accession of king Phing in B.C. 770. From that time, the kings of *K*âu sank nearly to the level of the princes of the states, and the poems collected in their domain were classed among the 'Lessons of Manners from the States,' though still distinguished by the epithet 'royal' prefixed to them.

ODE 1, STANZA 1. THE SHÛ LÎ.

AN OFFICER DESCRIBES HIS MELANCHOLY AND REFLECTIONS ON SEEING THE DESOLATION OF THE OLD CAPITAL OF *K*ÂU, MAKING HIS MOAN TO HEAVEN BECAUSE OF IT.

There is no specific mention of the old capital of *K*âu in the piece, but the schools of Mâo and *K*û are agreed in this interpretation, which is much more likely than any of the others that have been proposed.

There was the millet with its drooping heads;
There was the sacrificial millet coming into blade[1].
Slowly I moved about, In my heart all-agitated.
Those who knew me Said I was sad at heart.
Those who did not know me, Said I was seeking
for something. O thou distant and azure Heaven[2]!
By what man was this (brought about)[3]?

---

[1] That is, there where the ancestral temple and other grand buildings of Hâo had once stood.

[2] 'He cried out to Heaven,' says Yen Ȝ*h*an, 'and told (his distress), but he calls it distant in its azure brightness, lamenting that his complaint was not heard.' This is, probably, the correct explanation of the language. The speaker would by it express his grief that the dynasty of *K*âu and its people were abandoned and uncared for by Heaven.

[3] Referring to king Yû, whose reckless course had led to the destruction of Hâo by the *Z*ung, and in a minor degree to his son, king Phing, who had subsequently removed to the eastern capital.

ODE 9, STANZAS 1 AND 3. THE TÂ *K*Ü.

A LADY EXCUSES HERSELF FOR NOT FLYING TO HER LOVER BY HER FEAR OF A SEVERE AND VIRTUOUS MAGISTRATE, AND SWEARS TO HIM THAT SHE IS SINCERE IN HER ATTACHMENT TO HIM.

His great carriage rolls along, And his robes of rank glitter like the young sedge. Do I not think of you? But I am afraid of this officer, and dare not (fly to you).

While living we may have to occupy different apartments; But, when dead, we shall share the same grave. If you say that I am not sincere, By the bright sun I swear that I am [1].

BOOK X. THE ODES OF THANG.

THE odes of Thang were really the odes of 3in, the greatest of the fiefs of *K*âu until the rise of *Kh*in. King *Kh*ăng, in B.C. 1107, invested his younger brother, called Shû-yü, with the territory where Yâo was supposed to have ruled anciently as the marquis of Thang, in the present department of Thâi-yüan, Shan-hsî, the fief retaining that ancient name. Subsequently the name of the state was changed to 3in, from the river 3in in the southern part of it.

ODE 8, STANZA 1. THE PÂO YÜ.

THE MEN OF 3IN, CALLED OUT TO WARFARE BY THE KING'S ORDER, MOURN OVER THE CONSEQUENT SUFFERING OF THEIR PARENTS, AND LONG FOR THEIR RETURN TO THEIR ORDINARY AGRICULTURAL PURSUITS, MAKING THEIR APPEAL TO HEAVEN.

Sû-sû go the feathers of the wild geese, As

---

[1] In the 'Complete Digest' this oath is expanded in the following way:—'These words are from my heart. If you think that they are not sincere, there is (a Power) above, like the bright sun, observing me;—how should my words not be sincere?'

they settle on the bushy oaks[1]. The king's affairs must not be slackly discharged, And (so) we cannot plant our millets;—What will our parents have to rely on? O thou distant and azure Heaven[2]! When shall we be in our places again?

ODE 11. THE KO SHĂNG.

A WIFE MOURNS THE DEATH OF HER HUSBAND, REFUSING TO BE COMFORTED, AND DECLARES THAT SHE WILL CHERISH HIS MEMORY TILL HER OWN DEATH.

It is supposed that the husband whose death is bewailed in this piece had died in one of the military expeditions of which duke Hsien (B.C. 676–651) was fond. It may have been so, but there is nothing in the piece to make us think of duke Hsien. I give it a place in the volume, not because of the religious sentiment in it, but because of the absence of that sentiment, where we might expect it. The lady shows the grand virtue of a Chinese widow, in that she will never marry again. And her grief would not be assuaged. The days would all seem long summer days, and the nights all long winter nights; so that a hundred long years would seem to drag their slow course. But there is not any hope expressed of a re-union with her husband in another state. The 'abode' and the 'chamber' of which she speaks are to be understood of his grave; and her thoughts do not appear to go beyond it.

The dolichos grows, covering the thorn trees; The convolvulus spreads all over the waste[3]. The

[1] Trees are not the proper place for geese to rest on; and the attempt to do so is productive of much noise and trouble to the birds. The lines would seem to allude to the hardships of the soldiers' lot, called from their homes to go on a distant expedition.

[2] See note 2 on ode 1 of Book vi, where Heaven is appealed to in the same language.

[3] These two lines are taken as allusive, the speaker being led by the sight of the weak plants supported by the trees, shrubs, and tombs, to think of her own desolate, unsupported condition. But they may also be taken as narrative, and descriptive of the battle-ground, where her husband had met his death.

man of my admiration is no more here;—With whom can I dwell? I abide alone.

The dolichos grows, covering the jujube trees; The convolvulus spreads all over the tombs. The man of my admiration is no more here;—With whom can I dwell? I rest alone.

How beautiful was the pillow of horn! How splendid was the embroidered coverlet[1]! The man of my admiration is no more here;—With whom can I dwell? Alone (I wait for) the morning.

Through the (long) days of summer, Through the (long) nights of winter (shall I be alone), Till the lapse of a hundred years, When I shall go home to his abode.

Through the (long) nights of winter, Through the (long) days of summer (shall I be alone), Till the lapse of a hundred years, When I shall go home to his chamber.

Book XI. The Odes of *Kh*in.

The state of *Kh*in took its name from its earliest principal city, in the present district of *Kh*ing-shui, in *Kh*in *K*âu, Kan-sû. Its chiefs claimed to be descended from Yî, who appears in the Shû as the forester of Shun, and the assistant of the great Yü in his labours on the flood of Yâo. The history of his descendants is very imperfectly related till we come to a Fei-ȝze, who had charge of the herds of horses belonging to king Hsiâo (B.C. 909–895), and in consequence of his good services was invested with

[1] These things had been ornaments of the bridal chamber; and as the widow thinks of them, her grief becomes more intense.

the small territory of *Kh*in, as an attached state. A descendant of his, known as duke Hsiang, in consequence of his loyal services, when the capital was moved to the east in B.C. 770, was raised to the dignity of an earl, and took his place among the great feudal princes of the kingdom, receiving also a large portion of territory, which included the ancient capital of the House of *K*âu. In course of time *Kh*in, as is well known, superseded the dynasty of *K*âu, having gradually moved its capital more and more to the east. The people of *Kh*in were, no doubt, mainly composed of the wild tribes of the west.

ODE 6, STANZA 1. THE HWANG NIÂO.

LAMENT FOR THREE WORTHIES OF *KH*IN, WHO WERE BURIED IN THE SAME GRAVE WITH DUKE MÛ.

There is no difficulty or difference in the interpretation of this piece; and it brings us down to B.C. 621. Then died duke Mû, after playing an important part in the north-west of China for thirty-nine years. The Ʒo *K*wan, under the sixth year of duke Wăn, makes mention of Mû's requiring that the three brothers here celebrated should be buried with him, and of the composition of this piece in consequence. Sze-mâ *Kh*ien says that this barbarous practice began with Mû's predecessor, with whom sixty-six persons were buried alive, and that one hundred and seventy-seven in all were buried with Mû. The death of the last distinguished man of the House of *Kh*in, the emperor I, was subsequently celebrated by the entombment with him of all the inmates of his harem.

They flit about, the yellow birds, And rest upon the jujube trees[1]. Who followed duke Mû in the grave? Ʒze-*k*ü Yen-hsî. And this Yen-hsî Was a man above a hundred. When he came to the

[1] It is difficult to see the relation between these two allusive lines and the rest of the stanza. Some say that it is this,—that the people loved the three victims as they liked the birds; others that the birds among the trees were in their proper place,—very different from the brothers in the grave of duke Mû.

grave, He looked terrified and trembled. Thou azure Heaven there! Could he have been redeemed, We would have given a hundred (ordinary) men for him[1].

Book XV. The Odes of Pin.

Duke Liû, an ancestor of the *K*âu family, made a settlement, according to its traditions, in B.C. 1797, in Pin, the site of which is pointed out, 90 lî to the west of the present district city of San-shui, in Pin *K*âu, Shen-hsî, where the tribe remained till the movement eastwards of Than-fû, celebrated in the first decade of the Major Odes of the Kingdom, ode 3. The duke of *K*âu, during the minority of king *Kh*ăng, made, it is supposed, the first of the pieces in this Book, describing for the instruction of the young monarch, the ancient ways of their fathers in Pin; and subsequently some one compiled other odes made by the duke, and others also about him, and brought them together under the common name of 'the Odes of Pin.'

Ode 1, Stanza 8. The *Kh*î Yüeh.

DESCRIBING LIFE IN PIN IN THE OLDEN TIME; THE PROVIDENT ARRANGEMENTS THERE TO SECURE THE CONSTANT SUPPLY OF FOOD AND RAIMENT,—WHATEVER WAS NECESSARY FOR THE SUPPORT AND COMFORT OF THE PEOPLE.

If the piece was made, as the Chinese critics all suppose, by the duke of *K*âu, we must still suppose that he writes in the person of an old farmer or yeoman of Pin. The picture which it gives of the manners of the Chinese people, their thrifty, provident ways, their agriculture and weaving, nearly 3700 years ago, is

---

[1] This appeal to Heaven is like what we met with in the first of the Odes of the Royal Domain, and the eighth of those of Thang.

full of interest; but it is not till we come to the concluding stanza that we find anything bearing on their religious practices.

In the days of (our) second month, they hew out the ice with harmonious blows[1]; And in those of (our) third month, they convey it to the ice-houses, (Which they open) in those of (our) fourth, early in the morning A lamb having been offered in sacrifice with scallions[2]. In the ninth month, it is cold, with frost. In the tenth month, they sweep clean their stack-sites. (Taking) the two bottles of spirits to be offered to their ruler, And having killed their lambs and sheep, They go to his hall, And raising

[1] They went for the ice to the deep recesses of the hills, and wherever it was to be found in the best condition.

[2] It is said in the last chapter of 'the Great Learning,' that 'the family which keeps its stores of ice does not rear cattle or sheep,' meaning that the possessor of an ice-house must be supposed to be very wealthy, and above the necessity of increasing his means in the way described. Probably, the having ice-houses by high ministers and heads of clans was an innovation on the earlier custom, according to which such a distinction was proper only to the king, or the princes of states, on whom it devolved as 'the fathers of the people,' to impart from their stores in the hot season as might be necessary. The third and fourth lines of this stanza are to be understood of what was done by the orders of the ruler of the tribe of *K*âu in Pin. In the Official Book of *K*âu, Part I, ch. 5, we have a description of the duties of 'the Providers of Ice,' and the same subject is treated in the sixth Book of 'the Record of Rites,' sections 2 and 6. The ice having been collected and stored in winter, the ice-houses were solemnly opened in the spring. A sacrifice was offered to 'the Ruler of Cold, the Spirit of the Ice,' and of the first ice brought forth an offering was set out in the apartment behind the principal hall of the ancestral temple. A sacrifice to the same Ruler of Cold, it is said, had also been offered when the ice began to be collected. The ceremony may be taken as an illustration of the manner in which religious services entered into the life of the ancient Chinese.

the cup of rhinoceros horn, Wish him long life,—that he may live for ever[1].

---

[1] The custom described in the five concluding lines is mentioned to show the good and loyal feeling of the people of Pin towards their chief. Having finished all the agricultural labours of the year, and being now prepared to enjoy the results of their industry, the first thing they do is to hasten to the hall of their ruler, and ask him to share in their joy, and express their loyal wishes for his happiness.

THE HSIÂO KING

OR

CLASSIC OF FILIAL PIETY.

THE HSIÂO KING

OR

CLASSIC OF FILIAL PIETY.

INTRODUCTION.

CHAPTER I.

THE NAME OF THE CLASSIC; ITS EXISTENCE BEFORE THE HAN DYNASTY; ITS CONTENTS, AND BY WHOM IT WAS WRITTEN.

1. The Chinese character pronounced Hsiâo, which we translate by 'Filial Piety,' and which may also perform the part of an adjective, 'filial,' of a verb, 'to be filial,' or of an adverb, 'filially,' is one of the composite characters whose meaning is suggested by the meanings of their constituent parts combined together. It is made up of two others,—one signifying 'an old man' or 'old age,' and beneath it the character signifying 'a son.' It thus, according to the Shwo Wăn, the oldest Chinese dictionary (A. D. 100), presents to the eye 'a son bearing up an old man,' that is, a child supporting his parent. Hsiâo also enters as their phonetical element into at least twenty other characters, so that it must be put down as of very early formation. The character King has been explained in the Introduction to the Shû King, p. 2; and the title, Hsiâo King, means 'the Classic of Filial Piety.'

Meaning of the character Hsiâo.

2. Many Chinese critics contend that this brief treatise was thus designated by Confucius himself, and that it received the distinction of being styled a King before

any of the older and more important classics. For the preservation of the text as we now have it, we are indebted to Hsüan 3ung (A. D. 713–755), one of the emperors of the Thang dynasty. In the preface to his commentary on it there occurs this sentence:—'The Master said, "My aim is seen in the *Kh*un *Kh*iû; my (rule of) conduct is in the Hsiâo King."' The imperial author quotes the saying, as if it were universally acknowledged to have come from the sage. It is found at a much earlier date in the preface of Ho Hsiû (A. D. 129–182) to his commentary on the *Kh*un *Kh*iû as transmitted and annotated by Kung-yang. The industry of scholars has traced it still farther back, and in a more extended form, to a work called Hsiâo King *K*ü-ming *K*üeh,—a production, probably, of the first century of our era, or of the century before it. It was one of a class of writings on the classical books, full of mysterious and useless speculations, that never took rank among the acknowledged expositions. Most of them soon disappeared, but this subsisted down to the Sui dynasty (A. D. 581–618), for there was a copy of it then in the Imperial Library. It is now lost, but a few passages of it have been collected from quotations in the Han writers. Among them is this:—'Confucius said, "If you wish to see my aim in dispensing praise or blame to the feudal lords, it is to be found in the *Kh*un *Kh*iû; the courses by which I would exalt the social relations are in the Hsiâo King."' The words thus ascribed to Confucius were condensed, it is supposed, into the form in which we have them,—first from Ho Hsiû, and afterwards from the emperor Hsüan 3ung. Whether they were really used by the sage or not, they were attributed to him as early as the beginning of our Christian era, and it was then believed that he had given to our classic the honourable name of a King.

Was the treatise called the Hsiâo King by Confucius?

3. But the existence of the Hsiâo King can be traced several hundred years farther back;—to within less than a century after the death of Confucius. Sze-mâ *Kh*ien, in his history of the House of Wei, one of the three marquisates into which the

The Hsiâo King existed before the Han dynasty.

great state of *K*in was broken up in the fifth century B.C., tells us that the marquis Wăn received, in B.C. 407, the classical books from Pû Ȝze-hsiâ, and mentions the names of two other disciples of Confucius, with whom he was on intimate terms of friendship. There remains the title of a commentary on the Hsiâo King by this marquis Wăn; and the book was existing in the time of Ȝhâi Yung (A.D. 133-192), who gives a short extract from it in one of his treatises.

The contents of the classic, and by whom it was written.

4. The recovery of our classic after the fires of *Kh*in will be related in the next chapter. Assuming here that it was recovered, we look into it, and find a conversation, or memoranda, perhaps, of several conversations, between Confucius and his disciple Ȝăng-ȝze. The latter, however, is little more than a listener, to whom the sage delivers his views on Filial Piety in its various relations. There are two recensions of the text;—one in eighteen chapters, and the other in twenty-two. As edited in eighteen chapters, each of them has a very brief descriptive heading. I have given this in the subjoined translation, but the headings cannot be traced back beyond the commentary of the emperor Hsüan.

The saying attributed by Ho Hsiû and others to Confucius would seem to indicate that he had himself composed the work, but the reader of it sees at once that it could not have proceeded from him. Nor do the style and method of the treatise suggest a view which has had many advocates,—that it was written by Ȝăng-ȝze, under the direction of the master. There is no reason, however, why we should not accept the still more common account,—that the Hsiâo came from the school of Ȝăng-ȝze. To use the words of Hû Yin, an author of the first half of our twelfth century:—'The Classic of Filial Piety was not made by Ȝăng-ȝze himself. When he retired from his conversation (or conversations) with *K*ung-nî on the subject of Filial Piety, he repeated to the disciples of his own school what (the master) had said, and they classified the sayings, and formed the treatise.'

CHAPTER II.

THE RECOVERY OF THE HSIÂO KING UNDER THE HAN DYNASTY, AND ITS PRESERVATION DOWN TO THE PUBLICATION OF THE COMMENTARY OF THE THANG EMPEROR HSÜAN ȜUNG.

1. The Hsiâo King suffered, like all the other Confucian books except the Yî, from the fires of *Kh*in. Its subsequent recovery was very like that of the Shû, described on pp. 7, 8. We have in each case a shorter and a longer copy, a modern text and an ancient text.

In the Catalogue of the Imperial Library, prepared by Liû Hin immediately before the commencement of our Christian era, there are two copies of the Hsiâo:—'the old text of the Khung family,' which was in twenty-two chapters, according to a note by Pan Kû (died A. D. 92), the compiler of the documents in the records of the western Han; and another copy, which was, according to the same authority, in eighteen chapters, and was subsequently styled 'the modern text.' Immediately following the entry of these two copies, we find 'Expositions of the Hsiâo by four scholars,'—whose surnames were *K*ang-sun, *K*iang, Yî, and Hâu. 'They all,' says Pan Kû, 'had laboured on the shorter text.'

Recovery of the Hsiâo King.

The copy in eighteen chapters therefore, we must presume, had been the first recovered; but of how this came about we have no account till we come to the records of the Suì dynasty. There it is said that, when the *Kh*in edict for the destruction of the books was issued, his copy of the Hsiâo was hidden by a scholar called Yen *K*ih, a member, doubtless, of the Yen family to which Confucius' favourite disciple Yen Hui had belonged. When the edict was abrogated in a few years, *K*ăn, a son of *K*ih, brought the copy from its hiding-place. This must have been in the second century B. C., and the copy, transcribed, probably by *K*ăn, in the form of the characters then used, would pass into the charge of the board of 'great scholars' appointed to preserve the

The shorter or modern text.

ancient books, in the reigns of the emperors Wăn and *K*ing, B.C. 179–141.

The old or longer text.

The copy in the ancient text was derived from the tablets found in the wall of the Confucian house in the time of the emperor Wû (B.C. 140–87), and is commonly said to have been deciphered, as in the case of the tablets of the Shû, by Khung An-kwo. An-kwo wrote a commentary himself on the Hsiâo, which does not appear in Hin's Catalogue, just as no mention is made there of his commentary on the Shû. We find it entered, however, among the books in the Sui Library with the following note:—'The work of An-kwo disappeared during the troubles of the Liang dynasty (A.D. 502-556), and continued unknown till the time of Sui, when a copy was found in the capital, and came into the possession of a scholar called Liû Hsüan.' Hsüan made his treasure public, and ere long it was acknowledged by the court, while many scholars contended that it was a forgery of his own, and ascribed by him to An-kwo. Whatever opinion we may form on this matter, the discovery of the old text, and the production of a commentary on it by Khung An-kwo, can hardly be called in question.

Was another copy in the old text discovered?

It might be argued, indeed, that another copy in the old text was found in the first century B.C. In a memorial addressed about the Shwo Wăn dictionary to the emperor An, in A.D. 121, by Hsü *K*ung, a son of the author, he says that the Hsiâo King which his father used was a copy of that presented, by 'a very old man of Lû,' to the emperor *K*âo (B.C. 86–74)[1]. Many Chinese critics, and especially Wang Ying-lin

[1] The language of the memorial is:—'The Hsiâo King' (used by my father in the composition of his dictionary) 'was what San lâo of Lû presented in the time of the emperor *K*âo.' The San lâo most readily suggests to the reader the idea of 'three old men;' but the characters may also mean, in harmony with Chinese idiom, 'the three classes of old men,' or 'an individual from those three classes.' The classical passage to explain the phrase is par. 18 in the first section of the sixth Book in the Lî *K*î, where it is said that king Wăn feasted the San lâo and Wû kang, 'the three classes of old men and five classes of men of experience,' in his royal college. The three classes of old men were such as were over 80, 90, and 100 years respectively. It was from a man of one of these classes that the emperor received the Hsiâo in the old

(better known as Wang Po-hâu, A.D. 1223–1296), say that this is a different account of the recovery of the old text from that with which the name of Khung An-kwo is connected. It is difficult to reconcile the two statements, as will be seen on a reference to the note below[1]; and yet it

text. According to the account given in the next note this man was Khung 3ze-hui; and in the Books of Sui that is given as the name of the individual of the Khung family, who had hidden the tablets on the appearance of the *Kh*in edict for the destruction of all the old books.

[1] The Catalogue Raisonné of the Imperial Libraries commences its account of the copies of the Hsiâo with a description of 'the Old Text of the Hsiâo with the Commentary of Khung An-kwo,' obtained from Japan; but the editors give good reasons for doubting its genuineness. There is a copy of this work in the Chinese portion of the British Museum, an edition printed in Japan in 1732, which I have carefully examined, with the help of Professor R. K. Douglas and Mr. A. Wylie. It contains not only the commentary of Khung An-kwo, but what purports to be the original preface of that scholar. There it is said that the bamboo tablets of the copy in 'tadpole characters,' found in the wall of Confucius' old 'lecture hall, in a stone case,' were presented to the emperor by Khung 3ze-hui, 'a very old man of Lû.' The emperor, it is added, caused two copies to be made in the current characters of the time by 'the great scholars,' one of which was given to 3ze-hui, and the other to General Ho Kwang, a minister of war and favourite, who greatly valued it, and placed it among the archives of the empire, where it was jealously guarded.

This account makes the meaning of the phrase 'the San lâo of Lû' quite clear; but there are difficulties in the way of our believing that it proceeded from Khung An-kwo. No mention is made of him in it, whereas, according to the current narrations, the tablets with the tadpole characters were first deciphered by him; nor is the name of the emperor to whom Khung 3ze-hui presented the tablets given. No doubt, however, this emperor was *K*âo, with whom Ho Kwang was a favourite. If the preface were genuine, of course An-kwo was alive after 3ze-hui went to court with the tablets. Now, the tablets were discovered in the period Thien-han, B.C. 100–97, and *K*âo reigned from B.C. 86 to 74. An-kwo died at the age of sixty, but in what year we are not told. He had studied the Shih under Shăn Kung, whose death can hardly be placed later than in B.C. 135. If An-kwo were born in B.C. 150, he would have been more than sixty years old—the age assigned to him at his death—at the accession of *K*âo. I cannot believe, therefore, that the preface in the Japanese Hsiâo was written by him; and if we reject the preface, we must also reject the commentary before which it stands.

The text of the Hsiâo in the work is nearly identical with that of Sze-mâ Kwang, mentioned below on p. 458; but to the chapters there are prefixed the headings (which Kwang did not adopt), that cannot be traced farther back than the Thang dynasty. This might be got over, but the commentary throws no new light on the text. 'It is shallow and poor,' say the editors of the Catalogue Raisonné, 'and not in the style of the Han scholars.' I must think with them that Khung An-kwo's commentary, purporting to have been preserved in Japan, is a forgery.

is possible that the difficulty would disappear, if the details of the discovery and the subsequent dealing with the tablets had come down to us complete.

Certainly, in the first century B.C. there were two copies of the Hsiâo King in the Imperial Library of Han. If those copies, catalogued by Liû Hin, were the actual text, presented by Yen *K*ăn, and a faithful transcript in the current Han characters of the ancient text discovered in the wall of Confucius' old lecture hall, we should be able to say that the evidence for the recovery of the Hsiâo, as it had existed during the *K*âu dynasty, was as satisfactory as we could desire; but there are some considerations that are in the way of our doing so.

Can we rely fully on the copies catalogued by Liû Hin?

According to the records of Sui, after the old text came into the possession of the court, and the differences between it and the text earlier recovered were observed, Liû Hsiang (B.C. 80–9), the father of Hin, was charged by the emperor (*Kh*ăng, B.C. 32–7) to compare the two. The result of his examination of them was that 'he removed from the modern text what was excessive and erroneous, and fixed the number of the chapters at eighteen.' It does not appear that previously there was any division of *K*ăn's copy into chapters. What Hsiang did in the case of the old text we are not told. A note by Yen Sze-kû of the Thang dynasty, appended to Hin's Catalogue, quotes from him that 'one chapter of the modern text was divided into two in the old, another into three, and that the old had one chapter which did not appear in the other.' This missing chapter, it is understood, was the one beginning, 'Inside the smaller doors leading to the inner apartments,' which I have appended, from the current old text, to my translation of the classic as published by Hsüan Ȝung; and yet the Sui account says that that chapter was in the Hsiâo of *K*ang-sun, one of the four early commentators on the modern text.

The copies catalogued by Hin were made after the examination and revision of the two texts by his father. There are suspicious resemblances between the style and method of the present classic and those of the original works of

Hsiang that have come down to us. It is impossible to say, from the want of information, what liberties he took with the documents put into his charge. The differences between the two texts as we now have them are trivial. I believe that the changes made in them by Hsiang were not important; but having them as they came from his revision, we have them at second hand, and this has afforded ground for the dealing with them by *K*û Hsî and others in the manner which will be described in the next chapter.

From Khung An-kwo to the emperor Hsüan Ȝung.

2. I have said above (p. 450) that for the text of the classic,—the modern text, that is,—as we now have it, we are indebted to the labours of the emperor Hsüan Ȝung of the Thang dynasty. *K*û Î-tsun, of the *Kh*ien-lung period (1736–1795), in his work on the classics and the writings on them, has adduced the titles of eighty-six different works on our classic, that appeared between Khung An-kwo and Hsüan Ȝung. Not a single one of all these now survives; but the enumeration of them shows that the most distinguished scholars during the intervening centuries exercised their powers on the treatise, and would keep a watch on one another in the preservation of the text. Moreover, several of the works continued through the Thang dynasty, and on into that of Sung. The Catalogue of the Sui Library contains the titles of nineteen in its list.

Hsüan Ȝung's work.

The emperor Hsüan says, in his preface, that in the making of his commentary he had freely used the commentaries of six earlier writers, whom he names. They were, Wei *K*âo, Wang Sû, Yü Fan, and Liû Shâo, all of our second and third centuries; Liû Hsüan, of our sixth century, who laboured on the commentary of Khung An-kwo, which, as I have already stated, is said to have been discovered in his time and presented to him; and Lû *Kh*ang, rather earlier than Liû, who dealt critically with the commentary attributed to *K*ăng Khang-*kh*ăng. 'But,' says the imperial author, 'if a comment be right in reason, why need we enquire from whom it came? We have therefore taken those six writers, considered wherein they agreed and differed, and decided between their interpretations by reference to the general scope of the five (great) King. In compendious style, but with extensive examination of the subject, we have made the meaning of the classic clear.'

The emperor says nothing himself about the differences between the ancient and modern texts, though we know that that subject was vehemently agitated among the scholars of his court. The text as commented on by him is in eighteen chapters, which do not include the chapter to which I have referred on p. 455 as having been in the copy of *K*ang-sun in the first century B.C. It is said, and on sufficient authority, that this chapter was excluded through the influence of the scholar and minister Sze-mâ *K*ăn. To each of his chapters the emperor prefixed a brief heading or argument, which I have retained in the translation. These headings, probably, were selected by him from a variety proposed by the scholars about the court.

The text employed in this imperial commentary might now be considered as sufficiently secured. It was engraved, in less than a century after, on the stone tablets of Thang, which were completed in the year 837, and set up in Hsî-an, the Thang capital, where they remain, very little damaged, to this day[1]. And not only so. The emperor was so pleased with the commentary which he had made, that he caused the whole of it to be engraved on four large tablets or pillars of stone in 745. They are still to be seen at Hsî-an, in front of the Confucian College.

[1] These tablets are commonly said to contain the thirteen classics (Shih-san King). They contained, however, only twelve different works,—the Yî, the Shû, the Shih, the *K*âu Lî, the Î Lî, the Lî *K*î, and the amplifications of the *Kh*un *Kh*iû,—by 3o *Kh*iû-ming, by Kung-yang, and by Kû-liang. These form 'the nine King.' In addition to these there were the Lun Yü, the Hsiâo King, and the *R*' Yâ. According to Kû Yen-wû (1613-1682), the characters on the tablets were in all 650,252. Mr. T. W. Rhys Davids (Buddhism, p. 19) estimates that our English Bible contains between 900,000 and 950,000 words. The first Psalm, in what is called the Delegates' version, very good and concise, contains 100 Chinese characters, and in our English version 130 words. The classics of the Thang tablets, if the translator were a master of both languages, might be rendered in English so as to form a volume not quite so large as our Bible.

It is hardly necessary to say more on the preservation of the Hsiâo King. In A. D. 996 the second emperor of the Sung dynasty gave orders for an annotated edition of it to be prepared. This was finally completed in 1001, under the superintendence of Hsing Ping (932–1010), with a large critical apparatus, and a lengthened exposition, both of the text and of Hsüan Ȝung's explanation. This work has ever since been current in China.

The work of Hsing Ping.

CHAPTER III.

CRITICISM OF THE HSIÂO SINCE THE THANG DYNASTY.

1. Notwithstanding the difficulty about one chapter which has been pointed out on p. 455, Hsüan Ȝung's text was generally accepted as the representative of that in modern characters, recovered in the second century B. C. There were still those, however, who continued to advocate the claims of 'the old text.' Sze-mâ Kwang, a distinguished minister and scholar of the Sung dynasty (1009–1086), presented to the court in 1054 his 'Explanations of the Hsiâo King according to the Old Text,' arguing, in his preface and in various memorials, for the correctness of that text, as recovered by Liû Hsüan in the sixth century. Fan Ȝû-yü (1041–1098), a scholar of the same century, and in other things a collaborateur of Kwang, produced, towards the end of his life, an 'Exposition of the Hsiâo King according to the Old Text.' He says in his preface:—'Though the agreement between the ancient and modern texts is great, and the difference small, yet the ancient deserves to be preferred, and my labour upon it may not be without some little value [1].'

Works on the old text by Sze-mâ Kwang and Fan Ȝû-yü.

[1] In the Hsiâo King, as now frequently published in China, either separately by itself, or bound up with *K*û Hsî's Hsiâo Hsio, 'the Teaching for the Young,' we find the old text, without distinction of chapters. The commentaries of Hsüan Ȝung and Sze-mâ Kwang, and the exposition of Fan Ȝû-yü, however, follow one another at the end of the several clauses and paragraphs.

Sceptical criticism. Views of *K*û Hsî.

2. But our classic had still to pass the ordeal of the sceptical criticism that set in during the Sung dynasty. The most notable result of this was 'the Hsiâo King Expurgated,' published by *K*û Hsî in 1186. He tells us that when he first saw a statement by Hû Hung (a minister in the reign of Kâo Ʒung, 1127–1162), that the quotations from the Book of Poetry in the Hsiâo were probably of later introduction into the text, he was terror-struck. Prolonged examination, however, satisfied him that there were good grounds for Hû's statement, and that other portions of the text were also open to suspicion. He found, moreover, that another earlier writer, Wang Ying-*kh*ăn, in the reign of Hsiâo Ʒung (1163–1189), had come to the conclusion that much of the Hsiâo had been fabricated or interpolated in the Han dynasty. The way was open for him to give expression to his convictions, without incurring the charge of being the first to impugn the accepted text.

The fact was, as pointed out by the editors of the Catalogue Raisonné of the Imperial Library of the present dynasty, that *K*û had long entertained the views which he indicated in his expurgated edition of the Hsiâo, and his references to Hû and Wang were simply to shield his own boldness. He divided the treatise into one chapter of classical text, and fourteen chapters of illustration and commentary. But both parts were freely expurgated. His classical text embraces the first six chapters in my translation, and is supposed by him to form one continuous discourse by Confucius. The rest of the treatise should not be attributed to the sage at all. The bulk of it may have come from Ʒăng-ʒze, or from members of his school, but large interpolations were made by the Han scholars. Adopting the old text, *K*û discarded from it altogether 223 characters.

Attention will be called, under the several chapters, to

Some portions also are in a different order from the arrangement of Hsüan Ʒung and Hsing Ping, which I have followed in my translation. As has been already said, the difference between its text and that of the Thang emperor is slight,—hardly greater than the variations in the different recensions of our Gospels and the other books of the New Testament.

some of the passages which he suppressed, and to the reasons, generally satisfactory, which he advanced for his procedure. Evidently he was influenced considerably by the way in which *Kh*ăng Î (1033-1107), whom he called 'his master,' had dealt with the old text of 'the Great Learning;' but he made his innovations with a bolder pencil and on a more extensive plan, not merely altering the arrangement of paragraphs, and supplementing what was plainly defective, but challenging the genuineness of large portions of the treatise, and removing them without scruple.

Under the Yüan dynasty, Wû *Kh*ăng (1249-1333), the greatest of its scholars, followed in the wake of *K*û Hsî, yet with the independence characteristic of himself. As *K*û had preferred the old text, Wû decided—and, I believe, more correctly—in favour of the modern, arguing that the copy of Khung An-kwo's text and commentary, said to have been recovered and published in the sixth century by Liû Hsüan, was a fabrication. He adopted, therefore, Hsüan Ȝung's text as the basis of his revision, which appeared with the title of 'the Hsiâo King, in paragraphs and sentences[1].' He adopted *K*û's division of the treatise into classical text and commentary. The chapter of classical text is the same as *K*û's; the chapters of commentary are only twelve. He discarded, of course, the chapter peculiar to the old text, which has been referred to more than once, united Hsüan Ȝung's eleventh chapter with another, and arranged the other chapters differently from *K*û. His revision altogether had 246 characters fewer than the old text.

Views of Wû *Kh*ăng.

3. *K*û Î-tsun gives the titles of nearly 120 works on our classic that appeared after the volume of Wû *Kh*ăng, bringing its literary history down to the end of the Ming dynasty. The scholars of the present dynasty have not been less abundant in their labours on it than their predecessors. Among the col-

Later works on the Hsiâo.

[1] The title of this work in the Catalogue of the Imperial Libraries is 'Settlement of the Text of the Hsiâo King.'

lected works of Mâo *Kh*î-ling (1623–1713) is one called 'Questions about the Hsiâo King,' in which, with his usual ability, and, it must be added, his usual acrimony, he defends the received text. He asserts—and in this he is correct—that there is no difference of any importance between the ancient and modern texts; when he asserts further that there never was any such difference, what he affirms is incapable of proof. He pours scorn on *K*û Hsî and Wû *Kh*ăng; but he is not so successful in defending the integrity of the Hsiâo as I have allowed him to be in vindicating the portions of the Shû that we owe to Khung An-kwo.

The Hsiâo King has always been a favourite with the emperors of China. Before Hsüan Ȝung took it in hand, the first and eighth emperors of the eastern *K*in dynasty (317–419), the first and third of the Liang (502–556), and the ninth of the northern Wei (386–534) had published their labours upon it. The Manchâu rulers of the present dynasty have signalised themselves in this department. In 1656 the first emperor produced in one chapter his 'Imperial Commentary on the Hsiâo King,' and in 1728 the third published a 'Collection of Comments' on it. Between them was the long reign known to us as the Khang-hsî period (1662–1722), during which there appeared under the direction of the second emperor, the most distinguished of his line, his 'Extensive Explanation of the Hsiâo King,' in 100 chapters. The only portion of the text which it gives in full is *K*û Hsî's chapter of Confucian text; but most of the topics touched on in *K*û's supplementary chapters, added, as he supposed, by some later hand, are dealt with in the course of the work, the whole of which will amply repay a careful study.

Conclusion regarding the genuineness and integrity of the Hsiâo.

4. It will have been seen that the two great scholars, *K*û Hsî and Wû *Kh*ăng, who have taken the greatest liberties with the text of our classic, allow that there is a Confucian element in it, and that more than a fifth part of the whole, containing, even as expurgated by *K*û, about 400 characters, may be correctly ascribed to the sage. I agree with them

in this. All the rest of the treatise, to whomsoever it may be ascribed, from Ȝăng-ȝze, the immediate disciple of Confucius, down to Liû Hsiang (B.C. 80–9), took its present form in the first century before our Christian era. The reader will fail to see in it a close connexion between the different chapters, and think that the author or authors try to make more of Filial Piety than can be made of it. The whole, however, is a valuable monument of antiquity, and an exhibition of the virtue which Chinese moralists and rulers, from the most ancient times, have delighted to celebrate as the fundamental principle of human virtue, the great source of social happiness, and the bond of national strength and stability.

Note on the Translation.

In preparing the translation of the Hsiâo King for the present work, I have made frequent reference to four earlier translations.

Two of them were made by myself;—the one about thirty years ago, simply as an exercise for my own improvement in Chinese; the other four years ago, when I was anxious to understand fully the Confucian teaching on the subject of Filial Piety, but without reference to my earlier version.

The third is a translation in the fourth volume of the Chinese Repository, pp. 345–353 (1835), for the accuracy of which much cannot be said. Very few notes are appended to it. The fourth is in the 'Mémoires concernant les Chinois' (Paris, 1779), being part of a long treatise on the 'Ancient and Modern Doctrine of the Chinese about Filial Piety,' by P. Cibot. In a preliminary notice to his version of our classic, he says:—'P. Noel formerly translated the Hsiâo King into Latin. Our translation will necessarily be different from his. He laboured on the old text, and we on the new, which the scholars of the Imperial College have adopted. Besides this, he has launched out into paraphrase, and we have made it our business to present the text in French such as it is in Chinese.' I have not been able to refer to P. Noël's translation in preparing that now given to the public; but I had his work before me when writing out my earliest version. The difference between the old and modern texts is too slight to affect the character of translations of them, but P. Noël's version is decidedly periphrastic. The title of his work is:—'SINENSIS IMPERII LIBRI CLASSICI SEX, nimirum Adultorum Schola, Immutabile Medium, Liber sententiarum, Mencius, Filialis Observantia, Parvulorum Schola, e Sinico idiomate in Latinum traducti à P. Fr. Noël, S. J. (Prague, 1711).' The present version, I believe, gives the text in English, such as it is in Chinese, more accurately and closely than P. Cibot's does in French.

THE HSIÂO KING.

Chapter I.

The Scope and Meaning of the Treatise.

(Once), when *K*ung-nî[1] was unoccupied, and his disciple 3ăng[2] was sitting by in attendance on him, the Master said, 'Shăn, the ancient kings had a perfect virtue and all-embracing rule of conduct, through which they were in accord with all under heaven. By the practice of it the people were brought to live in peace and harmony, and there was no ill-will between superiors and inferiors. Do you know what it was[3]?' 3ăng rose from his mat, and said, 'How

---

[1] *K*ung-nî was the designation or marriage-name of Confucius. We find it twice in the Doctrine of the Mean (chh. 2 and 30), applied to the sage by 3ze-sze, his grandson, the reputed author of that treatise. By his designation, it is said, a grandson might speak of his grandfather, and therefore some scholars contend that the Classic of Filial Piety should also be ascribed to 3ze-sze; but such a canon cannot be considered as sufficiently established. On the authorship of the Classic, see the Introduction, p. 451.

[2] 3ăng-ȝze, named Shăn, and styled 3ze-yü, was one of the most distinguished of the disciples of Confucius. He was a favourite with the sage, and himself a voluminous writer. Many incidents and sayings are related, illustrative of his filial piety, so that it was natural for the master to enter with him on the discussion of that virtue. He shares in the honour and worship still paid to Confucius, and is one of his 'Four Assessors' in his temples.

[3] Both the translator in the Chinese Repository and P. Cibot have rendered this opening address of Confucius very imperfectly.

should I, Shăn, who am so devoid of intelligence, be able to know this?' The Master said, '(It was filial piety). Now filial piety is the root of (all) virtue[1], and (the stem) out of which grows (all moral) teaching. Sit down again, and I will explain the subject to you. Our bodies—to every hair and bit of skin—are received by us from our parents, and we must not presume to injure or wound them:—this is the beginning of filial piety. When we have established our character by the practice of the (filial) course, so as to make our name famous in future ages, and thereby glorify our parents:—this is the end of filial piety. It commences with the service

---

The former has:—'Do you understand how the ancient kings, who possessed the greatest virtue and the best moral principles, rendered the whole empire so obedient that the people lived in peace and harmony, and no ill-will existed between superiors and inferiors?' The other:—'Do you know what was the pre-eminent virtue and the essential doctrine which our ancient monarchs taught to all the empire, to maintain concord among their subjects, and banish all dissatisfaction between superiors and inferiors?' P. Cibot comes the nearer to the meaning of the text, but he has neglected the characters corresponding to 'through which they were in accord with all under heaven,' that are expounded clearly enough by Hsüan Ʒung. The sentiment of the sage is, as he has tersely expressed it in the Doctrine of the Mean (ch. 13), that the ancient kings 'governed men, according to their nature, with what is proper to them.'

[1] 'All virtue' means the five virtuous principles, the constituents of humanity, 'benevolence, righteousness, propriety, knowledge, and fidelity.' Of these, benevolence is the chief and fundamental, so that Mencius says (VII, ii, ch. 16), 'Benevolence is man.' In man's nature, therefore, benevolence is the root of filial piety; while in practice filial piety is the root of benevolence. Such is the way in which *K*û Hsî and other critical scholars reconcile the statements of the text here and elsewhere with their theory as to the constituents of humanity.

of parents; it proceeds to the service of the ruler; it is completed by the establishment of the character.

'It is said in the Major Odes of the Kingdom,
"Ever think of your ancestor,
Cultivating your virtue[1]."'

Chapter II.

Filial Piety in the Son of Heaven.

He who loves his parents will not dare (to incur the risk of) being hated by any man, and he who reveres his parents will not dare (to incur the risk of) being contemned by any man[2]. When the love and reverence (of the Son of Heaven) are thus carried to the utmost in the service of his parents, the lessons of his virtue affect all the people, and he becomes

---

[1] See the Shih King, III, i, ode 2, stanza 4. *K*û Hsî commences his expurgation of our classic with casting out this concluding paragraph; and rightly so. Such quotations of the odes and other passages in the ancient classics are not after the manner of Confucius. The application made of them, moreover, is often far-fetched, and away from their proper meaning.

[2] The thing thus generally stated must be understood specially of the sovereign, and only he who stands related to all other men can give its full manifestation. Previous translators have missed the peculiarity of the construction in each of the clauses. Thus P. Cibot gives:—'He who loves his parents will not dare to hate any one,' &c. But in the second member we have a well-known form in Chinese to give the force of the passive voice. Attention is called to this in the Extensive Explanation of the Hsiâo (see p. 461):—'Wû yü zăn does not mean merely to hate men; it indicates an anxious apprehension lest the hatred of men should light on me, and my parents thereby be involved in it.'

a pattern to (all within) the four seas[1]:—this is the filial piety of the Son of Heaven[2].

It is said in (the Marquis of) Fû on Punishments[3], 'The One man will have felicity, and the millions of the people will depend on (what ensures his happiness).'

CHAPTER III.

FILIAL PIETY IN THE PRINCES OF STATES.

Above others, and yet free from pride, they dwell on high, without peril; adhering to economy, and carefully observant of the rules and laws, they are full, without overflowing. To dwell on high without peril is the way long to preserve nobility; to be full without overflowing is the way long to preserve riches. When their riches and nobility do not leave their persons, then they are able to preserve the altars of their land and grain, and to secure the harmony of their people and men in office[4]:—this is the filial piety of the princes of states.

---

[1] Chinese scholars make 'the people' to be the subjects of the king, and 'all within the four seas' to be the barbarous tribes outside the four borders of the kingdom, between them and the seas or oceans within which the habitable earth was contained—according to the earliest geographical conceptions. All we have to find in the language is the unbounded, the universal, influence of 'the Son of Heaven.'

[2] The appellation 'Son of Heaven' for the sovereign was unknown in the earliest times of the Chinese nation. It cannot be traced beyond the Shang dynasty.

[3] See the Shû, V, xxvii, 4, and the note on the name of that Book, p. 254.

[4] In the Chinese Repository we have for this:—'They will be able to protect their ancestral possessions with the produce of their lands;' 'They will make sure the supreme rank to their

It is said in the Book of Poetry[1],

'Be apprehensive, be cautious,
As if on the brink of a deep abyss,
As if treading on thin ice.'

CHAPTER IV. FILIAL PIETY IN HIGH MINISTERS AND GREAT OFFICERS.

They do not presume to wear robes other than those appointed by the laws of the ancient kings[2]; nor to speak words other than those sanctioned by their speech; nor to exhibit conduct other than that exemplified by their virtuous ways. Thus none of their words being contrary to those sanctions, and none of their actions contrary to the (right) way,

---

families.' But it is better to retain the style of the original. The king had a great altar to the spirit (or spirits) presiding over the land. The colour of the earth in the centre of it was yellow; that on each of its four sides differed according to the colours assigned to the four quarters of the sky. A portion of this earth was cut away, and formed the nucleus of a corresponding altar in each feudal state, according to their position relative to the capital. The prince of the state had the prerogative of sacrificing there. A similar rule prevailed for the altars to the spirits presiding over the grain. So long as a family ruled in a state, so long its chief offered those sacrifices; and the extinction of the sacrifices was an emphatic way of describing the ruin and extinction of the ruling House.

[1] See the Shih, II, v, ode 1, stanza 6.

[2] The articles of dress, to be worn by individuals according to their rank, from the sovereign downwards, in their ordinary attire, and on special occasions, were the subject of attention and enactment in China from the earliest times. We find references to them in the earliest books of the Shû (Part II, Books iii, iv). The words to be spoken, and conduct to be exhibited, on every varying occasion, could not be so particularly described; but the example of the ancient kings would suffice for these, as their enactments for the dress.

from their mouths there comes no exceptionable speech, and in their conduct there are found no exceptionable actions. Their words may fill all under heaven, and no error of speech will be found in them. Their actions may fill all under heaven, and no dissatisfaction or dislike will be awakened by them. When these three things—(their robes, their words, and their conduct)—are all complete as they should be, they can then preserve their ancestral temples[1]:—this is the filial piety of high ministers and great officers.

It is said in the Book of Poetry[2],

> 'He is never idle, day or night,
> In the service of the One man.'

Chapter V. Filial Piety in Inferior Officers.

As they serve their fathers, so they serve their mothers, and they love them equally. As they serve their fathers, so they serve their rulers, and they reverence them equally. Hence love is what is chiefly rendered to the mother, and reverence is what is chiefly rendered to the ruler, while both of these things are given to the father. Therefore when they serve their ruler with filial piety they are loyal; when they serve their superiors with reverence they are obedient. Not failing in this loyalty

[1] Their ancestral temples were to the ministers and grand officers what the altars of their land and grain were to the feudal lords. Every great officer had three temples or shrines, in which he sacrificed to the first chief of his family or clan; to his grandfather, and to his father. While these remained, the family remained, and its honours were perpetuated.

[2] See the Shih, III, iii, ode 6, stanza 4.

and obedience in serving those above them, they are then able to preserve their emoluments and positions, and to maintain their sacrifices[1]:—this is the filial piety of inferior officers[2].

It is said in the Book of Poetry[3],

'Rising early and going to sleep late,
Do not disgrace those who gave you birth.'

Chapter VI.

Filial Piety in the Common People.

They follow the course of heaven (in the revolving seasons); they distinguish the advantages

---

[1] These officers had their 'positions' or places, and their pay. They had also their sacrifices, but such as were private or personal to themselves, so that we have not much information about them.

[2] The Chinese Repository has here, 'Such is the influence of filial duty when performed by scholars;' and P. Cibot, 'Voilà sommairement ce qui caractérise la Piété Filiale du Lettré.' But to use the term 'scholar' here is to translate from the standpoint of modern China, and not from that of the time of Confucius. The Shih of feudal China were the younger sons of the higher classes, and men that by their ability were rising out of the lower, and who were all in inferior situations, and looking forward to offices of trust in the service of the royal court, or of their several states. Below the 'great officers' of ch. 4, three classes of Shih—the highest, middle, lowest—were recognised, all intended in this chapter. When the feudal system had passed away, the class of 'scholars' gradually took their place. Shih (士) is one of the oldest characters in Chinese, but the idea expressed in its formation is not known. Confucius is quoted in the Shwo Wăn as making it to be from the characters for one (一) and ten (十 . A very old definition of it is—'The denomination of one entrusted with affairs.'

[3] See the Shih, II, iii, ode 2, stanza 6.

afforded by (different) soils[1]; they are careful of their conduct and economical in their expenditure;—in order to nourish their parents:—this is the filial piety of the common people.

Therefore from the Son of Heaven down to the common people, there never has been one whose filial piety was without its beginning and end on whom calamity did not come.

Chapter VII.

Filial Piety in Relation to the Three Powers[2].

The disciple Ȝăng said, 'Immense indeed is the greatness of filial piety!' The Master replied[3],

---

[1] These two sentences describe the attention of the people to the various processes of agriculture, as conditioned by the seasons and the qualities of different soils.

With this chapter there ends what *K*û Hsî regarded as the only portion of the Hsiâo in which we can rest as having come from Confucius. So far, it is with him a continuous discourse that proceeded from the sage. And there is, in this portion, especially when we admit *K*û's expurgations, a certain sequence and progress, without logical connexion, in the exhibition of the subject which we fail to find in the chapters that follow.

[2] 'The Three Powers' is a phrase which is first found in two of the Appendixes to the Yî King, denoting Heaven, Earth, and Man, as the three great agents or agencies in nature, or the circle of being.

[3] The whole of the reply of Confucius here, down to 'the advantages afforded by earth,' is found in a narrative in the Ȝo *K*wan, under the twenty-fifth year of duke *Kh*âo (B.C. 517), with the important difference that the discourse is there about 'ceremonies,' and not about filial piety. Plainly, it is an interpolation in the Hsiâo, and is rightly thrown out by *K*û and Wû *Kh*ăng. To my own mind it was a relief to find that the passage was not genuine, and had not come from Confucius. The discourse in the Ȝo *K*wan, which is quite lengthy, these sentences being only the com-

'Yes, filial piety is the constant (method) of Heaven, the righteousness of Earth, and the practical duty of Man[1]. Heaven and earth invariably pursue the course (that may be thus described), and the people take it as their pattern. (The ancient kings) imitated the brilliant luminaries of heaven, and acted in accordance with the (varying) advantages afforded by earth, so that they were in accord with all under heaven; and in consequence their teachings, without being severe, were successful, and their government, without being rigorous, secured perfect order.

---

mencement of it, is more than sufficiently fanciful; but it is conceivable that what is here predicated of filial piety might be spoken of ceremonies, while I never could see what it could have to do with filial piety, or filial piety with it. After the long discourse in the Ȝo *K*wan one of the interlocutors in it exclaims, 'Immense, indeed, is the greatness of ceremonies!'—the same terms with which Ȝăng-ȝze is made to commence this chapter, saving that we have 'ceremonies' instead of 'filial piety.' There can be no doubt that the passage is interpolated; and yet the first part of it is quoted by Pan Kû (in our first century), in a note to Liû Hin's Catalogue, and also in the Amplification of the First Precept of the Khang-hsî Sacred Edict (in our eighteenth century). Pan Kû may not have been sufficiently acquainted with the Ȝo *K*wan to detect the forgery; that Chinese scholars should still quote the description as applicable to filial piety shows how liable they are to be carried away by fine-sounding terms and mysterious utterances.

P. Cibot gives a correct translation of the first part in a note, but adds that it carries the sense of the text much too high, and would bring it into collision with the prejudices of the west, and he has preferred to hold to the more common explanation:—'Ce qu'est la régularité des monuments des astres pour le firmament, la fertilité des campagnes pour la terre, la Piété Filiale l'est constamment pour les peuples!'

[1] An amusing translation of this sentence is found in Samuel Johnson's 'Oriental Religions, China,' p. 208, beginning, 'Filial Piety is the Book of Heaven!' Mr. Johnson does not say where he got this version.

'The ancient kings, seeing how their teachings [1] could transform the people, set before them therefore an example of the most extended love, and none of the people neglected their parents; they set forth to them (the nature of) virtue and righteousness, and the people roused themselves to the practice of them; they went before them with reverence and yielding courtesy, and the people had no contentions; they led them on by the rules of propriety and by music, and the people were harmonious and benignant; they showed them what they loved and what they disliked, and the people understood their prohibitions.

'It is said in the Book of Poetry [2],

"Awe-inspiring are you, O Grand-Master Yin,
And the people all look up to you."'

Chapter VIII. Filial Piety in Government.

The Master said, 'Anciently, when the intelligent kings by means of filial piety ruled all under heaven, they did not dare to receive with disrespect the ministers of small states;—how much less would they do so to the dukes, marquises, counts, and barons!' Thus it was that they got (the princes of) the myriad states with joyful hearts (to assist them) in the (sacrificial) services to their royal predecessors [3].

---

[1] Sze-mâ Kwang changes the character for 'teachings' here into that for 'filial piety.' There is no external evidence for such a reading; and the texture of the whole treatise is so loose that we cannot insist on internal evidence.

[2] See the Shih, II, iv, ode 7, stanza 1.

[3] Under the *K*âu dynasty there were five orders of nobility, and the states belonging to their rulers varied proportionally in size.

'The rulers of states did not dare to slight wifeless men and widows;—how much less would they slight their officers and the people! Thus it was that they got all their people with joyful hearts (to assist them) in serving the rulers, their predecessors [1].

'The heads of clans did not dare to slight their servants and concubines;—how much less would they slight their wives and sons! Thus it was that they got their men with joyful hearts (to assist them) in the service of their parents.

'In such a state of things, while alive, parents reposed in (the glory of) their sons; and, when sacrificed to, their disembodied spirits enjoyed their offerings [2]. Therefore all under heaven peace and harmony prevailed; disasters and calamities did not occur; misfortunes and rebellions did not arise.

'It is said in the Book of Poetry [3],

"To an upright, virtuous conduct
All in the four quarters of the state render obedient
homage."'

There were besides many smaller states attached to these. The feudal lords at stated times appeared at the royal court, and one important duty which then devolved on them was to take part in the sacrificial services of the sovereign in the ancestral temple.

[1] These services were also the sacrifices in the ancestral temples of the rulers of the states and of the chiefs of clans,—the feudal princes and the ministers and great officers of chapters 3 and 4.

[2] In the Chinese Repository we read here:—'Parents enjoyed tranquillity while they lived, and after their decease sacrifices were offered to their disembodied spirits.' To the same effect P. Cibot:—'Les pères et mères étoient heureux pendant la vie, et après leur mort leurs âmes étoient consolées par des Tsî (sacrifices).' I believe that I have caught the meaning more exactly.

[3] See the Shih, III, iii, ode 2, stanza 2.

Chapter IX. The Government of the Sages[1].

The disciple Ȝăng said, 'I venture to ask whether in the virtue of the sages there was not something greater than filial piety.' The Master replied, 'Of all (creatures with their different) natures produced by Heaven and Earth, man is the noblest. Of all the actions of man there is none greater than filial piety. In filial piety there is nothing greater than the reverential awe of one's father. In the reverential awe shown to one's father there is nothing greater than the making him the correlate of Heaven[2]. The duke of *K*âu was the man who (first) did this[3].

---

[1] 'The sages' here must mean the sage sovereigns of antiquity, who had at once the highest wisdom and the highest place.

[2] See a note on p. 99 on the meaning of the phrase 'the fellow of God,' which is the same as that in this chapter, translated 'the correlate of God.' P. Cibot goes at length into a discussion of the idea conveyed by the Chinese character P'ei, but without coming to any definite conclusion; and indeed Tâi Thung, author of the dictionary Liû Shû Kû, says that 'its original significancy has baffled investigation, while its classical usage is in the sense of "mate," "fellow."' The meaning here is the second assigned to it on p. 99. In the Chinese Repository we find:—'As a mark of reverence there is nothing more important than to place the father on an equality with heaven;' which is by no means the idea, while the author further distorts the meaning by the following note:—'T'ien, "Heaven," and Shang Tî, the "Supreme Ruler," seem to be perfectly synonymous; and whatever ideas the Chinese attach to them, it is evident that the noble lord of *K*âu regarded his ancestors, immediate and remote, as their equals, and paid to the one the same homage as the other. In thus elevating mortals to an equality with the Supreme Ruler, he is upheld and approved by Confucius, and has been imitated by myriads of every generation of his countrymen down to the present day.'

[3] It is difficult to say in what the innovation of the duke of *K*âu

'Formerly the duke of *K*âu at the border altar sacrificed to Hâu-*k*î as the correlate of Heaven, and in the Brilliant Hall he honoured king Wăn, and sacrificed to him as the correlate of God[1]. The

---

consisted. The editors of the Extensive Explanation of the Hsiâo say:—'According to commentators on our classic, Shun thinking only of the virtue of his ancestor did not sacrifice to him at the border altar. The sovereigns of Hsiâ and Yin were the first to sacrifice there to their ancestors; but they had not the ceremony of sacrificing to their fathers as the correlates of Heaven. This began with the duke of *K*âu.' To this explanation of the text the editors demur, and consider that the noun 'father' in the previous sentence should be taken, in the case of the duke of *K*âu, both of Hâu-*k*î and king Wăn.

[1] The reader of the translations from the Shih must be familiar with Hâu-*k*î, as the ancestor to whom the kings of *K*âu traced their lineage, and with king Wăn, as the acknowledged founder of their dynasty in connexion with his son, king Wû. Was any greater honour done to Hâu-*k*î in making him the correlate of Heaven than to king Wăn in making him the correlate of God? We must say, No. As is said in the Extensive Explanation, 'The words Heaven and God are different, but their meaning is one and the same.' The question is susceptible of easy determination. Let me refer the reader to the translations from the Shih on pp. 317 and 329. The tenth piece on the latter was sung, at the border sacrifice to Heaven, in honour of Hâu-*k*î; and the first four lines of it are to the effect--

'O thou, accomplished, great Hâu-*k*î!
To thee alone 'twas given
To be, by what we trace to thee,
The correlate of Heaven;'

while the fifth and sixth lines are—

'God had the wheat and barley meant
To nourish all mankind.
None would have fathomed His intent,
But for thy guiding mind.'

The seventh piece on the former page was used at the sacrifice, in the Brilliant Hall, to king Wăn, as 'the correlate of God.' The first three lines have been versified by—

consequence was that from (all the states) within the four seas, every (prince) came in the discharge of his duty to (assist in those) sacrifices. In the virtue of the sages what besides was there greater than filial piety?

'Now the feeling of affection grows up at the parents' knees, and as (the duty of) nourishing those parents is exercised, the affection daily merges in awe. The sages proceeded from the (feeling of) awe to teach (the duties of) reverence, and from (that of) affection to teach (those of) love. The teachings of the sages, without being severe, were successful, and their government, without being rigo-

---

'My offerings here are given,
A ram, a bull.
Accept them, mighty Heaven,
All-bountiful;'

and the sixth and seventh lines by—

'From Wăn comes blessing rich;
Now on the right
He owns those gifts to which
Him I invite.'

Since 'Heaven' and 'God' have the same reference, why are they used here as if there were some opposition between them? The nearest approach to an answer to this is found also in the Extensive Explanation, derived mainly from *Kh*ăn Hsiang-tâo, of the Sung dynasty, and to the following effect:—'Heaven (Tien) just is God (Tî). Heaven is a term specially expressive of honour, and Hâu-*k*î was made the correlate of Heaven, because he was remote, far distant from the worshipper. God is a term expressive of affection, and king Wăn was made the correlate of God, because he was nearer to, the father of, the duke of *K*âu.' Hsiang-tâo concludes by saying that the sacrifice at the border altar was an old institution, while that in the Brilliant Hall was first appointed by the duke of *K*âu. According to this view, Heaven would approximate to the name for Deity in the absolute,—Jehovah, as explained in Exodus xv. 14; while Tî is God, 'our Father in heaven.'

rous, was effective. What they proceeded from was the root (of filial piety implanted by Heaven).

'The relation and duties between father and son, (thus belonging to) the Heaven-conferred nature, (contain in them the principle of) righteousness between ruler and subject[1]. The son derives his life from his parents, and no greater gift could possibly be transmitted; his ruler and parent (in one), his father deals with him accordingly, and no generosity could be greater than this. Hence, he who does not love his parents, but loves other men, is called a rebel against virtue; and he who does not revere his parents, but reveres other men, is called a rebel against propriety. When (the ruler) himself thus acts contrary to (the principles) which should place him in accord (with all men), he presents nothing for the people to imitate. He has nothing to do with what is good, but entirely and only with what is injurious to virtue. Though he may get (his will, and be above others), the superior man does not give him his approval.

---

[1] We find for this in the Chinese Repository:—'The feelings which ought to characterise the intercourse between father and son are of a heavenly nature, resembling the bonds which exist between a prince and his ministers.' P. Cibot gives:—'Les rapports immuable de père et de fils découlent de l'essence même du Tien, et offrent la première idée de prince et de sujet;' adding on the former clause this note:—'Les commentateurs ne disent que des mots sur ces paroles; mais comment pourroient ils les bien expliquer, puisqu'ils ne sauroient en entrevoir le sens supreme et ineffable? Quelques-uns ont pris le parti de citer le texte de Tâo-teh King (ch. 42), "Le Tâo est vie et unité; le premier a engendré le second; les deux ont produit le troisième; le trois ont fait toutes choses;" c'est-à-dire, qu'ils ont tâchè d'expliquer un texte qui les passe, par un autre où ils ne comprennent rien.' But there is neither difficulty in the construction of the text here, nor mystery in its meaning.

'It is not so with the superior man. He speaks, having thought whether the words should be spoken; he acts, having thought whether his actions are sure to give pleasure. His virtue and righteousness are such as will be honoured; what he initiates and does is fit to be imitated; his deportment is worthy of contemplation; his movements in advancing or retiring are all according to the proper rule. In this way does he present himself to the people, who both revere and love him, imitate and become like him. Thus he is able to make his teaching of virtue successful, and his government and orders to be carried into effect[1].

'It is said in the Book of Poetry[2],

"The virtuous man, the princely one,
Has nothing wrong in his deportment."'

Chapter X. An Orderly Description of the Acts of Filial Piety.

The Master said, 'The service which a filial son does to his parents is as follows:—In his general conduct to them, he manifests the utmost reverence; in his nourishing of them, his endeavour is to give them the utmost pleasure; when they are ill, he feels the greatest anxiety; in mourning for them (dead), he exhibits every demonstration of grief; in sacrificing to them, he displays the utmost solemnity. When a son is complete in these five things (he may be pronounced) able to serve his parents.

[1] This paragraph may be called a mosaic, formed by piecing together passages from the Ʒo *K*wan.

[2] See the Shih, I, xiv, ode 3, stanza 3.

'He who (thus) serves his parents, in a high situation, will be free from pride; in a low situation, will be free from insubordination; and among his equals, will not be quarrelsome. In a high situation pride leads to ruin; in a low situation insubordination leads to punishment; among equals quarrelsomeness leads to the wielding of weapons.

'If those three things be not put away, though a son every day contribute beef, mutton, and pork[1] to nourish his parents, he is not filial.'

CHAPTER XI. FILIAL PIETY IN RELATION TO THE FIVE PUNISHMENTS.

The Master said, 'There are three thousand offences against which the five punishments are directed[2], and there is not one of them greater than being unfilial.

'When constraint is put upon a ruler, that is the disowning of his superiority; when the authority of the sages is disallowed, that is the disowning of (all) law; when filial piety is put aside, that is the disowning of the principle of affection. These (three things) pave the way to anarchy.'

CHAPTER XII. AMPLIFICATION OF 'THE ALL-EMBRACING RULE OF CONDUCT' IN CHAPTER I.

The Master said, 'For teaching the people to be affectionate and loving there is nothing better than Filial Piety; for teaching them (the observance of) propriety and submissiveness there is nothing better than Fraternal Duty; for changing their manners

[1] Compare with this the Confucian Analects, II, vii.

[2] See the Shû, p. 43, and especially pp. 255, 256.

and altering their customs there is nothing better than Music: for securing the repose of superiors and the good order of the people there is nothing better than the Rules of Propriety.

'The Rules of Propriety are simply (the development of) the principle of Reverence. Therefore the reverence paid to a father makes (all) sons pleased; the reverence paid to an elder brother makes (all) younger brothers pleased; the reverence paid to a ruler makes (all) subjects pleased[1]. The reverence paid to one man makes thousands and myriads of men pleased. The reverence is paid to a few, and the pleasure extends to many;—this is what is meant by an "All-embracing Rule of Conduct."'

Chapter XIII. Amplification of 'the Perfect Virtue' in Chapter I.

The Master said, 'The teaching of filial piety by the superior man[2] does not require that he should go to family after family, and daily see the members of each. His teaching of filial piety is a tribute of reverence to all the fathers under heaven; his teaching of fraternal submission is a tribute of reverence to all the elder brothers under heaven; his teaching of the duty of a subject is a tribute of reverence to all the rulers under heaven.

---

[1] We must understand that the 'reverence' here is to be understood as paid by the sovereign. In reverencing his father (or an uncle may also in Chinese usage be so styled), he reverences the idea of fatherhood, and being 'in accord with the minds of all under heaven,' his example is universally powerful. And we may reason similarly of the other two cases of reverence specified.

[2] The *K*ün-ȝze, or 'superior man,' here must be taken of the sovereign. P. Cibot translates it by 'un prince.'

'It is said in the Book of Poetry[1],

"The happy and courteous sovereign
Is the parent of the people."

'If it were not a perfect virtue, how could it be recognised as in accordance with their nature by the people so extensively as this?'

CHAPTER XIV. AMPLIFICATION OF 'MAKING OUR NAME FAMOUS' IN CHAPTER I.

The Master said, 'The filial piety with which the superior man serves his parents may be transferred as loyalty to the ruler; the fraternal duty with which he serves his elder brother may be transferred as submissive deference to elders; his regulation of his family may be transferred as good government in any official position. Therefore, when his conduct is thus successful in his inner (private) circle, his name will be established (and transmitted) to future generations.'

CHAPTER XV. FILIAL PIETY IN RELATION TO REPROOF AND REMONSTRANCE.

The disciple Ȝăng said, 'I have heard your instructions on the affection of love, on respect and reverence, on giving repose to (the minds of) our parents, and on making our names famous;—I would venture to ask if (simple) obedience to the orders of one's father can be pronounced filial piety.' The Master replied, 'What words are these! what words are these! Anciently, if the Son of Heaven had seven ministers who would remonstrate with him,

[1] See the Shih, III, ii, ode 7, stanza 1. The two lines of the Shih here are, possibly, not an interpolation.

although he had not right methods of government, he would not lose his possession of the kingdom; if the prince of a state had five such ministers, though his measures might be equally wrong, he would not lose his state; if a great officer had three, he would not, in a similar case, lose (the headship of) his clan; if an inferior officer had a friend who would remonstrate with him, a good name would not cease to be connected with his character; and the father who had a son that would remonstrate with him would not sink into the gulf of unrighteous deeds[1]. Therefore when a case of unrighteous conduct is concerned, a son must by no means keep from remonstrating with his father, nor a minister from remonstrating with his ruler. Hence, since remonstrance is required in the case of unrighteous conduct, how can (simple) obedience to the orders of a father be accounted filial piety[2]?'

Chapter XVI. The Influence of Filial Piety and the Response to it.

The Master said, 'Anciently, the intelligent kings served their fathers with filial piety, and therefore they served Heaven with intelligence; they served their mothers with filial piety, and therefore they served Earth with discrimination[3]. They pursued

---

[1] The numbers 7, 5, 3, 1 cannot be illustrated by examples, nor should they be insisted on. The higher the dignity, the greater would be the risk, and the stronger must be the support that was needed.

[2] Compare the Analects, IV, xviii, and the Lî *K*î, X, i, 15.

[3] This chapter is as difficult to grasp as the seventh, which treated of Filial Piety in Relation to 'the Three Powers.' It is indeed a sequel to that. Heaven and Earth appear as two Powers, or as

the right course with reference to their (own) seniors and juniors, and therefore they secured the regulation of the relations between superiors and inferiors (throughout the kingdom).

'When Heaven and Earth were served with intelligence and discrimination, the spiritual intelligences displayed (their retributive power[1]).

'Therefore even the Son of Heaven must have some whom he honours; that is, he has his uncles of his surname. He must have some to whom he concedes the precedence; that is, he has his cousins, who bear the same surname, and are older than himself. In the ancestral temple he manifests the utmost reverence, showing that he does not forget his parents; he cultivates his person and is careful of his conduct, fearing lest he should disgrace his predecessors.

'When in the ancestral temple he exhibits the

---

a dual Power, taking the place of Heaven or God. We can in a degree follow the treatise in transferring the reverence paid by a son to his father to loyalty shown by him to his ruler; but it is more difficult to understand the development of filial piety into religion that is here assumed and described. Was it not the pressing of this virtue too far, the making more of it than can be made, that tended to deprave religion during the *K*âu dynasty, and to mingle with the earlier monotheism a form of nature-worship?

Hsing Ping, in his 'Correct Meaning,' makes the 'discrimination' here to be 'an ability to distinguish the advantages of the earth;'—showing how he had the sixth and seventh chapters in his mind.

[1] 'The Spiritual Intelligences' here are Heaven and Earth conceived of as Spiritual Beings. They responded to the sincere service of the intelligent kings, as Hsing Ping says, with 'the harmony of the active and passive principles of nature, seasonable winds and rain, the absence of epidemic sickness and plague, and the repose of all under heaven.' Compare with this what is said in 'the Great Plan' of the Shû, pp. 147, 148.

utmost reverence, the spirits of the departed manifest themselves[1]. Perfect filial piety and fraternal duty reach to (and move) the spiritual intelligences, and diffuse their light on all within the four seas;—they penetrate everywhere.

'It is said in the Book of Poetry[2],

"From the west to the east,
From the south to the north,
There was not a thought but did him homage."'

Chapter XVII. The Service of the Ruler.

The Master said, 'The superior man[3] serves his ruler in such a way, that when at court in his presence his thought is how to discharge his loyal duty to the utmost; and when he retires from it, his thought is how to amend his errors. He carries out with deference the measures springing from his excellent qualities, and rectifies him (only) to save him from what are evil. Hence, as the superior and inferior, they are able to have an affection for each other.

'It is said in the Book of Poetry[4],

"In my heart I love him;
And why should I not say so?
In the core of my heart I keep him,
And never will forget him."'

---

[1] The reader will have noticed many instances of this, or what were intended to be instances of it, in the translations from the Shih, pp. 365–368, &c.

[2] See the Shih, III, i, ode 10, stanza 6.

[3] 'The superior man' here can only be the good and intelligent officer in the royal domain or at a feudal court.

[4] See the Shih, II, viii, ode 4, stanza 4.

THE SHÛ KING

OR

BOOK OF HISTORICAL DOCUMENTS.

CHAPTER XVIII.

FILIAL PIETY IN MOURNING FOR PARENTS.

The Master said, 'When a filial son is mourning for a parent, he wails, but not with a prolonged sobbing; in the movements of ceremony he pays no attention to his appearance; his words are without elegance of phrase; he cannot bear to wear fine clothes; when he hears music, he feels no delight; when he eats a delicacy, he is not conscious of its flavour:—such is the nature of grief and sorrow.

'After three days he may partake of food; for thus the people are taught that the living should not be injured on account of the dead, and that emaciation must not be carried to the extinction of life:—such is the rule of the sages. The period of mourning does not go beyond three years, to show the people that it must have an end.

'An inner and outer coffin are made; the grave-clothes also are put on, and the shroud; and (the body) is lifted (into the coffin). The sacrificial vessels, round and square, are (regularly) set forth, and (the sight of them) fills (the mourners) with (fresh) distress[1]. The women beat their breasts, and the men stamp with their feet, wailing and weeping, while they sorrowfully escort the coffin to the grave. They consult the tortoise-shell to determine the grave and the ground about it, and

[1] These vessels were arranged every day by the coffin, while it continued in the house, after the corpse was put into it. The practice was a serving of the dead as the living had been served. It is not thought necessary to give any details as to the other different rites of mourning which are mentioned. They will be found, with others, in the translations from the Lî *K*î.

there they lay the body in peace. They prepare the ancestral temple (to receive the tablet of the departed), and there present offerings to the disembodied spirit. In spring and autumn they offer sacrifices, thinking of the deceased as the seasons come round.

'The services of love and reverence to parents when alive, and those of grief and sorrow to them when dead:—these completely discharge the fundamental duty of living men. The righteous claims of life and death are all satisfied, and the filial son's service of his parents is completed.'

The above is the Classic of Filial Piety, as published by the emperor Hsüan in A.D. 722, with the headings then prefixed to the eighteen chapters. Subsequently, in the eleventh century, Sze-mâ Kwang (A.D. 1009-1086), a famous statesman and historian, published what he thought was the more ancient text of the Classic in twenty-two chapters, with 'Explanations' by himself, without indicating, however, the different chapters, and of course without headings to them. This work is commonly published along with an 'Exposition' of his views, by Fan Ȝû-yü, one of his contemporaries and friends. The differences between his text and that of the Thang emperor are insignificant. He gives, however, one additional chapter, which would be the nineteenth of his arrangement. It is as follows:—'Inside the smaller doors leading to the inner apartments are to be found all the rules (of government). There is awe for the father, and also for the elder brother. Wife and children, servants and concubines are like the common people, serfs, and underlings.'

TRANSLITERATION OF ORIENTAL ALPHABETS ADOPTED FOR THE TRANSLATIONS OF THE SACRED BOOKS OF THE EAST.

CONSONANTS.	MISSIONARY ALPHABET. I Class.	II Class.	III Class.	Sanskrit.	Zend.	Pehlevi.	Persian.	Arabic.	Hebrew.	Chinese.
Gutturales.										
1 Tenuis	k	...	....	क	𐬐	𐭪	ک	ك	כּ	k
2 „ aspirata	kh	...	....	ख	𐬑	𐭧	...	...	כ	kh
3 Media	g	...	....	ग	𐬔	𐭢	گ	...	גּ	...
4 „ aspirata	gh	...	....	घ	𐬖	𐭢	...	...	ג	...
5 Gutturo-labialis	q	...	....	...	....	...	ق	ق	ק	...
6 Nasalis	ṅ (ng)	...	....	ङ	{ 𐬣 (ng) / 𐬤 (N) }	...	...	...	...	...
7 Spiritus asper	h	...	....	ह	𐬵 (𐬓 hv)	𐭧	ه	ه	ה	h, hs
8 „ lenis	'	...	....	...	....	...	ا	ا	א	...
9 „ asper faucalis	‘h	...	....	...	....	...	ح	ح	ח	...
10 „ lenis faucalis	‘h	...	....	...	....	...	ع	ع	ע	...
11 „ asper fricatus	...	‘*h*	....	...	....	...	خ	خ	ח	‘...
12 „ lenis fricatus	...	‘*h*	....	...	....	...	...	...	...	...
Gutturales modificatae (palatales, &c.)										
13 Tenuis	...	*k*	....	च	𐬗	𐭰	چ	...	...	*k*
14 „ aspirata	...	*kh*	....	छ	....	...	...	...	...	*kh*
15 Media	...	*g*	....	ज	𐬘	𐭰	ج	ج	...	...
16 „ aspirata	...	*gh*	....	झ	....	...	ژ	ژ	...	...
17 „ Nasalis	...	*ñ*	....	ञ	....	...	...	...	...	...

CONSONANTS (*continued*).	MISSIONARY ALPHABET. I Class.	II Class.	III Class.	Sanskrit.	Zend.	Pehlevi.	Persian.	Arabic.	Hebrew.	Chinese.
18 Semivocalis	y	...	...	य	[illegible], init. [illegible]	[illegible]	ي	ي	י	y
19 Spiritus asper	...	($\acute{y}$)	...	...	...	...	...	...	...	...
20 „ lenis	...	($\grave{y}$)	...	...	...	...	...	...	...	...
21 „ asper assibilatus	...	*s*	...	श	[illegible]	[illegible]	ش	ش	...	...
22 „ lenis assibilatus	...	*z*	...	...	[illegible]	[illegible]	ژ	...	...	*z*
Dentales.										
23 Tenuis	t	...	...	त	[illegible]	[illegible]	ت	ت	תּ	t
24 „ aspirata	th	...	...	थ	[illegible]	...	...	...	ת	th
25 „ assibilata	...	...	TH	...	...	...	ث	ث	...	...
26 Media	d	...	...	द	[illegible]	[illegible]	د	د	דּ	...
27 „ aspirata	dh	...	...	ध	[illegible]	...	...	...	ד	...
28 „ assibilata	...	...	DH	...	...	...	ذ	ذ	...	...
29 Nasalis	n	...	...	न	[illegible]	[illegible]	ن	ن	נ	n
30 Semivocalis	l	...	...	ल	...	[illegible]	ل	ل	ל	l
31 „ mollis 1	...	*l*	...	ळ	...	...	...	...	...	...
32 „ mollis 2	...	...	L	...	...	...	...	...	...	...
33 Spiritus asper 1	s	...	...	स	[illegible]	[illegible]	س (ث)	س	שׂ	s
34 „ asper 2	...	...	s (ʃ)	...	...	...	...	...	ס	...
35 „ lenis	z	...	...	...	[illegible]	[illegible]	ز (ذ)	ز	ז	z
36 „ asperrimus 1	...	...	z (ʒ)	...	...	...	ص	ص	צ	ʒ, ʒh
37 „ asperrimus 2	...	...	ẓ (ʒ̣)	...	...	...	ض	...	...	...

Dentales modificatae (linguales, &c.)										
38 Tenuis	...	*t*	....	ट	....	...	ط	ط	ט	...
39 „ aspirata	...	*th*	....	ठ	....	...	ظ	ظ	...	...
40 Media	...	*d*	....	ड	[illegible]	[illegible]	...	...	...	...
41 „ aspirata	...	*dh*	....	ढ	....	...	...	ض	...	...
42 Nasalis	...	*n*	....	ण	[illegible]	...	...	...	...	...
43 Semivocalis	r	...	....	र	[illegible]	[illegible]	ر	ر	ר	...
44 „ fricata	...	*r*	....	...	....	...	...	...	...	*r*
45 „ diacritica	...	...	R	...	....	...	...	...	...	...
46 Spiritus asper	sh	...	....	ष	[illegible]	[illegible]	...	...	...	sh
47 „ lenis	zh	...	....	...	....	...	...	...	...	...
Labiales.										
48 Tenuis	p	...	....	प	[illegible]	[illegible]	پ	...	פּ	p
49 „ aspirata	ph	...	....	फ	....	...	...	...	פ	ph
50 Media	b	...	....	ब	[illegible]	[illegible]	ب	ب	בּ	...
51 „ aspirata	bh	...	....	भ	....	...	...	...	ב	...
52 Tenuissima	...	*p*	....	...	....	...	...	...	...	...
53 Nasalis	m	...	....	म	[illegible]	[illegible]	م	م	מ	m
54 Semivocalis	w	...	....	...	[illegible]	...	...	...	...	w
55 „ aspirata	hw	...	....	...	....	...	...	...	...	...
56 Spiritus asper	f	...	....	...	[illegible]	[illegible]	ف	ف	...	f
57 „ lenis	v	...	....	व	»	[illegible]	و	و	ו	...
58 Anusvâra	...	*m*	....	अं	[illegible] ã	...	...	...	...	...
59 Visarga	...	*h*	....	अः	....	...	...	...	...	...

VOWELS.	MISSIONARY ALPHABET.			Sanskrit.	Zend.	Pehlevi.	Persian.	Arabic.	Hebrew.	Chinese.
	I Class	II Class.	III Class.							
1 Neutralis	0	. . .	. . . .	. . .	. . . .	. . .	. . .	. . .	ְ	ă
2 Laryngo-palatalis	ĕ	. . .	. . . .	. . .	. . . .	. . .	. . .	. . .	. . .	. . .
3 „ labialis	ŏ	. . .	. . . .	. . .	. . . .	ا fin.	. . .	. . .	. . .	. . .
4 Gutturalis brevis	a	. . .	. . . .	अ	𐬀	𐬀 init.	ـَ	ـَ	ַ	a
5 „ longa	â	(*a*)	. . . .	आ	𐬁	𐬀	ـَا	ـَا	ָ	â
6 Palatalis brevis	i	. . .	. . . .	इ	𐬌	. . .	ـِ	ـِ	ִ	i
7 „ longa	î	(*i*)	. . . .	ई	𐬍	و	ـِي	ـِي	ִי	î
8 Dentalis brevis	*li*	. . .	. . . .	ऌ	. . . .	. . .	. . .	. . .	. . .	. . .
9 „ longa	*lî*	. . .	. . . .	ॡ	. . . .	. . .	. . .	. . .	. . .	. . .
10 Lingualis brevis	*ri*	. . .	. . . .	ऋ	. . . .	. . .	. . .	. . .	. . .	. . .
11 „ longa	*rî*	. . .	. . . .	ॠ	. . . .	. . .	. . .	. . .	. . .	. . .
12 Labialis brevis	u	. . .	. . . .	उ	𐬎	. . .	ـُ	ـُ	ֻ	u
13 „ longa	û	(*u*)	. . . .	ऊ	𐬏	ا	ـُو	ـُو	וּ	û
14 Gutturo-palatalis brevis . . .	e	. . .	. . . .	. . .	𐬈 (e) 𐬉 (*e*)	. . .	. . .	. . .	ֶ	e
15 „ longa . . .	ê (ai)	(*e*)	. . . .	ए	𐬆, 𐬇	و	. . .	. . .	ֵ	ê
16 Diphthongus gutturo-palatalis	âi	(*ai*)	. . . .	ऐ	. . . .	. . .	ـَيْ	ـَيْ	. . .	âi
17 „ „	ei (ĕi)	. . .	. . . .	. . .	. . . .	. . .	. . .	. . .	. . .	ei, êi
18 „ „	oi (ŏu)	. . .	. . . .	. . .	. . . .	. . .	. . .	. . .	. . .	. . .
19 Gutturo-labialis brevis	o	. . .	. . . .	. . .	𐬊	. . .	. . .	. . .	ָ	o
20 „ longa	ô (au)	(*o*)	. . . .	ओ	𐬋	ا	. . .	. . .	וֹ	. . .
21 Diphthongus gutturo-labialis	âu	(*au*)	. . . .	औ	𐬀𐬎 (*au*)	. . .	ـَوْ	ـَوْ	. . .	âu
22 „ „	eu (ĕu)	. . .	. . . .	. . .	. . . .	. . .	. . .	. . .	. . .	. . .
23 „ „	ou (ŏu)	. . .	. . . .	. . .	. . . .	. . .	. . .	. . .	. . .	. . .
24 Gutturalis fracta	ä	. . .	. . . .	. . .	. . . .	. . .	. . .	. . .	. . .	. . .
25 Palatalis fracta	ï	. . .	. . . .	. . .	. . . .	. . .	. . .	. . .	. . .	. . .
26 Labialis fracta	ü	. . .	. . . .	. . .	. . . .	. . .	. . .	. . .	. . .	ü
27 Gutt[illegible]labialis f[illegible]	ö̈									